Politics and Religion
in the United States

Politics and Religion in the United States

Michael Corbett
Ball State University

Julia Mitchell Corbett
Ball State University

Garland Publishing, Inc.
A member of the Taylor & Francis Group
New York & London
1999

Library of Congress Cataloging-in-Publication Data

Corbett, Michael, 1943–
     Politics and religion in the United States / by Michael Corbett
and Julia Mitchell Corbett.
        p.   cm. — (Garland reference library of social
science ; v. 1197)
     Includes bibliographical references and index.
     ISBN 0-8153-3141-X (alk. paper). — ISBN 0-8153-3143-6
(pbk. : alk. paper)
     1. Religion and politics—United States.   I. Corbett, Julia
Mitchell.   II. Title.   III. Series.
BL2525.C68   1999
322'.1'0973—dc21   98-19364
                                         CIP

Paperback cover design: Robert Vankeirsbilck

Printed on acid-free, 250-year-life paper
Manufactured in the United States of America

We dedicate this book with love to
Hinda and Dave
Mikel and Troy

Contents

PART II
Religion and the First Amendment

CHAPTER 5

CHAPTER 9

Religion and Politics Among Black Americans 297

PART IV

Effects of Religious Influences in Politics

PREFACE

Politics and Religion in the United States provides a comprehensive view of the ways in which politics and religion have interacted with each other in the United States from the days of the early colonial period through the 1990s.

Politics and Religion is unique in that it sets the contemporary discussion of this important and engrossing topic in the larger context of the entire scope of United States history. By tracing significant themes through a long span of time, this text enables students to see that the events of the 1990s have their roots in a long process of development.

At the same time, *Politics and Religion* offers students and teachers an excellent means of keeping up with contemporary developments virtually as rapidly as they occur. Each chapter gives the addresses of several relevant World Wide Web sites. The authors also have developed their own website (http://bsuvc.bsu.edu/~øøamcorbett/relpol.htm) to be used in conjunction with the book (see page xxi). It makes available many links and includes an update area in which important new developments will be posted.

Politics and Religion is also unique in that it is written by college professors with scholarly expertise, prior textbook publications, and teaching experience in both political science and religious studies. Michael Corbett's areas of teaching and research expertise include political science research methods and public opinion, as well as introduction to political science. Julia Corbett has research and teaching expertise in religion in the United States, research methods, and comparative religion. This unique collaboration makes for a book unlike any other in the depth as well as the breadth of its coverage.

We do not advocate particular points of view in this book. Rather, we describe, discuss, and explain, and we leave it up to the readers to make decisions about the merits of what is presented. We encourage students to think for themselves rather than relying on the viewpoints of others.

Students will find the book student-friendly. Sophisticated material is dealt with in a straightforward manner. We do not overwhelm the student with technical jargon or unnecessary detail. Rather we focus on major trends and ideas presented simply and concretely, but without oversimplification. Figures and tables are included to increase comprehension of important data. In addition to the websites listed, each chapter offers a limited number of suggestions for further reading—enough to enable students to investigate beyond the scope of the textbook but not enough to be overwhelming. Lists of important terms and review questions help students to organize their studying.

Instructors will also find this a valuable classroom tool. The material is presented in a clear, concise, and organized manner that facilitates teaching as well as learning. The inclusion of website references lends itself to assignments that encourage students to explore both the content and the medium of the World Wide Web.

The importance and volatility of the interface of religion and politics is well illustrated by events that occurred during the time that we were doing the final revisions on this manuscript. As they worked to complete their work for the 1997 term, the United States Supreme Court justices handed down two decisions that had a direct impact on religion and two others that concerned issues on which religious groups and individuals had strong opinions. In *Agostino* v. *Felton,* the high court reversed its earlier ruling (in *Aguilar* v. *Felton*) to allow public school teachers to offer remedial instruction on property belonging to parochial schools. Both these cases are discussed in Chapter 6. In *City of Boerne, Texas* v. *Flores,* the Court ruled that the Religious Freedom Restoration Act, signed into law in 1993 to bolster freedom of religion, was itself unconstitutional. The Religious Freedom Restoration Act and its subsequent reversal are also discussed in Chapter 6.

In two other decisions concerning issues on which people's opinions had been affected by their religious beliefs, the Court also refused to restrict free speech on the Internet to help curb the availability of pornographic material to children, and reinstated two state bans on physician-assisted suicide, saying that there is no constitutional right to such a measure for the terminally ill.

This book had its beginning when David Estrin, then senior editor at Longman, invited the two of us to collaborate on a book that would draw on the fields of expertise of both of us. Its history beyond that point, as editors came and went and publishing houses were bought and sold, and one of us suffered a major health crisis, could almost be the plot for another book. For suggesting the initial idea, David Estrin, now an editor at Garland Publishing, gets a special thank you.

As is always the case, this book is the product of far more labor than just our own. We benefited greatly from the suggestions of a number of people who reviewed the manuscript, and we wish to express our gratitude to the manuscript reviewers.

Finally, a collaborative writing project is always a challenge to all the authors, as they work to reconcile different visions of what the book will be, dissimilar modes of working, varied conceptualization and writing styles, and partially compatible word processing programs. When the collaborating authors also share a home and a marriage, it adds a whole new set of dynamics to the project.

THE POLITICS AND RELIGION WEBSITE

The authors have created this website as a base from which students can access relevant politics-and-religion websites listed in the textbook. For each of the chapters (except the introduction and the conclusion) we have provided a list of other websites that are relevant to that chaper. Some of these provide information and others provide viewpoints about politics and religion. As time goes by, we will add more links. We also have a general section that will include links to political websites and religious websites. Further, the website provides a means of updating students on some recent occurrences (e.g., a Supreme Court decision that affects religious-political relationships).

The website can be accessed at http://bsuvc.bsu.edu/~øøamcorbett/relpol.htm

Our plan is to continue the website in this location and to maintain and update the site.

Politics and Religion in the United States

INTRODUCTION

In his 1997 inaugural address, President Clinton used a metaphor from the Hebrew scriptures when he said, "Guided by the ancient vision of a promised land, let us set our sights upon a land of new promise." Presidents from George Washington onward have relied on religious imagery to engage not only people's minds but their hearts in support of presidential goals.

In the colonial period and afterward, many thousands of African blacks were brought to the United States as slaves. In 1993, a case before the U.S. Supreme Court dealt with the religious practices of a church that traces its roots back to the native religions of Africa *(Church of the Lukumi v. Hialeah)*.

Religious arguments and justifications have been used by *both* sides in many significant political issues in the United States, including slavery, Prohibition, women's rights, gay rights, war, and the abortion controversy, to name but a few.

As the above examples indicate, religion and politics have been woven together throughout the history of the United States, from the very beginning of the colonial period to the present. *Politics and Religion in the United States* provides a comprehensive view of the ways in which politics and religion have interacted with each other in the United States. This ongoing story is told in several sections.

- This introduction lays the groundwork by *defining the terms of the relationship,* by providing working descriptions of both religion and politics and demonstrating why they are necessarily related in the United States. It also provides a brief typology of the logical possibilities for this relationship.

- Part I, *Religion and History,* examines the *nature of these relationships in the past.* Individual chapters deal with the colonial experience, the intentions of the founders, the time period between 1800 and 1959, and 1960 through the present. The specific issues vary over time, but the relationship between religion and politics is a continuing motif throughout our history.

- Part II, *Religion and the First Amendment,* concerns the history of the *legal relationship* between politics and religion. The legal separation of governmental institutions and religious institutions in the United States has meant—and continues to mean—that their relationship must always be in a process of being defined anew as new situations arise. Separate chapters deal with the establishment clause and the free exercise clause, and the tension between the two clauses is examined.

- Part III, *Religion and Public Opinion,* uses information from leading public opinion surveys to explore *how the relationship between religion and politics is reflected in the social and political views of people today.* A chapter on religion and public opinion is followed by separate chapters that analyze religious-political links among white Americans and among black Americans, since these two groups differ dramatically in how religion and politics are linked.

- Part IV, *Effects of Religious Influences in Politics,* consists of two chapters that examine *how this relationship plays out today* as religious groups try to affect public policy and as people reflect on what the relationship between them should be.

- Two appendices profile religious groups in the United States, with particular attention to features that influence their *participation in the relationship between politics and religion* and also provide the wording of the questions of the survey used in our analysis.

Alongside the overarching theme of the relationships between politics and religion, several groups of questions and issues reoccur throughout many of the above sections. Some, though not all, are enumerated below.

- Waging war and understanding or rationalizing it: From the American Revolution through the Persian Gulf War, religion has influenced peoples' views about warfare and has been used both to voice antiwar protest and to justify participation in war.
- The regulation of personal life: From Puritan restrictions on what one could and could not do on Sunday to today's religiously based views on what consenting adults may do in the privacy of their own homes, people have sought to have laws passed that would make their views applicable to all.
- Relationships between groups of people: For example, religion was used to promote both slavery and abolition, as it was used to promote both racial segregation and integration.
- In the United States, religion has most often been generally supportive of government. But throughout history, individuals and groups have raised serious challenges to specific actions of government or, less frequently, to the legitimacy of government itself on the basis of their religious views.
- Religion and the electoral process: Religion has played a role, along with other factors, in people's voting behavior throughout history. Catholics and Jews, for example, have tended to vote Democratic more frequently than Protestants. It has also affected how candidates and elected officials present their causes to the voting public.

Religion and Politics: Working Definitions

In order to describe relationships between politics and religion, we need to first be clear about the definition of each of the two terms in the relationship. The definitions we develop below are certainly not the only good definitions; they are, however, definitions that are useful for understanding this topic. They help us to understand how religion and politics are related and why this relationship is unavoidable in the United States.

Definition of Religion

We will define religion this way: "A religion is an integrated system of beliefs, lifestyle, ritual activities, and institutions by which people give meaning to (or find meaning in) their lives by orienting themselves to what they take to be holy, sacred, or of ultimate value" (Corbett, 1997: 7). This definition is grounded in the social sciences in that it deals with human behavior in groups and with the beliefs and rituals that help to define those groups. It is also based in the humanities in its emphasis on the meaning that religion has for those who participate in it.

To say that a religion is an *integrated system* means that its various dimensions work together and reinforce each other. At least ideally, there are no "loose ends." This system can be thought of as being made up of four parts: *beliefs, lifestyle, ritual,* and *social organizations.*

The beliefs of a religion are found in its sacred writings and stories as well as in its doctrines, creeds, and hymns. Religious beliefs include beliefs about the sacred or holy, about the meaning of life in the world, about ethical and moral values, and about what happens after death, to name but a few common themes. These beliefs may include explicit teachings about the proper relationship between the religious and the political orders.

Lifestyle and ritual are related in that they both have to do with activities. "Lifestyle" has to do with how people live on a day-to-day basis. It is the ethical and moral dimension of religion. It includes activities that must be done and other activities that must be avoided (for example, the Ten Commandments of both Judaism and Christianity). Sometimes the lifestyle prescribed by a religion serves to set its members apart from the rest of their culture, to a greater or lesser extent. It may include directives about food and clothing (for example, and dress codes, especially for female members in some branches of Christianity). It often prescribes participation in ritual (for example, encouraging private prayer and attendance at corporate worship). Questions about how religion may properly influence politics have arisen when members of a religious group have attempted to have their particular morality made into the law of the land.

Ritual, on the other hand, comprises those activities in which people focus explicitly on religion. In the United States, for example, attendance at corporate worship is a ritual in which people often participate. Rituals serve to make the sacred present and available to people. They also commemorate important historic events in the life of a community of faith, mark and celebrate the passages of the human life cycle, and celebrate and reinforce the connectedness of the community (again, to name but a few of their functions).

Social or institutional organization is an important aspect of any religion. Such organization is necessary to keep the life of the group going and to move it forward. The organizational structures of religious groups help express their self-understanding. It is often these institutional structures that interface with the political realm.

Religion is related to other activities in which people find meaning, while being distinct from them. Like family, peer groups, occupation, and leisure activities, religion is one of the things that make human life meaningful and rich for many people. The meaning that people gain from participation in religion is distinctive, however, in that it derives from the contact and interaction that people have in religion with what they take to be holy, sacred, or of ultimate value. It is the relationship with the sacred that sets religion apart from other human activities.

Definition of Politics

There are many different definitions of politics. Some political analysts have defined politics primarily around the concept of *government*. For example, V.O. Key (1958) defined politics in terms of the workings of government, the impact of governments on people, the ways in which governments operate, and the processes by which governmental leaders attain and retain authority.

A different approach focuses on the use of *power*. For example, Robert Dahl (1991: 3) defined politics in terms of human relationships that "involve to a significant extent, control, influence, power, or authority." Almost all political scientists would agree that politics involves the use of power. However, it can be argued that there are different types of power in society (e.g., political power, economic power, and social power) and, therefore, the power approach is too broad. What is it about the use of power in *political* matters that distinguishes political power from other forms of power?

Another approach focuses on the *allocation of values*. David Easton (1965) defined politics as the *authoritative allocation of values for a society*. This definition—or variations of it—is perhaps the most widely accepted definition of politics among political scientists. It is also the definition that we find most useful for the present work. In a sense, however, a related concept of politics was presented earlier by Harold Lasswell (1936), who defined politics in the title of his book *Politics: Who Gets What, When and How?*

We will use Easton's definition as a working definition of politics. Thus, politics concerns the allocation of values. *Values are beliefs about what is good or bad, right or wrong, desirable or undesirable.* People have many different values, such as wealth, power, health, religious values, freedom, patriotism, justice, equality, love, friendship, tolerance, adventure, wisdom, beauty, security, peace, conquest, individualism, community, and so on.

Politics exists because people have *conflict* concerning values. People might disagree on a value (e.g., the anti–abortion rights movement versus the pro-choice movement) and this leads to conflict. Conflict might also occur in situations in which people agree on a particular value. First, people might agree on a value but disagree on how that value should be achieved. For example, if widespread unemployment exists in American society, the great majority of people support action to decrease this problem. However, different people take different approaches to how the problem ought to be handled (e.g., increase government spending to create public sector jobs or decrease government spending to stimulate the private sector to create new jobs), and this leads to political conflict. Second, people might agree on a value but disagree on the priority of that value in relation to other values. For example, although the great majority of Americans are in favor of both clear air and economic growth, conflict arises when people must choose which of these values is more important in a particular situation. Third, conflict can occur when people agree on a value but are competing with one another to achieve that value for themselves. For example, people might try to get their taxes reduced by shifting the costs to other types of taxpayers.

Since there is conflict concerning values, not everyone can have everything that they want. Values must be *allocated*. In a particular situation, some people might win while others lose; alternately, a compromise might result in everyone both winning and losing to some degree. In order for there to be any allocation of values, however, there must be at least some degree of *cooperation* among people. Further, the process by which values are allocated has to be *authoritative:* people have to accept the allocation as being legitimate and binding. People might not agree with the allocation of values, but unless there is at least a minimal level of acceptance of the legitimacy of the allocation process, the political system will break down.

This, then, is our conception of politics. As we shall see, religious motivations have greatly affected the allocation of various values in American society. Further, the role of religion has itself been a value about which substantial political conflict has arisen in the American political system.

Religion and Politics:
Their Roles in Human Life

The Roles of Religion

Religion plays many roles in human life and in the life of societies and cultures. Its distinctive role for individuals is providing meaning that derives from human contact with what are believed to be sacred realities. Religion provides ways in which people can live their lives in conscious relationship with what is to them the highest value. It helps them recognize and celebrate the mysterious horizons that illuminate mundane existence. Religion also plays many other roles, only a few of which can be discussed here.

Certainly a major function, for both individuals and entire societies, is the provision and sanctioning of moral guidelines. Religion provides both the guidelines themselves and the sanction or warrant for them. It frequently also indicates punishments for disobedience and rewards for the obedient, thus reinforcing compliance. Religion also defines appropriate roles for different members of a culture. Religion helps to indicate the boundaries of what is acceptable individual and group behavior. These boundaries are defined and sanctioned with reference to perceived transcendent realities.

Religion contributes to the value system of societies and individuals in other ways. For example, Christianity and Judaism, the most common religions in the United States, both emphasize the importance of helping other people, an emphasis that has led to a great deal of volunteer work in our society. Both were also instrumental in the rise of public education.

Religion also provides support for its adherents, both for their daily lives and at special times of crisis and celebration. Being a part of a like-minded group of people helps to provide the human context that all of us need. For many people, alongside family, their religious group is the primary face-to-face contact group with whom they celebrate births and marriages and mourn their dead. In so doing, religion helps to answer the question of "what to do" in the face of such significant human events.

The Roles of Politics

Politics can play different roles in different societies, and we limit our discussion here to the American political system. Sometimes politics is conceived in terms of a means to achieve collective goals for a society; this conception places the emphasis on cooperation in relatively noncontroversial matters. And this is important. However, the most important role played by politics is one of conflict resolution. Conflicts that concern public issues ultimately achieve some sort of resolution. An issue arises, there is conflict concerning the issue, and sooner or later some sort of binding decision is made on the issue—although the decision might not be permanent. Further, in almost all cases in American politics, the allocation of values is considered to be legitimate and binding. The processes of a political system based on notions of representative democracy carry their own authority and legitimacy in the eyes of most citizens.

Given democratic theory and the slogans surrounding the American political system, politics plays a role of providing an avenue for people to express their values concerning public issues and to work toward the achievement of their values in the public arena. Even if people do not actually attempt to achieve their values in politics, the knowledge that they could try to do it might be intrinsically valuable to them and it might be a check on the power of political leaders. If people do make the effort and they fail, the process itself might be satisfying to them; sometimes people need to express their values even if it achieves nothing more than expressive goals.

Another role that politics plays for some people is that it helps to develop the citizen role. Although most citizens do not participate in politics beyond the minimal level of voting, politics can still make them more fully aware of their existence as part of a public whole. Politics can make people aware that there is more to life than just their private goals. Aristotle and some other political philosophers have advocated that people take a very active role in public life in order to more fully develop themselves. In this sense, at least for the minority who actively participate, politics is similar to religion in that it can help to give meaning to the lives of people.

Religion and Politics: Common Concerns

Although politics and religion are obviously not the same, their realms overlap. This is especially true with regard to values, and it is also true that both religion and politics concern *power* over the lives of people. Reichley (1985: 9) states that the chief thing that religion and politics have in common "is that both are concerned with the pursuit of values— personal, social, or transcendent" (emphasis added). Chidester (1988: 1) begins his book on religion and politics with the statement, "Religion and politics are dimensions of human experience engaged in the meaningful exercise of *power*" (emphasis added).

Religions teach people certain values and, thus, have some degree of power over how people live their lives. Politics leads to the allocation of values in society; the decisions made in this process are binding on people and have some degree of power over what people can or cannot do. Chidester (1988: 1) makes the further point that religion also provides an orientation for people to the powers that impinge upon their lives, and suggests that the way to distinguish between region and politics is that religion concerns sacred power while politics concerns ordinary, mundane, or profane power.

Religion and politics become intertwined in a variety of situations. The values taught by particular religions might become the authoritatively allocated values within the political system. Religious groups might attempt to use the power of the state to express or enforce their religious values. Different religious groups with different values might engage in political conflict in order to have their own values prevail. The values generated or supported within the political system might permeate religious views. Religious organizations might pursue their organizational interests (e.g., keeping church property exempt from property taxes) within the political system. Religion and politics each provides a point of reference by which the other can be judged, and the two may become intertwined as people engage in this evaluative behavior. (See, for example, our discussion of conscientious objection to warfare in Chapter 7.)

Politicians sometimes use religion to gain support for their own interests. Politicians eager for the support of black Americans have frequently cultivated the blessing of black churches, and the connection between the Republican Party and conservative religious groups is well known.

Both religion and politics are concerned with values and with power. Further, religion and politics are frequently intertwined in society. But different people have different views on what type of relationship there should be between these two realms. What kind of link should there be between religion and politics? The typology below surveys the different views on this subject.

A Typology of Views on the Proper Relationship of Religion and Politics

Believing with you that religion is a matter which lies solely between man and his God, that he owes account to none other for his faith or his worship . . ., I contemplate with sovereign reverence

that act of the whole American people which declared that their
legislature should . . . [build] *a wall of separation between church
and state.*

—Thomas Jefferson (1802) [emphasis added]

If a man is not a student of the Word of God and does not know
what the Bible says, I question his ability to be an effective leader.
Whatever he leads, whether it be his family, his church, or his
nation, will not be properly led without this priority.

—Jerry Falwell (1980: 17)

As these two quotations show, differences of opinion about the proper
roles of religion and politics with regard to one another have been a feature of the cultural life of the United States since the beginning, and the
discussion continues to this day.

We present below a typology of the ways in which people have understood this relationship (*see* Figure I.1). Some of the alternatives discussed have never been a part of historical experience in the United
States. Others have existed here, or exist now, sometimes in a modified
form. The typology allows the ways in which the proper relationship between religion and politics is conceived in the United States to be understood in a broader context. In addition, each of the alternatives presented
has had its advocates in the United States.

First, the two extremes of *theocracy* and *government suppression of religion* will be discussed. We will then consider the various types of *religious establishments*. Finally, views that typify the *separation of church and
state* will be addressed.

Complete Domination:
Theocracy and Secular Suppression of Religion

As different as they are in substance, theocracy and the complete suppression of religion by government are formally very similar. In each instance,
one of the two social systems completely overpowers the other, leaving it
virtually no freedom nor independent existence. Because they are extreme positions, they seldom occur in reality, and rarely, if ever, appear in
pure form. Neither has been a part of the historical experience in the
United States. While these extreme positions have few advocates, they
form the boundaries of the current discussion.

FIGURE 1.1

Typology of Church-State Relations

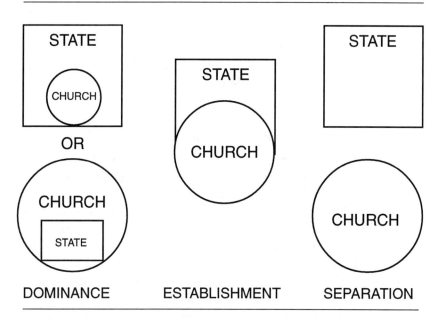

| DOMINANCE | ESTABLISHMENT | SEPARATION |

Theocracy

Theocracy is the government of a political unit by divine rule, usually thought of as operating through human rulers who receive immediate and direct guidance from God. As a type, theocracy assumes that religion and government have the same geographical boundaries, and that every resident is subject both to the government and to the religious hierarchy. In one possible variation, the government and its hierarchy may have some autonomy, but only as much as is granted by the religious hierarchy, which in turn may take it back at any moment. In a sense, the "state" in the usual political sense of the word does not exist, since all political as well as religious functions are performed by the religious group and all political power is ultimately held by the religious authorities. While such an arrangement belongs in this typology, its embodiment in the modern world is highly unlikely. It presupposes a degree of religious strength and agreement that simply does not exist in modern, developed societies.

An example of a society with a theocratic system was the government

of Moses among the early Israelites, as described in the Hebrew Bible and
the Christian Old Testament. There was no distinction between the religious and the political in the life of the early Israelites. They were subject
to the all-powerful sovereign God not only in their religious but also in
their political life.

A modern-day example of governmental and religious authority began in 1929 when the Catholic papacy and the Italian government
reached an agreement that made the pope the temporal ruler of the
Vatican City.

Governmental Suppression of Religion

In situations in which there is *governmental suppression of religion,* the
political state is a totalitarian entity, claiming jurisdiction over all dimensions of its subjects' lives and personhood. It is not so much a *denial* of
religion, usually, as it is a matter of the state trying to *become* religion, taking over those functions that in other cultures are performed by religion.
The state sets itself up as the highest value, the ultimate reality, in its subjects' lives. Usually such an arrangement has led to attempts to destroy
institutional religion, since religion's claim on its members' ultimate loy-
alties makes it especially inconvenient for a totalitarian state.

Well-known instances of such totalitarian regimes have occurred in
recent history. Although in Germany under Adolf Hitler's National Socialist Party the Christian churches remained somewhat intact institutionally, their leadership was subject to constant attack. People who re-
sisted the Third Reich on grounds of conscience were often killed. Hitler's
program was also a direct attack on a particular religious group, the Jews
and their sympathizers, with the goal of total extermination.

Soviet Russia under Joseph Stalin provides another example. For centuries an integral part of Russian life and culture, the Russian Orthodox
Church was forced underground during the Stalinist regime. This latter
example points up an important distinction: the suppression of religious
institutions by a totalitarian government does not necessarily mean the
extinction of *religion,* although it certainly lessens its public presence. Orthodoxy continued to exist underground in Stalinist Russia, as did an
evangelical Protestant movement.

Another modern-day example of a direct attack on religion by a totalitarian government was Maoist China. In the 1966 Cultural Revolution, there was an all-out attempt to destroy all forms of religious practice: religious books were burned, temples destroyed, and religious

leaders exiled or killed. Death was the penalty for those who chose to continue to practice their religion.

Establishments of Religion

A wide range of theories and actual practices comes under the heading of "establishments of religion." However, the basic principle is the same in all of them: The civil government supports religion, whether directly or indirectly. *An establishment of religion is an arrangement in which the civil government supports religion.* Establishments of a stronger or weaker sort have existed at various times and places in the United States and in the colonies that preceded statehood. Establishment also continues to have its advocates.

Protestant reformers Martin Luther in Germany and John Calvin in Switzerland advocated government support of religion, as did Henry VIII in England. The Catholic Church has often enjoyed favorable relationships with government. All were important predecessors of prominent religious groups in the United States today. Luther's teaching underlies the beliefs and practices of the Lutheran churches, and Calvinism gave rise to Presbyterianism, as well as influencing a number of other denominations. Catholics account for about a quarter of the population of the United States. However, none of these denominations today advocate establishment. The most direct influence in the United States, however, comes from Puritanism—to be examined in Chapter 1. Before discussing the others, we will describe some different types of establishment.

In the first place, government support for religion may be *prescriptive* or *permissive.* A prescriptive government position holds that the residents of a given locale must support the religion favored by the government, by paying taxes to support its clergy, for example, or by attending its worship services. On the other hand, a permissive stance simply allows for the dominance of a particular religion, by allowing its holy days and festivals to be celebrated in the public schools, for example.

Establishments may also exist *with or without tolerance for other religions.* An example of the former is the situation in which one religion receives support from tax monies while others are allowed to exist but receive no support from tax monies. In other circumstances, however, nonestablished religions are not even allowed to exist.

Establishments may be *exclusive, dual,* or *multiple.* An exclusive establishment permits the existence of only the officially favored religion. At some points in the development of state constitutions in the United

States, two different religions received the same treatment under a dual establishment. In other states during the very early statehood period, multiple establishments existed, in which taxes were paid to support whichever religious organization the taxpayer chose.

A final distinction can be made between *general* and *specific* establishments. General establishments are very broad. Full religious and political freedom might be granted to "all who believe in Jesus Christ," for example. On the other hand, specific establishments call for allegiance to a particular denomination.

One *historic Catholic view* began with the dramatic conversion of the Emperor Constantine in 312 C.E. and the subsequent establishment of Christianity as the official religion of the Roman Empire by 381 C.E. The Christian Church thus began a long history of favorable relationships with civil government. In the Roman Empire, for example, nonbelievers were barred from holding positions of authority, and the clergy (ordained church officials) received special privileges. The church had the backing of the government in its quest to make converts. The Roman emperor was declared the supreme authority in both civil and religious matters.

The Catholic Church was *the* Christian church in the Western world until the Protestant reform movements of the sixteenth century and later. Historically, Catholicism often took the position that the government must uphold the true religion, which, from the standpoint of the Catholicism of that time, was Catholicism.

The Catholic Church's Second Vatican Council in the early 1960s will be discussed in the section on disestablishment. While the pro-establishment Catholic view has been superseded in the teaching of the Church, it lingers as a source of uneasiness and sometimes prejudice in the minds of many non-Catholics in the United States who fear that Catholic loyalty to Rome undercuts Catholic loyalty to the United States.

We might think that, along with other sweeping religious reforms undertaken by Martin Luther (b. 1483) and John Calvin (b. 1509), they would have proposed doing away with the connection between church and state that was so much a part of the Catholicism of their time. In fact, *both Martin Luther and John Calvin supported some type of establishment for the churches that they helped found.*

The pattern that finally prevailed in Luther's Germany and the Scandinavian countries was one of state churches, supported by the government. The prince of each state in the region had the right to select the religion that would be established in his kingdom, on the principle of the ruler's religion prevailing in his territory. What this meant in practice was that most of northern Germany and the Scandinavian countries became Protestant (Lutheran), while many of the southern German states remained Catholic.

John Calvin's view of the proper relationship between church and state is similar to that of Luther. Calvin assigned a number of functions to civil government, some of which focus on the protection and advancement of religion: civil government is to "cherish" and protect the outward worship of God, to defend sound doctrine and protect the position of the church (Calvin, 1559: IV.xx.2). It is also responsible for preventing idolatry, sacrilege and blasphemy, as well as "other public offenses against religion." "I now commit to civil government," Calvin wrote in his *Institutes of the Christian Religion*, "the duty of rightly establishing religion" (Calvin, 1559: IV.xx.3). He also made civil officials responsible for enforcing the Ten Commandments as found in the Hebrew and Christian scriptures.

In Geneva, Calvin developed a form of both civil and church government based on what he believed was the pattern described in the Christian New Testament. The civil government was responsible in a very direct way for the affairs of the church. The line between the religious and the secular was blurred but not erased. The same consistory that advised the city council on its actions also governed the church. The government of both the church and the city was in the hands of an elected group of officials rather than a single ruler. Calvin's belief in the sinfulness of human beings led him to believe that "men's fault or failing causes it to be safer and more bearable for a number to exercise government" (Calvin, 1559: IV.xx.8). Luther, by contrast, favored a system in which princes ruled territories.

The *English Reformation* gave birth to the Church of England, which would become the Episcopal Church in the United States. The religious reforms of the English or Tudor reformation were, at least in the beginning, slight. However, abrupt changes occurred in the relationship between church and state. Catholicism had been the established church in England. The Supremacy Act of 1534 created a fully separate national church in England. It declared that "the King's Majesty justly and rightly is . . . the only Supreme Head in Earth of the Church of England." King Henry VIII had clearly become the head of a new national church. Under this arrangement, to go against the policies of the Church of England was to commit treason. Treason was usually punishable by death. There was nearly complete repression of Catholics, Lutherans, Calvinists, and

Anabaptists. (We will discuss the views of the Anabaptists in the section on disestablishment.)

In spite of the power that the monarch exercised over the church in this system, there were limitations. The monarch was a layperson (not a member of the church hierarchy). The monarch was in charge of appointing bishops and archbishops to their sees (area of church rule), but could not consecrate them as bishops, nor ordain men to the priesthood. The monarch was responsible for defending what the church taught was correct belief, but could not determine what correct belief was.

The Separation of Church and State

Disestablishment has to do with two basic principles: (1) Religion is a matter of personal conscience and cannot be coerced, either by the secular government or by a religious group. (2) Although peoples' religious beliefs may well influence their political behavior (as we will demonstrate throughout this book), there should be no formal, legal connection between religion and politics. There should, in other words, be no undue state regulation or support of the church. Nor ought the church to exercise undue influence on the state by any kind of coercion or support. Decisions in the political realm should be made on the basis of human reason and political considerations, not on the basis of the teachings of a specific religious group. *Disestablishment is legal separation between the institutions of religion and the institutions of government.* A variety of religious and secular models have contributed to the understanding of disestablishment in the United States. Let's look at some of these models in terms of four areas: the radical reformers, post–Vatican II Catholicism, Judaism, and humanism.

The Radical Reformers

Some of the Protestant reformers took a very different approach than did either Luther or Calvin. These were the *radical reformers* (also called Anabaptists) in Germany, Switzerland, Holland, and Moravia. They opposed not only the Catholicism of their time, but also much of what Luther and Calvin taught. Their central belief was that the Christian church must duplicate the pattern of the church at the time of the Christian New Testament, insofar as that was possible. The church is to be a voluntary association of believers, and ties with the government destroy its very being (Dillenberger and Welch, 1988: 50). The ways in which

Luther, Calvin, and Henry VIII had linked church and state were as unacceptable to them as was the Catholic viewpoint.

Most radical reformation Christians did acknowledge the necessity of civil government and realized that they, too, benefited from it. But they withdrew from taking any active part in it. They believed that a Christian could not be a magistrate and remain truly Christian. They refused to swear oaths. Nor did they participate in warfare. These positions set them against both the church and the civil government of their day, and many died because of their beliefs.

Baptist Christians are the most direct inheritors of the Anabaptist belief in the separation of church and state. As we will discuss more fully in chapter two, they were a significant part of a coalition that formed in support of religious liberty around the time of the Revolution. Those who, for religious reasons, favored separation of church and state to protect religion from government interference (Baptists, for example) joined with those who sought to protect government from the incursion of religion (Thomas Paine) and with those who simply favored individual autonomy in matters of conscience (Jefferson, for example) (Mead, 1978).

Post–Vatican II Catholicism

Much later, in the 1960s, *post–Vatican II Catholicism* emerged as a strong supporter of disestablishment. Vatican II (1962–1965) was called together by Pope John XXIII in order to modernize and update the Catholic Church. Of the many documents coming out of Vatican II, its "Declaration on Religious Freedom" is one of the most striking. It is addressed to the world at large, not just to the Catholic Church. We will summarize its main points.

The Declaration declares that anything less than full freedom of religion violates the essential freedom and dignity of human nature. This right is derived from both human reason (first) and God's will for humankind made known in the Christian Bible. People may not be forced to act in ways that are contrary to their beliefs, nor may they be prevented from acting on those beliefs, within due limits of the law. Human nature is so constituted that people have both freedom and the responsibility that goes with it. Thus, we have a moral obligation to search for and live by the truth. Fulfilling this moral obligation requires freedom from both external and psychological coercion.

Both the nature of religion and the social nature of human beings require that people be free to form and associate with religious groups. The same freedoms that apply to individuals apply to the groups of which they are a part, as long as these groups operate within just laws. The "Declaration on Religious Freedom" stipulates that under certain circumstances the government may accord special preference to one particular religion. In that case, all others must also have the benefits of full toleration. It also recognizes that a "society has the right to defend itself against possible abuses committed on pretext of freedom of religion." Such protection must be carried out with great care not to interfere more than is necessary with religious freedom ("Declaration on Religious Freedom," 1966).

The Declaration also indicates that legal ties between religion and government are bad for the church. It does not take the position that Christians must withdraw from worldly involvement, but specifies that the church can be what the church is intended to be only when it is free of unjustified government restraint and coercion.

The Vatican Council's Declaration in many ways carries forward and systematizes Pope John XXIII's encyclical "Pacem in Terris" (1963). The encyclical, in its turn, built on some of Pope Pius XII's writing. The Catholic Church moved from a long history of being the established religion, through acceptance of disestablishment in cultures in which it had no choice, to a carefully worded and thorough statement of the principle of freedom of religion.

Judaism

Those of Jewish faith have usually been a persecuted minority, without full civil rights, wherever they have lived since the Babylonian exile in 578 to 538 B.C.E. Due in part to this history, many major Jewish thinkers have developed theories that advocate full separation of religion and government for the benefit of *all* persons.

The work of Jewish theologian Richard L. Rubenstein (1964) is an example. He notes that, ideologically, Judaism calls for a union between religion and government. (See our discussion of Israelite theocracy, above.) However, the realities of historical experience have led Jews to be nearly unanimous in their support for very strong guarantees that the religious and the political orders will remain separate. According to this view, absolute political neutrality regarding religion is the only way that equality for all people can be guaranteed. Judaism seeks more than simply the right of individuals to believe and practice their religion as they choose. It seeks their right to participate fully in the communities of which they are a part, without encountering any kind of prejudice. This can come about only when governments maintain strict neutrality in matters of religion.

Rubenstein notes that absolute separation is not possible on an institutional level and certainly not in the minds of most individuals. However, it is important that the ideal be maintained as a goal and as a standard by which all actual practical arrangements are to be judged. Anything less threatens the civil rights of all.

Humanism

Although not a religion, *humanism* occupies a position in the lives of humanists that is similar to that of religion in the lives of the more religiously oriented. Humanism endorses the complete separation of religion and government both in the interest of protecting the government and of guaranteeing individual rights in matters of conscience and religion.

"A Secular Humanist Declaration" (1980) is one of the most recent documents that attempts to lay out the humanist viewpoint. Its authors advocate the complete separation of church and state, and list several specific points:

- Religious authorities ought not to be allowed to make their particular views into law for everyone.
- Tax money should not be used to support religious institutions.
- People should not be taxed to support religions in which they do not believe, and should be free to give financial support to organizations whose views they do share.
- Church properties should pay their fair share of taxes.
- Compulsory prayers and religious oaths in public educational or political settings violate the principle of separation. (Kurtz et al., 1980: 12)

American Civil Religion

The discussion of the separation of church and state and its implications continues throughout the entire book. We now turn briefly to a model of church-state relationships that has grown out of the American experience of disestablishment. We can term it the *collaboration and cooperation* model. It sees church and state as parallel institutions, institutionally independent of one another, but cooperating to accomplish shared goals. It is embodied in "American civil religion" as well as in some views of "mainline" or "mainstream" religion.

The idea of a *civil religion* did not begin with sociologist Robert Bellah, but his work brought it to scholarly attention and ultimately to the American popular mind. In a 1967 essay, Bellah wrote that in the United States

> there actually exists alongside of and rather clearly differentiated from the churches an elaborate and well-institutionalized civil religion in America. . . . This public religious dimension is expressed in a set of beliefs, symbols, and rituals that I am calling the American civil religion (Bellah, 1967: 1 and 4).

The existence of a public religious dimension in the United States begins with the founding documents of the nation, and is carried forward through presidential addresses and similar utterances that articulate the nation's "official" vision of itself. The existence of a religious dimension in American public life is reflected in Washington's declaration of November 26 as a national day of "public thanksgiving and prayer," as well as George Bush's declaration of February 3, 1991, as a national day of prayer during the Persian Gulf War. President Bill Clinton's speeches have repeatedly invoked God's blessing on the United States.

This dimension of national life has its own set of symbols such as the American flag and the Liberty Bell. It has rituals such as those national holidays at which religious sentiments are often invoked, as well as customs such as opening governmental sessions with prayer. It is reflected in public support for military and congressional chaplains at public expense. It also appears in such songs as "The Star-Spangled Banner," "America the Beautiful," and "God Bless America."

The public schools are the primary place where the beliefs and practices of American civil religion are learned. If not the "church" of American civil religion, the public schools certainly comprise its "religious education department."

Bellah's assertion of a common civil faith has been challenged, but there remains little doubt that in the minds of most citizens that there is a religious dimension to the United States itself. It functions as a genuine means of perceiving a sacred dimension to national life. The inclusion of the phrases "In God we trust" on money and "One nation under God" in the Pledge of Allegiance is criticized by some people as a violation of the constitutional separation of church and state. The fact that the phrases remain indicates that civil religion does enjoy a type of "permissive establishment" in the United States.

The concept of *mainline or mainstream religion* does not have a single agreed-upon definition. The mainline has grown and expanded, particularly since the 1960s. However, the features of it with which we are most concerned here are clear. Mainline religion is that which is "dominant" and "culturally established" (Roof and McKinney, 1987). It is religion that has a relatively easy relationship with public life and helps to shape its beliefs, morality, and values.

Summary and Conclusions

We can draw two conclusions from this preliminary discussion:

- Politics and religion are, by their very natures, unavoidably related. This relationship can take many forms, as we have seen in the typology, but there will always be a relationship.
- Disestablishment—the legal separation of the institutions of government and those of religion—means that in the United States this relationship between government and religion can never be in a final sense "settled." It is always up for negotiation. The rest of this book can be seen as an exploration of this negotiation.

In this introduction we have defined both politics and religion, discussed their common concern with power and the provision of meaning in people's lives, and provided a typology of the relationships between politics and religion. We will now turn to the relationships of politics and religion throughout history, beginning with the colonial experience and the intentions of the founders. We then trace this relationship during the periods 1800 through 1959 and 1960 through the 1990s. Throughout this historical section, we will demonstrate the relationship of politics and religion as it is reflected in a variety of movements and issues. These include, but are not limited to:

•war and peace,

•the regulation of personal life,

•relationships between groups of people, and

•the electoral process.

Important Terms

Religion

Politics

Values

Typology

Theocracy

Establishment

Civil religion

Mainline religion

Disestablishment

Review Questions

1. How does the book define religion? Politics? Why are they necessarily related?
2. Distinguish between a prescriptive and a permissive establishment of religion and give an example of each.
3. Distinguish among exclusive, dual, and multiple establishments of religion.
4. What is disestablishment?
5. What is American civil religion?
6. What is "mainline" religion and why is it important in this context?

Discussion Questions

1. What might be the advantages and disadvantages of an establishment of religion? Of religion's being disestablished?
2. How important do you think the civil religion is in American life?
3. What are the advantages and dangers of collaboration and cooperation between government and religion?

References

Bellah, Robert. 1967. "Civil Religion in America." *Daedalus,* Winter: 1–21.

Calvin, John. 1559. *Institutes of the Christian Religion.* In John T. MacNeill (Ed.), *Library of Christian Classics.* 1960. Trans. Ford Lewis Battles et al. Philadelphia: Westminster Press.

Chidester, David. 1988. *Patterns of Power: Religion and Politics in American Culture.* Englewood Cliffs, NJ: Prentice Hall.

Corbett, Julia M. 1997. *Religion in America, 3rd. ed.* Upper Saddle River, New Jersey: Prentice Hall.

Dahl, Robert A. 1991. *Modern Political Analysis. 5th. ed.* Englewood Cliffs, New Jersey: Prentice Hall.

"Declaration on Religious Freedom." 1966. In Walter M. Abbott and Joseph Gallagher (Eds.), *Documents of Vatican II.* New York: Guild Press.

Dillenberger, John, and Claude Welch. 1988. *Protestant Christianity: Interpreted Through Its Development. 2nd. ed.* New York: Macmillan.

Easton, David. 1965. *A Systems Analysis of Political Life.* New York, NY: Wiley.

Falwell, Jerry. 1980. *Listen, America!* New York, NY: Doubleday.

Jefferson, Thomas. 1802. "Letter to Danbury Baptist Association." In Saul K. Padover (Ed.), *The Complete Jefferson,* 1943. New York: Books for Libraries.

Key. V. O. 1958. *Politics, Parties, and Pressure Groups. 4th. ed.* New York, NY: Thomas Y. Crowell.

Kurtz, Paul (Ed). 1980. "A Secular Humanist Declaration." *Free Inquiry,* 1:1

Lasswell, Harold. 1936. *Politics: Who Gets What, When, and How?* New York: McGraw-Hill.

Mead, Sidney E. 1978. "American Protestantism During the Revolutionary Epoch." Pp. 162–180. In John M. Mulder and John F. Wilson (Eds.), *Religion in American History: Interpretive Essays.* Englewood Cliffs, New Jersey: Prentice Hall.

Reichley, A. James. 1985. *Religion in American Public Life.* Washington, D.C.: The Brookings Institution.

Roof, Wade Clark and William McKinney. 1987. *American Mainline Religion: Its Changing Shape and Future.* New Brunswick, New Jersey: Rutgers University Press.

Rubenstein, Richard L. 1964. "Church and State: The Jewish Posture." In Donald A. Gianella (Ed.), *Religion and the Public Order.* Chicago: University of Chicago Press.

Swieringa, Robert P. 1990. "Ethnoreligious Political Behavior in the Mid-Nineteenth Century: Voting, Values, Cultures." Pp. 146–171. In Mark A. Noll (Ed.), *Religion and American Politics: From the Colonial Period to the 1980s.* New York: Oxford University Press.

Whalen, William. 1981. *Strange Gods: Contemporary Religious Cults in America.* Huntington Indiana: Our Sunday Visitor.

Williams, Peter W. 1990. *America's Religions: Traditions and Cultures.* New York: Macmillan.

PART I

Religion and History

CHAPTER 1

The Colonial Experience

If any man after legal conviction shall have or worship any other god but the lord god, he shall be put to death.

If any man or woman or woman be a witch, (that is hath or consulteth with a familiar spirit,) They shall be put to death.

If any man shall Blaspheme the name of God, the father, Son or Holy ghost, with direct, express, presumptuous or high handed blasphemy, or shall curse god in the like manner, he shall be put to death.

—Selections from the *Capital Laws* part of *The Massachusetts Body of Liberties* of 1641 contained in the *Colonial Laws of Massachusetts*

Overview

The Puritans in the Massachusetts Bay Colony listed twelve crimes for which a person could be put to death, and the first three (listed above) concerned religious matters. During its heyday, the Puritan system leaned toward the theocracy model discussed in the Introduction. In this colony, the Puritan churches controlled the government and Puritans were very serious about using both religious and political organizations to create their vision of society modeled on their religious beliefs. As we will see in this chapter, religion and politics were very much intertwined in colonial times, but there were substantial variations from one colony to another—ranging from a leaning toward theocracy in Massachusetts Bay Colony to establishment in some colonies to disestablishment in Rhode Island.

This chapter concerns religion and politics in the colonies prior to the American Revolution, and the next chapter will examine religious-political linkages during the revolutionary era and the founding of the United States. To understand relationships between politics and religion in the development of the United States, we must first examine some important colonial roots. Religious and political experiences in the early colonies had an impact on the framing of the Declaration of Independence, the U.S. Constitution, and state constitutions. These arrangements in turn affected the course of the history of the United States. As we have shown in the Introduction, religion and politics both can be sources of meaning and power in people's lives; this was very much the case in the colonies.

We will begin with the Puritans in the Massachusetts Bay Colony and describe their legacy for political development. Next we will examine important developments in other British colonies, such as the growth of religious tolerance in Rhode Island, the pluralism of the middle colonies, and the weakness of religious establishments in the southern colonies. Then we turn to two important eighteenth-century forces that helped shape the future of politics and religion in the United States: the Great Awakening (a Calvinistic, evangelical religious revival—one that echoes today in Christian television broadcasts) and rational religion (focusing on reason). Here are some of the major questions to be approached in this chapter:

- What was the Puritan covenant and how did it influence the political development of the United States?
- What links were there between the Puritans' religious organization and their community's civil government?
- How did congregationalism among Puritans contribute to the development of democracy?
- What was the view of Puritans concerning religious tolerance?
- How did Rhode Island start and how did it become a symbol of religious tolerance?
- How did religious pluralism develop in the middle colonies?
- What was the Great Awakening and how did it affect religion and politics in the colonies?
- What was rational religion and how was it different from traditional religion?
- How did rational religion and the pietistic religion of the Great

Awakening join forces in order to support the American Revolution?

Throughout this examination, certain key issues are involved. As you read this chapter—and much of this entire book—keep in mind key issues that concern the proper relationship between:

- church and state
- the church and the individual
- the state and the individual
- different groups with conflicting religious beliefs.

Some Qualifications About the Examination of Colonial America

The colonies that we will examine eventually became the original United States. Thus, developments in these colonies have had the greatest influence in shaping the history of political-religious linkages in the United States. These colonies were all British, although New York was Dutch until 1664 and other immigrants (e.g., Swedish) preceded the British in some colonial areas. Further, the colonists were primarily Protestants. However, there were other, non-British or non-Protestant influences during this period that affected the development of the United States as we know it today.

First, when European settlers came to this country, it had already been "discovered" and was already occupied. At the time in which Europeans began to settle what is now the United States, there were millions of Native Americans who had already settled it. While the diverse religious views of Native Americans do not seem to have had a direct, pronounced effect on political-religious practices in the United States, it seems likely that the interactions of European settlers and Native Americans produced at least some effect on political-religious developments in the U.S.

Second, British Protestants were not the first settlers in the new world. Spanish Catholics led the way; the oldest permanent European settlement in the United States was in St. Augustine, Florida, in 1565 by Spanish Catholics. Further, French Catholics were busy making settlements later in areas that eventually became part of the United States. Thus, while the British Protestant colonies became the original United

States, French and Spanish settlements were added later. Further, settlers also came from other countries such as Germany, Sweden, and Holland.

Third, during the colonial period (and afterward) many thousands of black Africans of diverse cultural backgrounds were brought to this country as slaves. The interactions of European settlers with black slaves influenced the political-religious development of the United States. As we will describe further in Chapter 9, slaveowners sometimes used religion to bring about acceptance and compliance among black slaves; however, this religion also provided support for black Americans in their quest for racial equality (e.g., the crucial role of black churches in the civil rights movement in the 1950s and 1960s).

The Massachusetts Bay Colony: Puritans
Motives for the Colony

The Puritan colonists who founded the Massachusetts Bay Colony came to the new world at least partly for religious motives. They came here from England in order to live their lives more in accord with their own religious views than had been possible in England.

Prior to the sixteenth century, the Catholic Church was *the* church in Europe. During the sixteenth century, men such as Luther and Calvin brought about the Protestant Reformation. Following the Reformation, some countries (e.g., Spain) were still Catholic and some became Protestant. In England, for personal rather than religious motives, King Henry VIII broke relations with the Catholic Church, established the Church of England (the Anglican Church), and made himself the head of this church.

The Puritans were Protestants who wanted to *purify* the Church of England. While some Puritans (e.g., the Pilgrims) wanted to separate from the Church of England completely, the Puritans who settled the Massachusetts Bay Colony wanted to continue their formal affiliation with the Church of England while at the same time practicing their own beliefs about what this church ought to be. During the hostile reigns of James I and Charles I, many Puritans decided it would be better to go elsewhere to practice their beliefs. Thus, Puritans established the Massachusetts Bay Colony in 1630; over the next decade, more than twenty thousand Puritans migrated to this colony.

The Puritans in the Massachusetts Bay Colony were *congregationalists*. Various settlements in this area had their own churches, each of which was based around the congregation. Each congregation selected its own minister and made its own decisions, within limits. All congregations were tied together by an overall structure and a fairly uniform set of beliefs and practices; no congregation was free to break off from the others.

The Covenant

The Puritans saw themselves in a very special light. In the biblical exodus, Jews escaped from Egypt to travel to a new land promised to them by God. The Puritans saw themselves as the new chosen people and the new world was the new Israel; the old world was the old Egypt from which they were escaping. They made a covenant with God: if God took them safely to the new world, they would build a society governed by divine laws. John Winthrop, the first governor of the Massachusetts Bay Colony, likened the colony to a "City upon a Hill" with the eyes of the world upon it. The Puritans would set an example for the world. This kind of thinking has persisted in the United States: Americans often view themselves as having a special mission to serve as an example for the rest of the world.

Given the conspicuous position of the Puritan experiment in the eyes of the world, God would punish the colony severely for transgressions. The covenant was an agreement of the colonists with each other and with God; thus, this contract obligated the whole community. This covenant was to be reflected in both religious and political organizations. While separate institutions, the church and the state were each to support and protect the other. Church attendance was required for everyone, and everyone contributed to the financial support of the church.

This concept of a covenant among people became very important in the later political history of the country. When the Founders wrote the Declaration of Independence, the concept of a *social contract* was crucial: individuals entered into a contract with government in which they gave their consent to be governed in return for protection of their inalienable rights. This social contract was very different from the Puritan covenant and it was based on the writings of John Locke rather than the ideas of the Puritans. However, two points are in order. First, covenant theology preceded the work of John Locke and probably influenced his thinking about the social contract between citizens and the government. Second, the covenant theology of the Puritans had prepared people to think in terms of a social contract. The covenant theology prepared people to think of commitment to agreements and obligations to God and other members of the community in return for certain benefits for all within the community. The social contract shifted the emphasis to a covenant between the individual and the government.

The Elect and Citizenship

In the Puritan covenant, church members elect the government. Thus, there is a democratic tendency here. Cowing (1971: 39) notes that there were three classic forms of church organization (episcopal, presbyterian, and congregational) and that many people associated these three (respectively) with monarchy, republicanism, and democracy in the secular world. The idea that the congregation is the basic source of governance for the church definitely has implications for later notions of democracy. However, only the full-covenant church members could elect the government and full-covenant church members constituted only a small fraction of the population—no more than one-fifth of the population (Miller and Johnson, 1938: 191), and perhaps only about 8 percent (Reichley, 1985: 56), or maybe even only 6 percent (Fowler 1985: 14).

In order to be a full-covenant church member, a person had to demonstrate spiritual regeneration. Based on Calvinism, the Puritans believed that some people—the *elect*—had been selected by God to receive regeneration and that others had been passed over. This was God's choice and it had nothing to do with the behavior of the individual. A person could not earn salvation through good works; God elected people to receive grace regardless of their actions; once they had received spiritual regeneration, they lost any liberty except to do God's will. Those who had received grace became a community of living saints and were under a sacred obligation to act accordingly.

Even though the members of the church were saints, this did not mean that they were without sin. The *depravity of human nature*—based on the concept of original sin—is a constant theme in Puritan thought. Puritans believed that people are sinful by nature and that no one can escape sinfulness; thus, human behavior is tainted by sin. However, the Puritan covenant community was to follow divine law as much as was humanly possible.

Everyone in the community was a member of the congregation and must attend church and support the church. Only those who went through the arduous process of demonstrating their spiritual regeneration could become full members of the church—and thus gain a say in the civil government as well. The civil government had authority over everyone in the community, but it was controlled only by those who were full church members.

Puritan Intolerance

The Puritans believed that they had a mission, and they wanted to keep their efforts on track; thus, they enforced strict conformity to their beliefs. Efforts to maintain this religious conformity resulted in intolerance, persecution, and exile (Gaustad, 1990: 65). In addition to conformity in religious views, Chidester (1988: 34) points out that everyone had to attend church, people had to live in a family setting rather than singly, everyone had to learn to read in order to read the Bible, their personal behavior and dress were carefully regulated, and they were expected to monitor each other's moral behavior. Chidester (1988: 34) concludes that as a result of this tight network of social relationships, any departure from the established pattern was regarded as a danger to the entire social fabric.

The Puritans did not believe in religious tolerance; on the contrary, the Puritans rejected the idea of religious tolerance (Miller and Johnson, 1938; Miller, 1989; Reichley, 1985; Chidester, 1988). They believed that only the truth should be heard, and that it was dangerous and immoral to allow false religious ideas to be expressed. And they were hardly alone in this idea. At that time, support for the idea that a society should tolerate diverse religions was rare in the world—except perhaps in Holland. The Puritans' intolerance of religious diversity was not simply due to ignorance; on the contrary, the Puritans placed great emphasis upon learning—as the establishment of universities such as Harvard and Yale indicates.

The Puritans did not come to the new world to practice religious toleration; they came to practice their own religious views. Religious liberty in the eyes of the Puritans was the liberty of non-Puritans to keep away, as indicated by the following quotation from Nathaniel Ward (1647: 97):

> I dare take it upon me, to be the Herauld of New-England so farre, as to proclaime to the world, in the name of our Colony, that all Familists, Antinomians, Anabaptists, and other Enthusiasts, shall have free Liberty to keep away from us, and such as will come to be gone as fast as they can, the sooner the better.

Believing that their own religious views represented God's will, the Puritans took pride in punishing transgressors. Miller and Johnson (1938: 185) describe the puzzlement of Puritans at the end of the seventeenth century when the idea of religious toleration was becoming more acceptable in the world:

They could hardly understand what was happening in the world, and they could not for a long time be persuaded that they had any reason to be ashamed of their record of so many Quakers whipped, blasphemers punished by the amputation of ears, Antinomians exiled, Anabaptists fined, or witches executed.

The banishment of fellow Puritans Roger Williams and Anne Hutchinson is, of course, well known. The conduct of the Puritans in the Salem witch trials is also quite well known. At first, Quaker missionaries who came to Massachusetts to spread their views were simply banished. However, the Quakers kept coming, and harsher punishments were introduced for them, such as cutting off their ears or boring a hole in their tongues with a hot iron—and then banishing them. This didn't stop the Quaker missionary activity; so the death penalty was added. Between 1659 and 1661, four Quakers were put to death by the Puritans (Miller, 1976: 40). It appeared that persecution of Quakers would become even more deadly; however, in 1661, King Charles II intervened and prohibited corporal (and capital) punishment of Quakers.

Once again, keep in mind the framework of the Puritans. They were the new chosen people in the new Israel. They had a covenant with God to establish religious and political institutions in accord with divine law. This covenant community of saints had to be kept as pure as humans could make it. The Puritans worked hard and led ascetic, self-disciplined lives to produce their City upon a Hill. It could not be corrupted by false religions. The religious intolerance they demonstrated was not new in the world; on the contrary, it was very typical of much of the world.

Some version of the Puritan view that links right social order to right religion is at work in most establishments of religion, as we described in the Introduction. As we will see in Chapter 4, such a vision is very much at work in the 1990s in the thinking of the New Christian Right.

The Erosion of Puritanism

By the eighteenth century, "pure" Puritanism had faded, and religious rationalism and evangelism were replacing it as the dominant forces in colonial religious life. As the first generations of Puritans passed on, Puritanism was unable to retain its original form or original ardor. In 1684, England took away the charter of the Massachusetts Bay Colony and brought it under control of the home British government; this lessened the power of the Puritans. Further, the idea of religious toleration was becoming more acceptable in the world, and the British Act of Toleration of

1689 extended religious tolerance to all Protestants. Finally, church membership ceased to be a prerequisite for voting for civil government, and as religious zeal decreased, church membership began to dwindle.

Miller and Johnson (1938: 192) argue that a very serious problem developed with regard to the covenant idea as time passed. As religious ardor cooled, it became more and more difficult to distinguish between citizens (in the original Puritan sense of full-covenant church membership as a requirement for citizenship) and inhabitants. As this happened, many people began to view the covenant in a different way—as a compact among people rather than as a compact of people with God; this moved the covenant concept closer to the idea of a *social* contract. This lessened the importance of Puritanism on both religious and civil matters.

As Puritanism in its original form declined, some of the church leaders took a pragmatic approach to try to save as much of it as they could (Cowing, 1971: 17). Given less interest among people in achieving full church membership, the Half Way Covenant was introduced. This plan reduced the requirements for a kind of partial membership in the church. Baptized Christians received this type of membership until they could demonstrate their spiritual regeneration. For many, this was the final plateau of membership; they did not attempt to go on to the more difficult task of demonstrating that they had received spiritual regeneration. Allowing people to become partial church members in this way did increase the membership of the churches. Ultimately, however, the predominance of Puritan thought in the colonies could not be maintained. According to one estimate, on the eve of the American Revolution, only 22 percent of the population of Massachusetts were members of church congregations, and in all the colonies combined only about one fifth of the congregations were congregational (Finke and Stark, 1992).

Puritanism's Legacy

Most Americans today reject certain features of Puritanism (e.g., religious intolerance). However, some Puritan beliefs have had an impact on American political-religious development and culture. We will briefly reiterate several of these ideas.

Covenant Theology and the Social Contract

As indicated before, the covenant concept—that the Puritans had formed a compact with God and with each other to establish a society in accord with divine law—preceded and perhaps influenced John Locke's social contract views, which were so important in the Declaration of Independence. The social contract in the Declaration of Independence was quite different from the Puritans' covenant, but the Puritans had laid the groundwork for thinking in terms of a covenant among humans and the government as the basis for society.

The City upon a Hill and American Destiny

The Puritans came to the new world thinking of themselves as the chosen people with a mission. The new world was the new Israel and the old world was the new Egypt. The Puritans had formed a covenant with God and with each other to build a society based on divine law. They were to stand as a City upon a Hill with all the eyes of the world upon them. Today many people in the United States think of the country as having a special mission and providing an example to the world. Many Americans feel that the United States is the chosen land to which God has given grace. This view is reflected, for example, in President Clinton's 1997 Inaugural Address when he said: "Guided by the ancient vision of a promised land, let us set our sights upon a land of new promise."

Congregationalism and Democracy

Within limits, the individual congregations in the Massachusetts Bay Colony made their own decisions; these decisions were made democratically by the full members of the church. Further, church members also elected the civil government. Also, individuals were under an obligation to learn; everyone, for example, was required to learn to read in order to be able to read the Bible. These practices contributed to the groundwork for democracy in the civil government. On the other hand, full participation in the civil government was limited to the tiny minority who were full church members. Also, except for the elements of democracy practiced by the relatively few who were church members, church leaders rejected democracy as a form of government for either church or state. Chidester (1988: 34) cites Governor John Winthrop's statement that democracy is the "meanest and worst forms of government." Even so, congregationalism probably fostered support for the idea that humans could make their own political decisions.

Original Sin and Limited Government

The Puritans believed in original sin and that human depravity was a fact of life. This negative view of human nature has carried over into the political culture of American life. While the Declaration of Independence did not emphasize this negative view, the writers of the Constitution—notably James Madison—were affected by it. In recent times, there has been criticism of *gridlock* in American government; it appears very difficult to get all branches of the government to agree enough in order to solve the problems of the country. The preconditions for this gridlock, however, were deliberately built into the constitutional framework by the Founders. Given a negative view of human nature, they formulated a limited government with restrictions, checks and balances, and separation of powers. The Founders did not have faith in full-fledged, unlimited democracy; the system they invented provided a limited degree of democracy and—even at that—it was hemmed in by restrictions and counterbalanced forces.

The Other British Colonies

Puritanism was not limited to the Massachusetts Bay Colony; in one form or another it permeated most of the colonial settlements. While the biggest influence on American political-religious development came from the Puritans in the Massachusetts Bay Colony, there were also important developments in the other colonies.

Plymouth: The Pilgrims

The Pilgrims who settled Plymouth in 1620 were Puritans of a different sort. The Pilgrims, for example, were more tolerant of religious diversity than the Massachusetts Bay Colony Puritans were (Cowing, 1971: 6). Also, unlike their neighbors, the Pilgrims were separatists; they completely separated from the Church of England and formed their own church whereas the Bay Puritans maintained official ties with the Church of England.

The Pilgrims were a relatively small group and, as a group, never became a major force. In the late seventeenth century, they became part of the broader Massachusetts colony. Their covenant, the Mayflower Compact, is very well known. This social and religious compact is very similar to the covenant discussed earlier. It was signed by the colonists while they were still on board the Mayflower, and it provided the social and religious organization for the colony.

Rhode Island and Religious Liberty

Roger Williams was a Puritan minister who arrived in Boston from England in 1631 and was officially banished from the Massachusetts Bay Colony in 1635. In January 1636, Williams was to be arrested and returned to England; however, he fled the colony. Later that year, he bought some land from Native Americans and founded Providence.

Gaustad (1990: 65–66) describes three differences that Williams had with Puritan leaders that led to his banishment. First, Williams advocated separation of church and state in order to purify the church even further. Second, Williams wanted to break completely with the Church of England. Third, Williams was concerned that the Puritans had simply taken land from the Native Americans without any agreement with the Native Americans or any compensation for the land; he further argued that King Charles I had no right to give the land to the Puritans because the land did not belong to him in the first place.

Roger Williams and the Rhode Island experiment are today associated with religious tolerance. However, Williams did not start out quite this way; his views evolved out of a quest for an even purer form of Puritanism than existed in the Massachusetts Bay Colony. Miller and Johnson (1938: 186) explain Williams' evolution this way:

> Williams evolved from an orthodox Puritan into the champion of religious liberty because he came to see spiritual truth as so rare, so elevated, so supernal a loveliness that it could not be chained to a worldly establishment and a vested interest.

In Rhode Island, Roger Williams carried out his evolving political-religious views. First, he bought the land from the Native Americans rather than simply getting title for the land from the British government. Second, he helped to found a church that was not tied to the Church of England. Third, there was no established church in Rhode Island; the government had a role to play in providing for the social order, but it was not to control religious life. It was Roger Williams—not Thomas Jefferson—who first used the metaphor of the wall of separation between church and state, but his purpose was to protect the church from being corrupted by the world (Howe, 1965).

Despite his own strong religious convictions, Williams argued for religious liberty and for separation of church and state. As we noted in the Introduction, one of the arguments for the legal separation of church and state is that this will protect religion from governmental interference.

Williams felt that efforts by the state to compel people to accept certain religious beliefs would only lead to hypocrisy; he also felt that it was morally wrong to persecute people for their religious beliefs. The state, governed by democratic means, provided for the public order; within that state, people were to be free to hold their own religious beliefs.

As a result of this religious liberty in Rhode Island, the colony became diverse in terms of Protestant religious beliefs. Roger Williams helped to found a Baptist church and was a Baptist himself for a while. In addition to Baptists, there were Quakers and, later, Anglicans and Congregationalists. A variety of Protestant viewpoints were represented, and eventually there were also Jews and Catholics in Rhode Island.

Religious Pluralism in the Middle Colonies

The New England pattern discussed with regard to Massachusetts also applied to a great extent to New Hampshire and Connecticut—but not Rhode Island. In the South were the Carolinas, Georgia, and Virginia. In the middle were New York, New Jersey, Pennsylvania, Delaware, and Maryland. These middle colonies contained the greatest degree of religious diversity, and this degree of religious diversity no doubt had a great impact on the development of sentiments for religious tolerance during the eighteenth century.

Pennsylvania was founded by William Penn, a Quaker, as a "Holy Experiment." Penn believed that people should receive spiritual salvation voluntarily rather than through an established church. He believed strongly in religious toleration, and he deliberately incorporated religious diversity into the development of Pennsylvania. Penn did not intend to establish a colony for just Quakers; on the contrary, he intended to have a diversity of religious groups within Pennsylvania—although he did enforce the Quakers' views of moral standards on all residents. He actively recruited people. In addition to Quakers, there were Mennonites, Amish, German Lutherans, German Reformed, Scotch-Irish Presbyterians, Welsh Baptists, free African Methodists, Irish Catholics, deists, Anglicans, and others (Gaustad, 1990: 91–92; Miller, 1976: 49). Religious diversity helped to protect religious freedom. Further, to the surprise of some, the colony thrived.

In New York and New Jersey, religious diversity occurred despite official efforts against it. New York (originally New Netherlands), for example, was originally settled by the Dutch West India Company, and the Dutch Reformed Church became the established church. The Dutch, however, were fairly tolerant and loose in their religious establishment. At any rate, the area was filled by people of diverse religious views. When the director general (Peter Stuyvesant) later tried to reduce the diversity (e.g., by keeping Jews out and by punishing Quakers), he was rebuked by the West India Company and by his own people. In 1664, the British captured New Netherlands and, under the control of the duke of York, it became New York. For a while, there was even greater religious tolerance in the colonies because of the Catholic sympathies of the duke. But, after he became King James II and was overthrown in the Glorious Revolution of 1688, the Church of England was eventually established in New York. However, the governors of New York were not able to bring about religious uniformity by establishing the Anglican Church; the religious diversity that frustrated Peter Stuyvesant continued to frustrate efforts to create a unified church (Gaustad, 1990: 85).

Maryland was originally intended to be a haven for Catholics, but it was not a haven for long. Cecil Calvert (Lord Baltimore), a Catholic, founded Maryland in 1634. He wanted to attract both Catholics and Protestants to Maryland. However, the Protestants soon outnumbered the Catholics. In 1649, Calvert persuaded the Maryland Assembly to pass the Toleration Act, which provided religious liberty for all persons who professed to believe in Jesus Christ. Eventually, however, Protestants took control of Maryland and excluded Catholics from holding public office. Further, after the Glorious Revolution of 1688, Maryland became a royal province, and the Church of England was later established as its official church.

The Southern Colonies

The first permanent British colony in what is now the United States was Jamestown, Virginia, in 1607. The colony was settled in order to seek profit (and thus to strengthen the British empire) and to spread the Church of England. The Anglican Church was the established church; people were usually required to attend church and to help pay for its support. For at least the first half of the century, however, the Anglican Church was very weak. The resources of the church were not great and the great expanses of territory meant that the influence of the church was spread very thin. Adding to this is the fact that there were few Anglican clergy and these were apparently neither industrious nor particularly good role models. Generally, the only clergy who could be persuaded to leave England and come to Virginia were those who wished to escape from problems (e.g., debts) in the old country (Gaustad, 1990: 43). The situation improved in the second half of the century and the Anglican organization became stronger. However, after the British Act of Toleration of 1689, Protestant diversity increased in Virginia. During the eighteenth century Baptists, Presbyterians, and Methodists flowed into Virginia. Because of the persecution which resulted, Virginia gave rise to men such as Jefferson and Madison who were firmly committed to religious liberty.

In 1663, King Charles II gave to some of his supporters the land that was to be called Carolina, which was later divided into North Carolina and South Carolina. Settlements in this area were very slow. Gaustad (1990: 99) reports that by the end of the seventeenth century the population in Carolina was only about eight thousand and half of these people were black slaves. The owners of Carolina were concerned with profit rather than religion, and they granted religious freedom to anyone who would come to settle in this area. In this "wild, sparsely settled and ill-governed expanses of early Carolina," churches had a very weak hold (Ahlstrom, 1972: 196). The Anglican Church was the primary church in the Carolinas, but attempts to establish it were unsuccessful. There was too much (Protestant) religious diversity and too much cultural diversity for a relatively weak church to impose uniformity.

Georgia, the last of the British colonies to be established in what is now the United States, was not founded until 1733. While the Anglican Church was the official church, it was weak. By the time of the American Revolution, the population of Georgia was small, diverse, and relatively scattered.

The Great Awakening

By the end of the seventeenth century, the British empire had taken control of all the colonies. While this strengthened the official position of the Anglican Church in some areas, the British Act of Toleration of 1689 helped to undercut the forces of religious intolerance. During the eighteenth century, two important forces occurred that each had strong implications for the American Revolution and for religious liberty: the Great Awakening and religious rationalism. This section discusses the Great Awakening and the next section concerns religious rationalism.

Solomon Stoddard (1643–1729) and Jonathan Edwards (1703–1758)

The Great Awakening was a Calvinistic, evangelical religious revival that occurred during the 1730s and 1740s. The movement was expansive in the sense that it attempted to bring into the church many who would not have qualified under older Puritan standards—and it did succeed in bringing in more people into the church. This religious movement was also marked by highly emotional and dramatic preaching; the movement appealed to the emotions rather than to religious reasoning. Conversion in the evangelical religious movement was perceived as a sudden, dramatic process that occurred quickly and changed the person through religious rebirth.

The beginning of much of the Great Awakening can be attributed to the prior efforts of Solomon Stoddard, the Congregational minister in Northampton, Connecticut (Cowing, 1971: 41–45). In essence, Stoddard brought people into the congregation by not discriminating between those who could demonstrate that they had received God's grace and those who had not. The congregation included both those who had been saved and those who wanted to be saved, and Stoddard did not make distinctions between the two groups in communion. The approach was to bring practically everyone into the church and then convert them to God.

Stoddard's approach to converting people to God was unusual for its time. The substance of his preaching was not much different from traditional Puritan ideas, but his style was evangelistic. Stoddard's approach is represented in his often quoted statement: "The Word is as a hammer and we should use it to break the Rocky Hearts of Men" (Cowing, 1971: 43). In order to convert souls, Stoddard skillfully and dramatically invoked fear of damnation on one hand and the possibility of heaven on the other hand. Stoddard first terrorized people (this is what God will do to those who aren't saved) and then gave them the good news (here is how you can be saved).

Stoddard's work was carried on in part by his famous grandson, Jonathan Edwards, who is well known for his sermon "Sinners in the Hands of An Angry God." After Stoddard died, Edwards took over his pulpit in Northampton. While Edwards was less dramatic than Stoddard, he apparently developed a very effective style of expressing well-developed theological ideas in a plain manner so that they were easily understood. Edwards has been classified by some (e.g., Noll et al., 1989) as the most important theologian of the Great Awakening.

Reichley (1985: 71–72) argues that Edwards' chief influence on politics was his part in relating the millennial expectations aroused by the Great Awakening to the American nationalism that was developing. While believing that human society is corrupt, Edwards also believed that civil society could be used to achieve—very gradually—God's kingdom on earth. He believed that as time passed, progress toward this goal would be achieved. This belief in gradual progress toward a better society was very important in the beliefs of American evangelical Christians in the eighteenth century and it had an impact on the political culture; as we will see in Chapter 4, this belief continues to be evidenced today (e.g., in the work of Evangelicals for Social Action).

George Whitefield (1714–1770)

The greatest preacher of the Great Awakening—and the most widely known person in all the colonies—was George Whitefield. Whitefield traveled around the colonies preaching between 1738 and 1770, and he was very instrumental in the evangelical, Calvinistic religious revival of those times. He also had a gentler message than the terrifying theme presented by some Calvinists (Cowing, 1971: 60).

Whitefield apparently was a spellbinding speaker and had great power over those who heard him. His powerful voice could reach crowds of thousands of people who gathered to hear him; Benjamin Franklin calculated that Whitefield's voice could reach thirty thousand people at one time. While Whitefield was not the theologian that Jonathan Edwards was, he provided a model for revivalist preachers and he carried the revival message to the people more effectively than others had done.

Effects of the Great Awakening

Whitefield's revivals represented the peak of the Great Awakening, and many people attested that this revival movement had substantial effects in the colonies. Noll et al. (1989: 52) argue that the Great Awakening had three effects: it converted many new Christians; it energized many churches and made them more active; and it had an effect on colonial culture (e.g., a greater interest in education for both religious and secular purposes). Chidester (1988: 50–52) argues that Protestant pietism (the personalized, inner emotional experience of religious power) in the Great Awakening supported a more democratic distribution of political power.

This pietism of the eighteenth century was used to undergird the efforts of the American Revolution. Cowing (1971: 224) concludes that the large evangelical component in the colonial population was crucial in the American Revolution and in legalizing religious freedom. We can draw

arguments from Cowing (1971), Heimert (1966), and Chidester (1988) to
show how the Great Awakening eventually supported the revolution.

- The pietism of the movement gave people a sense of personal religious power; this feeling of religious power led to feelings of individual power in the rest of society, and this supported more democratic political practices.
- In clashing with more traditional religious establishments,
  evangelicals strove to achieve religious freedom. This in turn led
  to support for political freedom and it supported independence
  of the colonies from Great Britain and the Anglican Church.
- Those who accepted the millennialism of the movement—the belief that progress would be made toward achieving God's kingdom on earth—were eager to help bring this about by establishing a better social order.

There is no doubt that the pietism supplied much of the religious
and emotional fervor for the American Revolution. The intellectual rationale was supplied by a different movement: *rationalism*.

Rational Religion
The European Enlightenment in the Colonies

The European Enlightenment, starting primarily in the seventeenth century, revolved around the use of reason to discover and understand the
laws that governed nature and society. This movement encompassed a
range of thinkers—from those whose primary accomplishments were in
the physical realm (e.g., Newton) to those whose primary contributions
were in the philosophical realm (e.g., Locke). This approach to understanding all aspects of the universe—whether the laws of motion or the
laws of God—was to use reason in order to study, analyze, and understand those aspects. Rationalists expected that their approach would lead
to progress in improving the human condition.

Obviously, European rationalism would not be adopted by the average
working person in the colonies. While the Puritan background valued
learning and required people to be able to read, the average person in the
colonies would not know about or care about the currents of intellectual
thought in Europe. However, the relatively well-to-do families did have the

resources and the time to partake of the European Enlightenment. Men like Thomas Jefferson and Benjamin Franklin are outstanding examples of the application of rationalism to both the physical world (in terms of their inventions) and to the social world (in terms of their political theories). Many of the elite who adopted Enlightenment viewpoints developed a very nontraditional view toward religion; religion itself was to be analyzed rationally. This led to the development of religious approaches that have been termed "rational religion" or "religious rationalism."

Enlightenment Religion

Some clergy in the colonies were educated at colleges in which they were exposed to Enlightenment philosophy. Their liberal, rational religion rejected the older traditional Calvinist outlook with its emphasis on the depravity of human nature, predestination, and the necessity of conversion. Instead, rational religion took a more benign view of human nature and human prospects; the emphasis was not on the next life, but on what people do in this life. What should a human being do in order to lead a good life? How should people treat one another? Ahlstrom (1972: 356–358) notes that there was no uniformity in the ideas of Enlightenment theology, but there were certain ideas that were widely shared, and he describes seven chief characteristics of "enlightened Christianity." We will briefly paraphrase these seven characteristics here.

1. It emphasized the role of humans in their own redemption and it rejected predestination.
2. It emphasized simplicity in Christian beliefs.
3. It placed emphasis on getting people to lead ethical lives.
4. It placed little value on sacraments and the ministry except for moral instruction.
5. It placed great emphasis on reason and downplayed the limitations imposed on humans by historical circumstances.
6. It emphasized the idea of human progress in secular and religious terms.
7. It viewed God as an impersonal power that ruled the universe through natural laws, rather than as a personal God who related to humans.

Rational Religion and Revolutionary Politics

This rational religion, of course, was naturally suited for a political system that expanded political power beyond the few. Rational religion and Enlightenment philosophy were very much in tune with the establishment of new ways of doing things in the governance of human beings. First, of course, they had to throw off the old ways of doing things: this occurred to a very large extent in the American Revolution. By itself, the thrusts of rational religion could not have achieved the Revolution. Rational religion and pietistic, evangelical religion were in accord in certain ways—for example, the belief in progress toward some ideal state of affairs on earth—and they joined forces temporarily for the revolution (Mead, 1978).

The American Revolution did not, by itself, establish anything new. That task came later when the Constitution went into effect. The Constitution has changed greatly over time, but there is still great concern over the meaning attached to it at the time of its inception. Thus, the next chapter will consider the intentions of the Framers; in this examination, we will delve further into the effects of rational religion on those who framed the initial government structure of the United States.

Summary and Conclusions

Religion played an important role in the colonial development of this country, and the effects of this role continue to affect political-religious linkages in the United States. Religious motives combined with economic motives in the settlement of much of the original colonial lands. Puritan thought dominated religion in the early colonies, and certain aspects of Puritan thought (e.g., the concept of the covenant, the view of human nature) have permeated the American political culture. As the dominance of the relatively pure strain of Puritan doctrine faded, two other religious movements (the Great Awakening and rational religion) occurred and temporarily joined forces to support the American Revolution; these two movements subsequently influenced American political development in different ways. We turn now to a closer examination of the political-religious intentions of the Founders of the United States.

Important Terms

Puritanism
Massachusetts Bay Colony
City upon a Hill
Social contract
Puritan covenant

The elect
Depravity of human nature
Great Awakening
European Enlightenment
Enlightened Christianity

Review Questions

1. Briefly describe each of the key issues involved in the nature of religion and politics in the colonies prior to the Revolution.
2. Why was the Massachusetts Bay Colony begun?
3. What effects did Puritanism have on American political-religious development and culture?
4. Why did religious liberty develop in Rhode Island to the extent that it did?
5. Why were the middle colonies as religiously diverse as they were?
6. What effects did the Great Awakening have on religion and politics?
7. What was rational religion, and what were its effects on religion and politics?

Discussion Questions

1. Puritanism presents one view of human nature. What kind of government is best if you agree with this view of human nature? What kind of government is best if you take a completely opposite view of human nature?
2. Should we in the United States look upon our nation as a City upon a Hill? What are the benefits and harms that might occur from thinking of the United States in this way?
3. What kinds of consequences does enlightened religion have for views concerning government?

For Further Reading

Ahlstrom, Sydney E. 1972. *A Religious History of the American People.* New Haven: Yale University Press.

    This work contains a good discussion of the colonial background of religion and politics.

Chidester, David. 1988. *Patterns of Power: Religion and Politics in American Culture.* Englewood Cliffs, New Jersey: Prentice-Hall.

    Chapter 2 is relevant to theocracy and Puritanism.

Finke, Roger, and Rodney Stark. 1992. *The Churching of America, 1776–1990: Winners and Losers in Our Religious Economy.* New Brunswick, New Jersey: Rutgers University Press.

    The first two chapters provide an interesting approach to religious adherence in the colonies and present a somewhat different view of the relevance of religion during colonial times.

Noll, Mark A., Nathan O. Hatch, and George M. Marsden. 1989. *The Search for Christian America.* Colorado Springs: Helmers & Howard.

    This book concerns Christianity in the development of the U.S., starting with the colonial period.

Reichley, A. James. 1985. *Religion in American Public Life.* Washington, D.C.: Brookings Institution.

    Chapter 3 contains background that is relevant to the colonial connection between religion and politics.

Relevant World Wide Websites

Important Note: For many of the topics covered in this book there are websites that will give you additional information or provide interesting viewpoints. We have listed some of these websites in this book, but they can change quickly. Thus, we will also maintain a website that contains additional links. Please visit our website at http://bsuvc.bsu.edu/~00amcorbett/relpol.htm

http://www.gty.org/~phil/hall.htm The Hall of Church History site contains interesting historical information about a variety of different religious groups, including the Puritans.

http://members.aol.com/calebj/dir.html The Mayflower Web Pages site gives extensive information about the Pilgrims.

http://earlyamerica.com/_Archiving Early America The Archiving Early America site contains information about and documents from the eighteenth century.

http://www.usia.gov/usa/oah/toc.htm An Outline of American History site includes precolonial period through current history.

http://www.msstate.edu/Archives/History/USA/usa.html History of the United States site includes colonial period through current history.

References

Ahlstrom, Sydney E. 1972. *A Religious History of the American People.* New Haven: Yale University Press.

Chidester, David. 1988. *Patterns of Power: Religion and Politics in American Culture.* Englewood Cliffs, New Jersey: Prentice-Hall.

Cowing, Cedric B. 1971. *The Great Awakening and the American Revolution: Colonial Thought in the 18th Century.* Chicago: Rand McNally.

Finke, Roger, and Rodney Stark. 1992. *The Churching of America, 1776–1990: Winners and Losers in Our Religious Economy.* New Brunswick, New Jersey: Rutgers University Press.

Fowler, Robert Booth. 1985. *Religion and Politics in America.* Metuchen, New Jersey: American Theological Library Association.

Gaustad, Edwin Scott. 1990. *A Religious History of America.* San Francisco: Harper and Row.

Heimert, Alan. 1966. *Religion and the American Mind: From the Great Awakening to the Revolution.* Cambridge, Massachusetts: Harvard University Press.

Howe, Mark DeWolfe. 1965. *The Garden and the Wilderness: Religion and Government in American Constitutional History.* Chicago: University of Chicago Press.

Mead, Sidney E. 1978. "American Protestantism During the Revolutionary Epoch." Pp. 162–180 in John M. Mulder and John F. Wilson (Eds.), *Religion in American History: Interpretive Essays.* Englewood Cliffs, New Jersey: Prentice-Hall.

Miller, Glenn T. 1976. *Religious Liberty in America: History and Prospects.* Philadelphia: Westminster Press.

Miller, Perry, and Thomas H. Johnson (Eds.). 1938. *The Puritans.* New York: American Book Company.

Miller, Robert. 1989. "Religious Conscience in Colonial New England." Pp. 9–24 in James E. Wood, Jr. (Ed.), *Readings on Church and State.* Waco, Texas: J.M. Dawson Institute of Church-State Studies.

Noll, Mark A., Nathan O. Hatch, and George M. Marsden. 1989. *The Search for Christian America.* Colorado Springs: Helmers & Howard.

Reichley, A. James. 1985. *Religion in American Public Life.* Washington, D.C.: Brookings Institution.

Ward, Nathaniel. 1647. "The Simple Cobbler of Aggawam." Reprinted in pp. 95–108 of Perry Miller (Ed.), *The American Puritans: Their Prose and Poetry.* Garden City, New York: Doubleday, 1956.

Wilson, John F. 1990. "Religion, Government, and Power in the New American
    Nation." Pp. 77–91 in Mark A. Noll (Ed.), *Religion and American Politics: From
    the Colonial Period to the 1980s*. New York: Oxford University Press.

CHAPTER 2

Religion and Politics

Intentions of the Founders

Religion and the Founding of the United States: Two Views

The Founders of the United States were Christians, and they intended the government to support and encourage Christianity in a nonsectarian fashion.

The Founders of the United States were not Christians, and they intended to create a secular government with a wall of separation between itself and religious institutions.

Overview

Which of the above views do you think more accurately reflects what occurred during the founding of the United States? Both these positions have been argued with great passion at times in American history. In relatively recent history, for example, some members of what is broadly called the New Christian Right have argued that the United States was created as a Christian—and specifically Protestant—nation, that we have strayed from our roots, and that we must return to those roots. On the other hand, a number of individuals and groups support the second viewpoint—that the Founders intended to create a secular government that should stay out of religion. This second viewpoint is reflected in some important decisions by the Supreme Court during this century, but (as you will see in Chapters 5 and 6) the Supreme Court has not been completely consistent in reflecting a particular view on this matter.

Which view is correct? This chapter will examine the Founders and the context in which the United States was founded. We will show that the issue of the intentions of the Founders cannot be resolved simply. Both of the conflicting views presented at the beginning of this chapter are correct to some extent and both are incorrect to some extent. We will provide some perspective for this issue, but there is no single perspective on this issue with which all scholars would agree. There is enough complexity and ambiguity in the reality of the founding of the United States that different scholars, each earnestly pursuing a faithful description of the intentions of the Founders, can come to different conclusions. Cobb (1970) and Malbin (1978), for example, take the first view and argue that the Founders supported Christianity and meant to prevent preferential treatment of one religion over the rest. On the other hand, Swomley (1987: 17) takes the other view when he states: "The Constitution of the United States provides for a wholly secular government." At the same time, Levy (1995: xix), whose sympathies lie with the separationist view, cautions that the historical evidence does not permit complete certainty about the intentions of the Founders (also known as Framers).

This chapter concerns the time from the eve of the American Revolution to a few years after the United States Constitution went into effect. We selected this range of time in order to highlight the role of the establishment issue from the time just prior to the Declaration of Independence—when most colonies had some provision for religious establishments—to the years after the enactment of the Constitution when most states individually moved toward disestablishment. Here are some major questions to be addressed in this chapter:

- What led to the American Revolution and what religious matters contributed to it?
- What led two very different religious groups (pietists and religious rationalists) to form a coalition to carry out the American Revolution?
- Where does religion fit in the Declaration of Independence?
- What were the views of the Founders on religion and the proper mix of religion and politics?
- On the eve of the American Revolution, what was the relationship between church and state in the individual colonies?
- How did James Madison and Thomas Jefferson lead the way in

disestablishment and religious liberty in Virginia?

- What did the original (before amendments) U.S. Constitution say about religion and why did it say so little?

- What does the First Amendment say about religion?

The Revolutionary Era
Overview of Events

During the years leading up to the American Revolution, several different political, economic, and religious factors contributed to tensions between Great Britain and the thirteen North American colonies that ultimately rebelled and declared their independence. The political tensions were due partly to an increasing feeling among the colonies that they could rule themselves and that they needed neither the benefits nor the restraints of a government in which they had no say. Both political and economic tensions were generated by the efforts of the British empire to recover some of its economic losses by taxing the colonists. The debt of the British government was staggering, and much of it was a result of costs involved in defending its colonies—especially the costs of the French and Indian War which ended in 1763. In order to shift more of the costs of maintaining the empire to the colonies themselves, the British government enacted the Sugar Act in 1764, the Stamp Act in 1765, and the Tea Act in 1773. Because of both political and economic motives, many of the colonists strongly opposed these taxes, and this gave birth to the "No Taxation Without Representation" slogan.

Religious motivations became intertwined with such political and economic issues as the tax issues. However, two particular factors more directly related to religious establishments led to tension between the colonists and Britain. First, *there was fear among some colonists that Britain would appoint an Anglican bishop for the colonies.* Recall that the Church of England (the Anglican Church) was the official, established church in England. Some Anglican colonists wanted Britain to appoint an Anglican bishop for the colonies; however, there were many other people (including many Anglicans) who feared such external control of religious institutions. Second, *the Quebec Act of 1774 caused an uproar among many colonists.* Having acquired Quebec from the French as a result of the French and Indian War, the British came to an agreement with the French Catholic population of Quebec. This agreement gave the Catholics some degree of autonomy (e.g., the ability to raise tax money for schools) and the kind of status that Catholics had in Catholic countries in Europe. This was viewed by many British colonists as an establishment of a hostile religion in the region—a possible precedent that might cause problems for the colonies. Many Protestant colonists were strongly anti-Catholic and many were opposed to the establishment of religion—at least to the external establishment of religion—and they were especially opposed to the establishment of the Catholic Church.

As a result of political, economic, and religious issues, a period of colonial resistance against the British government began. For example, this resistance took the form of defiance of British tax laws and harassment of tax collectors. In response, the British government accelerated its use of force in order to enforce laws and collect taxes. This escalation of force led to greater resistance from the colonists and to an increase in the acceptability of the idea of declaring independence from the British empire.

The process of declaring political independence from Britain changed church-state relations within the colonies. In the first place, the emphasis in political and religious rhetoric on the autonomy of the individual carried over into the debates on the proper relationships among the individual, religious institutions, and political institutions. Further, as the colonies declared their independence from Britain, they transformed themselves into independent states, and this process opened certain questions for debate. As each of these newly transformed states created its own constitution, questions of church-state relations were often raised and debated. On the eve of the American Revolution, most colonies had some provision for an establishment (or multiple establishments) of religion, and often these provisions were simply carried over into the new state constitutions. However, most of these establishment provisions were eliminated by the end of the century.

After declaring independence, the states formed a loose confederation under the Articles of Confederation; after the war was over, this government continued functioning. However, there were some leaders in the states who wanted a stronger federal government for various reasons (e.g., to aid economic development and to present a stronger front in international relations). With great political skill, these leaders brought about a new Constitution. The development of the original Constitution and the Bill of Rights had implications for individual-church-state relationships then and later. Further, individual-church-state relationships were affected because of the creation of a larger political entity with much greater overall religious diversity than existed within the individual states.

Rationalists and Pietists in the Revolutionary Coalition

The American Revolution was not a result of just one single political or religious viewpoint. The motives and viewpoints of those who carried out the revolution were diverse and conflicting. Further, within almost any religious grouping, some supported the Revolution and some did not. However, an informal coalition was formed that managed to agree on independence from Britain and a substantial degree of autonomy for the individual. Two major components of this coalition were discussed in the previous chapter: the pietistic evangelical Christians and the religious rationalists. We will reiterate some basic points about these two groups and then expand the discussion of deists as a subgroup of religious rationalists.

Pietists

The evangelical pietists who emerged out of the Great Awakening emphasized the role of the individual in achieving salvation. This emphasis gave people a feeling of personal power in religious matters which could be transferred to their roles in society. In their clashes with traditional religious establishments, the pietists worked to achieve religious freedom. This support for religious freedom for themselves led them to support a broader conception of religious freedom at that time, and it led to support for independence from Britain. Further, many pietists held a millennial view of society in the colonies: breaking with Britain was a step toward creating a better social order in which gradual progress could be made toward achieving God's kingdom on earth.

Religious Rationalists

Religious rationalism grew out of the European Enlightenment. Here we will briefly paraphrase several characteristics of "enlightened Christianity" discussed by Ahlstrom (1972: 356–358). Religious rationalism placed a great deal of emphasis on the use of reason in religion and in other matters as well. Through the use of reason, people could make progress in both religious and secular terms. In order for reason to be used in religion, religious doctrines had to be simplified and the unnecessary theological baggage needed to be discarded. It also placed the emphasis on getting people to lead moral, ethical lives. Along these lines, predestination was rejected—the lives and fate of people were not determined in advance by God. God was seen as an impersonal power that ruled the universe rather than as a personal God who related to humans.

Deism

Not all religious rationalists shared the same outlook. Miller (1976: 58–59) discusses three responses to the European Enlightenment. The first response consists of conservatives and evangelicals; these groups placed the emphasis on revealed faith rather than reason, and they were the least responsive to the ideas of the Enlightenment. Miller's other two categories are two varieties of religious rationalists: liberals and deists. In this context, religious liberals are religious rationalists who attempted to reconcile traditional Christian beliefs with ideas from the Enlightenment. On the other end were the deists, who—to varying degrees—did not necessarily attempt to retain anything at all from traditional Christianity or from any other religion.

While deism did not attract great numbers of people, some of those who were attracted to deism (e.g., Jefferson, Madison, and Franklin) were among the most important Founders. While not all deists shared the same beliefs, we will list some of the basic ideas generally associated with deism.

- Deists believe in a deity (a god) who created the universe.
- This deity was sometimes simply called God, but more often this deity was referred to by such terms as the *Creator*, the *God of Nature, Nature's God*, the *Governor of the Universe, the Author of Existence*, the *Great Architect*, or the *Great Legislator*.
- The nature of this deity was beyond the ability of human nature to comprehend.
- This deity did not intervene in human affairs.
- This deity governed through the laws of nature rather than through personal intervention. Albanese (1976: 118) describes this process thus: "The Creator God had wound the springs of a great natural machine which worked according to prescribed and predictable laws."
- These laws of nature through which this deity governed could be discovered through reason.
- Humans had a duty to use their reason and talents in order to improve the lot of humanity.

Such a religious viewpoint obviously prescribes a great deal of freedom—and obligation—for the individual. Albanese (1976: 114) cleverly expresses this deistic view of human freedom from the deity: "The greatest Governor governs least." Humans are left free to shape their own destinies.

The Founders who were deists usually did not publicize their views—with the exception of some such as Thomas Paine. Men such as Jefferson and Franklin usually kept their religious views to themselves and were "outwardly conforming" (Mead, 1978; Miller, 1976). Given the unorthodox nature of their views, they kept quiet in order to avoid unnecessary battles with those who held more orthodox religious views and to avoid further attacks on themselves. When Jefferson ran for president in 1800, he was attacked for his religious views, but he did not respond to the attacks.

The Basis of the Coalition

Various scholars (e.g., Miller, 1976; Mead, 1978; Albanese, 1976; Chidester, 1988) basically concur on the fundamental factor that led to a temporary alliance between many religious rationalists (including deists) and many evangelical, pietistic Christians: *the emphasis on individual autonomy in both civil and religious matters.* Miller (1976: 57) argues that people of the time around the Revolution were beginning to think of themselves as free beings who did not need to be directed by either the church or the state: "Would not things be better, they reasoned, if men could be trusted to attain their own goals, find their own religion, manage their own economy, and even govern themselves?"

The coalition between rationalism and pietism lasted long enough to bring about a substantial degree of religious freedom and separation of church and state. Mead (1976: 162) argues that only after this achievement "did pietism discover its latent incompatibility with rationalism, divorce itself, and remarry traditional orthodoxy."

Wrapping the Revolution in Religion

Patriot leaders used religious appeals to identify the revolution with religion (Reichley, 1985; Albanese, 1976; Chidester, 1988). The justifications for the war were often wrapped in religious reasons and images. Again using the analogy based on the biblical account of Jews escaping from Egypt to seek the new land promised to them by God, the new nation became the new Israel and Britain became the new Egypt. The pietist side of the revolutionary coalition provided the religious ardor for the coalition and the rationalist side provided the intellectual rationale, but both parts of the coalition wrapped the revolutionary effort in religious language.

The cultural environment of that time was infused with the pietism from the Great Awakening and the rationalism from the Enlightenment. The pietists spoke of what Albanese (1976) terms the God of History or Jehovah; the rationalists spoke of the God of Nature. Given the common goal of the revolutionary coalition, given the infusion of the environment with both pietism and rationalism, and given the emotionally charged situation, an interesting blurring of gods sometimes happened. Albanese (1976: 139) states that during the revolutionary era: "Both leaders and followers acknowledged the God of Nature, while many of the leaders and most of the followers cheerfully venerated Jehovah as well." Albanese argues that the people of this time often moved comfortably between the God of History and the God of Nature and sometimes did not perceive any difference; the identities of the two became fused into two-Gods-in-one in much of the thinking and rhetoric of that time. This is an important point to keep in mind when trying to interpret the religious motives of leaders during that time. For example, sometimes a rationalist such as Jefferson might use the language of traditional Christianity and sometimes a pietist might use some of the God of Nature imagery.

The Declaration of Independence

Which God—the God of History or the God of Nature—is invoked in the Declaration of Independence? The document mentions deities in four places using four different terms: Nature's God, Creator, Supreme Judge of the World, and divine Providence. Overall, these terms sound much more like the God of Nature than the God of History. Further, they were written primarily by Thomas Jefferson, who was in the rationalist camp. On the other hand, the religious terminology used is such that traditional, orthodox Christians could assent to it as well.

What is in the Declaration of Independence? One way to view it is in terms of five sections as follows:

- The first paragraph says that the representatives of the United States of America are declaring independence from Britain and this document will give the reasons for the separation.
- The second paragraph presents the political theory justifying the right of the colonies to declare their independence.

- The next twenty or so paragraphs list specific grievances against the king of Great Britain.
- The next two paragraphs say that the colonies have repeatedly asked for a redress of grievances and received only further injury in return.
- The last paragraph declares the independence of the colonies from Britain and declares that each of the colonies is now an independent state with all the rights and powers of independent states.

The political theory in the second paragraph is extremely important because, although it was not included in the Constitution later, it has become a semi-official rationale for the United States government; many people refer to the ideas within the Declaration of Independence as if they were official or perhaps even sacred. These ideas have come to form the justification for *liberal government*—for government in which individuals are given a great deal of liberty. In writing this concise summary of his political theory, Thomas Jefferson borrowed heavily from John Locke. At the same time, we can also see the possible influence of covenant theology transposed into the social contract basis of government. Let's briefly list the basics of this theory.

- All men are created equal.
- Men are endowed by their Creator with certain unalienable rights, among which are life, liberty, and the pursuit of happiness.
- Governments are created among men for the purpose of securing these rights.
- Governments derive their powers from the consent of the governed.
- If a government doesn't secure the rights of men, it is the right of people to alter it or to abolish it and to institute a new government.

Note that the political theory of Jefferson (and John Locke) was male-oriented. The term *men* in the Declaration of Independence or the Constitution did not apply to both men and women. Further, the phrase *all men* did not mean all men. At that time, approximately one third of all the people in the southern colonies were slaves; in Jefferson's state, Virginia, 39 percent of the population in the first Census (in 1790) were slaves, and Jefferson himself owned slaves. Despite the universal rhetoric, Jefferson really meant *all white men who owned enough property so that they had the resources and time to develop their reasoning ability.* This view was later reflected in the voting requirements of most states: only white males who owned property could vote.

Thus, the liberal theory underlying the Declaration of Independence was republican rather than democratic. In a republic, political participation is much wider than in an aristocracy or a monarchy, but not everyone can participate. Over time, the original restrictions on political participation have been eliminated; thus, the United States has evolved from a (representative) republic to a (representative) democracy in which basically any adult citizen has the right to participate in politics.

The Founders

This section will present brief profiles of some important leaders involved with the Declaration of Independence and the Constitution. By examining the views of some of the greatest leaders of that time, we can more fully understand the intentions of the Founders with regard to the proper relationships among the individual, the state, and religious institutions. There is, however, an extremely important qualification that needs to be made: the Founders were engaged in politics and, as it often does, politics requires compromise. While there is every reason to believe that the Founders were highly principled, they were also very goal-oriented and pragmatic. In order to achieve their goals, they sometimes bent their principles, hid their true views on matters, or compromised one principle completely in order to achieve a more important principle. In short, our Founders were expert politicians, and the United States might have suffered a very different fate if they had not been.

Thomas Jefferson (1743–1826)

As the son of a wealthy Virginia planter, Jefferson had the time and resources to develop his education broadly and deeply. He was very familiar with—and affected by—the currents of the European Enlightenment. Cousins (1958: 114) notes that Jefferson's library contained books on art, architecture, music, history, science, poetry, belles-lettres, religion, and philosophy. Aside from his other pursuits, Jefferson was deeply involved in state and national politics—and in the question of the proper relationship between church and state. The inscription on Thomas Jefferson's epitaph reads: AUTHOR OF THE DECLARATION OF INDEPENDENCE, OF THE STATUTE

OF VIRGINIA FOR RELIGIOUS FREEDOM, AND FATHER OF THE UNIVERSITY OF VIRGINIA. All three of these accomplishments involve religion and politics in one way or another. We have already discussed the Declaration of Independence, and we will return to the Statute for Religious Freedom later.

Jefferson was a deist—although at various times he also referred to himself as a "theist," a "unitarian" or a "rational Christian" (Reichley, 1985: 94) and his political enemies labeled him an atheist. As a deist and as a creature of the Enlightenment, he placed great emphasis on the use of reason in order to improve the lot of humanity.

Jefferson was also a Christian, but not in any orthodox sense. He was a Christian in that he strongly believed in the moral teachings of Jesus; he ascribed to Jesus "all human excellence." He rejected the divinity of Jesus along with most of the other traditional orthodoxy of Christianity. Thus, Jefferson saw Jesus in terms of ethics and morality rather than in terms of spirituality or divinity. Jefferson believed that there was great wisdom in the teachings of Jesus, but this wisdom had been perverted by others (e.g., the clergy and organized religious institutions) for selfish reasons. He wanted to demystify and simplify the teachings of Jesus. He argued that people should read the Bible in the same way that they read any other book; they should take the gems of wisdom from it and discard the wrong parts. Thus, Jefferson culled from regular Bibles (using Greek, Latin, French, and English versions) his own slim "Jefferson Bible" which was entitled *The Life and Morals of Jesus*. He discarded the great bulk of the Bible and selected only a small portion from the four gospels which he felt was actually correct and useful.

Given his distrust of the clergy and religious establishments, Jefferson believed strongly in freedom of conscience and separation of church and state. The famous phrase "wall of separation between church and state" comes from a letter written by Jefferson in 1802 while he was president; he used the term in response to a question from the Baptist Association in Danbury, Connecticut, asking about the interpretation of the First Amendment. In this letter, Jefferson affirmed his views on religious liberty for the individual and gave his interpretation that the religious clauses of the First Amendment (to which we will return later) built a wall of separation between church and state.

While Jefferson distrusted the clergy and opposed the establishment of religion, he nevertheless advocated religion as a useful support for achieving civic virtue. This view was shared by most political and religious leaders of whatever persuasion. In order to encourage people to act in a moral and responsible fashion, Jefferson felt that it was necessary that people view their liberties as a divine gift. It might very well be that Jefferson—despite his own religious rationalism—had no problem with the idea that the commoner might be brought to act virtuously by the fear of God. Rational religion was not necessarily a good thing in the hands of those who might use it licentiously; some who held rationalist views in religion did not believe that this kind of religion would be adequate to restrain the behavior of the commoner.

While Jefferson believed strongly in individual liberty, he also strongly believed that people—for the good of society and for their own good—needed to act in a moral and responsible fashion. Religion helped to achieve this objective. At any rate, Jefferson was concerned more about the behavior of people than their beliefs; he once stated that it did him no harm whether people believed in one god or twenty gods or no god. Gaustad (1990: 126) notes the emphasis on deeds rather than words when Jefferson says that if he were to found a religious sect, the fundamental principle would be the opposite of Calvinism; that is, the principle would be that people could be saved by their good works, not by their faith.

James Madison (1751–1836)

James Madison, the Father of the Constitution and the fourth president of the United States, was very quiet about his personal religious views, especially as he drifted away from orthodox Christianity (Murrin, 1990: 34), even though he had studied theology for several years at Princeton. Madison strongly believed in individual freedom, and he was very concerned about possible oppression from either political or religious institutions.

As the chief architect of the Constitution, Madison helped to construct a government structure with countervailing forces to prevent it from becoming too powerful and to prevent it from oppressing individual freedom. In the *Tenth Federalist*, he put forth a negative view of human nature which some argue is based on the concept of original sin. Without restraints, the selfishness of human nature would lead to government policies in which factions would trample upon the rights of other people. The masses might, for example, use the power of the government to stifle unpopular opinions or to undermine the property rights of the wealthy. On the one hand, protection from such abuses was to be promoted by the sheer size and diversity of the new nation; given the number of different factions within the new nation, it would be difficult for any faction to gain enough power to become oppressive. Thus, political pluralism—the existence of a great number of competing factions—would help to prevent tyranny. On the other hand, there were structural safeguards built into the Constitution: the separation of powers in the three branches of government and the system of checks and balances so that each branch could counterbalance the power of the other branches. Further, within the legislative branch, the method of dividing power between the two houses—the Senate favoring the small states and the House favoring the large states—would also provide countervailing forces.

Reimer (1989) argues that Madison's earlier experience with the religious liberty issue provided him with the political pluralism ideas for the national government. In his 1785 fight in the Virginia legislature against religious establishment and for religious liberty, Madison had come to the conclusion that religious pluralism—based on the variety of different religious sects—would protect the religious freedom of individuals provided that there was no oppressive coalition among these sects. Thus, in both religion and politics, *pluralism*—the existence of a variety of different competing groups—was to help safeguard the freedom of the individual.

Madison strongly opposed official religious establishments whether they were establishments of a single church—such as had been the case when the Anglican Church was the official church in Virginia—or a multiple establishment—such as would have been the case if Patrick Henry had succeeded during the mid-1780s in establishing the Christian religion in Virginia. In Virginia, Madison and Jefferson together succeeded in preventing the reestablishment of any church and in giving official sanction to a broad concept of religious liberty. We will discuss these important events in Virginia further later.

Madison opposed the establishment of any religion (or coalition of religions) and he also supported a line of separation between church and state. Notice, however, that Madison has a *line* of separation between church and state rather than Jefferson's *wall* of separation (Mead, 1989). Thus, Madison did not try to avoid church-state overlap as much as Jefferson did.

George Washington (1723–1799)

George Washington's religious views are open to various and contradictory interpretations; his speeches and religious observances contain enough vagueness and generality that some have claimed that he was an orthodox Christian and some have claimed he was a deist (Cousins,

1958). On the one hand, he attended church, favored the reestablishment of religion in Virginia, made frequent religious references in his public speeches, required his soldiers to attend religious services on Sunday unless they were on active duty, and as president issued proclamations of national thanksgiving to God. On this basis, one might certainly conclude that Washington was a fairly orthodox Christian. On the other hand, his church attendance was infrequent (less than ten times a year), his religious references were "ecumenical rather than specifically Protestant or even Christian" (Reichley, 1985: 103), he "rarely cited the Bible and never spoke of Jesus Christ" (Gaustad, 1990: 123), he opposed oppression of one religious group by another, and he sometimes spoke of God in terms (e.g., the Grand Architect, the Great Ruler of Events, the Governor of the Universe) that resembled the language of deism more than the language of traditional Christianity. Washington was even labeled an atheist by some during his presidency. In short, there are conflicting claims about the religious views of Washington.

There is also some degree of ambiguity about Washington's views on church-state relationships. On the one hand, Washington supported Patrick Henry's failed attempt to restore a religious establishment in Virginia, he asked Congress to institute chaplains in the military, and as president he proclaimed national religious holidays. On the other hand, he apparently supported the restoration of a religious establishment in Virginia only because it would be a very broad establishment encompassing Christian churches in general; as military commander during the Revolution, he was very careful to avoid any partiality or offense with regard to the various religious views of the soldiers; as the first president of the United States, he set the tone for religious freedom in the future by making it quite clear that the government would not support religious bigotry or persecution.

After Washington became president, various religious groups (e.g., Catholics, Jews, Baptists) that had been the targets of persecution and discrimination in the colonies wrote to him to determine what his view would be on bigotry and persecution. One by one, he responded to their queries by writing that the government would not support bigotry and persecution. His August 17, 1790, response to a Jewish group summarizes his position well: "For happily the Government of the United States, which gives bigotry no sanction, to persecution no assistance, requires only that they who live under its protection should demean [behave] themselves as good citizens, in giving it on all occasions their effectual support."

Benjamin Franklin (1706–1790)

Benjamin Franklin—politician, writer, inventor—can probably best be described within our present examination as a gentle, tolerant Christian deist who felt that religion—all religions in general, but especially Christianity—served a good purpose in society. His own basic beliefs are indicated in his *Autobiography* and in a March 9, 1790 letter—written shortly before Franklin's death—to Ezra Stiles, president of Yale University. In that letter, Franklin expressed what he considered to be the fundamental principles of all sound religion: "I believe in one God, Creator of the Universe. That he governs it by his Providence. That he ought to be worshiped. That the most acceptable service we render to him is doing good to his other children. That the soul of man is immortal, and will be treated with justice in another life respecting its conduct in this."

Franklin continued in this letter that he believed that the system of morals and religion left by Jesus were the best in the world, but that they had been corrupted by others. Further, Franklin doubted the divinity of Jesus but had not really given much attention to the question; he also indicated that he would not busy himself with the question now since he would soon know the truth with less trouble. In line with his view that religion helped support a moral society, Franklin indicated that he saw no harm in people believing that Jesus was divine. He added that he didn't believe "the Supreme" punished the unbelievers of the world. Franklin also added that he had experienced the goodness of that Being in this life and he had no doubt that it would continue in the next.

As indicated before, many deists conformed to a greater or lesser degree to the religious customs around them. It was not their goal to convert people to religious rationalism. They were very concerned about the protection of religious liberty; they did not want the religious views of others imposed on them and they did not attempt to impose their views on others. At various times, many of the Founders such as Franklin, Washington, and Jefferson were labeled as atheists. In order to avoid fights over such matters, they usually kept their views to themselves. This is very evident in the postscript to the letter to Stiles, in which Franklin requests: "I hope you will not expose me to criticism and censure by publishing any part of this communication to you." Franklin asserted that he himself had always let others hold their own religious sentiments without criticism even when he felt their religious views were insupportable. He had contributed money to many religious groups in his area to help build their places of worship. And since he had never opposed any of their doctrines, he hoped to go out of the world in peace with all of them.

Franklin felt that religious views should be judged on the basis of their effectiveness in making people good citizens (Chidester, 1988: 67). Along with some other deists such as Jefferson, he believed that many ordinary people were weak and required religion to restrain vices and support virtues (Mead, 1978: 166). Any religious doctrine that contributed to this goal was good.

John Adams (1735–1826)

Like Jefferson, John Adams, the second president of the United States, could also be described as a Christian deist: a deist who believed in the moral teachings—but not divinity—of Jesus. In Massachusetts, Adams was one of the religious liberals who split off from the orthodox Congregationalists to become a Unitarian. He believed that the Christian religion was the best, but he viewed this in terms of its promotion of moral behavior; in his July 26, 1796 diary entry, he referred to Christianity as the religion of wisdom, virtue, equity, and humanity. These qualities concern human characteristics rather than dealing with divinity or salvation. In a diary entry on August 14, 1796, Adams wrote that one great advantage of the Christian religion was that it was able to spread to everyone the great principle of the law of nature and nations: Love your neighbor as yourself, and do to others as you would that others should do to you. Like Jefferson and Franklin, Adams put the emphasis on the behavior of people rather than their religious beliefs. Adams believed that all good men (whatever their religious beliefs) were Christians; this is different from saying that a man had to be a Christian in order to be good.

At the same time, Adams was very critical of what he viewed as the perversion of Christianity through institutional religion (although he believed that people should go to church) and the theological disputes that went on forever. In a December 27, 1816 letter to F.A. Van Der Kemp, Adams indicated that this perversion had made the Christian religion and the Jewish religion the most bloody religions that had ever existed, and he indicated that many cultural achievements had been prostituted for the detestable purposes of superstition and fraud.

Adams believed in—and worked for—religious freedom. He did not believe that any group had a right to impose its religious doctrines on others. The human mind was to be left free from dogmatism. In a May 22, 1821 letter to David Sewall, Adams expressed the view that progress had been made in various areas during his lifetime; the list of such areas included the abatement of superstition, persecution, and bigotry.

In his August 28, 1811 letter to Benjamin Rush, Adams stated an idea that he had long held: religion and virtue are the foundations of republican government and all free governments and the basis for social happiness under all governments. Adams believed very strongly in the use of religion to support both individual morality and civic virtue; religion made people responsible and moral in terms of their behavior as individuals in everyday life and in terms of their duties as citizens. Without religion as a support, a republican government could not exist.

Brief Comments on Other Founders

At this point, certain patterns have developed with regard to the Founders discussed so far. They tended to be religious rationalists—and probably deists—who believed strongly in religious freedom but also saw religion—especially Christianity—as a source of moral and ethical guidance that was needed to make a decent society and support republican government. While religious rationalists tended to keep their religious views to themselves, the religious language they used in particular circumstances was sometimes chosen to avoid attack or to make necessary coalitions with more orthodox Christians. While the Founders supported religious liberty, they almost unanimously believed that religion was a necessary support for a free society.

These kinds of patterns applied to many of the Founders; in some cases the patterns are less accurate than in other cases. With regard to Alexander Hamilton, for example, the patterns do not apply so well as they do for Jefferson. Hamilton was more orthodox in his religious views than most of the other major Founders. On the other hand, there were a few orthodox Christians among the Founders, such as John Jay and Patrick Henry (Noll et al., 1989: 72). John Jay, the first chief justice of the Supreme Court, was a conservative in politics and religion. Nevertheless, while Jay held orthodox Christian religious views, he was in accord with religious rationalists such as Jefferson, Franklin, Adams, and Madison in their support for religious liberty. On the other hand, Samuel Adams held orthodox Puritanical Christian religious views and ridiculed the religious views of others such as Catholics or Quakers (Cousins, 1958: 344).

With Samuel Adams on one end of the religious continuum, Thomas Paine (and perhaps Ethan Allen) occupied the opposite end. Paine's deism was much more pronounced and explicitly proclaimed than the religious rationalism of any of the other Founders. In *The Age of Reason*, written in 1794, Paine put forth his deistic views, criticized organized religions, and ridiculed the Bible and revealed religion. To him, all religious institutions of whatever kind were tools by which some humans terrified, enslaved, and exploited other humans. Most deists among the Founders did not attempt to convert others to their way of thinking about religious matters; they had other political goals, and in the religious realm they simply tried to bring about religious liberty for everyone. However, by the time he wrote *The Age of Reason*, Paine was different in this respect; he did want people to turn away from traditional religion and become deists. Instead of turning away from traditional religion, however, many people turned away from Paine.

Overall, it could be argued that the most effective Founders were religious rationalists who made use of the emphasis on reason from the Enlightenment but did not use confrontational tactics in response to traditional religious orthodoxy. Those who took an orthodox viewpoint aggressively (e.g., Samuel Adams) and those who pushed the deistic viewpoint aggressively (e.g., Thomas Paine) were more limited in the impact that they could have in the new national environment. In the next section, we will examine the environment within the states with regard to the establishment and disestablishment of religious institutions.

Establishment and Disestablishment in the States
Establishments in the States

On the eve of the American Revolution, almost all colonies had some sort of provision for the establishment or multiple establishments of religion. In New England, the Congregational Church was established in Massachusetts, Connecticut, and New Hampshire. The Anglican Church (the Church of England) was established in North Carolina, South Carolina, Virginia, Georgia, Maryland, New York, and New Jersey. Rhode Island, Pennsylvania, and Delaware had no established religion. Further, many colonies had a *religious test for public office—in order to hold public office a person must belong to a particular religious group or swear to certain religious doctrines.* Aside from discrimination of one Protestant group against another, in almost all the colonies there was discrimination against Catholics and Jews, who were usually not allowed to vote or hold public office (Curry, 1986: 80).

When the colonies declared their independence from Britain, most of them drew up new constitutions. Some of these constitutions carried over the basic church-state arrangements that had existed before independence, but changes occurred—sooner for some and later for others—in almost all the arrangements.

Virginia had an established Anglican Church before the Revolution, and there were later attempts to restore an establishment in the form of a broader Christian establishment. However, from 1776 to 1785, Virginia went though a series of steps that eventually led to rejection of established religion and to the legal protection of religious liberty. The experience of Virginia is important because it helped to set the stage for the development of the national constitution later and because other states also eventually eliminated religious establishments and religious tests for public office. We will pay particular attention to the case of Virginia later, but first let's examine other state establishments of religion after the Revolution.

New England

New Hampshire's new constitution did not even mention religion, but it left intact the old colonial law which made the church a town institution (Cobb, 1970: 500). The church was supported by a public tax and the law discriminated in favor of Protestant churches. Each town, based on the particular religious preferences within the town, established and supported a church; some towns had multiple establishments. For example, New Hampshire had multiple establishments of religion.

In addition to an established state church (Congregational), Connecticut had a multiple Protestant establishment in which the members of each established church were taxed to support their own church. Thus, the state church coexisted with other Protestant churches. Those who did not belong to a Protestant church were taxed to support the state church (Swomley, 1987: 36).

Massachusetts also had a multiple establishment. Individuals were taxed to support a church, but they were allowed to specify which church was to receive the money. If a person did not specify a choice, then the money went to the state Congregational Church.

Rhode Island did not have an established church. It continued the tradition of the comparatively high degree of religious liberty which had distinguished its history.

The Middle States

Pennsylvania and Delaware had very similar provisions. Neither state had an established religion and neither collected any taxes to support religion.

However, in both cases there was a religious test for full citizenship and for public office (Cobb, 1970: 503). In Pennsylvania, civil rights were limited to those who acknowledged the existence of God; in Delaware, civil rights were limited specifically to Christians. In both cases, the oath for public offices required them to affirm a belief in God and a belief in the divine inspiration of both the Old and New Testaments.

In New York and New Jersey, the Anglican establishment was abolished after the Declaration of Independence. While both states had a tradition of relatively high religious freedom, there were some qualifications. In New York, one article of the state constitution was apparently intended to exclude Catholics from full citizenship, and another article excluded clergymen from public office; in New Jersey, only Protestants were allowed to hold public office (Cobb, 1970: 502).

The South

Maryland ended its Anglican establishment and provided for religious liberty for all who professed the Christian religion. It also provided in its constitution for a multiple establishment arrangement in which people would be taxed to support the church of their choice; however, this taxing provision in the constitution was not actually implemented through specific legislation (Swomley, 1987: 35). Maryland also excluded clergymen from public office and required public officeholders to affirm a belief in Christianity. Further, Maryland developed a state prayer and required the clergy who refused to use this prayer to pay additional taxes or leave the state (Cobb, 1970: 504).

North Carolina ended its Anglican establishment and guaranteed freedom of conscience. However, in order to hold public office, one had to affirm belief in God, the Protestant religion, and the divine authority of the Old and New Testaments.

South Carolina replaced its Anglican establishment by establishing the "Christian Protestant religion." Thus, South Carolina set up a multiple establishment of Protestant churches. It guaranteed religious and civil liberties for all Protestants, but the clergy were excluded from holding most state offices.

Georgia replaced its Anglican establishment with a multiple establishment arrangement in which people could not be forced to support any church but their own. Religious liberty was granted, but only Protestants could serve in the state legislature.

Miller (1976: 62) argues that there was a trend throughout the nation during this time: states moved from the formal establishment of one religion to the informal establishment of denominational Christianity. Different Protestant churches were to be given equal treatment, and general Christian (Protestant) values were to be incorporated into government.

Disestablishment and Religious Liberty in Virginia

Eventually those states that had religious establishments eliminated them—along with the religious tests for public office. The process in Virginia is especially important because some argue–and some disagree—that Virginia provided a model of sorts for other states to follow later. And it is of special interest because of the contestants involved: Thomas Jefferson and James Madison versus Patrick Henry and George Washington. Also, in the process of fighting establishment in Virginia, Jefferson and Madison provided important arguments for religious liberty. Mead (1978: 175) declares that the fundamental documents of American religious freedom are two documents produced during this fight: Madison's *Memorial and Remonstrance* and Jefferson's *An Act for Establishing Religous Freedom*.

The Reestablishment Effort in Virginia

Prior to the Revolution, the Anglican Church was established in Virginia, and it was supported by taxes and by tracts of land (glebes) given to it by the government. Other Protestant churches were allowed to exist, and this had attracted a number of Baptists and Presbyterians. With the coming of the Revolution, the Anglican Church (based on the Church of England) came to be called the Protestant Episcopal Church. At this point, the Episcopalians constituted only 35 percent of all church members according to the first U.S. Census taken in 1790. There were almost as many Baptists (30 percent) and there was a substantial group of Presbyterians (22 percent). Further, there were other smaller religious groups such as Quakers (7 percent) and Methodists (2 percent).

When the state constitutional convention met in 1776, George Mason proposed that the Virginia Declaration of Rights include a phrase providing for "the fullest Toleration in the Exercise of Religion." James Madison wanted the language to go beyond the concept of toleration. To some such as Madison, the concept of toleration implies that those who have greater power will put up with and indulge those who have less power; Madison wanted a fuller expression of the acceptance and equality of the range of the groups which made up the religious pluralism of Virginia. Thus, he succeeded in getting the following phrase in Virginia's Declaration of Rights: "All men are equally entitled to the free exercise of religion according to the dictates of conscience." This put the emphasis on individual rights rather than on governmental toleration of the religious views of people.

This statement did not totally and unequivocally settle the question of state support for the church. However, the legislature began suspending the Act for the Support of the Clergy and made this suspension permanent in 1779 (Miller, 1976: 64). Ultimately, then, the Anglican Church had been disestablished for all practical purposes. However, when Jefferson first proposed his *Bill for Establishing Religious Freedom* in 1779, it was defeated by being tabled. Among other things, this bill would have made it very clear that the state would not have any established church. The failure of the bill to pass left the question of possible religious establishment in limbo.

In 1784 Patrick Henry, with the support of George Washington, introduced an assessment bill that would create a broad establishment of the Christian religion and provide for its tax support. The proposed arrangement was similar to the multiple establishments of Christian churches in several other states. People would be taxed to support Christian churches and they could specify which church was to receive their money.

This bill was popular and Patrick Henry apparently had enough votes to get it passed. Madison, however, led the opposition and was successful in getting the vote on the bill postponed and in getting the bill submitted to the public for its opinions. By the time the bill came up for a vote, Madison had activated the opposition to it. He mustered the coalition of religious rationalists and two religious groups—pietists (mostly Baptists) and Presbyterians—who had been the brunt of discrimination under the Anglican establishment, and he provided an extensive rationale for religious freedom in his *Memorial and Remonstrance.*

Madison's *Memorial and Remonstrance*

In his *Memorial and Remonstrance,* Madison presented fifteen arguments against the bill to make Christianity the established religion in Virginia and to provide tax support for it. Let's consider some of the basic ideas in Madison's reasoning.

- Religion should be directed by reason and conviction, not by force or violence, and the free exercise of reason and conviction is the unalienable right of every person.

- We should be careful of any infringement of our civil liberties; any infringement might grow into a much larger usurpation of our freedom.

- By giving favored status to the religious views of some people, the bill violates the principle of equality of all citizens.

- When a church is supported by the state, the clergy become corrupt and lazy.

- The Christian religion does not need state support; it has existed and flourished without the support of laws and even in spite of opposition from laws.

- The bill would actually hurt the spread of Christianity by making unconverted people defensive toward it; further, it would hurt Christianity by creating disharmony among religious groups.

- On the economic development level, Madison argued that by providing a less hospitable environment for religious diversity, the bill might cause possible immigrants not to come here and it might cause some residents to move elsewhere.

- The enforcement of a law considered obnoxious and invalid by so many people will undermine respect and obedience for the laws in general and weaken the legitimate powers of government.

- If the legislature can infringe on freedom of religion, then it can infringe on other individual rights as well.

Some of Madison's arguments were not specific to the question of religious freedom per se. He argued, for example, that if a state can infringe on a freedom a little now, it might completely usurp that freedom later. Some arguments concerned practical consequences (e.g., possible increases in religious disharmony and possible economic development problems resulting from decreased immigration and increased emigration). At the core, however, Madison argued that religious establishments were not good for the individual, the state, or religion itself. Individuals have an unalienable right to freedom of conscience, and their religious beliefs should be developed from their own reasoning and faith rather than being imposed upon them by a state church. State establishments violate the rights of those who don't share the established religion and this violates the principle of equality of citizens. When the state involves itself in religion, political leaders tend to use religion to achieve political goals and this corrupts the state. Further, when the state enforces laws in favor of one religion, it alienates some people and reduces its own legitimacy in their eyes; this makes it more difficult to obtain the compliance of citizens for laws in general. Further, the established churches and their clergy are harmed by establishment because they become corrupted by their position of power.

Madison's arguments helped to win the fight against Patrick Henry's religious assessments bill. Further, in the aftermath of this victory, the time was right to reintroduce Jefferson's *Bill for Establishing Religious Freedom*.

Jefferson's *Bill for Establishing Religious Freedom*

Soon after Patrick Henry's assessment bill was defeated, Jefferson's *Bill for Establishing Religious Freedom* was called up again, and the state legislature enacted it—in slightly modified form—into law in 1785 by an overwhelming majority. Jefferson's statute had three sections.

The first section provided a rationale for the law. Let's examine—in paraphrased form—some of Jefferson's ideas expressed in the first section of the statute. He first argued that God had created the human mind free and wanted to keep it that way. Attempts to force people to believe certain things only result in hypocrisy and meanness, and such attempts are not in accord with the plan of the deity. The deity's plan was to have people accept religion through their own reason. It is an "impious presumption" of civil and religious leaders—who are themselves fallible and uninspired—to impose their views on others. Compelling people to help pay for the propagation of religious views with which they disagree is sinful and tyrannical. It is even wrong to force people to contribute to their own religious institutions; such contributions should be voluntary. It is wrong to deprive someone of civil rights—or prevent them from holding public office—simply because of the person's religious views. By making rights and privileges dependent upon holding certain religious views, the religion itself is corrupted because people are "bribed" to hold those views—if they hold certain religious views, they receive certain civil rights and privileges.

It is not the object of civil government to control the opinions of people. When government tries to control the religious views of people, this destroys all religious liberty. If the opinions of people break out into acts against peace and good order, it is at that point that the government can act. Finally, the truth is great and will prevail unless free argument and debate have been taken away from people. To a very great extent, Jefferson's arguments for freedom of religion are arguments for freedom of expression; the history of freedom of expression has often revolved around religious freedom issues.

The second section constitutes the actual policy. It provides a very extensive statement of religious liberty. The first part is put in the negative—as a restriction on what can be done to the individual:

> ... [N]o man shall be compelled to frequent or support any religious worship, place, or ministry whatsoever, nor shall be enforced, restrained, molested, or burthened in his body or goods, or shall otherwise suffer, on account of his religious opinions or belief;

The second part is put in the positive—as a statement of what the individual is free to do:

> ... but that all men shall be free to profess, and by argument to maintain, their opinions in matters of religion, and that the same shall in no wise diminish, enlarge, or affect their civil capacities.

The third section begins by acknowledging that it would be futile for the present legislature to try to keep future legislatures from revoking this statute. However, the present legislature does declare that the rights in this statute are natural rights; if any future legislature repeals this statute or narrows it, such action would be an infringement of natural right.

Thus, Virginia went from a colony with an established Anglican Church prior to the Revolution to the forefront of religious liberty on the eve of the development of the United States Constitution. Three of the men involved in the fights in Virginia—Madison, Jefferson, and Washington—went on to have a substantial voice in individual-state-church relations in the national arena. Now let's examine the issue of individual-state-church relationships in the formulation of the initial Constitution and the Bill of Rights, which was added to it very quickly.

Religious Clauses in the United States Constitution

The Unamended Constitution

A Secular Document

The United States Constitution is essentially a secular document that is neutral toward religion. We need to note, however, that some would disagree with the preceding statement.

The original Constitution—prior to the addition of the Bill of Rights—says almost nothing about religion. With the exception of the phrasing in the date ("the Seventeenth Day of September in the Year of our Lord one thousand seven hundred and Eighty seven"), the Constitution makes no mention of any god whatsoever—neither the orthodox God of History nor the deistic God of Nature.

Religion is only mentioned once in the Constitution. In the last paragraph of Article 6, it is first stated that United State senators and representatives, members of the state legislatures, and all state and federal executive and judicial officers "shall be bound by Oath or Affirmation" to support the Constitution. Of significance here is the fact that people could use either an oath or an affirmation; oaths imply a religious basis while affirmations do not. After this clause, Article 6 continues by prohibiting religious tests for national office: "[N]o religious Test shall ever be required as a Qualification to any Office or public Trust under the United States."

At the time the Constitution was signed, a number of states still had religious tests—in order to hold public office, a person had to swear to a belief in certain religious ideas. Typically, this meant that only Protestants could hold public offices in the states. Article 6 did not prohibit such religious tests for *state* offices; it applied only to *national* offices. Eventually, however, the states that had religious tests either eliminated them or ignored them.

Not everyone at the Constitutional Convention favored the prohibition on religious tests. A few of the delegates favored restricting public office to Protestants. Curry (1986: 195) provides quotes to show that several delegates opposed allowing the following to hold public office: Jews, heathens, infidels, pagans, deists, "Mahometans" (Muslims), and "Papists" (Catholics).

Why a Secular National Government?

Given the use of religious language and images by both religious rationalists and pietists during the Revolution, why did the Constitution avoid the matter completely except for the prohibition of religious tests for national office? Let's consider several reasons.

First, the Founders were well aware of the great religious pluralism that existed in the states. Perhaps in no country in the world at that time was there as much religious diversity as there was in the combined population of the different states within the United States. Any attempt by the delegates at the Constitutional Convention to establish religion or require religious tests for public office would have led to intense opposition within the convention itself and in later efforts to obtain ratification.

Second, the Founders were also well aware of religious persecution that had taken place in the colonies and in the world generally; they had seen how established churches had treated dissenters. Thus, they did not want to provide any basis for one religious group to harass another religious group.

Third, the Founders were primarily interested in achieving their central goal—the creation of a stronger central government—and they did not want to raise issues which might derail their primary goal. Wilson (1990: 84) states: "The Founding Fathers' overriding concern was to neutralize religion as a factor that might jeopardize the achievement of a federal government." Thus, the Founders' avoidance of religious concerns in the Constitution constituted neither support nor opposition to religious values; it was a very pragmatic strategy of avoiding stirring up a hornets' nest of religious issues. This is demonstrated somewhat oddly in the reaction to Benjamin Franklin's request that each day's session of the Constitutional Convention be opened with a prayer; the unsuccessful request was opposed by Alexander Hamilton. Recall that Franklin was a deist and Hamilton was more orthodox. Yet Franklin had called for prayer and Hamilton opposed it. Despite his deism, Franklin felt that this religious observance might help lift the convention out of the deadlock it was in at that particular time. Hamilton opposed the measure on pragmatic grounds: the action might signal to the rest of the country that the convention was having problems (Murrin, 1990: 30).

Fourth, the Founders generally shared the belief that religious liberty was good for religion itself (Castelli, 1988: 10; Reichley, 1985: 107). Therefore, any promotion of a particular religion within the Constitution would have had negative effects on religion rather than positive effects. Keep in mind, also, that most Founders, regardless of whether they held rationalist or orthodox religious views, believed that religion provided a necessary support for government—especially republican government.

Fifth, given the concern of many at the convention with the economic development of the country and given the need for the country to deal with other nations, it was very pragmatic for the delegates to avoid the matter of religion in the Constitution. The establishment of any religion might have prevented immigration to this country, discouraged foreign investors, and made it more difficult to enter into agreements and treaties with other countries. Noll et al. (1989: 131) emphasize the importance of the wording in the 1797 treaty with the Islamic nation of Tripoli. This treaty—which was negotiated under President Washington, ratified later by the Senate, and signed by President John Adams—states that the harmony between the two countries would not be interrupted for religious reasons because the United States "is not in any sense founded on the Christian Religion."

Adding the Bill of Rights
Motivations and Background

The Constitution required ratification by nine of the thirteen states. After the Constitution had been written and signed, the job of getting the individual states to ratify it began. Proponents and opponents of the proposed stronger central government marshaled their arguments to persuade the undecided. One issue that was raised was a lack of a bill of rights in the Constitution.

Most of the Founders at the Constitutional Convention apparently felt that a bill of rights was not needed because the Constitution was not giving the government any power to act in this area anyway, because the governmental power was to be hemmed in by checks and balances, because many of the state constitutions already had some sort of bill of rights, and because listing some of the rights of individuals in the Constitution might imply that those were the only rights individuals possessed. Nevertheless, there were strong objections to the absence of a bill of rights in the Constitution. Some who raised this objection (e.g., Patrick Henry) apparently did so simply in order to help prevent the ratification of the Constitution; others (e.g., Thomas Jefferson) were genuinely concerned about the absence of a bill of rights in the Constitution (Curry, 1986: 194). In discussions of the need for a bill of rights, one recurrent theme was the need for a guarantee of religious freedom.

The absence of a bill of rights was causing a problem for ratification of the Constitution. While he did not originally think a bill of rights was necessary, Madison changed his mind and promised that this would be one of the first actions of the new government. After the Constitution was ratified, the new United States government began in 1789, and Madison was elected to the first House of Representatives. In June, Madison submitted a list of amendments to the House; after debate and modification of the amendments in the House and Senate, the final list of ten amendments was passed on September 25. These first ten amendments, the Bill of Rights, were ratified by the states and took effect on December 15, 1791.

The first Congress had many problems with which to deal and many of its members did not want to spend a great deal of time on developing a bill of rights. As a result, the amendments were modified, compromised, and passed without a great deal of debate. The language of the amendments was often very general and this left the amendments open for future generations to interpret. However, there was some debate and Madison kept notes on this debate. Let's examine the development of the religious clauses in the First Amendment.

Religion and the Formulation of the First Amendment

The "first freedom" of the First Amendment prohibits Congress from making any laws concerning an establishment of religion or from prohibiting the free exercise of religion: "Congress shall make no law respecting an establishment of religion, or prohibiting the free exercise thereof." Thus, at the national level, there is to be no religious establishment and individuals are to have religious freedom.

Note that this amendment applies only to Congress; it did not apply to the states and, as discussed earlier, there were still states at that time that had religious establishments—usually multiple establishments of Protestant Christian churches. Thus, it was still possible for a state to establish a church; further, several states still had religious tests for public office and did not give full citizenship rights to people who were not Protestants.

In a later chapter, we will discuss the way in which the Bill of Rights was eventually held to apply to state actions as well as the national government as a result of the passage of the Fourteenth Amendment. However, such interpretations of the religious clauses of the First Amendment were not made until this century. Cobb (1970: 510) wrote in *The Rise of Religious Liberty in America* (originally published in 1902) that even then if a state wanted to, it could set up a state church and support it with tax money, and the national government would have no power to prevent it.

Swomley (1987: 44) states that the debate concerning the religious clauses in the First Amendment was not between supporters and opponents of religion; it had already been decided in the Constitutional Convention not to give the national government any power in this area. Since the national government had not been given any power in this area, some thought it was unnecessary to deal with the subject in the Bill of Rights. However, Swomley (1987: 44) describes the problem for Congress thusly: define a prohibition against the use of federal power in religious matters in such a way that no future Congress could assume any power in this area. Similarly, Curry (1986: 216) argues that, since the Constitution had not given the national government any power to deal with religious matters, passage of the religious clauses of the First Amendment was a symbolic act: "an assurance to those nervous about the federal government that it was not going to reverse any of the guarantees for religious liberty won by the revolutionary states."

The wording of the final religious clauses in the First Amendment came about after a series of changes and compromises. Madison's original provisions concerning religion in the Bill of Rights were broader. He originally proposed two amendments concerning religious freedom. The first would prohibit any violation of civil rights of people on the basis of religious beliefs or practices, prohibit any national religious establishment, and guarantee full and equal rights of conscience: "The civil rights of none shall be abridged on account of religious belief or worship, nor shall any national religion be established, nor shall the full and equal rights of conscience be in any manner, or on any pretext, infringed." These ideas were modified and compressed into the final wording of the religious clauses in the First Amendment.

Madison's second amendment relating to freedom of religion, and other rights, extended the idea of religious freedom to the states: "No state shall violate the equal rights of conscience, or the freedom of the press, or the trial by jury in criminal cases." Madison himself considered this to be the most important amendment in his whole list of amendments (Curry, 1986: 204). While this proposed amendment passed in the House of Representatives, it was rejected in the Senate. Thus, the Bill of Rights applied only to the national government.

The debates concerning the religious clauses of the First Amendment indicate that there was not just a single viewpoint about church-state relations on which everyone agreed. Further, given the religious pluralism and the variety of church-state relationships in the individual states, Congress tried to avoid much controversy in the proposed amendments because it was necessary to have amendments ratified by three fourths of the states. Perhaps the clearest agreement among members of Congress during the debates about the religious clauses was the idea that the national government had no power whatsoever to deal with religious matters. The states did have power to deal with religious matters, and Madison did not succeed with his proposed amendment to prohibit the states from violating the equal rights of conscience of individuals. The religious clauses in the Constitution had little significance except on a symbolic basis until after the 1868 ratification of the Fourteenth Amendment which, among other things, placed restrictions on what the states could do.

Summary and Conclusions

Part of the difficulty that we have today in interpreting the intentions of the Founders with regard to individual-church-state relationships is that they did not speak with a single voice. There was a variety of viewpoints on the proper mix of religion and politics. Further, this situation was complicated by the fact that, during the process of making a revolution and the process of making a nation, people who wanted to make a revolution or make a nation had to form coalitions among groups who held conflicting views on religion and the proper church-state relationship.

Thus, the deist Thomas Jefferson wrote the Declaration of Independence in such a way that it could garner support from both religious rationalists like himself and those who held pietistic or orthodox religious views; the God in the Declaration of Independence was general enough to be interpreted as either the God of History or the God of Nature. The coalition that created the Constitution, on the other hand, was held together partly as a result of taking a neutral stance toward religion; it avoided mention of either the God of History or God of Nature. In formulating the religious clauses in the First Amendment, Congress simply affirmed that the Constitution had never given the national government any power to deal with religious matters.

Despite the problems in attributing a single set of intentions to the Founders, we can say that the major figures among them shared a certain set of beliefs about relationships between the individual, the church, and the state. Let's list these beliefs.

- Individuals have an inherent, unalienable right to form their own religious views without compulsion from either church or state.
- There should not be an established church arrangement—neither a single established church nor a multiple establishment. Support for churches should be completely voluntary.

- There should be no religious test for public office, and individuals should not be deprived of any of their rights on account of the religious views they held.
- Individuals should have the right to practice their own religious beliefs provided that such practices did not cause any harm to anyone else.
- Any religion that helped to bring about moral behavior in people was good, and they believed that the Christian religion was the best religion in this respect.
- A republican government required a fairly high level of morality and ethical conduct from citizens.
- Religion was needed to provide support for government—especially a republican government in which a comparatively large proportion (in relation to other forms of government at that time) of the population would have a say in public policy.

Overall, while concerned with the necessary compliance of people with rules needed to provide for the social order, the Founders gave great emphasis to the freedom of the individual in both religion and government.

This chapter concerned developments in linkages between politics and religion up through the first few years under the new Constitution. In the next chapter, we will see how this framework played out in the historical period from 1800 through 1959 as the nation engaged such issues as slavery, Prohibition, and issues of war and peace. Then Chapter 4 will take this historical examination from 1960 to the present.

Important Terms

American Revolution	*Memorial and Remonstrance*
Deism	*An Act for Establishing Religious Freedom*
Declaration of Independence	Bill of Rights
Constitution	First Amendment
Jefferson Bible	God of History
Religious establishment	God of Nature

Review Questions

1. What groups made up the informal coalition that supported the American Revolution? Why was each group in support of this move?

2. What was the "fundamental factor" that motivated them?

3. Compare and contrast the God of Nature and the God of History.

4. What are the basics of the theory of government that Jefferson borrowed from Locke?

5. What role did each of the following play in shaping the Declaration of Independence and the Constitution: Thomas Jefferson, James Madison, George Washington, Benjamin Franklin, and John Adams?

6. Why is the establishment and later disestablishment experience of Virginia particularly important for our topic in this chapter?

7. Compare and contrast *Memorial and Remonstrance* and *An Act for Establishing Religious Freedom*.

8. Since both religious rationalists and pietists had used religious language and imagery during the Revolution, why did they draft the original Constitution with so little religious language?

9. Why was the Bill of Rights added to the Constitution?

Discussion Questions

1. What do you think of the religious ideas of the deists?

2. The American Revolution was "wrapped in religion," that is, religious appeals were used to justify the Revolution. Can you think of any more recent wars in which this happened?

3. We noted that "certain patterns" are evident in the religious outlooks of the founders. Why do you think they held these sorts of viewpoints?

4. How important is religious liberty to you, personally? Why?

For Further Reading

Ahlstrom, Sydney E. 1972. *A Religious History of the American People.* New Haven: Yale University Press.
> Parts of this book are very relevant to the historical aspects of religion and politics covered in this chapter.

Castelli, Jim. 1988. *A Plea for Common Sense: Resolving the Clash between Religion and Politics.* San Francisco: Harper and Row.
> Parts of this book are very relevant to the question of the intentions of the founders of the U.S.

Cousins, Norman. 1958. *In God We Trust: The Religious Beliefs and Ideas of the American Founding Fathers.* New York: Harper and Brothers.
> This is an informative and interesting discussion of religion and politics among the founders of the U.S.

Curry, Thomas J. 1986. *The First Freedoms: Church and State in America to the Passage of the First Amendment.* New York: Oxford University Press.
> This work examines the background of the U.S. in terms of the development of religious and political freedom.

Swomley, John M. 1987. *Religious Liberty and the Secular State.* Buffalo: Prometheus Books.
> Parts of this work concern the early political and religious connections in the U.S.

Relevant World Wide Websites

Remember to visit our website for updates and additional links at
http://bsuvc.bsu.edu/~øøamcorbett/relpol.htm

http://www.th-jefferson.org/ Interpreting Thomas Jefferson

http://sln.fi.edu/franklin/ Benjamin Franklin: Glimpses of the Man

http://xroads.virginia.edu/~CAP/ham/hamilton.html The Rise and Fall of Alexander Hamilton

http://odur.let.rug.nl/~usa/P/ This site consists of information on U.S. presidents, including Washington, Adams, Jefferson, and Madison.

http://www.mediapro.net/cdadesign/paine/ Thomas Paine National Historical Association

http://www.usia.gov/usa/oah/toc.htm An Outline of American History site includes

http://www.usia.gov/usa/oah/toc.htm An Outline of American History site includes precolonial period through current history.

http://www.msstate.edu/Archives/History/USA/usa.html History of the United States site includes colonial period through current history.

http://www.deism.com/ World Union of Deists site provides a more extensive view of deism.

References

Ahlstrom, Sydney E. 1972. *A Religious History of the American People.* New Haven: Yale University Press.

Albanese, Catherine L. 1976. *Sons of the Fathers: The Civil Religion of the American Revolution.* Philadelphia: Temple University Press.

Castelli, Jim. 1988. *A Plea for Common Sense: Resolving the Clash between Religion and Politics.* San Francisco: Harper and Row.

Chidester, David. 1988. *Patterns of Power: Religion and Politics in American Culture.* Englewood Cliffs, New Jersey: Prentice-Hall.

Cobb, Sanford H. 1970. *The Rise of Religious Liberty in America.* New York: Burt Franklin.

Cousins, Norman. 1958. *In God We Trust: The Religious Beliefs and Ideas of the American Founding Fathers.* New York: Harper and Brothers.

Curry, Thomas J. 1986. *The First Freedoms: Church and State in America to the Passage of the First Amendment.* New York: Oxford University Press.

Gaustad, Edwin Scott. 1990. *A Religious History of America.* San Francisco: Harper and Row.

Levy, Leonard. 1995. *The Establishment Clause, Second Edition.* Chapel Hill: University of North Carolina Press.

Malbin, Michael J. 1978. *Religion and Politics: The Intentions of the Authors of the First Amendment.* Washington, D.C.: American Enterprise Institute.

Mead, Sidney E. 1978. "American Protestantism During the Revolutionary Epoch." Pp. 162–180 in John M. Mulder and John F. Wilson (Eds.), *Religion in American History: Interpretive Essays.* Englewood Cliffs, New Jersey: Prentice-Hall.

Mead, Sidney E. 1989. "Neither Church nor State: Reflections on James Madison's 'Line of Separation.'" Pp. 41–54 in James E. Wood, Jr. (Ed.), *Readings on Church and State.* Waco, Texas: J.M. Dawson Institute of Church-State Studies.

Miller, Glenn T. 1976. *Religious Liberty in America: History and Prospects.* Philadelphia: Westminster Press.

Murrin, John M. 1990. "Religion and Politics in America from the First Settlements to the Civil War." Pp. 19–43 in Mark A. Noll (Ed.), *Religion and American Politics: From the Colonial Period to the 1980s.* New York: Oxford University Press.

Noll, Mark A., Nathan O. Hatch, and George M. Marsden. 1989. *The Search for Christian America.* Colorado Springs: Helmers and Howard.

Reichley, A. James. 1985. *Religion in American Public Life.* Washington, D.C.:
    Brookings Institution.
Reimer, Neal. 1989. "Religious Liberty and Creative Breakthroughs: The Contribu-
    tions of Roger Williams and James Madison." Pp. 15–24 in Charles W. Dunn
    (Ed.), *Religion in American Politics.* Washington, D.C.: CQ Press.
Swomley, John M. 1987. *Religious Liberty and the Secular State.* Buffalo: Prometheus
    Books.
Wilson, John F. 1990. "Religion, Government, and Power in the New American
    Nation." Pp. 77–91 in Mark A. Noll (Ed.), *Religion and American Politics: From
    the Colonial Period to the 1980s.* New York: Oxford University Press.

CHAPTER 3

Religion and Politics in United States History, 1800–1959

[Slavery] was particularly burdensome to the white women of the South because it was they who had the daily responsibility of oversight, especially of the house servants. . . . Many also came to see that as women they were in many ways as much in thrall to their husbands and brothers as the slaves were.
 —Frank G. Kirkpatrick, "From Shackles to Liberation: Religion, the Grimke Sisters and Dissent"

Overview

In the previous two chapters we discussed the cultural, religious, and political framework that provided the beginnings of religious and political linkages in the United States. This chapter briefly reviews the effects of religion and religious groups on political actions and movements in the United States from 1800 through 1959.

In this brief analysis, we cannot cover everything relating to religion and politics during those years. Thus, we will focus on the roles that religion and religious groups played in certain crucial issues: the slavery debate, the Prohibition controversy, movements for broad social reform, and matters of war and peace. Here are some of the major questions we will address:

- In what ways did religion and religious groups affect the political process?

- What particular social movements involved linkages between religion and politics?
- What religious divisions resulted from the slavery issue and what were the long-term effects of these divisions?
- What role did religious groups play in the temperance movement and the push for prohibition of alcohol?
- What kinds of social reforms were advocated by religious groups?
- What were the religious-political ramifications of the New Deal during the 1930s?
- What different views of war have been supported by religious groups?
- What effects did the Revolutionary War have on churches?
- What views have religious groups taken toward particular wars?

Background

Religion and religious groups have affected the political process throughout American history in at least three ways (Swieringa, 1990):

1. Religious groups were important reference groups on which people relied.
2. Religious groups worked to extend their influence in the larger society and to protect their interests from attack by using the political process.
3. Religious beliefs themselves affected political choices.

Social reform movements—organized movements that attempt to bring about change in social institutions or behavior through deliberate action— did not come into being in the United States until the late eighteenth century. Beginning in the early nineteenth century, however, such reform movements became the main avenue for social change. Three shifts in people's viewpoint brought this about: (1) People came to believe that they could bring about effective social change, rather than having a passive attitude toward it. (2) They began to think of religion in terms of both personal piety and social action, rather than limiting it to the personal, private dimensions of life. (3) They came to think that maintaining the social order and making needed changes in it was everyone's obligation rather than just being the responsibility of religious and political leaders.

The Benevolent Empire

The term Benevolent Empire is sometimes used to refer to the reforming organizations and movements that harnessed the religious energies loosed by the Second Great Awakening (approximately 1790 through the 1830s) to bring about significant social reforms. The Society of Friends—more commonly known as Quakers—were among the first religious groups to link personal piety with the responsibility for improving the social order. Quaker laity and leaders alike were active early on in their distinctive peace witness and in movements for poor relief, prison reform, temperance, and abolition.

A number of general movements to better society through improved education and strengthened morals began in New England in the early 1800s, sponsored primarily by Congregationalists and Presbyterians. Most focused on the distribution of Bibles and religious tracts, along with teaching literacy so that people could read them. Similar groups were sponsored by other religious organizations. In addition, the Unitarians—whom the Congregationalists and Presbyterians regarded as heretics—sponsored humanitarian reform efforts of their own, believing that such work was the most and perhaps the only genuine piety. Unitarians were active in the establishment of public education and in working for more humane care for mentally ill, deaf, and blind persons (Cayton, 1988: 1430–1434).

Revival and Perfectionism

A second religious movement played into the growing reform movement as the Benevolent Empire peaked in the 1830s. Revivalists such as Charles Grandison Finney, a New York Presbyterian, preached perfectionism and holiness. These new doctrines held that people could avoid sinning in this life, and that perfection and moral holiness were indeed possible for human beings. Further, Finney emphasized that religious conversion, genuine spiritual rebirth, would be accompanied by renewed zeal to reform society. The perfectionist reformers primarily advocated peace, temperance or prohibition, and abolition (Cayton, 1988: 1434–1435). Finney's list of political issues that the churches must address included "Abolition of Slavery, Temperance, Moral Reform, Politics, Business Principles, Physiological and Dietetic Reform" (Sweet, 1988: 893).

Despite his insistence that the churches must address a number of pressing social issues, Finney avoided direct political involvement. Government reforms, he believed, were useless without the regeneration of people's souls. He thought it best to rely on preaching, conversion, and sanctification of each individual to gradually eliminate social evils. William Lloyd Garrison, on the other hand, who followed Finney into the abolition movement, thought preaching and conversion important, but believed that churches should engage in direct political action as well, lobbying government to get abolitionist views made into law (Dunn, 1984).

The Social Gospel Movement

During the period between 1865 and 1930, several general trends developed. Religious organizations became increasingly involved with social reform and developed active programs to better social conditions. Perhaps the best known of these efforts is the Social Gospel movement. In the wake of the election of Theodore Roosevelt, with his progressive social views, "new progressive suggestions from Christians for more comprehensively reforming the social and economic order" arose (Marsden, 1991: 29). What was distinctive about the Social Gospel movement was that it understood the Christian Gospel as *essentially* social in its message, rather than seeing social reform as a by-product of individual conversion. Its central message was social. The churches were divided, however, by theological differences between liberals and moderates, on the one hand, and fundamentalists on the other. The latter accused the Social Gospel advocates of heresy, since they did not share the fundamentalists' adherence to a literal view of sacred scripture. Secular social reform efforts also increased (Mayer, 1988: 1441–1442).

The dramatic "revolution in morals" in the 1920s brought about a "climate of crisis" that led to a deep theological division within Protestantism (Marsden, 1991: 55–56), a division that would be echoed in Christianity in the United States in the latter half of the twentieth century. The 1920s form took shape as a schism between fundamentalism and modernism. The "central symbol" that focused the concerns of the fundamentalists was the Darwinian theory of biological evolution (Marsden, 1991: 57).

The Climate of Crisis and Its Results

The campaign against evolution was essentially a political one, since it focused on attempts to prohibit the teaching of evolution in the public schools. Looking ahead, this prefigures the attempt in the 1980s and 1990s to require the teaching of creationism or creation science alongside or instead of evolution. There was no clear "winner" in the Tennessee battle over evolution. The anti-evolution law was not overturned. On the other hand, the media's treatment of fundamentalism and its portrayal of fundamentalists seriously discredited them in the minds of many people.

The 1920s looked in some ways like the end of fundamentalism, but they certainly were not, as subsequent chapters will show. Fundamentalists, by and large, returned to what had always been their strength—evangelization and building local congregations—to reemerge as an important political force in the closing decades of the century.

An important result of this development was that United States Protestantism was divided into a politically and theologically conservative branch and a politically progressive and theologically liberal camp, in a reversal of previous alignments between evangelical Christianity and social reform impulses. It would be the mid- to late 1900s before evangelicalism and progressive social action views would be realigned (see Chapter 4).

Another change occurred during this period that was of the greatest importance for the role of religion in political and social reforming movements in succeeding years. At the beginning of this time period, the language of social reform was religious even if not explicitly theological; it assumed a common set of agreed-upon religious beliefs. By the end of this era, the language used to address the issues had become secular. The growth of pluralism played a role in this; there was no longer a common religious base, and if necessary coalitions were to be formed, the language had to appeal widely and avoid potentially divisive theological implications. Scientific, secular language gained in prestige, as well. The search for and implementation of change came to rely more upon the modern, secular university than upon the religious institutions (Mayer, 1988: 1460).

Between the Great Depression and 1959, Protestantism in the United States was closely bound up with the prevailing culture, producing a high level of complacency. In addition, the economic crisis of the Depression forced churches and synagogues to concentrate on their own economic survival while doing what they could to assist their own members in doing likewise. Not until the social upheaval of the 1960s did religion again become intimately involved in the process of political and social reform (Bucher and Tait, 1988: 1463).

Given this general examination of political-religious movements during the 1800–1959 time period, let's now turn to specific issues around which such movements developed. We will begin with the very important issue of slavery.

Religion and the Slavery Question

Slaveholding had been a fact of life in most of the colonies, both in the South and in the North. The little opposition that existed had come mainly from the Friends (Quakers) and Mennonites, both small and often disadvantaged groups. Apparently the first written public protest against slavery was that published by the Monthly Meeting of Friends in Germantown, Pennsylvania, in 1688 (Edel, 1987). As the abolition movement grew stronger, it would see increasing participation on the part of the Friends, whose belief in the inviolability of each individual's conscience made slaveholding anathema. The Friends banned slaveholding among their own members and worked actively in the Underground Railroad in explicit defiance of the federal Fugitive Slave Law. Widespread opposition to slaveholding did not begin to appear until the 1770s, when spreading agitation for freedom from English rule began to seem incongruous with the denial of freedom to the slaves. As one early writer put it in the Massachusetts *Spy*: "The patriots in every town throughout the province are weekly telling us how highly they value freedom . . . yet at the same time they are stopping their ears to the cries of their poor unhappy suffering brethern [sic]," (Hyneman and Lutz, 1975: 1:183).

Both Sides Cited the Bible

Both proslavery and abolition advocates cited the Christian Bible and the teachings of their churches in support of their views. The slavery issue proved quite disruptive for the churches, in large part because stridently vocal proslavery and antislavery movements existed side by side in denominations and sometimes in local congregations. Nor were proslavery sentiments found exclusively in the South, nor abolitionist forces exclusively in the North. Although many southern churches upheld slavery as a necessary and even beneficial institution (especially as a part of the cotton economy), and most of the northern churches decried it, there were exceptions. Typical of the apologists for slavery was Baptist spokesperson Richard Furman (1755–1825). Furman declared that "the right of holding slaves is clearly established in the Holy Scriptures, both by precept and example." On the other side of the discussion, the Presbyterian General Assembly of 1818 stated that slavery was "utterly inconsistent with the law of God" and "totally irreconcilable with the spirit and principles of the Gospel of Christ." In a different vein, South Carolina Lutherans believed that churches should not interfere in economic issues. They cited the "impropriety and injustice of the interference or intermeddling of any religious or deliberative body with the subject of slavery or slaveholding, emancipation or abolition."

Denominational Differences

What of the fates of the individual denominations? In the twenty years preceding the Civil War, the Presbyterians, Methodists, and Baptists all divided over this matter.

The Methodist Church was the first to suffer division over the slavery question. The immediate problem was whether a slaveholding minister could be appointed a bishop. Although its founder, John Wesley, had spoken out against slavery and the founding conference of the church had provided for the expulsion of slaveholders who refused to free their slaves, Methodism backed away from his view as it extended its membership into the slaveholding South. The General Conference of 1836 named slavery as an evil, but also condemned abolitionism. Two conferences later, in 1844, the church adopted a strong antislavery position. It was inevitable at that point that the simmering conflict would erupt into division, and the Methodist Episcopal Church, South, formally separated with a proslavery platform.

The Presbyterian Church did not actually divide until after the political division between the Union and the Confederacy, officially dividing in 1857, but slavery was one of the issues underlying the Old School versus New School controversy in the late 1830s. The Old School was solidly centered in the South, while the New School drew its strength from the North. In 1849, the official statement produced by the General Assembly was that slavery was a matter for the civil government to deal with, and the church should stay out of it. The division into what would become the Presbyterian Church, United States, and the United Presbyterian Church in the United States of America would not be overcome until 1983 when the two major Presbyterian bodies reunited after long and tortuous discussion.

The Baptists, the third major denomination with strength in both North and South, were in a somewhat different position. While both the Methodists and the Presbyterians had national judicatories that made decisions and set policies for the entire church, Baptist church polity was altogether congregational. By the mid-1800s, however, churches in both the North and the South had become more strident in their views. In 1845, the southern churches seized the opportunity to break away and form their own, more connectional association, with a proslavery stance, becoming what would eventually be known as the Southern Baptist Convention. Meanwhile, the northern churches had also consolidated into a closer union, although still without the connectionalism of the southern church, eventually becoming the American Baptist Churches, with the exclusion of proslavery members.

The Disciples of Christ were so thoroughly local in their organization that there was literally nothing on the national level to divide. This meant that the Disciples escaped any serious division over slavery. Another group of churches was not particularly disrupted because they did not have membership in both regions. The Congregationalists, Unitarians, and Universalists were restricted to the North. They each moved easily into the abolitionist camp. Most Quakers were without question abolitionists, although some did own slaves and John Woolman's *Considerations on the Keeping of Negroes* (1754) dealt with how to keep slaves most humanely without considering the humanity of slavekeeping. The Lutheran, Episcopal, and Catholic churches remained practically undivided until the country split, despite their each having both membership in both regions and devoted proponents of both points of view. Catholic churches, particularly, tended to regard slavery as a civil matter that was best left to the government. Various social and church-governmental factors prevented church division prior to national division. Judaism's congregational polity helped it avoid division, as well. As a general rule, Jewish congregations tended to identify with whatever view prevailed around them.

The perfectionist theological tendencies described above were especially prominent among the major denominations that divided over the slavery issue, as well as among the Lutherans, whose territorial organization kept them together by preventing a clash of opinions in any national meeting. Increasingly, perfectionists of whatever denomination came to identify slaveholding as the sin of sins, utterly incompatible with religious conversion. By the early 1800s, however, many of the perfectionists had adopted the attitude that the churches should deal with spiritual matters and leave civil matters in the hands of civil governments. They focused more of their efforts on the spiritual care of slaves and provision for their physical welfare as well.

Women played an important role in the abolition movement. Harriet Beecher Stowe, daughter of a minister and a skilled lay theologian in her own right, awakened the conscience of many people with her impassioned *Uncle Tom's Cabin* (1852). After the Civil War began, Julia Ward Howe wrote "The Battle Hymn of the Republic," couching the conflict in apocalyptic imagery. Howe's work became as much the anthem of the northern cause as "Dixie" was for the South. Other, less-known and unknown women contributed greatly in terms of organizing ability, time, and money, often taking on roles and responsibilities that reached beyond what were common for women to assume at that time.

Long-Term Effects

The antislavery movement was the site of the first open conflict between the more conservative religious reformers and the more radical perfectionists, as outright abolitionism emerged from the humanitarian movement that intended to simply improve the lot of the slaves, not to abolish the institution of slavery. It was a split that would be echoed by divisions between advocates of temperance and advocates of complete prohibition, as well as between the moderate and radical factions within the peace movement (while the moderates wanted to concentrate on peace, the radicals came to see any participation in civil government as alien to Christian perfection).

What were the long-term effects of the interaction between religion and politics during this era? Charles Dunn (1984: 31–34) lists thirteen, of which the following seem to us to be the most important. (1) In all likelihood, the abolition movement would have been seriously slowed down without the energies of church people. (2) Perhaps most important of all, the abolition movement left the churches with a legacy of direct political action as a tool for religiously-based action, a legacy that continues to have an impact right up through the present. Religious groups emerged as political interest groups, a position they would continue to occupy. (3) The different views of theological liberals (direct action) and conservatives (indirect action) of what was appropriate laid the groundwork for similar patterns of action that continued through the 1970s. As a result, until that time, the main religious lobbies in Washington were liberal. (4) The concepts of equality and its corollary, social reform, raised during this era laid the groundwork for the continuing political emphasis on these issues, and the formation of political party platforms that emphasized them. (5) Emancipation brought with it identification of blacks with Lincoln's party (Republican), but the social reform emphasis set things up for the majority of blacks to become Democrats in the Franklin Roosevelt era when Democratic policies were of greater benefit to them than those of the Republicans.

Religion, Temperance, and Prohibition

The crusade for regulation of liquor or for total prohibition was part of a much larger middle-class support for "social Christianity" that aligned itself with Theodore Roosevelt's politics, especially his Square Deal and Bull Moose platforms. The 1912 Progressive Party convention used "Onward, Christian Soldiers" as its theme song. The advocated reforms included "direct primaries, women's suffrage, the initiative, referendum, recall, regulation of interstate commerce, revision of banking and currency laws, effective antitrust legislation, municipal ownership of public utilities, the income tax, the eight-hour day, prohibition of child labor, safeguards against industrial accidents and occupational diseases, and either strict regulation of the liquor traffic or its outright prohibition" (Hudson and Corrigan, 1992: 303). The liquor industry was cited as "the most dangerous and predatory of all big business" (Hudson and Corrigan, 1992: 306). Strong drink came to occupy in its time a place similar to that which had been held by slaveholding in an earlier time—regarded as the clearest evidence of an unconverted life.

Two strands of religious thought came together in the campaign against "Demon Rum." Progressive social Christianity was motivated more by the harm people saw being done by the overuse of alcohol, by the strains on families and on society that resulted from the unregulated sale and consumption of liquor. This often gave rise to working for temperance and regulation, without total prohibition. Temperance advocates often distinguished between wine and beer, on the one hand, and distilled spirits on the other hand, and encouraged moderation in the use of the former with total avoidance of the latter. Perfectionist evangelicalism was motivated more by its view that any use of alcohol was clear evidence of an unredeemed life, and anything short of prohibition was evidence of an unredeemed society. Temperance was not enough; prohibition was the only adequate approach.

A Protestant Crusade

The push for prohibition was largely a Protestant crusade, and it involved both liberal and conservative Protestants. One author has dubbed the Anti-Saloon League, founded in 1895, as "virtually a branch of the Methodist and Baptist churches" (Dabney, 1949: 35). American Protestants were solidly behind prohibition, with a couple of exceptions. Neither German Lutherans nor the Episcopalians officially supported the prohibition cause, although both were strong temperance advocates. Individual Episcopal parishes and leaders did support prohibition, and Scandinavian Lutherans of a more pietistic frame of heart did as well (Ahlstrom, 1972: 902). Congregationalists and Quakers had been strong supporters of prohibition almost from the beginning. Even as evangelical Protestantism became more acculturated and less critical of the society in which it existed and less crusading as well, its determination to see a prohibition amendment enacted remained (Sweet, 1988: 892).

Conflict between Irish and German Catholics had festered in the United States at least since the Civil War, and the prohibition movement intensified this conflict. German Catholics, like their German Lutheran counterparts, felt that prohibition amounted to fanaticism. Irish Catholic leaders in general—and those who advocated rapid assimilation into American culture in particular—were in favor of it. They regarded the drinking habits of Irish Catholic laity as a serious obstacle to progress and integration into American culture and called for prohibition as an ally in their cause. Division over prohibition within Catholicism continued until Protestant domination of the movement and passage of a constitutional amendment brought about nearly unanimous Catholic opposition (Ahlstrom, 1972: 831).

Jews were usually in the forefront of reform movements well into the 1900s, including the fight for temperance. Jewish participation in such efforts was usually disproportionate to the size of the Jewish population, for a number of reasons. The prophetic tradition of the Hebrew scriptures emphasizes social justice and providing for the needs of the entire human community. The continuing persecution of Jews sharpens their survival instincts. As one Jewish author puts it, "The Jewish outlook . . . prods Jews constantly to strive for a better world, to be in the thick and at the front of movements for social reform" (Bernstein, 1950: 419). Secular and Reform Jews, especially, for whom the essence of Judaism lay in its ethical directives, supported temperance as being of benefit to the entire community. On the other hand, many were not wholly favorable toward prohibition, because it advocated an extent of asceticism and self-denial that was and is foreign to Judaism.

Women and Prohibition

We discussed women's involvement in the antislavery movement above. Women were also deeply involved in the temperance movement, again in ways that reached beyond commonly accepted norms of the day. The Women's Christian Temperance Union, better known as the WCTU, founded in 1874, was the "first nondenominational mass women's organization." Led by founder Frances Willard, whose concerns reached far beyond prohibition, the organization provided women with a "base for their participation in reformist causes, [and served] as a sophisticated avenue for political action, as a support for demanding the ballot, and as a vehicle for supporting a wide range of charitable activities." There was a conscious attempt to "integrate women's moral outlook into the public policy arena" (Mayer, 1988: 1447). Women who had begun to gain a sense of their own power and effectiveness in the WCTU were also involved in working more directly for women's rights, including suffrage.

Involvement in the abolition and temperance crusades had made women more aware than before of their political power and its potential. Involvement in the antislavery movement had made them aware of *their* bondage as well, and of the churches' complicity in that bondage. On the one hand, the institutional church and its male clergy were often a major obstacle in the cause of women's rights, invoking divine sanction to preserve past traditions. On the other hand, churches were training grounds for leadership. When the first women's rights convention convened at Seneca Falls, New York, in 1848, the motif was discontent with both social systems that subordinated women and theologies that justified subordination.

The Churches and Broad Programs for Social Reform

Religious organizations and people were heavily involved in single-issue efforts throughout history. Many times, however, they formulated very broad, far-reaching programs for social reform. We have already seen this tendency in the theology of the Social Gospel. Two cases in point are the 1919 U.S. Catholic "Bishops' Program of Social Reconstruction" and the statement "The Social Ideals of the Churches," adopted by the Federal Council of Churches (predecessor of the National Council of Churches of Christ in the U.S.A., and, like it, closely identified with liberal Protestantism) in 1908.

The "Bishops' Program of Social Reconstruction"

The organization of the Catholic Church is such that the U.S. Catholic bishops, especially during the time period under consideration here, rarely if ever published official pronouncements such as this document without the approval of Rome, and the views outlined in it are in full agreement with mainstream Catholic teaching. Catholicism has always taught an *organic* view of society, in which all people and all aspects of society are intimately related, in contrast to the more Protestant emphasis on *individualism*. This theological position has often been the foundation for Catholic support of social programs.

The 1919 "Bishops' Program of Social Reconstruction" includes a number of points that touch on many social issues. In the face of proposals for a general wage reduction, the bishops supported labor's efforts to resist such reductions on grounds of both justice and economics. While acknowledging that the government could not continue to build public housing at the rate that it had for war workers earlier, they did make it government's responsibility to provide decent housing for all, especially in the cities. While eschewing government price controls, they championed continued reduction of the cost of living, primarily by the prevention of monopolies. They promoted the concept of a legal minimum wage and of government-provided insurance against "illness, invalidity, unemployment, and old age."

The bishops also supported labor's right to organize and to deal with management through representatives chosen by the workers, as well as labor's right to have a say in how production was carried out. They advocated extension of workplace safety and sanitation regulations, and of vocational training, along with the elimination of child labor.

They did not want to see the capitalist system become a collectivist or socialist system, but they did cite three major defects of the system as it existed: it was inefficient and wasteful in both production and distribution; it provided inadequate incomes for the majority of workers; and at the same time, it provided "unnecessarily large" incomes for the privileged few.

The Social Ideals of the Churches

The Federal Council of Churches list in 1932, which in many ways echoed a social statement approved by the Methodist Church about a quarter of a century earlier, was even longer. Several points involve the "practical application of the Christian principle of social well-being" to various aspects of the economic system: credit, the monetary system itself, the acquisition of capital, a fairer distribution of wealth, and a minimum wage, among others.

Worker safety in both industry and agriculture, and insurance, including unemployment insurance are also listed. The Council approved a reduction in the number of hours worked daily, and encouraged all employers to limit their employees' workweek to six days, "with a shorter working week in prospect." The legitimacy of labor organizations and the right of collective bargaining are upheld. Economic justice for farmers and the extension of the cultural opportunities available in cities to those in rural areas are listed.

Special regulations that would safeguard working women were included, as was the complete abolition of child labor and "protection of the family by a single standard of purity" and "educational preparation for marriage, homemaking, and parenthood." The Council sought to protect society from the effects of "any traffic" in alcohol or illegal drugs, and encouraged reform of the criminal court and prison systems.

They also wanted to foster the building of a "cooperative world order" by the renunciation of war and dramatic armament reductions, as well as the establishment of international agencies for settling disputes. More generally, they embraced toleration and goodwill toward all, along with the safeguarding of the rights and responsibilities of free speech, free assembly, and a free press, holding the "free communication of mind with mind as essential to the discovery of truth."

Two things stand out when we look at either of these documents. First, they were written over a half century ago and yet many of the problems still exist. Second, the solutions suggested then are very similar to those being suggested now; for example, government-funded health insurance appears in both documents and in the health care reform package that was proposed by President Bill Clinton in the 1990s.

Religious Liberals, Conservatives, and Franklin Roosevelt's New Deal

During the Great Depression of the 1930s, President Roosevelt changed the role of government to one of greater responsibility for the economic welfare of individuals and society. His New Deal included programs to assist people in terms of jobs, disabilities, pensions (Social Security), and other matters. As had religious involvement in the earlier Civil War and abolition era, religious involvement in the politics of Roosevelt's New Deal had ramifications that would reach into our own time. Following Dunn (1984: 50–52), we can identify several effects.

First, religious liberals had carried the day, largely because their more conservative counterparts did not make common cause with political conservatives, believing that "religion's business is religion."

Second, theological liberals had used the power of the pulpit, which had earlier been much more on the conservative side, to influence public opinion and the political process. Both of these trends would continue into the 1970s, when religious conservatism would again find its political voice.

Third, the Catholic, Jewish, and black votes became strategically important, and would continue to be so. These important components of Roosevelt's New Deal coalition retain their importance today, and we will return to this in Chapters 8 and 9.

Fourth, this particular time period drew battle lines between religious liberals and conservatives on what type of government each favored, lines that still exist. While liberals sought to use the power of government to bring about social reforms, the conservatives advocated a much more limited role for government and continued to promote individualism. This difference, too, is still a factor in the late twentieth century, as exemplified in the current discussion of welfare and other entitlements.

Fifth, the ascendance of religious liberalism contributed to the rise of internationalism, conservative religion having historically favored nationalism over international participation.

Sixth, Prohibition's defeat during the New Deal era signaled a reduction in the role personal morality played in the political involvement of religion—a reduction that would last until the last quarter of the twentieth century when it would be reactivated by the women's rights movement and the abortion controversy.

Religion, Peace, and War
Three Approaches to War

The religious roots of American attitudes toward peace and war are to be found in the scriptures of Judaism and Christianity; these scriptures have given rise to three basic approaches to warfare: the *holy war*, the *just war*, and *pacifism* (Endy, 1988: 1409). Since Christianity has been dominant in shaping attitudes in the United States, our cultural attitudes toward war can be summarized as follows: Until the reign of Constantine, *pacifism* was the dominant Christian position. Aside from that, two nonpacifist positions can be noted. The *just war* doctrine states that Christians may take part in war—and in fact may be obligated to do so—as long as the war is declared by a proper authority and certain ethical requirements are met in the conduct of the war. The idea of the *crusade* or *holy war* came into being during the Middle Ages, but never became the predominant view. Usually, Christians have put the claims of their nation above those of their religion when it came to participating in war (Ferguson, 1978: 121–122).

Holy War

The *crusade* or *holy war* approach has been a significant aspect of attitudes toward some wars in the United States. As used here, a holy war is one waged by the righteous on behalf of God against unbelievers or heretics—political *or* religious. When it came to interpreting and making sense out of the Civil War, the model of the crusade apparently worked for both sides, although understandably somewhat better for the North (Ahlstrom, 1972: 684). It was easy enough for the victors to regard their victory as God's vindication of their antislavery position, and the South's defeat as the enactment of divine wrath. For the punished, it was harder to see God's hand at work in what appeared to be the destruction of their entire way of life. Many people regarded World War II as a war of the godly against the godless as well.

Just War: The Predominant Model

The predominant model that has shaped people's attitudes has been one or another version of the *just war*. Providing that a war is declared by the proper authorities, and providing that it is carried out justly, people may in good conscience participate; in fact, they may be obligated to do so. Protestant reformers Martin Luther and John Calvin each supported a version of just war doctrine. According to Luther, the sword is a legitimate weapon of the state. Calvin was somewhat more militant: The state was responsible for supporting the church, and Calvin comes close to describing warfare to this end as a holy war. However, in the long run, his emphasis is on the right of taking up arms in a just cause, including the defense of "true religion."

Summarizing the elements of just war theory as it developed in Christianity, John Ferguson (1978) lists eight:

1. A just war is one that is declared by proper authority.

2. The cause must be just.

3. The intention must be to increase good and decrease evil.

4. It must be fought by proper means.

5. It must be directed at the guilty, not the innocent.

6. The innocent should not suffer more than is absolutely necessary.

7. War must be a last resort, after all other measures have failed.

8. There must be a reasonable chance of success.

The alert reader will immediately grasp the difficulty of being certain about whether these criteria are in fact being met in the conduct of an actual war; none except the first is easily decided, and even the first is subject to some ambiguity as well.

Ferguson points out that Christian advocacy of the just war view replaces the distinguishing Christian view with ideas taken over from Greek philosophy or Roman law. It does not result in a distinctively Christian approach to participation in war (Ferguson, 1978: 111).

Pacifism

Within the United States, the primary locus of *pacifism,* the third viewpoint, has been the "historic peace churches," along with certain other Christian denominations. These are the churches that have been present in the United States from early in its history—the Society of Friends, the Mennonites, the Brethren, and others. One of the Friends' "Queries" serves as an example of this perspective: "Are you faithful in maintaining our testimony against all war as inconsistent with the spirit and teaching of Christ? Do you live in the life and power that takes away the occasion of all wars?" The Seventh-day Adventists and the Jehovah's Witnesses are later pacifist denominations (although the Witnesses say they will fight in "God's war," and so are not in the same sense pacifists).

The Fellowship of Reconciliation, founded in December 1914, is the primary interdenominational Christian pacifist organization. It was founded on five principles (paraphrased):

1. Love, as shown in the life and death of Jesus Christ, is the only power strong enough to overcome evil with good, and the only sufficient basis for human society.

2. In order to establish a world order based on this love, people must accept the principle fully, even though this means taking risks, since most of the world does not accept the law of love.

3. As Christians we cannot participate in war, and must instead live a life based on love in all aspects of life, as an embodiment of our national loyalty and our loyalty to Jesus Christ.

4. The power, wisdom, and love of God are far greater than we know, and are always seeking to be embodied in human life in more decisive ways.

5. God works in the world through people, and therefore we offer ourselves to Him for whatever use He will make of us.

Attitudes Toward Particular Wars

Given the three approaches to war, what attitudes have Americans held toward particular wars? Let's consider some of the major wars.

The Revolutionary War

In the Revolutionary War there was religious support for both England and the revolutionaries, but in general there was greater support for the revolutionaries. We noted in the previous chapter that the Revolution was wrapped in religion, and that it received support from a coalition of very different religious camps—the pietists and the religious rationalists. The "Protestant disposition" of the colonists led to their "viewing the king and English rule with suspicion," (Ahlstrom, 1972: 361). This was true even for supporters of the Church of England. There was another factor that greatly enhanced colonial religious support for the Revolution. There had not been a resident Church of England bishop in the colonies. Prior to the Revolutionary War, support grew in England for sending a resident bishop to oversee the religious life of the colonies. This threat to the religious independence of the colonies evoked strong opposition (on religious grounds) that contributed to support for forging greater political independence (Bridenbaugh, 1962).

The Revolutionary War had a tremendous impact on the churches as well. Following Ahlstrom (1972: 365–384) we can note four primary effects.

1. The disruption and devastation of the war and the periods leading up to and following it contributed to an overall decline in the churches, a "religious depression," in the new nation. Problems of politics claimed people's attention more than matters of religion.

Church membership fell, and such membership as remained was increasingly nominal.

2. Enlightenment philosophy, deism, and secularism, on the other hand, flourished. Rationalism and liberalism became the dominant ways of looking at things, and even the religious had little use for the doctrines of revealed religion.

3. Of course, the Church of England suffered particularly devastating losses. Nonetheless, all the churches had to reorganize to meet the demands of the new situation. This made further demands on energy already sapped by the war itself.

4. At the same time, independence brought new opportunities for religion, particularly because of new relationships between religion and government. Religious freedom promoted more vigorous development of the churches as increasing separation of church and state made new opportunities and choices available. *Denominationalism—a concept of the church in which many varieties of Christianity could be included and within which there was at least some level of tolerance for differences*—became the organizing principle of Christianity in the United States.

These things together meant that the churches now had to rely on a voluntary membership. Even more, they had to rely on voluntary financial support. In response to this new "consumer market" in religion, the churches became less formal in worship, less otherworldly and intellectual in their theology, more democratic and local in their organization, and more practical in their goals. It was also the pervading patriotic spirit of the time that gave rise to the beginnings of what would be called "American civil religion," that union of religion and nationalism that would in later years provide a counterweight to increasing religious diversity.

The Civil War

Both North and South, supporters of the Union and of the Confederacy, slaveholders and abolitionists, used religious rationales in support of their positions in the Civil War. Religious historian Sydney Ahlstrom has described the Civil War as a uniquely "moral war," not because one side was clearly in the right and the other clearly in the wrong, but because "it sprang from a moral impasse on issues on which Americans in the mid-nineteenth century could no longer avoid or escape," (Ahlstrom, 1972: 649). Chaplains supported soldiers and consoled those at home on both sides. They organized noncombatant services. The war became a central topic of sermons and pastoral prayers. Revivals were a frequent feature of military camp life.

We have already noted that "holy war" ideology and the rhetoric of judgment and punishment helped many to make sense of the war and its carnage. There were other, more theologically sophisticated views. Horace Bushnell saw it as a war in which the nation's divisions were purged and its oneness strengthened. He compared it with Jesus' atoning sacrifice, in which suffering and death brought salvation. Historian Philip Schaff interpreted it as divine judgment on the entire nation's implication in the institution of slavery and as an event that made the nation ready to play a decisive role in the extension of human freedom. Abraham Lincoln believed the war to have been an ordeal to test the nation's moral purpose, leading to a new birth of freedom (Ahlstrom, 1972: 685–688).

World War I

When England and France, with their allies, declared war on Germany and its allies, religious leaders and laity were divided in their opinions of the war effort. Divisions were not along religious lines as much as over the morality and long-term consequences of the war. President Wilson's declaration of United States involvement in World War I in 1917 received nearly the full support of religious groups, even of those usually committed to pacifism. His depiction of U.S. involvement as completely disinterested and entering the conflict solely to uphold human rights made it easier to accept. Even those who had been pro-German earlier in the European conflict changed their minds. It was seen as one of those situations in which war was a necessary evil, the only way to ensure peace. Religious organizations and their leaders very shortly were caught up in feverish support of the war effort. It became a crusade: God called the nation into the battle, to promote the final triumph of "Christian civilization," and the combatants were glorified as champions of the right over against the devil's minions (Endy, 1988).

Protestant, Catholic, and Jewish religious organizations and chaplains served both the needs of military personnel and their families. World War I was the first time that significant non-Christian services had been available to military personnel and their families. Concerned not only with spiritual needs, religious organizations worked alongside secular ones to help provide for the various needs that the wartime situation engendered. The American Friends Service Committee was formed in 1917 both to counsel and assist Quakers and others to remain strong in their peace witness and to support humanitarian activity for the benefit of all engaged in the war. It has endured to the present day as an outstanding peace and humanitarian service organization.

The Selective Service Act of 1917 did provide exemptions from combatant service for clergy and seminary students. Members of the historic peace churches were exempt as well. Interestingly, although many thousands were granted certificates of exemption, only a fraction used them. The majority of those drafted went to war. Two things together were probably responsible: the churches' hold on their members had weakened, and there was fervent public condemnation of those who did refuse to fight.

Religious support for the peace movement increased in the interval between World War I and World War II, among both Protestants and Catholics. The Fellowship of Reconciliation grew to twelve thousand members by the 1930s. The Catholic Association for International Peace was formed in 1927. Peace activism was not limited to the peace churches, but drew support from mainstream religion as well. Churches worked on new ways to counsel and provide assistance and support to conscientious objectors.

World War II

Prior to the Japanese bombing of Pearl Harbor in 1941, almost all groups opposed the United States becoming involved in yet another European conflict. However, the attack on the U.S. base led to widespread religious support for intervention in World War II. Just war ideology carried the day for justification and support, focusing on the necessity of opposing the fascist threat but not making this war into a crusade against demonic evil. Religious organizations responded in two wide-ranging ways (Gaustad, 1990). Protestant, Catholic, and Jewish chaplains (over eight thousand of them) led worship, encouraged the living, comforted the dying, and provided spiritual comfort. Their assistance went beyond what is usually defined as "spiritual," however. They also helped provide for the physical and emotional needs of soldiers and families. The second approach centered on humanitarian efforts intended to soften the war's effects. Clothing, food, housing, and medicine were all provided. Religious organizations also helped deal with the tremendous refugee problem.

Mennonites, Brethren, and Friends helped run Civilian Public Service work camps where those who claimed conscientious objector standing could do alternative service. The Selective Training and Service Act of 1940 extended the right of conscientious objection to members of any religious organization who "by religious training and belief" objected to all warfare. This meant, for example, that Seventh-day Adventists came to play a much greater role; they made up between one fourth and one half of the noncombatants. The Jehovah's Witnesses were more difficult for the draft boards to deal with, since they did not oppose *all* wars, but only ones of human origin. When God's final battle of Armageddon came, they anticipated being on the front lines. Many were imprisoned for their beliefs, even after the 1942 Selective Service Act provided for them to be granted ministerial standing if these duties occupied them for at least eighty hours a month. Beyond these groups, conscientious objection became an option for members of mainline religious organizations. Methodists and Baptists accounted for the majority of mainstream Protestants claiming such standing. Some Catholics and a very few Jews also joined in this form of peace activism. Since Nazi persecution of Jews (as well as others) had virtually turned World War II into a holy war for Jews, conscientious objectors were often regarded as traitors by their fellow Jews.

World War II had an immensely unifying effect on the United States Jewish community, as it did on Jews throughout the world. As the atrocities of the Nazi death camps came to light, Jews, who before had been divided in their support for a Jewish state of Israel, came to favor it nearly unanimously. One of Theodor Herzl's key points in *Der Judenstadt* [*The Jewish State*], the book that gave the first voice to the Zionist movement in the late 1800s, was that Judaism would not be safe in the world until a permanent Jewish homeland was established. The Holocaust made his point more urgent. Jews in the United States as elsewhere laid aside differences in order to focus on supporting this crucial task.

When the United States dropped atomic bombs on Hiroshima and Nagasaki in 1945, it not only brought a rapid end to World War II, but an end to any possibility of thinking of wars as "just" on the grounds discussed above. The widespread killing of innocents and the unimaginable horror of near-total destruction make a mockery of all talk of just war criteria. From the perspective of religious thought, discussion of "just wars" was replaced by discussions of the circumstances under which war might be "justified." For example, although religious thinkers differed in their assessment of the Korean War, most believed it to be justified in order to contain the spread of communism.

The development of nuclear weapons added to the impossibility of maintaining a just war ideology. In the mid-1950s, United States and Soviet Union testing of nuclear weapons, fear of nuclear fallout, and the very real prospect of worldwide destruction led to a resurgence of peace activism. Liberal religious leaders, especially, joined scientists in SANE, the National Committee for a Sane Nuclear Policy.

Summary and Conclusions

As we have seen, religion played important roles in political movements between 1800 and 1959. Religion figured prominently in:

- slavery and abolition
- temperance and prohibition efforts
- movements for broad, progressive social reform, and
- war and peace.

One conclusion that we can draw at this point is that in many ways events during this period laid the foundations for the relationships between religion and politics that still exist in our own time. Perhaps the most important of these was the churches' discovery of the political process as a way of enacting the social reforms that they sought. Fundamental differences in how conservative and liberal religion relate to politics were also laid out during this time. Also of crucial significance was the firm establishment of the principle that religion *would* relate to the political order, for the most part. There were then and there are now religious groups that try to limit their contact with politics, but they do not represent the main thrust of religion in the United States anymore.

Beyond these broad principles, however, issues that echo those of this historical period reappear in the period from 1960 to the present: The wide-ranging social programs espoused by many religious liberals as well as by the evangelical political progressives (e.g., Sojourners) are quite similar to those of the Catholic "Bishops' Program of Social Reconstruction" and the Federal Council of Churches' "The Social Ideals of the Churches." On the other hand, the concern with personal morality that marked the advocacy of temperance and prohibition echoes in the late 1900s in conservative's support for traditional values in the area of family and sexual relationships. The fundamentalist-modernist controversy reappears, with modifications, in the "culture wars" of the late 1900s, as well.

Events that took place during this period continue to affect the relationship between politics and religion as we approach the new millennium. The experience of slavery and emancipation, for example, helps to explain differences in how religion and political views are related among white and black Americans, to be discussed in Part III.

Another important conclusion to be drawn from our discussion of the relationship of religion and politics from 1800 through 1959 is that those relationships are never simple and straightforward. Those who differ on religious matters may be drawn together in a common social or political cause—a phenomenon that has continued until our own time. Similarly, as we will see in Chapter 9, those who agree on religious questions do not necessarily agree on political questions.

Important Terms

Perfectionism   Prohibition

Social Gospel movement   Holy War

Abolition movement   Just War

Temperance   Pacifism

Review Questions

1. What three shifts in people's viewpoint made movements for social reform possible?
2. What were the long-term effects of the interaction between religion and politics during the Civil War and abolition era?
3. What were the long-term effects of the interaction between religion and politics during the Prohibition era?
4. What are the differences between the holy war approach, the just war approach, and pacifism?
5. What are the traditional criteria for a just war?
6. Describe the impact that the Revolutionary War had on the churches.

Discussion Questions

1. Do you believe that a just war was ever possible? Why or why not?
2. If you believe that a just war was once possible, is it still possible in the face of the development of nuclear and biological weapons?
3. *Should* religion work to promote social justice? Why or why not?

4. If you think that religion should work to promote social justice, do you believe that it should function as an interest group alongside other interest groups in the political process? Or should it rely, as Finney said, on the conversion of individual souls and trust that these individuals would then work for social reform?

5. Should religious groups attempt to legislate things that many people regard as matters for personal choice (for example, the use of alcoholic beverages)?

6. Why do you think that we as a nation are still dealing with the problems addressed in the "Bishops' Program of Social Reconstruction" and "The Social Ideals of the Churches"?

For Further Reading

Dunn, Charles W. (Ed.). 1984. *American Political Theology: Historical Perspective and Theoretical Analysis.* New York: Praeger.
> Thorough history combined with careful analysis make this a valuable book in this area.

Edel, Wilbur. 1987. *Defenders of the Faith: Religion and Politics from the Pilgrim Fathers to Ronald Reagan.* New York: Praeger.
> A good survey treatment of this topic.

Marsden, George M. 1991. *Understanding Fundamentalism and Evangelicalism.* Grand Rapids, Michigan: William B. Eerdmans.

Noll, Mark (Ed.). 1990. *Religion and American Politics: From the Colonial Period to the 1980s.* New York: Oxford University Press.

Relevant World Wide Websites

Remember to visit our website for updates and additional links at
http://bsuvc.bsu.edu/~00amcorbett/relpol.htm

http:// www.usia.gov/usa/oah/toc.htm An Outline of American History site includes precolonial period through current history.

http://www.msstate.edu/Archives/History/USA/usa.html History of the United States site includes colonial period through current history.

http://grid.let.rug.nl/~welling/usa/adams/ad_ch1.html A Hypertext on American History

References

Ahlstrom, Sydney E. 1972. *A Religious History of the American People*. New Haven: Yale University Press.

Bernstein, Philip S. 1950. *What Jews Believe*. New York: Farrar, Straus, and Young.

Bridenbaugh, Carl. 1962. *Mitre and Sceptre: Transatlantic Faiths, Ideas, Personalities, and Politics: 1689–1775*. New York: Oxford University Press.

Bucher, Glenn R., and L. Gordon Tait. 1988. "Social Reform Since the Great Depression." Pp. 1463–1475 in Charles H. Lippy and Peter W. Williams (Eds.), *Encyclopedia of the American Religious Experience: Studies of Traditions and Movements*. New York: Charles Scribner's Sons.

Cayton, Mary A. 1988. "Social Reform from the Colonial Period Through the Civil War." Pp. 1429–1440 in Charles H. Lippy and Peter W. Williams (Eds.), *Encyclopedia of the American Religious Experience: Studies of Traditions and Movements*. New York: Charles Scribner's Sons.

Dabney, Virginius. 1949. *Dry Messiah: The Life of Bishop Cannon*. New York: Alfred A. Knopf.

Dunn, Charles W., ed. 1984. *American Political Theology: Historical Perspective and Theoretical Analysis*. New York: Praeger.

Edel, Wilbur. 1987. *Defenders of the Faith: Religion and Politics from the Pilgrim Fathers to Ronald Reagan*. New York: Praeger.

Endy, Melvin B., Jr. 1988. "War and Peace." Pp. 1409–1429 in Charles H. Lippy and Peter W. Williams (Eds.), *Encyclopedia of the American Religious Experience: Studies of Traditions and Movements*. New York: Charles Scribner's Sons.

Ferguson, John. 1978. *War and Peace in the World's Religions*. New York: Oxford University Press.

Gaustad, Edwin Scott. 1990. *A Religious History of America, New Revised Edition*. San Francisco: Harper and Row.

Hudson, Winthrop S., and John Corrigan. 1992. *Religion in America: An Historical Account of the Development of American Religious Life*. New York: Macmillan.

Hyneman, Charles S., and Donald S. Lutz. 1978. *American Political Writing during the Founding Era, 1760–1805*. New York: Harper and Row.

Marsden, George M. 1991. *Understanding Fundamentalism and Evangelicalism*. New York: Oxford University Press.

Mayer, John A. 1988. "Social Reform after the Civil War to the Great Depression." Pp. 1441–1461 in Charles H. Lippy and Peter W. Williams (Eds.), *Encyclopedia of the American Religious Experience: Studies of Traditions and Movements*. New York: Charles Scribner's Sons.

Sweet, Leonard I. 1988. "Nineteenth-Century Evangelicalism." Pp. 875–899 in Charles H. Lippy and Peter W. Williams (Eds.), *Encyclopedia of the American Religious Experience: Studies of Traditions and Movements*. New York: Charles Scribner's Sons.

CHAPTER 4

Religion and Politics
Since 1960

Romer v. Evans [the 1996 case in which the Supreme Court struck down Colorado's attempt to block legislation that would ensure civil rights for gay people] is the unraveling of the rule of law in America. It is the end of connecting the law to any objective standard or natural law to which man-made law must be responsible.

—Charles Colson, *Christianity Today*

It is simply wrong and stupid to blame gay and lesbian people for the breakdown of the heterosexual family. . . . Their civil and human rights must also be honored, respected, and defended for a society to be good and healthy.

—Jim Wallis, *Sojourners*

Overview

This chapter examines relationships between religion and politics from the 1960s through the present. Several of the key issues during the 1960s through the early 1990s remind us of the questions dealt with in the previous chapter:

- The struggle over civil rights for blacks demonstrates that the abolition movement has in some ways not yet come to full fruition.

- The Vietnam War again raised questions about just wars and the limits of conscientious objection. (This topic will be considered from a First Amendment standpoint in Chapter 6.)
- The resurgence of political involvement on the part of Christian conservatives and the rise of the New Christian Right with its politics of individual, private morality echoed the temperance and prohibition crusades.
- At the same time, the emergence of social concern among Christian conservatives links this era with the broad social progressivism discussed in Chapter 3. Conservative social progressivism reflects considerations similar to those voiced by earlier movements for broad social reform.

As in that earlier period, religion and politics interact in complex ways; religion helps to shape both the political questions asked and the answers given.

We will look first at the decade of the 1960s itself, ten years that changed forever the ways that people in the United States experience and think about their world. We will then examine the positions taken by several religious lobbies in Washington. Having laid this foundation, we will turn to consideration of specific issues, such as the civil rights movement and the development of the New Christian Right, religious television, and conservative Christian social progressivism. Some of the major questions to guide this examination are:

- What dramatic events and trends that occurred during the 1960s affected religion and politics—and the American culture in general?
- During the time period from 1960 to the present, what major types of religious groups have been lobbying in Washington in efforts to have their values reflected in public policy?
- How were religion and politics very much intertwined in the civil rights movement?
- Why did the New Christian Right emerge and how has it evolved over time?
- How do conservative Christians translate their religious values into political stands?
- How did Christian television develop and what has its political involvement been?

The Decade of the Sixties

Following a relatively calm period following World War II, the 1960s was a decade of dramatic change. The implications of the social reorganization that characterized the 1960s are still being worked out in the closing years of the century.

The Civil Rights Movement

Although various analysts of that period give different lists of the social changes that are most significant, there are several on which nearly all agree. Certainly first among these is the civil rights movement, the concentrated effort by black people and their supporters to claim for black people the freedom and equality to which they are entitled under the Constitution. The civil rights movement shook the nation out of its complacency and brought about political and religious changes whose legacy continues today. The civil rights movement by black people was the first of what would become a series of such movements from the 1960s through the 1990s in which women, Hispanics, Asians, migrant farm workers, and homosexuals, along with others, claimed the rights that were enjoyed by the cultural majority. The 1970s, 1980s, and 1990s saw the continuing working out of charges that change had gone too far or not far enough, along with political attempts by religious groups and individuals to either increase change or rein it in.

The War in Southeast Asia and Questioning the "Establishment"

During the second half of the decade, the war in Vietnam became a divisive issue. Religious groups through their Washington offices weighed in on both sides of the argument. Both supporters and detractors cited religious rationales for their views and many believed that they were truly "on God's side." Although war had never been declared officially (by the Congress), it escalated by executive order, especially after the purported attack on U.S. warships in the Gulf of Tonkin in 1964. Many people opposed the war because they believed it to be illegitimate because undeclared. Others questioned the underlying "domino theory" that held if Vietnam fell to the Communists, then the rest of Southeast Asia would surely fall as well. Still others saw it as a "white man's war" on people of color (that is, Asians); it seemed to be a "white man's war" fought prima-

rily by black soldiers, too. People questioned the possible economic motives of defense industry contractors. Although the protest against the
war was outspoken and at times violent, it was not universal; a large percent of Americans supported the war as a way to hasten the downfall of
atheistic communism and "make the world safe for democracy."

Going along with questioning the war was an increasing rebellious-
ness on the part of some young people who more and more questioned
what they saw as a racist, militarist, materialistic, elitist, and essentially
meaningless culture. "The establishment" became the focus for everything that they believed needed to be done away with or radically
changed. Increasing awareness of and disillusionment with what seemed
to be enormous gaps between what was said and what was done, between
the ideal and the actual, joined with serious doubt that the existing social,
religious, educational, and political institutions were capable of doing
anything to close the distance. While some of these young people pro-
tested against the culture, others simply dropped out and retreated as far
as possible from any involvement with the culture.

Murders and Moral Mayhem

This single decade also witnessed the death by assassination of three well-
known and widely respected and beloved leaders—President John F.
Kennedy in 1963, and both Robert Kennedy and Martin Luther King, Jr.,
in 1968. Many, if not most, of those who were older than young teenagers
at the time can still recall exactly where they were and what they were doing when they heard that the president had been shot. Television made
people's individual grief over Kennedy's death into a truly national grief
in a way that had not happened before.

The "new morality" or *situation ethics* (from a book of that title by
Joseph Fletcher) shifted the groundwork of moral decision making for
many people, and helped to lay the foundation for some of the religious
and political conflicts that persisted into the nineties. Traditional moral
teaching holds that there are clear and unwavering moral laws that apply
in any and all situations. There are things that are right and those that are
wrong, and circumstances do not affect that. This view is sometimes described as an "ethic of the right," because of its emphasis on unalterable
moral rules. It is an ethic of polar opposites, right and wrong. Situation
ethics, as the name suggests, takes the situation much more into account.
It can be described as an "ethic of the good," because it seeks the best solution in a given situation. Flexible and alterable moral guidelines are

only one element of moral decision making; the other is the situation it-self. Not only does it *allow for* variations in specific situations; it *requires* that these variations be given a prominent place if the process of moral reasoning is to be legitimate. While some people welcomed this loosening of authority as a proper and fitting response for a "humanity come of age," others feared that it would bring moral chaos and anarchy. Perhaps both have proven true. At any rate, this revolution in moral thinking helped to set up the situation for the emergence of the religious-political right in the decades following the sixties.

Technology Outstripping Ethics

Finally, major technological advances that began in the sixties and spilled over into the following three decades changed the way in which people experienced their world. Humans went into outer space at the same time as advocates of psychedelic drugs claimed to have discovered inner space. The development and increasing use of computers and the beginnings of satellite transmission technology made communication much more rapid and far-reaching. The "industrial age" began to be superseded by the "age of communications." Medical advances greatly increased the ca-pacity to sustain physical life and soon outdistanced our capacity and willingness to think ethically about their meaning. While some techno-logical developments cast doubt on traditional ways of thinking about the end of life, others, in the areas of conception control and human fer-tility, made rethinking its beginning necessary.

We became aware of at least the beginnings of the "energy crisis" and the ways in which the surge of technology threatened the environment. We began to be aware of how people themselves threatened the entire sta-bility of Earth simply by there being too many of us. Nuclear weapons, known since the United States bombed Hiroshima and Nagasaki in 1945, proliferated, and fear of their use proliferated with them. Machines some-times displaced people in the labor force and increasingly dictated how people did their work. Technological advances have continued at a rapid pace, and have continued to raise questions that are addressed by both politics and religion.

In sum, the years between 1960 and 1970 witnessed social changes of a much greater magnitude than had been the case previously, transforma-tions that added up to a dramatic metamorphosis in the world in which people lived and worked. These changes required a rethinking of social and cultural arrangements, and of the role and purpose of human life itself, thus engaged both religion and politics. The rethinking that began in the 1960s continues as this book is written.

Religious Lobbies in Washington

We have said that perhaps the most important discovery that religious groups made during the 1800s through the first half of the 1900s was that they could use the political process to achieve their social, and sometimes religious, goals. This realization continues to be an important factor in the last half of the twentieth century. Religion has come to be increasingly characterized by the proliferation of special interest groups, a development that sociologist Robert Wuthnow calls "a significant form of social restructuring in American religion" (Wuthnow, 1988: 101). One notable outgrowth of this trend has been an increase in the importance of religious lobbies in Washington. Here we will describe certain aspects of such lobbies, and we will return to a fuller discussion of the behavior of religious groups as interest groups in Chapter 11.

On a brief historical note, the first significant involvement of a specific religious denomination in Washington was Methodist support for prohibition. The Methodist Building, built in 1923 across from the Capitol, became the locus of the Prohibition effort. Today, it houses the Washington offices of many liberal Protestant groups (Hertzke, 1988: 28).

Following Hertzke (1988: 28–43), we can identify six major religious groups whose views are distinctive. There is a great deal of disagreement about the proper use of the terms "evangelical" and "fundamentalist." In this section, we adopt Hertzke's use of those terms. These six groups reflect the major players in the interaction of politics and religion as it has developed since the 1960s. None of these is monolithic; all are composed of elites and rank-and-file constituencies with a variety of views on both religious and political matters, as well as on the proper relationship of the two. However, there is sufficient commonality to identify them as discrete clusters.

Liberal Protestants

We may describe liberal Protestantism as theologically liberal, socially and economically liberal, eager to build coalitions of like-minded groups, willing to question national policy in foreign affairs, and of the opinion that what consenting adults do behind closed doors is not the government's business. This group includes those Protestant denominations that have usually been called "mainline"—the Methodists, Presbyterians, Lutherans, American Baptists, Episcopalians, United Church of Christ. It includes as well others who share their concerns for peace and justice, such as the Mennonites, Friends, and Brethren. The National Council of Churches is representative of this group.

Working for socially and economically liberal causes within the liberal Protestant tradition goes back at least to the Social Gospel movement (discussed in the preceding chapter). This emphasis was supported and increased by the tide of liberal theology that swept seminaries in the 1920s, and was renewed in the 1960s as "radical theology" focused on the social dimension of Christianity, sometimes to the exclusion of nearly everything else. Liberal theology, with its emphasis on life in this world, its optimism about human beings and the world itself, its eagerness to accommodate religious thought to the demands of reason and science, and its willingness to cooperate with other like-minded groups, was well-placed to engage with social issues on a continuing basis.

As with so many other things, the civil rights movement of the 1960s dramatically increased the involvement of liberal Protestants in lobbying and other activities to promote social justice. The war in Vietnam provided another rallying point.

As Hertzke (1988: 31) states, the liberal Protestant view can be summarized as "peace and justice." This includes working for justice for the poor at home and abroad, including support for welfare here and Third World development abroad. Working for peace "translates into frequent criticism of American military and foreign policies, nuclear arms strategies, and military spending generally," on the grounds that money spent on armaments and weapons of mass destruction is diverted from its proper use in more humanitarian programs.

Liberal Protestants have consistently supported racial and gender equality, and other characteristically liberal social positions such as abortion rights and civil rights for homosexual persons.

Liberal Protestantism's leadership still provides a consistent witness to a progressive social position. However, it has been beset by at least three major problems in recent years.

- There are differences between clergy and laity on the social and political questions themselves. Increasingly, the people in the pews do not feel that their denominational officials speak for them.

- The laity are also more reluctant than the clergy themselves to have the clergy become involved in direct political action. This was true in the civil rights struggle of the 1960s and it is true now. Increasingly, the mood among what were once liberal and so-cially-activist Protestants seems to be "the business of religion is religion."

- These two things translate into a severe decline in financial sup-port for national denominational offices and especially for the National Council of Churches, all of which have had to curtail their staffs and initiatives sharply in the face of economic cut-backs.

Fundamentalists

The rallying cry for fundamentalist lobbies in Washington has been and continues to be "traditional values." They defend the traditional family, orthodox religion, strong patriotism conceived in conven-tional terms, and a Puritan approach to morality that emphasizes per-sonal moral uprightness. Their support for traditional values has ar-rayed them against such things as the changes in the family brought about by the liberalization of divorce laws and the movement of women into the paid work force, the increased availability of pornog-raphy, increased civil rights for gays and lesbians, and abortion rights. They support prayer in the schools, voucher programs that allow par-ents more freedom to choose their children's schools, and freedom of Christian schools to operate with minimal government interference. Like the Puritans of old, they want to see the values of traditional Christianity made the basis of the law of the land. Major groups rep-resentative of this category include the Moral Majority (now defunct), the Christian Coalition, Focus on the Family, and Concerned Women for America.

The problem as fundamentalists see it is not so much secularization in general as "elite secularization." The secular elites—the media, govern-ment, educational institutions, and other gate-keepers and agenda-set-ters—are more secular than is the mass public. This means that the elites that determine policy and make laws are out of touch with the values of the majority. These secular elites have set standards and made policy for too long, according to the fundamentalists; it is time to restore the values of the "moral majority."

Catholics

Traditionally, the official teaching of the Catholic Church has been politically conservative. In some ways symbolized by the life and work of Francis Cardinal Spellman (Archbishop of New York from 1939 to 1967), the church's impact on politics has until recently been quite traditional (Cooney, 1984). Spellman mirrored secular conservatism: anti-Communist, suspicious of labor and of civil rights, and strongly pro-military. A minority of the Catholic laity supported Spellman's views. Both the Father Coughlin movement and the McCarthy crusade were somewhat supported by Catholics. The John Birch Society, a secular right-wing organization, drew some support from Catholics, as well (Lipset, 1964).

There were, however, strong countervailing forces at work in the Catholic Church, especially among its elites. Robert F. Wagner, a senator from New York State, contributed significantly to establishing the welfare system in the United States (O'Brien, 1968). During the same time period that Spellman was leading a strongly conservative church, Dorothy Day co-founded the Catholic Workers movement, which identified the church with increasingly progressive social views, especially on issues affecting workers (Piehl, 1982). From the founding of that movement during the Depression until her death in 1980, Day and her colleagues worked tirelessly on behalf of the poor and oppressed. *The Catholic Worker,* the publication she founded in 1933, has been a consistent voice for very liberal Catholic social thought. In addition, at least some Catholic ethicists were increasingly involved in social ethics (Curran, 1982).

It is difficult to overestimate the role that the Second Vatican Council played in furthering this trend among Catholic leaders and laity. The Council, convened by Pope John XXIII during the years 1962–1965, did two things that directly stimulated the growth of liberal Catholic social involvement. The first was to encourage laity and leadership alike to apply their religious values to life in the world, and especially to the demands of social life in an increasingly shrinking world. The second was a reorganization of the Catholic Church in the United States that empowered the American bishops to establish the United States Catholic Conference. This helped to give the church a unified voice on social issues, along with a degree of autonomy for the American bishops. This organization has become a seedbed for Catholic social liberalism (Hanna, 1979).

The election of John F. Kennedy as president of the United States in 1960 was a final galvanizing for liberal involvement in politics on the part of American Catholics. For many Catholics, Kennedy's election meant that they had at last attained cultural parity with the Protestant majority. His espousal of socially liberal politics encouraged the trends that were already present.

Today's U.S. Catholic Conference is a multidimensional lobby in that it shares concerns with a number of other groups. Its focus can be described as "peace, justice, and traditional values." It is aligned with liberal Protestants on issues such as military spending and Third World development, but its social issues stands—on the ERA and abortion, for example—align it with conservative Protestants. This represents what is sometimes referred to as a "seamless garment" of concern for life that transcends theological differences among these groups.

Because the Catholic Church in the United States is historically a church of immigrants, it has always paid special attention to the marginalization of immigrants and immigrant rights. It is estimated that by the year 2000, 50 percent of all Catholics in the United States will be of Hispanic descent, and many will not be native speakers of English (Corbett: 1997). As a result, contemporary Catholic political involvement has often revolved around issues affecting the Hispanic and Chicano communities. César Chavez, who organized the Mexican-American migrant farm workers in California in the 1960s and 1970s, was a Catholic layperson. His work led to the founding of the National Farm Workers Union to protect the rights of migrant farm workers wherever they worked. A 1983 U.S. bishops' pastoral letter specifically addressed social concerns that are of particular relevance to Hispanics, including "voting rights, discrimination, immigration rights, the status of farm workers, bilingualism and pluralism." These issues, of course, do not affect only Hispanics; most of them apply as well, for example, to Asian immigrants, whose numbers are increasing in the United States.

The overall impact of Catholicism and the teachings of the church on the pluralistic political situation in the United States appears to be modest, in spite of strong organization, skilled representation in Washington, and willingness to engage in coalition building. Except for the ongoing abortion debate and gaining some state aid for parochial schools, there is neither Catholic cohesion nor strong impact. And some prejudice against Catholics remains, which undercuts coalition building (Fowler, 1985). Demographic trends among Catholic laity indicate that an increasing proportion of the faithful will continue to take most of their moral cues from American culture rather than from the teachings of their church (Corbett, 1997). This may suggest a widening gap between Catholic laity and leadership on issues that involve both politics and religion, a breach which parallels that experienced by liberal Protestants.

Jews

Jewish religious values and their historical experience have worked together to involve Jews in politics in numbers far higher than their proportion in the population. The "Jewish view" on political and social matters is more complex than it may seem at first, and not monolithic, just as Jewish religiousness is not monolithic. Secular Jewish intellectual and cultural leaders also have a far greater influence in formulating the Jewish viewpoint than is the case with either Protestantism or Catholicism. The "Jewish civil religion" (Woocher, 1986) that largely unifies America's religiously diverse Jewish population does not require that one be *religiously* Jewish in order to be Jewish. This view, nevertheless, deserves inclusion here because it represents Jewish religio-cultural interests.

Jewish groups usually side with liberal Protestants and with Catholics on many issues, including foreign policy, military policy, the ERA, national economic issues, civil rights, and church-state questions. Where some Jews and liberal Protestants differ is on Israel. Many liberal Protestants believe that any lasting Middle East peace must include justice for—and negotiations with—the Palestinians. These attitudes place them profoundly at odds with some Jews who believe that any compromise with the Palestinians means injustice for Jews (Hertzke, 1988).

Characteristically, though, Jews have had and continue to have, a very positive attitude toward social change, and toward the use of government as the primary means to bring about change (Fowler, 1985). For the most part, theirs is a view that has been considerably to the left of center on most sociopolitical issues. For at least some Jews, this view comes close to being a religious as well as a sociopolitical outlook (Fuchs, 1956; Sklare and Greenblum, 1967; Liebman and Cohen, 1990). This is one reason that the Democratic party held the allegiance of most Jews through the 1970s.

That social and political liberalism is an inherent aspect of Jewish religious thought has become a topic of debate among scholars in recent years. The relationship advanced by Fuchs (1956), Sklare and Greenblum (1967), and Liebman and Cohen (1990) has been questioned by scholars who have found that the most religiously observant Jews are also the most politically conservative (Cohen, 1983; Penn and Schoen, 1988; Lazerwitz, Winter, and Dashefsky, 1988). In our opinion, there remains ground for including social liberalism within the compass of the Jewish theological tradition. Theologically, social-issues liberalism arises from the prophetic stance of Judaism. Time after time, the Hebrew prophets have enjoined their people to care for the unfortunate, the oppressed, the widow and the orphan—as an integral aspect of their devotion to a God who is concerned for the welfare of all persons. That those Jews who are more religiously observant are the least politically liberal is not surprising: Religiously observant Judaism focuses at least as much on Judaism's ritual component, which the Orthodox hold to be of equal importance with the ethical commandments. The emphasis here is on the "vertical" dimension, people and God. Religiously liberal Judaism, epitomized in Reform and Reconstructionist Judaism, holds that *only* the ethical commandments are religiously binding. Religion virtually becomes ethics, and social ethics at that. The emphasis falls almost exclusively on the "horizontal," human-to-human relationship, as a way of embodying the religious relationship itself. In spite of being among the more affluent voting groups in the United States, Jews have tended less than other prosperous groups to vote for their own economic self-interest (Fisher, 1989; Fuchs, 1956).

The history of persecution endured by those of Jewish faith, and their continuing minority status, have led them to be ardent champions of individual civil liberties and the separation of church and state. Their concern for civil liberties led them to be early allies of blacks in the civil rights movement. Tensions did arise between the Jewish and black communities with the establishment of affirmative action programs, which gave advantages to blacks. To Jews, often the victims of exclusivist "quota systems," affirmative action seemed to give unjust advantage to one group over another. When Jews allied themselves with those who opposed affirmative action programs as a means of racial advancement, blacks leveled charges of racism, in response to which some Jews accused the blacks of anti-Semitism.

Tensions also arose within the Jewish community and between the Jewish and gentile communities over relations with Israel, as indicated above. In 1975, the United Nations declared that Zionism—Jewish support for the creation and maintenance of a Jewish homeland in Palestine—was a form of racism, and compared the actions of the Israeli Jews against the Palestinians to the actions of white South Africans against blacks. This declaration further eroded relationships between Jews and blacks in the United States.

These issues, and others less important, caused a small number of Jewish intellectuals to begin to rethink the traditional Jewish commitment to political liberalism and to the Democratic party. This reevaluation became more important during Jesse Jackson's 1984 presidential campaign, during which he was accused of anti-Semitic slurs. As a result of his perceived antagonism toward Jews, they did not support his candidacy. There is continuing evidence that, while Jews remain among the most liberal of political interest groups, they are less economically liberal than they once were. As we will see further in Chapter 8, on issues of individual civil liberties, most Jews remain firmly in favor of individual freedom. They have very high support for abortion rights, gender equality, and homosexual rights, for example.

Evangelical Protestants

The word "evangelical" has many meanings within Protestant thought, and modern-day evangelicals do not comprise a monolithic group. For our purposes here, we will use the word to mean those Protestants whose approach to religion is conservative without having the aggressive and sometimes separatist character displayed by fundamentalists. They affirm traditional Christian religious and moral teachings and reject liberal theology and its liberal moral stands without the militancy of many fundamentalists. Many Baptists fit into this category, as do a substantial proportion of Methodists, Lutherans, Presbyterians, and others.

Evangelical lobbying began with a concern to protect freedom of religion. Their concerns are now considerably more broad, but church-state issues still occupy an important place in their work. They perceive a threat to religious liberty both from the "right," in the form of fundamentalist militancy that would dictate religious expression for everyone and from the "left," in the form of restrictive applications of the establishment clause that have the result of restricting religious freedom, especially for evangelicals concerned to make a public witness to their faith.

On some issues, evangelicals have aligned with the more separatist fundamentalists, but on others have made common cause with liberal Protestants, Catholics, and Jews. Their focus is "peace, justice, *and* traditional values" (Hertzke, 1988: 42), a phrase that also describes the Catholic Church's viewpoint.

Evangelicals also believe there is a genuine biblical imperative for social action on behalf of the poor and oppressed both here and overseas. Peacemaking has assumed an increasingly larger role. On social, economic, peacemaking, nuclear disarmament, and similar issues, they have often sided with liberal Protestants and Catholics. They are, nonetheless, much more concerned than are liberals to make certain that their stands are tied directly and visibly to the Bible. Unlike the Catholics, they do not ground their views in the tradition of the church. On the other hand, their support for traditional morality often aligns them with fundamentalist Protestants, Mormons, Catholics and very conservative Jews on issues such as abortion and homosexual rights.

Black Evangelicals

Within the evangelical approach, black evangelicals occupy a unique place. Most of the historically black churches (e.g., the African Methodist Episcopal, African Methodist Episcopal Zion, Christian Methodist Episcopal, and several black Baptist churches) maintain their own Washington offices, as well as working with other evangelical groups. They continue to press for civil rights and justice for black people, as well as other minorities and disadvantaged groups.

None of the religious interest groups described above are monolithic in outlook, nor are these the only religious interest groups represented in the political life of the United States. We have described the general tendencies of some of the largest and best-known among the religious groups, as these are reflected in their Washington lobbies.

Politics, Religion, and Civil Rights

The civil rights movement has been called "the most important recent example of a political movement where religious forces played a tremendous role" (Fowler, 1985: 154). While it is true that religion and religious people were in the forefront of the movement for civil rights for blacks from its inception, many also opposed civil rights. An event in May 1954 was at the center of the beginning of the civil rights movement. In *Plessy v. Ferguson* (1896), the United States Supreme Court held that racially segregated facilities, such as schools and accommodations, were constitutional as long as the facilities provided were of equal quality. In 1954, in *Brown v. Board of Education of Topeka, Kansas,* the Court held that separate facilities by definition were not equal, and hence were illegal acts of discrimination. The Court ordered that school desegregation proceed as rapidly as possible.

The following year, in an atmosphere already tension-charged, Rosa Parks, a Montgomery, Alabama, domestic worker, boarded a city bus to return home after a tiring day. Finding no seats available at the rear of the bus, where black people were required to sit, she took a seat nearer the front. She refused the driver's order to move to the rear, where she would have had to stand, and was arrested. Dr. Martin Luther King, Jr., pastor of Montgomery's Dexter Avenue Baptist Church, was soon thrust into the leadership of what would become known as the Montgomery bus boycott, a year-long protest of segregated seating by blacks, who were the primary users of the city's bus system.

King's tireless leadership of the civil rights movement continued into the following decade. King's religious outlook combined warm Baptist piety and enthusiasm with a personalist theology acquired during his graduate school days. His approach was guided by his commitment to positive change at as rapid a pace as possible, on the one hand, and his equally strong commitment to nonviolent methods. In studying the lives and teachings of Jesus of Nazareth and Mohandas Gandhi, the Indian reformer, King had concluded that the way to lasting results was through cooperation and nonviolent confrontation, coupled with a readiness to accept the consequences of one's actions.

King's Approach
Nonviolent Civil Disobedience

King and his followers made use of the nonviolent technique of "civil disobedience." There are, he said, four steps in such an effort (1963, "Letter from Birmingham Jail"):

- careful collection of the facts to verify that injustice does exist
- negotiation—always to be carried out before more confrontational methods are used
- self-purification—a necessary prelude to civil disobedience so that participants are clear about their own motives and strong enough within themselves not to return violence for violence
- direct action—marches, sit-ins, protests.

The purpose of direct action is to force a community or group to confront an issue that they have refused to confront, about which they have refused to negotiate. Such an approach had worked for Gandhi in freeing India from British colonial rule. Privileged groups seldom if ever relinquish their privilege voluntarily; freedom is seldom given by the oppressor without something to force the issue. This is where nonviolent protest as a form of political action comes into the picture.

Laws That Are Just

As a general matter, King said, people should obey just laws. Equally, however, God calls people to engage in civil disobedience against unjust laws. How do we distinguish between a just and an unjust law?

- a just law squares with the law of God
- a just law is equally binding on all, while one that is unjust is made to apply to a minority, who had no part in bringing it into being, by the majority
- a just law may be unjust in its application.

The Black Church and Civil Rights

The roots of King's political action were sunk deeply into his religious convictions and experience. One of the results of the actions that were taken between the midfifties and the midsixties was the passage of the Civil Rights Act in 1964. In addition to King's influence, the vast majority of white religious leaders in Washington worked for its passage, as they had stood arm in arm with King and other black religious leaders in Selma and Montgomery. It is notable that a white Catholic priest, Theodore Hesburgh of Notre Dame University, came to serve as chair of the federal Civil Rights Commission in 1969.

The role of the black church in the civil rights movement can hardly be overestimated. Not only Martin Luther King, Jr., but Ralph Abernathy, Andrew Young, Jesse Jackson, and other charismatic leaders were drawn from the ranks of the black clergy. Before abolition, black religion had helped the slaves retain some sense of being "somebody" in God's eyes, a powerful antidote to being "nobody" in the eyes of the slaveholding world. After emancipation, it had provided necessary services to assist freed slaves, and continued to strengthen the sense of peoplehood and worth. And it provided a structure in which the yearning for freedom could find expression and organization, with no outside support from the white culture.

In addition, black churches became the "command centers" of the movement. They organized transportation for people who were not riding buses. They had dedicated people who were ready to volunteer. They became information centers, emergency housing coordinators, food providers, and places of encouragement.

A Diversity of Views

There was a variety of views within the black churches themselves, from those who believed that the "business of religion is religion" to those whose members and leaders believed that they should be in the forefront of the movement. Studies done during the 1960s found that there were at least three types of attitudes among black clergy, reflected among black laity as well. *Traditionalists* held to a view that churches should be about religion and spiritual things and stay out of political involvement altogether. *Moderates*, while believing that religion must be deeply concerned with worldly as well as spiritual affairs, preferred to work for change gradually, without causing any disruption or disturbance. *Militants* believed that God called them to direct political action, including disruption and disturbance, if that was what was needed to get the job done. A minority even condoned violence (Johnstone, 1969; Marx, 1969).

The diversity of views notwithstanding, some black church scholars understand political action as an inherent aspect of black religion, as an embodiment of its prophetic mandate to criticize society in the name of God (e.g., Paris, 1985).

Other scholars point to the transformation of the "Negro" church by its participation in the civil rights movement. In answering the call to full personhood posed by the civil rights movement, the church of the American "Negro" (who was defined by the dominant white culture as less than a person) had to die, in order that the "contemporary Black Church" could rise, "bold, strident, [and] self-conscious" (Frazier and Lincoln, 1974).

While there was widespread support from leaders of white churches and synagogues, their support was far from universal. Their disagreements were not so much over whether an integrated society should become a reality—a point on which most agreed—but over how best to go about it, and what roles were appropriate for clergy to play. As a general rule, the more theologically conservative groups, and laypeople more than clergy, favored very gradual change brought about by the passage of resolutions and proclamations, without direct action and certainly without the involvement of their clergy in such direct action.

In its effect on mainline religion, the civil rights movement precipitated an increase in direct political action on the part of the elites, which then led to dissent by many laypeople. It also heightened conflict between more conservative and more liberal religious groups. The more conservative sought to mold public values and influence society indirectly, while the more liberal took the more direct route of political action (Wuthnow, 1988: 145–148). This tension, which echoes the tension within the prohibition movement described in the previous chapter, is still a source of some conflict between religious groups, but to a lesser extent, as more conservative groups have espoused direct action as well. The most obvious example of this trend in the 1990s was the proportion of conservative Christians involved in blockades and picket lines outside abortion clinics.

The New Christian Right

A particular intersection of religion and politics gave rise to the New Christian Right, beginning in the 1970s (although some of its roots go back to colonial times). It is the result not only of the "swing toward conservatism" in religion in the 1970s but of conservative religion asserting its political voice.

The Emergence of the New Christian Right

Why did the New Christian Right emerge when it did? There are any number of explanations, some theological and some sociopolitical. It is not possible here to survey all of them, nor to trace their historical development in detail. We can, however, suggest the broad outlines. A thorough analysis of these developments can be found in sociologist Robert Wuthnow's *The Restructuring of American Religion: Society and Faith Since World War II* (1988), on whose analysis we draw in the discussion that follows.

The rise of the New Christian Right and the widening chasm between conservative and liberal religion in the 1970s and 1980s is in some ways the *legacy of the fundamentalist-modernist controversy* discussed in the previous chapter. However, the relationship is not direct. The earlier controversy provides only a beginning point, a legacy that has been dramatically modified over time. Yet the legacy is important.

By the 1950s, religion in the United States was marked by divisions between Christians and Jews, between Catholic and Protestant Christians, and between various Protestant denominations. Conservative religion was consciously moving away from fundamentalism while liberals were moving away from modernism; both were approaching a more centrist position. Further, most were agreed that the "business of religion is religion," that their focus should be on gaining new converts.

The Decade of the 1960s

The 1960s dramatically altered the picture. The civil rights movement and United States involvement in the war in Southeast Asia helped bring about a sharp division in the style of religious activism: liberals came to be known as those who advocated direct action—sit-ins and other sorts of demonstrations—while conservatives believed that religion's role was to influence individual consciences. This division cut across denominational lines, laying the groundwork for the intradenominational divisions that have characterized subsequent decades.

Growth in science, technology, and the expansion of higher education played an important role. This expansion brought about a shift in values and attitudes, as attitudes on a wide range of lifestyle and personal morality issues changed decisively, as we discussed above. The importance of this shift for the development of the New Christian Right is that these changes helped bring about the perception of a culture divided into the "ordinary people" and an "elite class." The elites were said to be characterized by egalitarianism, liberal attitudes, and permissiveness. Whereas in the 1950s there had been a positive correlation between education and indicators of traditional religiousness, that correlation reversed in the 1960s. Increasing education came to be positively associated with liberalizing tendencies.

Thus, at the end of the 1960s, a new "cultural cleavage" along educational lines was in place, one that cut across denominational lines.

Into the 1970s and the 1980s

The 1970s and 1980s were a time for the consolidation of this cleavage, which made the time ripe for the development of the New Christian Right. The educational divide continued, and the breach between religious liberals and religious conservatives widened.

These developments, again, were a result of both religious and social forces at work. Religious conservatism gained a national identity with the founding of a number of "parachurch" organizations such as the Campus Crusade for Christ and the founding in 1942 of the National Association of Evangelicals as an umbrella organization for those denominations that were dissatisfied with the theological liberalism of the National Council of Churches. The national prominence of Billy Graham's crusades added to this identity.

Interestingly, the mass media and the use of polling techniques also contributed to this sense of national identity. Polls made it possible to measure conservative religious sentiment and commitment with new precision. It was announced that anywhere from one fifth to one third of the population regarded themselves as religious conservatives (depending upon the criteria for inclusion). These figures easily gained the attention of the mass media.

Jimmy Carter's candidacy for the presidency and his subsequent victory in 1976 also helped bring conservative Christianity front and center in the public consciousness. *Time* and *Newsweek* declared 1976 as the "year of the evangelical." This was underscored further by the fact that the opponent in 1976 (Gerald Ford) and both opponents in 1980 (Ronald Reagan and John Anderson) also openly professed their born-again status. A movement had arrived.

Private Morality and Public Life

Perhaps of even greater importance was the change in the issues that were at the forefront of political discussion. The abortion question, differences in opinion about the morality of artificial birth control, even more pressing doubts about the morality of newer and more dramatic reproductive technologies, questions about gender roles, and about the relationship between church and state all entered the arena of public discourse. Public morality became an issue, especially in the wake of Watergate. The Supreme Court decision legalizing abortion (*Roe* v. *Wade*, 1973) also heightened the discussion about the relationship of morality and public life.

Conservative Christians had always seen a close connection between personal morality and public life, between individual moral choices and the fortunes of the nation. In addition, conservatives were in much greater agreement on moral issues then they were over matters such as the Vietnam War or race relations.

The New Christian Right and the Republican Party

The questions that became central to the political agenda in the 1970s continued into the 1980s and the 1990s. A particularly interesting turn of events concerns the increasingly close relationship between the New Christian Right and the Republican Party in the late 1970s and 1980s. This association did not begin in the late 1970s; the relationship between Billy Graham and Dwight Eisenhower is well known, for example, as are the White House "prayer breakfasts" of the Nixon years. However, it reached a new level with the Reagan candidacy and presidency. The following is not an exhaustive list, but it is illustrative:

- Almost immediately after the nominating convention, Reagan endorsed the work of Christian conservatives in a speech to a ministerial meeting in Texas.
- The news media gave extensive coverage to the Moral Majority during the Reagan campaign.
- Several New Christian Right favorites were appointed to political office by Reagan.
- In a 1983 speech to the National Religious Broadcasters, Reagan supported tax credits for parents whose children attended parochial schools and the return of prayer to the schools, and condemned *Roe* v. *Wade*, all items close to the heart of the New Christian Right.
- Also in 1983, a new political action group, the American Coalition for Traditional Values, was founded to get out the conservative vote for the Reagan-Bush ticket in 1984. Its focus was the registration of religiously conservative voters, and it received direct support from the Reagan White House in the form of a million-dollar grant through Leadership '84 (Jorstad, 1993).

The relationship proved less useful to the New Christian Right than its leaders and rank and file had hoped, however. In the election of 1986, New Christian Right–supported candidates for Congress lost at the state and national levels. Robert Bork's failure to gain confirmation as a Supreme Court justice despite vigorous support from the New Christian Right, and the Iran-Contra debacle further eroded the connection. Reagan did not offer Oliver North the pardon requested by his New Christian Right supporters. Nor did Reagan support the New Christian Right's bid to keep Congress from withholding tax funding to Pennsylvania's Grove City College for its racially discriminatory policies. Pat Robertson's failed bid for nomination as a presidential candidate was yet another blow (Jorstad, 1990).

The Evolution of the New Christian Right

What of the New Christian Right now? A recent essay describes four phases in its development (Moen, 1996). Moen's thesis is that even as the New Christian Right has shaped politics, the demands of political life have shaped the New Christian Right. The 1970s through 1984 were the *expansionist period*, marked by steady growth in both numbers and organizations, and by reliance on direct-mail fundraising. A brief *transition phase* ran from 1985 through 1986, and was a time distinguished by retrenchment. Although the New Christian Right's effectiveness seemed to wane during this time, its leaders were working toward the next major stage.

Moen names this stage the *institutionalization phase,* dating it from 1987 through 1994. This stage was notable for the continued existence of stable organizations that were well positioned to accomplish their goals. Their financial situation was more stable with less reliance on direct-mail fundraising. Several of the organizations matured into genuine membership organizations (e.g., Concerned Women for America and Focus on the Family) having regular membership lists, meetings, dues, and benefits for members. Theological orientations within the New Christian Right diversified. Further, the New Christian Right gained political savvy, learning to frame issues so as to garner public support. Last, it gathered strength at the grass roots level.

The current stage in its development is the *devolutionary phase,* which began with the 104th Congress in 1995–1996. In most ways it is similar to the preceding phase, except that the locus of action has shifted from the national scene to the states and compromise is seen as increasingly necessary and acceptable on certain issues. The Republican emphasis on curbing the power of the federal government in favor of state and local government power accords well with the New Christian Right's own beliefs that "big government" harms families while government closer to home helps them (Moen, 1995). The Republican and the New Christian Right emphases thus come together.

Moen (1994: 353) summarizes the present day New Christian Right this way:

> [It] now consists of a variety of well-established membership organizations, whose leaders use mainstream language and organize followers in the grassroots. The strident campaign to "put God back in government" has been replaced by a quiet effort to rally sympathetic citizens and win elections. The Christian Right has adjusted itself to the traditional practices of American politics.

What has not changed is the New Christian Right's support for the causes that were defined in the earlier decades of its existence. They stand unwaveringly behind:

- A call for a return to traditional values, including traditional family structures: clearly defined gender roles, restrictions on abortion, limitations on homosexual rights, support for in-home care for the elderly, and restraint on governmental interference with how parents raise their children

- Education issues: support for prayer and devotional exercises in the public schools, the teaching of creation science, elimination of teaching about unconventional lifestyles, and the establishment of a network of Christian schools free from government regulation
- Military issues: support for the United States as the primary world military power
- Economic issues: less government regulation of business and industry, shifting responsibility for welfare from the federal government to the private sector and strict limitations on welfare benefits
- Crime issues: a tough "law-and-order" position
- Directly political goals: lobbying, voter registration, funding candidates with whose priorities they agree, and making certain that information is available on congressional officeholders' voting records (Corbett, 1997).

Although their focus has shifted significantly to the level of state and local politics, they are still active on the national level as well. They are still concerned to see a constitutional amendment pass that would protect the flag against desecration. They want legislation on the national level that will allow for student-led prayer in public schools and provide vouchers to help parents send their children to private schools.

The New Christian Right and the Heritage of Puritanism

In looking at the position the New Christian Right occupies in the political life of the United States, it is instructive to compare it with the approach taken by the Puritans (Corbett, 1988), whose views were important in the colonial period and the early days of statehood (see Chapter 1). There are several similarities.

- Their goals are similar. Both call for the United States to be a nation in conformity to the laws and will of God, as they understand it. Both public and private morality must conform to the teachings of the Bible, interpreted conservatively.
- Both want to use the legislative process to ensure that civil law conforms to religious law, and applies to believers and nonbelievers alike.
- Both see the public schools as a primary agent for training children in their views, after home and church.

- These goals are rooted in theological understandings that are very similar. There is but one absolute truth, revealed to people by a God whose primary attributes are sovereignty and power. Human beings are sinful and utterly lost without God. The United States is God's chosen nation, intended to be an example of godly living for the world.

Conservatives and Social Action

Beginning in the 1970s, the conservative Christian community came to be characterized by increasing diversity. One result of this diversification was an increase in individuals and groups who combined religious conservatism with political progressivism. As described by Evangelicals for Social Action, their vision is that "every Christian be a faithful disciple— marked by service to the poor and powerless, reverence for life, care for creation, and passionate witness to Jesus Christ." The heretofore unquestioned link between conservative religion and conservative social views and politics was being questioned from within the ranks of conservative religion itself. This development also carries the broad-based social reform concerns described in Chapter 3 into the late twentieth century.

The Religiously Conservative Social Progressives: Stands on the Issues

Evangelicals for Social Action and Bread for the World are two representative organizations. A recent survey of their membership provides a portrait of the issue stands taken by groups and individuals who combine religious conservatism with social progressivism (Smidt et al., 1994). A majority of the respondents in these two organizations agreed with the following views:

- Alleviating world hunger is a priority even if it means raising taxes.
- Government should help those in need, again even if taxes have to be raised.
- There should be a national health insurance program.
- The environment must be protected, even if doing so raises taxes and costs jobs.

A majority of those in Bread for the World also agreed that the United States needs the Equal Rights Amendment; among Evangelicals for Social Action members, 45 percent agreed. A majority of ESA and BFW members *also* agreed with the following:

- Local governments should prohibit the sale of pornography.
- Homosexuals should be allowed to teach in public schools.
- Birth control information should be made available in public schools.
- Capital punishment is morally wrong.

Like their socially and politically conservative counterparts in the New Christian Right, they strongly support the role of prayer and reliance on the guidance of the Holy Spirit in making social-action decisions (Sider, 1990). Religious factors are powerful influences in both groups. Unlike their NCR counterparts, they believe that true conservative Christianity requires the pursuit of progressivist social ideals, and they believe that government can and should play a central role in the achievement of a just and more economically equalitarian society.

Both groups put raising moral standards at the top of their agenda priorities. What is clear is that they have in mind different moral standards. Like the Social Gospel advocates described in the previous chapter, the progressives focus on social morality, while their NCR counterparts focus on the personal dimensions of morality. While both share the conviction that the biblical message has clear political implications, they differ radically on what those implications are. The right sees the political implications in terms of building a moral society focused on conservative family, gender, and sexual views. The progressive stance sees the implications in terms of standing squarely with the oppressed and socially disadvantaged against those social and political systems that oppress them at home and abroad.

Christian Television

We will not trace the history of religious broadcasting in detail here; this has been done elsewhere (Erickson, 1992; Peck, 1993). We do, however, wish to put the contemporary conservative Christian involvement with television in a longer-range historical perspective.

A Dramatic Shift: 1960 and Beyond

A crucial government decision in 1960 changed the landscape of religious programming forever. The FCC ruled that stations no longer had to provide free air time in the public interest. It also exempted religious programming from the "fairness doctrine," which had required reasonably equal representation of opposing viewpoints and removed previous restrictions on the solicitation of contributions (Peck, 1993). This suddenly made religious programming marketable and economically competitive; it also gave tremendous advantage to those individuals and groups that were able to garner extensive financial support for their efforts.

The development of cable television and UHF stations in the 1970s and 1980s, and the increasing development of satellite broadcasting in the 1980s and 1990s combine with a number of other factors to again change the face of religious programming. By the 1990s, the vast majority of religious broadcasting was provided by conservative Christian groups and showcased their concerns and "personality preachers."

Conservative Religion and Modern Technology: Natural Partners

There are other reasons for this predominance of conservative perspectives in Christian television, however. Protestant Christian history is replete with examples of the eagerness with which conservatives embraced new technologies in order to communicate their message more effectively and efficiently. It can be said that this trend goes back to the great Protestant reformer, Martin Luther (see the Introduction), who used the newly invented printing press to print religious tracts and Bibles relatively quickly and at less expense than had been possible prior to its invention. Because conversion has usually been a mainstay of conservative concern, conservative Christians have been open to using modern printing discoveries, radio, television, satellite technology, and now the Internet and the World Wide Web to achieve their goals.

We can also see Christian television as an extension of the revival method in conservative practice. The underlying theology and method of the Great Awakening (discussed in Chapter 1), the Second Awakening, and the urban revival movement fuse with the opportunities and constraints presented by television as medium.

This fusion is seen, for example, in the Oral Roberts and Billy Graham crusade broadcasts. It appears later in the television style of Jimmy

Swaggart (as well as in the work of many lesser-known persons). What Swaggart does before huge television audiences is not all that different from what the evangelists of the Awakenings did before their much smaller crowds. On the other hand, the talk-show format exemplified by the 700 Club (and many others) represents a much greater adaptation of religion to television (Peck, 1993).

Christian Television Summarized

Following Schultze (1991), we can summarize the salient features of Christian television this way:

- It is audience-supported, dependent on its viewers for financial backing. It must please its audience, a situation that may compromise the integrity of the message and the messengers.
- It revolves around the strong personalities of its leaders, for the most part, more so than do other types of religious organizations. Message and messenger may become difficult to separate. This also reflects the more general preoccupation of the culture with stars and celebrities.
- Like much of American culture, it is "experientially validated." It reflects an American cultural tendency to link truth to experience.
- As it has evolved, Christian television has become very sophisticated technologically. It has often been in the forefront of the use, and sometimes the development, of new and more powerful broadcast technologies.
- Because it must appeal to an audience, it has become entertainment-oriented as well as religious. It has adopted and adapted most of the formats that have proven themselves in secular television. Television preachers are performers.
- Finally, it has tended to become part of a cluster of institutions directed toward similar ends. It is growth-oriented. Programs become fundraisers for other projects. The expansion of Jerry Falwell's media and educational empire is a case in point. Beginning with a television program broadcast from a "regular" church, it expanded into sophisticated studio technology, a university, a lifelong learning program, a law school, and more.

The Meaning of Conservative Christian Television

What are we to make of the meaning of this phenomenon? We referred earlier in this chapter to the New Christian Right's perception that there is an elite class, including the media, that is seriously out of touch with the moral values of most Americans. Certainly one thing that viewers of Christian television find is entertainment and informational programming that reflects *their* values, not those of the commercial networks. This is seen in specifically religious programming and in the reruns of family-oriented serials that are a staple part of conservative programming.

As one analyst of Christian television points out, conservatism is not simply a lobby or a social movement—it is a religious orientation to life (Peck, 1993). As we discussed in the definition of religion, religions help to provide meaning for people's lives. Christian television is one of the ways in which these particular religious meanings are communicated and disseminated. Such communication and dissemination must occur if the belief system is to continue (Peck, 1993). Christian television does that, to a wide audience, in many formats, without requiring geographical proximity.

As Christian conservatism moved from the periphery to the center of culture in the United States, Christian television both facilitated and reflected that movement. Television is a central aspect of our life and culture. The vast majority of homes have at least one television set, and many have more than one. Both adults and children spend many hours a week watching television, and many people come to relate to television personalities as if they knew them in a personal way. It has become a primary means—perhaps *the* primary means—by which people get information about their world. It has taken on a legitimating function; people believe what they see reported on television. This makes television an ideal vehicle for the legitimation of religious conservatism in the culture, as well as a principal means of reflecting that increasing prominence.

Studies have indicated repeatedly that most people who watch Christian television already agree with the views being presented. Thus, it is not a good medium for converting others to the views of the New Christian Right. What it does very well is provide a constant flow of information and encouragement to people who agree with its views. It also has proven to be an excellent fundraiser for the groups involved with it (Corbett, 1997). It has been a key factor in establishing conservative religion as part of America's television-inspired popular culture.

For many of the reasons enumerated above, Christian television is an important instrument for communicating the social and political agenda of the New Christian Right to a receptive audience. By doing this, it helps to "transform audience members into social actors" (Peck, 1993: 108) who will vote, telephone their congressional representatives, and try to persuade their neighbors about the issues. It is thus a significant factor at the intersection of religion and politics.

Christian Television: Personalities and Politics

Many—not all—of the television preachers and evangelists have worked political messages and viewpoints into their broadcasts. The FCC regards these programs as religious broadcasts, however. As such, they are exempt from the requirement to present both sides equally that otherwise applies to political programming (Johnston, 1986). This means that, if they choose to do so, they need present only their own side of an issue. While some make an attempt at balance, most do not. In this way, they are an important feature of how religion and politics relate to each other in the United States.

There has, however, been a notable shift in the emphasis of television's personality-preachers in recent years, according to one religious media watcher. This shift may signal a partial move away from political concerns in the religious television industry. The televangelists whose prominence seems to be waxing are those whose programs focus on faith healing and pentecostal religious experience. A subsidiary theme for many of them is that sufficient faith brings with it prosperity as well as physical healing (Jorstad, 1993). It is far too soon to say if this shift is the beginning of a long-term trend or a minor deviation that will be followed by a return to more directly political broadcasts.

Summary and Conclusions

The decade of the 1960s was of major importance for the relationship between politics and religion in the United States. In some ways, that decade set an agenda that continued into the 1990s. Some of the major groups and attitudes that developed in the 1960s continue, while others have arisen in response to them, or as modifications of them. We saw that religion—among both blacks and whites—was instrumental in the civil rights movement, and in turn was deeply influenced by it. Cultural shifts resulted in the rise of the religious-political right, and shifts within the religious-political right led to the emergence of a new conservative social progressivism. The issues discussed in this chapter can safely be predicted to continue into the foreseeable future.

We saw how issues of this time period are reflected in the lobbying interests of religious groups at the national level. In Part III, "Religion and Public Opinion," we will see how these issues play out in the views of black and white Americans.

What conclusions can we draw from this survey of the relationship between politics and religion in the latter decades of the century? This chapter provides strong documentation for three major conclusions:

- This time period has witnessed an ever greater diversity of voices clamoring to be heard and to get their agenda on the table of national discussion. On the one hand, this has led to what may appear to be a "confusion of tongues." On the other, however, it has led to increased coalition building between religious groups and between political parties and religious groups. We can reasonably expect that this pattern will continue.

- A second inescapable conclusion is the resilience and adaptability of the conservative perspective in the United States. It has been a part of the American religious scene since the colonial period, and appears well positioned to continue to be a significant player at the junction of politics and religion well into the next century.

- A third conclusion seems to us to follow from the second. The concerns voiced by religious conservatives will continue to have a large influence—and perhaps an increasing influence—on American public life as we move into the next millennium. A recent U.S. Supreme Court decision (*Agostino* v. *Felton*, 1997), discussed in Chapter 5, bears this out.

In the climate of plurality and diversity that now exists in both religious and political perspectives in the United States, it is inevitable that viewpoints will clash. That is why the *legal relationship of religion and politics*, discussed in Chapters 5 and 6, is so crucial in the United States.

Important Terms

Civil rights movement

Catholic Worker Movement

New Christian Right

Christian television

Civil disobedience

Review Questions

1. What events during the 1960s were of particular importance for the relationship of politics and religion?
2. Briefly state the views of each of the groups discussed in the section, "Religious Lobbies in Washington."
3. Discuss the roles of religion in the civil rights movement, and the impact of that movement on religion.
4. What political views are usually associated with the religious-political right?
5. What is religiously conservative social progressivism, and what views does it advocate?

Discussion Questions

1. In a religiously plural society such as the United States, what role should religion play in shaping the culture?
2. Is civil disobedience an appropriate tactic to use?
3. Should clergy be actively involved in politics? For example, should they run for public office? Campaign for others who are running? Be involved in sit-ins, picket lines, and the like?
4. Are the views of the New Christian Right or those of social progressivism based on conservative religion more appealing to you? Why?

For Further Reading

Billingsley, K.L. 1990. *From Mainline to Sideline: The Social Witness of the National Council of Churches.* Washington, D.C.: Ethics and Public Policy Center.
Thorough review of the development of mainline social thought.

Bork, Robert H. 1996. *Slouching Toward Gomorrah: Modern Liberalism and American Decline.* New York: HarperCollins.
A thoughtful statement that cites religious liberalism as a primary cause of the decline of traditional morality and decency in American life.

Green, John C., James L. Guth, Corwin E. Smidt, and Lyman A. Kellstedt. 1996. *Religion and the Culture Wars: Dispatches from the Front.* Lanham, Maryland: Rowman and Littlefield.

A collection of essays that examines the influence of religion in the political life of the United States as we approach the end of the millennium. Based on the presupposition that religion does matter deeply in politics.

Hertzke, Allen D. 1988. *Representing God in Washington: The Role of Religious Lobbies in the American Polity*. Knoxville: University of Tennessee Press.

The "who, what, and why" of religious lobbies.

Martin, William. 1996. *With God on Our Side: The Rise of the Religious Right in America*. New York: Bantam Doubleday.

The subtitle well describes the book's focus. A companion volume to a PBS television series of the same name, one of the book's strengths is its reliance on extensive interviews with participants.

Rozell, Mark J., and Clyde Wilcox. 1995. *God at the Grass Roots: The Christian Right in the 1994 Elections*. Lanham, Maryland: Rowman and Littlefield.

Examines the role of the Christian Right in the 1994 elections, its contribution to the "Republican revolution," in a state-by-state analysis.

Schultze, Quentin J. 1991. *Televangelism and American Culture: The Business of Popular Religion*. Grand Rapids, Michigan: Baker Book House.

A careful examination of televangelism as business, as religion, and as a significant form of American popular culture, and what this may mean for each.

Wallis, Jim. 1996. *Who Speaks for God? An Alternative to the Religious Right—A New Politics of Compassion, Community, and Civility*. New York: Delacorte.

The counterpoint to the Bork book. Wallis believes that the old ideologies and the divisions they support no longer suffice, that Americans are looking for a "new politics" beyond inflammatory rhetoric and division.

Relevant World Wide Websites

Remember to visit our website for updates and additional links at:
http://bsuvc.bsu.edu/~00amcorbett/relpol.htm

Many websites could be listed for this chapter. Here we include four good sites that contain lists of relevant links.

http://www.isrp.org/linkslft.html Politically left-oriented links

http://www.pfaw.org/link2pg.htm More left links

http://www.isrp.org/linksrt.html Politically right-oriented links

http://www.pfaw.org/link2rr.htm More right links

A number of organizations that have Washington lobbies also have websites. Some examples include:

http://shamash.org/reform/uahc/ The Union of American Hebrew Congregations

http://ncccusa.org/ The National Council of Churches

http://nae.goshen.net/ The National Association of Evangelicals

http://cc.org/ The Christian Coalition

The J.M. Dawson Institute for Church-State Studies is located at Baylor University. Its site is very informative on this important topic:

http://www.baylor.edu/~Church_State/

References

Cohen, Steven M. 1983. *American Modernity and Jewish Identity*. New York: Tavistock.

Cooney, John. 1984. *The American Pope*. New York: Times Books.

Corbett, Julia Mitchell. 1988. "The New Puritanism: We Must Say 'No' Again." *The Humanist* 48 (No. 5): 19–23, 48.

Corbett, Julia Mitchell. 1997. *Religion in America, Third Edition*. Upper Saddle River, New Jersey: Prentice Hall.

Curran, Charles E. 1982. *American Catholic Social Ethics: Twentieth Century Approaches*. Notre Dame, Indiana: University of Notre Dame Press.

Erickson, Hal. 1992. *Religious Radio and Television in the United states, 1921–1991: The Programs and Personalities*. Jefferson, North Carolina: McFarland and Company.

Fisher, Alan M. 1989. "Where the Jewish Vote Is Going." *Moment* 14: 41–43.

Fowler, Robert Booth. 1985. *Religion and Politics in America*. ATLA Monograph Series No. 21. Metuchen, New Jersey: American Theological Library Association and Scarecrow Press.

Frazier, E. Franklin, and C. Eric Lincoln. 1974. *The Negro Church in America* and *The Black Church Since Frazier*. New York: Schocken Books.

Fuchs, Lawrence. 1956. *The Political Behavior of American Jews*. Glencoe, Illinois: Free Press.

Hanna, Mary T. 1979. *Catholics and American Politics.* Cambridge, Massachusetts: Harvard University Press.

Hertzke, Allen D. 1988. *Representing God in Washington: The Role of Religious Lobbies in the American Polity.* Knoxville: University of Tennessee Press.

Johnston, Michael. 1982. "The 'New Christian Right' in American Politics." *Political Quarterly* 53: 181–199.

Johnstone, Ronald L. 1969. "Negro Preachers Take Sides," *Review of Religious Research* 11: 81–89.

Jorstad, Erling. 1990. *Holding Fast/Pressing On: Religion in America in the 1980s.* New York: Praeger.

Jorstad, Erling. 1993. "New Generation of Preachers Guiding Televangelism in the 1990s." *Religion Watch* 9 (No. 1): 3–4.

Lazerwitz, Bernard, J. Allen Winter, and Arnold Dashefsky, 1988. "Localism, Religiosity, Orthodoxy and Liberalism: The Case of Jews in the United States." *Social Forces* 67: 229–242.

Liebman, Charles S., and Steven M. Cohen. 1990. *Two Worlds of Judaism: The Israeli and American Experiences.* New Haven: Yale University Press.

Lipset, Seymour Martin. 1964. "Three Decades of the Radical Right: Coughlinites, McCarthyites, and Birchers," Pp. 373–446 in Daniel Bell (Ed.), *The Radical Right.* Garden City, New York: Doubleday Anchor.

Marx, Gary. 1969. "Religion: Opiate or Inspiration of Civil Rights Militancy Among Negroes." *American Sociological Review* 32: 64–72.

Moen, Matthew C. 1994. "From Revolution to Evolution: The Changing Nature of the Christian Right." *Sociology of Religion* 55: 345–357.

Moen, Matthew C. 1995. "The Fourth Wave of the Evangelical Tide: Religious Conservatives in the Aftermath of the 1994 Elections." *Contention* 5: 19–38.

Moen, Matthew C. 1996. "Evolving Politics of the Christian Right." *Political Science and Politics* XXIX: 461–464.

O'Brien, David J. 1968. *American Catholics and Social Reform: The New Deal Years.* New York: Oxford University Press.

Paris, Peter J. 1985. *The Social Teachings of the Black Churches.* Philadelphia: Fortress Press.

Peck, Janice. 1993. *The Gods of Televangelism: The Crisis of Meaning and he Appeal of Religious Television.* Cresskill, New Jersey: Hampton Press.

Penn, Mark J., and Douglas E. Schoen. 1988. "Prospects for the Jewish Vote in 1988." *Election Politics* 5: 24–26.

Piehl, Mel. 1982. *Breaking Bread: The Catholic Worker and the Origins of Catholic Radicalism in America.* Philadelphia: Temple University Press.

Schultze, Quentin J. 1991. *Televangelism and American Culture: The Business of Popular Religion.* Grand Rapids, Michigan: Baker Book House.

Sider, Ron. 1990. *Rich Christians in an Age of Hunger.* Dallas: Word Publishing.

Sklare, Marshall, and Joseph Greenblum. 1967. *Jewish Identity on the Suburban Frontier.* New York: Basic Books.

Smidt, Corwin, Lyman Kellstedt, John Green, and James Guth. 1994. "The Characteristics of Christian Political Activists: An Interest Group Analysis." Pp. 133–171 in William R. Stevenson, Jr. (Ed.). *Christian Political Activism at the Crossroads*. Lanham, Maryland: University Press of America.

Woocher, Jonathan S. 1986. *Sacred Survival: The Civil Religion of American Jews*. Bloomington: Indiana University Press.

Wuthnow, Robert. 1988. *The Restructuring of American Religion: Society and Faith Since World War II*. Princeton: Princeton University Press.

PART II

Religion and the First Amendment

CHAPTER 5

The Establishment Clause

Mr. Chairman, I am one of those persons . . . who gets carried away
by the Establishment Clause of the First Amendment. I get carried
away in awe by what it has wrought. And what it has wrought is a
nation which has more religious freedom, where the practice of
religion is healthier than anywhere else in the world and I suggest
that we all be proud of it and defend it.

> —Barry Ungar, Counsel, American Jewish Congress,
> testifying before the House Committee on Education
> and Labor, concerning the Equal Access Act, March 28, 1984

The Supreme Court, which so often finds an establishment of
religion where one does not exist and which often cannot see an
establishment of religion where it does exist . . .

> —Leonard W. Levy, establishment clause scholar, in *The
> Establishment Clause: Religion and the First Amendment*

Overview

The two quotations above indicate both the promise and the difficulty of
the establishment clause of the First Amendment. Religious liberty was
written into the United States Constitution from the beginning, with Article Six, which prohibits requiring religious qualifications for holding public office. It was substantially augmented when the Bill of Rights was added
in 1791. The First Amendment states the limits of the national
government's power to intervene in religious affairs: "Congress shall make

no law respecting an establishment of religion, or prohibiting the free exercise thereof. . . ." The freedoms of speech, of the press, and of peaceful assembly guaranteed in the First Amendment also enhance religious freedom.

In this chapter we will examine the application and interpretation of the establishment clause of the First Amendment to cases involving connections between religion and government. In the next chapter, we will examine the free exercise clause. The major questions to guide our examination of the establishment clause are:

- What was the constitutional background of the religious liberty clauses in the First Amendment?
- What major developments since the adoption of the Bill of Rights have affected the way in which the religious clauses of the First Amendment are applied and interpreted?
- What major principles have been applied by the Supreme Court in interpreting establishment clause cases?
- What are the major Supreme Court cases concerning establishment issues and what principles did these cases support?
- What principles guide government aid to religiously sponsored schools?
- What religious activities are permitted in public schools and what religious activities are not permitted? For example, is it legal for a student religious organization to hold meetings in public school buildings after school?
- How have taxation issues for religious organizations been decided? For example, are a religious organization's buildings exempt from taxes?
- How have religious holiday display issues been decided? For example, is it legal to have a nativity scene in city hall?

Background and Context
The First Amendment and Religious Liberty

As we discussed in Chapter 2, the Founders had differing ideas about the proper role of government in matters of religion. The language of the Constitution in general was often left somewhat vague in order to gain support from people who might not have agreed to more specific principles. However, we can say that *the Framers of the Constitution were in general agreement that the national government should not involve itself in religion.* The matter of whether religion ought to be the business of state governments is much less clear, and we will discuss the incorporation of religious liberty legislation at the state level below.

The First Amendment itself was drafted largely by three men from Virginia: James Madison, Thomas Jefferson, and George Mason. They were in no way hostile to religion, but rather believed that it should be a strictly private matter, completely outside the realm of government. Although they believed that a religious culture provided support for republican government, the Founders and some other people at the time believed that religion stood to gain nothing and lose much if it were officially linked with government. Likewise, government would lose if it were officially linked with religion.

Thomas Jefferson's statement that there should be a "wall of separation between church and state" has become well known and is often cited as the meaning of the First Amendment. However, as at least one author points out, James Madison wrote thirty years later that there should be a "line of separation between the rights of religion and the Civil authority" (Mead, 1977: 40–43). Madison's statement is more accurate, Mead says, since in the United States there is no single church (but a variety of churches and religious interest groups) and no single state (but rather the dispersal of civil authority throughout a wide range of agencies). The metaphor of a moving point drawing a constantly changing line also reflects more accurately than does the metaphor of the wall the reality of changing interpretation.

By including freedom of religion in the constitution, the Founders effectively removed religion on the national level from the realm of majority vote and made it subject instead to the courts. Writing for the majority of the Supreme Court in *West Virginia State Board of Education* v. *Barnette* (319 U.S. 624, 1943), Justice Robert H. Jackson stated this point succinctly:

> The very purpose of a Bill of Rights was to withdraw certain subjects from the vicissitudes of political controversy, to place them beyond the reach of majorities and officials and to establish them as legal principles to be applied by the courts. One's right to . . . freedom of worship . . . and other fundamental rights may not be submitted to vote; they depend on the outcome of no elections.

The authors of the Bill of Rights could never have imagined the great diversity of religious groups and individuals now present in the United States. Nor could they have envisioned the variety of conflicting demands that this diverse religious population would make. In the rough and tumble of practical decision making, the abstract nature of the amendment language leaves its meaning open to widely varying interpretations.

The vast majority of the religious liberty litigation to come before the Supreme Court has arisen out of the two religion clauses of the First Amendment—the establishment clause and the free exercise clause. In some instances, the First Amendment's two clauses concerning religion support each other, but in other cases, they oppose each other. What appears from one angle to be support for the free exercise of religion may well appear from a different angle to be an unacceptable establishment of religion. Similarly, what seems from one perspective to be support for the separation of religion and government may seem more like an interference with free exercise when seen from a different vantage point. We will discuss this tension in greater detail in Chapter 6, after you have had the opportunity to learn about the application of the free exercise clause. We will also see in Chapter 7 that this tension between the two clauses seems to be mirrored in the general public's attitudes toward the proper mix of religion and politics.

Developments Since the First Amendment

Developments have occurred since the First Amendment was written which dramatically affect its practical application. Following Weber (1990: 5–8), we can list five influential factors.

1. *Incorporation* under the Fourteenth Amendment made the religion clauses applicable at the state government level.

The First Amendment provisions dealing with religious liberty curtail the powers of Congress. The Bill of Rights was added to the Constitution to prevent encroachment on individual rights by the national government.

Beginning at the turn of the century, the Supreme Court began a process that came to be called "selective incorporation." This process gradually ensured that the freedoms guaranteed at the federal level would also be guaranteed at the state level. These freedoms came to be included under the Fourteenth Amendment's due process clause, which forbids state governments from depriving "any person of life, liberty, or property, without due process of law."

Incorporation of the Bill of Right's two specific provisions concerning religious liberty came in the 1940s. In 1940, the decision in *Cantwell* v. *Connecticut* incorporated free exercise of religion at the state level. In 1947, the establishment clause was incorporated in *Everson* v. *Board of Education*.

2. Both federal and state governments have become much more active and expansive bureaucracies, with "broad taxing, regulatory, and spending powers."

One example is the government regulation of schooling, with the accompanying issues concerning regulation of religiously-sponsored schools. Another example is the development of the welfare state. This has raised questions about the constitutionality of using government funds to pay for welfare programs that are sponsored by religious organizations. The expansion of taxation powers has led to questions regarding the taxation of the income and property that belongs to religious organizations.

3. As government has expanded, so has religion, increasing the variety of its activities and organizations.

Religious television programming distributed through high-tech satellite networks and financed largely by direct-mail fundraising (discussed in Chapter 4) is the most obvious example, but there is an array of others. Religious organizations themselves have become larger, more complex, and more bureaucratic. If religion were only an individual matter, there would be far less interface between government and religion. But, as we saw in the Introduction, religions have a significant social and institutional dimension, as well.

4. The invention of technologies such as those referred to above is in itself a change that strongly affects the interaction of religion and government.

When utilized by religious groups, are they subject to the same regulation as they are when used by other groups? Does the goal of protecting the public against fraud, for example, justify government surveillance of a religious organization's financial dealings? The government regulates what medical claims may be made by the manufacturers of nutritional supplements. Should it also oversee the claims made by religious healers?

5.   Within the last two decades, a proliferation of new religious groups and points of view has begun to question many of the usually accepted "rules of the game" in the area of religion and government.

Religious fundamentalists, for example, support a "social-political-economic-cultural vision" that integrates religious and governmental perspectives. Favoring broad accommodation, they tend to not see the issue of separation versus accommodation as particularly important.

Part of the legacy of the 1960s, discussed in Chapter 4, has been an increasing demand for freedom of religious practice by people in a variety of public settings such as schools and prisons. Prisons have routinely provided chaplains at government expense. To what extent are they required to provide chaplains of a wide variety of faiths? What rights do incarcerated persons have to follow the dietary rules of their religion? What about following other rituals of their faith, or the wearing of special clothing?

Three Types of Cases

Cases dealing with the relationship between religion and government fall into three categories (Drakeman, 1991: 112–114).

First, there are *pure establishment cases,* those in which there is an alleged establishment of religion without any attempt at justification on the grounds that it is necessary to protect free exercise. Examples include the public school prayer and Bible reading cases discussed below.

Second, there are the *pure free exercise cases,* in which it is claimed that certain activities are protected from government interference, without any accompanying establishment claim. The free exercise claims made for the use of peyote in a sacramental context by Native Americans exemplifies this type, as does a recent Florida case involving animal sacrifice (both of which are discussed in the following chapter).

Third, in between are the *mixed First Amendment cases,* those that illustrate the tension inherent in the two clauses of the First Amendment. An example is the provision of military and prison chaplains. Since they are paid by the government, establishment threatens to be an issue. However, they are necessary in order to preserve the free exercise of those who otherwise would be unable to practice their faith under the guidance of a clergyperson.

"Congress Shall Make No Law Respecting an Establishment of Religion"

Establishment clause cases have dealt mainly with two types of problems: support for church-related institutions (usually, schools) with tax monies or other public funds, and support for religious activities and rituals by agencies of the government (Morgan, 1972: 76). Examples of the former include the provision of buses and textbooks for parochial (church-sponsored) schools and, more recently, the controversy over the use of payment vouchers by the parents of children attending religiously-sponsored primary and secondary schools. Examples of the latter include mandated prayers and other devotional activities in the schools, and recently, student-led prayers at graduation ceremonies.

Three Principles for Establishment Clause Cases

The precise meaning of the establishment clause is far from clear, and the Court's interpretation of it has not been consistent. What is the exact meaning of the term "establishment"? What does "religion" mean in this context? And what degree of interaction violates the provision? Different courts and different justices have answered such questions differently. There have, however, been three identifiable principles that have guided the U.S. Supreme Court in its decisions in establishment clause cases (O'Brien, 1991: 643–644; Abraham, 1989: 118–124).

Strict Separation

Strict separation when applied to establishment clause cases holds that the government can offer no support whatsoever to religion. Justice Hugo Black wrote the majority opinion in *Everson* v. *Board of Education of Ewing Township* (330 U.S. 1, 1947), a case in which the court upheld the use of tax monies to provide transportation for children to parochial as well as to public schools. He stated this view as clearly as it has ever been stated:

> The "establishment of religion" clause of the First Amendment means at least this: Neither a state nor the Federal Government can set up a church. Neither can pass laws which aid one religion, aid all religions, or prefer one religion over another. Neither can force nor influence a person to go or to remain away from church against his will or force him to profess a belief or disbelief in any religion. No person can be punished for entertaining or profess-

ing religious beliefs or disbeliefs, for church attendance or non-attendance. No tax in any amount, large or small, can be levied to support any religious activities or institutions, whatever they may be called, or whatever form they may adopt to teach or practice religion. Neither a state nor the Federal Government can, openly or secretly, participate in the affairs of any religious organizations or groups and *vice versa*.

Strict Neutrality

Strict neutrality is similar to strict separation but allows for greater flexibility. In upholding property tax exemptions for buildings owned by religious organizations and used only for religious purposes (*Walz v. Tax Commission*, 397 U.S. 664, 1970), Chief Justice Warren E. Burger wrote an often cited statement of the principle of neutrality:

> [R]igidity could well defeat the basic purpose of these provisions [the religion clauses], which is to insure that no religion is sponsored or favored, none commanded, and none inhibited. The general principle deducible from the First Amendment and all that has been said by the Court is this: that we will not tolerate either governmentally established religion or governmental interference with religion. Short of these expressly proscribed governmental acts, there is room for play in the joints productive of a benevolent neutrality which will permit religious exercise to exist without sponsorship and without interference.

Accommodation

Accommodation or nonpreferentialism supports government support of all religions without discrimination among them. This view was stated by Edwin Meese, attorney general under President Ronald Reagan:

> [T]he First Amendment forbade the establishment of a particular religion or a particular church. It also precluded the federal government from favoring one church, or one church group over another. That's what the First Amendment did, but it did not go further. It did not, for example, preclude federal aid to religious groups so long as that assistance furthered a public purpose and so long as it did not discriminate in favor of one religious group over another (Meese, in his "Address before the Christian Legal Society" in San Diego, September 29, 1985, quoted in O'Brien, 1991: 640).

Major Establishment Cases

Most establishment cases have concerned activities in schools, both public and religiously-affiliated. The majority of these since 1960 have dealt with government aid to religiously-sponsored or affiliated private schools. We will first discuss those cases. This will be followed by a discussion of religious activities in public schools. We will then take up the interpretation of the establishment clause as it has affected secondary schools. Finally, other disestablishment cases will be considered.

One further point needs to be made before getting into specific cases. The decisions of the Supreme Court are sometimes unanimous. More often, however, they are not. We will focus on the majority opinions in the cases we present, since these are the ones that establish what is and is not legitimate under the Constitution. The fact that there are so often dissenting opinions, however, demonstrates that these are issues upon which reasonable people can be expected to disagree.

Everson v. *Board of Education*

One pre-1960 case must be mentioned here. *Everson* v. *Board of Education* (1947) was the first among the Court's major efforts at interpreting the establishment clause in regard to government aid to religiously affiliated schools. (Throughout this chapter, the term "religiously affiliated" or "religiously sponsored" school in used in preference to the more standard "parochial school." The former includes schools sponsored by any religious group, while the latter usually connotes Catholic schools.) The case concerned a New Jersey law that provided for tax reimbursement to parents for money spent on bus transportation of their children to schools, whether public or private. The reimbursements to parents of children in religiously-affiliated schools were challenged as an establishment of religion. The Court held, in a 5–4 decision, that the program simply did "no more than provide a general program to help parents get their children, regardless of their religion, safely and expeditiously to and from accredited schools."

There are two important elements in this case, as far as the precedent set is concerned. First, the aid was provided to parents without regard to religion, since the reimbursement was available to parents whose children attended public as well as private schools. Second, the assistance went directly to the parents, not to the school.

Lemon v. *Kurtzman* and the "Three-Part Test"

The Supreme Court has dealt with the question of the extent to which governments and their agencies may constitutionally assist the instructional efforts of religiously-affiliated schools repeatedly since 1960. *Lemon* v. *Kurtzman* is the definitive case with respect to establishment clause jurisprudence. Important distinctions were drawn in *Lemon* v. *Kurtzman*. Chief Justice Warren E. Burger, writing for the majority, stated that the Court had from *Everson* to *Allen* "permitted the States to provide church-related schools with secular, neutral, or nonideological services, facilities, or materials . . . [such as bus] transportation, school lunches, public health services, and secular textbooks . . ."

The *Lemon* case was different in that it dealt with the use of state monies to pay the salaries of teachers who were teaching secular subjects in religiously-affiliated schools. Justice William O. Douglas, with Justice Hugo T. Black joining, concurred with Burger's opinion and added:

> The surveillance or supervision of the States needed to police grants involved in these three cases, if performed, puts a public investigator into every classroom and entails a pervasive monitoring of these church agencies by the secular authorities. Yet if that surveillance or supervision does not occur, the zeal of religious proselytizers promises to carry the day and make a shambles of the Establishment Clause.

Lemon resulted in the definitive enumeration of the *three-part test* of constitutionality in cases of this type. After noting that "we can only dimly perceive the line of demarcation in this extraordinarily sensitive area of constitutional law," Justice Burger outlined the three parts:

- A statute must have a secular purpose.
- Its principal or primary effect must neither inhibit nor enhance religion.
- It must not lead to excessive entanglement between government and religion.

None of the three requirements of the *Lemon* test is easy to apply. In the nature of these cases, secular and religious purposes may be mixed. Exactly what constitutes a secular purpose? Not everyone agrees on the answer to this question, particularly in a country in which religion has been so thoroughly woven into public life. Even if a statute has a secular purpose, its end result might be to either enhance or inhibit religion (see our discussion of the peyote cases in Chapter 6, for example). The question of what constitutes a "principal or primary effect" is relevant—and not always easily decided—as well. Just exactly when government entanglement with religion becomes "excessive" is another difficulty in the application of *Lemon*. Although the application of the *Lemon* test has not been consistent, in part due to the problems described above, the Court has not definitively replaced it with anything else.

Refining the Differences

Tilton v. *Richardson,* decided on the same day as *Lemon,* illustrates two other significant points in the history of the Court's wrestling with this issue. While *Lemon* dealt with elementary and secondary schools, *Tilton* concerned a Catholic college. First, as a general rule, the Court has held that college and university students are less subject to undue influence by teachers than are those in the lower grades. Thus, assistance to religiously-affiliated post-secondary schools does not pose the threat to the establishment clause that it does in the lower grades. Second, buildings clearly exert far less influence than do teachers and books. Thus, aid for building construction has frequently been ruled constitutional.

Government Aid to Religiously Sponsored Primary and Secondary Schools

Several "working principles" have emerged in the last thirty-five years of the history of the Supreme Court's interpretation of what the establishment clause allows as far as government aid to primary and secondary schools:

- The same aid must be available to all students.
- The aid should not be paid directly to the school, but to the students or their parents.
- Excessive government entanglement must be avoided.
- There must be no religious content involved.

The Aid Must Be Available to All Students

The first of these can be stated this way: Aid to religiously sponsored education is permissible if the same aid is available to all, without regard to the type of school they attend.

Board of Education v. *Allen* (1968) firmly established this principle when the Court ruled that the provision of textbooks at no charge to students in religiously sponsored primary and secondary schools was constitutional because books were also provided free of charge to students in public schools. In *Wolman* v. *Walter* (1977), the Court held that supplying standardized tests and scoring to religiously sponsored schools was constitutional because identical assistance was provided to public schools. Similarly, *Committee for Public Education and Religious Liberty* v. *Regan* (1980) held that reimbursement of both religiously affiliated and secular nonpublic schools for state mandated testing and record keeping concerning purely secular subjects was constitutional because it served the secular purpose of quality education for all children. Finally, *Mueller* v. *Allen* (1983) established the constitutionality of a state income tax deduction for public and private school expenses, since it was allowed for parents of children in all types of schools, religious and secular, public and private.

Aid Should Not Be Paid Directly to the School

A second principle runs through many of these cases, as well as others: Aid is more acceptable if it goes directly to the students and/or their parents, rather than being paid to the school itself. Lemon v. Kurtzman (1971) dealt with the use of tax money to provide a salary supplement for teachers who taught secular subjects in religiously-sponsored schools and with the practice of state reimbursement of religiously-sponsored schools for the cost of textbooks. Both were ruled unconstitutional, in part because the assistance went directly to the school and thus amounted to direct aid to religion. In *Committee for Public Education and Religious Liberty* v. *Nyquist* (1973), the Court held that subsidies for maintenance and repair of religiously-sponsored primary and secondary schools could not pass establishment clause scrutiny for the same reason.

Nyquist differed from *Allen*, however, in that the Court ruled that tuition reimbursement for parents of religiously-sponsored primary and secondary school students was unconstitutional, even though the payments were made to the parents and not to the schools.

On the other hand, in *Zobrest* v. *Catalina Foothills School district* (1993) the use of public funds through the Individuals with Disabilities Education Act to pay for a sign-language interpreter for a student in a religiously-sponsored school was deemed constitutional on the grounds that, although it took place in a sectarian school, it provided a neutral service available to all students, rather than advancing religion.

Excessive Entanglement and Paying for Personnel

Lemon v. *Kurtzman* was also a case in which the principle that *an activity must not entail excessive entanglement between government and religion* was applied to education. The content of textbooks is fixed and can be determined. There is a substantially greater chance that a classroom teacher, even one teaching a secular subject, in the atmosphere of a religiously-sponsored school, will interject religion into what is taught. This has led to a further principle that assistance with paying for personnel is less acceptable than assistance with textbooks and the like. Chief Justice Warren E. Burger wrote the majority opinion in this case:

> Although the District Court found that concern for religious values did not inevitably or necessarily intrude into the content of secular subjects, the considerable religious activity of these schools led the legislature to provide for careful government controls and surveillance by state authorities in order to ensure that state aid supports only secular education. . . . [T]eachers have a substantially different ideological character from books. In terms of involving some aspect of faith or morals in secular subjects, a textbook's content is ascertainable, but a teacher's handling of a subject is not.

Wolman v. *Walter* (1977) provides an interesting perspective on the matter of school personnel and possible ideological involvement. The Court held that the possibility that state-supported persons providing speech, hearing, and psychological diagnostic services in religiously-sponsored schools might engage in conversation with students about religious topics was not great enough to make that support unconstitutional. Neither is the provision of therapeutic guidance and remedial services a violation of the establishment clause.

However, state provision of school buses to religiously-affiliated schools for field trips was held to lead to excessive entanglement because it required government supervision of the sectarian personnel involved in such trips. Later on, however, in *Aguilar* v. *Felton* (1985; superceded in 1997 in *Agostini* v. *Felton,* discussed below), it was held that public school personnel going into religiously-sponsored schools to provide remedial and guidance services violated the establishment clause as well as the excessive entanglement provision. The activity was said to take place in a pervasively sectarian atmosphere, thus requiring ongoing inspection to ensure that the teachers did not become involved in teaching religion.

In mid-1997, the Court reversed the ruling it had handed down in *Aguilar.* In essence, the Court held that decisions in its more recent cases have undermined the four assumptions on which the *Aguilar* case rested: (1) that any public school teacher teaching in a parochial school inevitably inculcates religion; (2) that public employees working on parochial school grounds create a symbolic union of church and state; (3) that public aid to a religious school necessarily finances religious education; and (4) that such employment creates an excessive entanglement between government and religion. The program at issue in *Agostini* (a New York City Title I program which allowed public school teachers to give remedial instruction to parochial school students on the grounds of the parochial school) was held to violate none of the currently operative criteria: it did not result in religious indoctrination, select recipients on the basis of religion, or create excessive entanglement. The decision was 5–4, and dissenting opinions indicated strong opposition based on concern about breaching the division between religion and government called for by the establishment clause.

There Must Be No Religious Content Involved

In order for the provision of services to religiously-affiliated schools to pass establishment clause muster, there must be a high degree of certainty that no religious content is involved. In *Levitt v. Committee for Public Education and Religious Liberty* (1973), state reimbursement of religiously-sponsored primary and secondary schools for expenses incurred in testing, grading, compiling, and reporting test scores when there was no means to ensure that the internally prepared tests were free of religious content was held to be unconstitutional. On the other hand, in *Wolman v. Walter* it was held to be constitutional for the state to supply standardized tests and scoring to religiously affiliated schools because these were the same ones used in the public schools.

Religious Activities in Public Schools
Devotional Activities

As indicated above, most of these cases are clear-cut establishment cases. Several concern prayer in the classroom or in connection with other school-sponsored activities. Perhaps the best-known is *Engel* v. *Vitale* (1962), sometimes referred to as the "New York Board of Regents prayer case." The New York State Board of Regents composed a nondenominational prayer and mandated its use at the beginning of every school day. School officials maintained that doing so was an aspect of the students' moral and spiritual training. The prayer was simple: "Almighty God, we acknowledge our dependence upon Thee, and we beg Thy blessings upon us, our parents, our teachers and our Country." Students did not have to repeat the prayer, but obviously peer pressure to participate was strong. The Court ruled the prayer in violation of the establishment clause. Justice Hugo L. Black's opinion was strongly worded and explicit:

> [We] think that the constitutional prohibition against laws respecting an establishment of religion must at least mean that in this country it is no part of the business of government to compose official prayers for any group of the American people to recite as part of a religious program carried on by government.

A similar case a year later, *Abington v. Schempp*, held that school board sponsorship of Bible reading and the recitation of the Lord's Prayer are clearly unconstitutional devotional exercises. Again, students whose parents wished it could ask to be excused from participation.

Two crucial principles came out of this case. In his majority opinion, Justice Tom C. Clark noted that some people insisted that a "religion of secularism" was being established in the schools unless such exercises were permitted. This same claim continues to be advanced in the discussions of the permissibility of "moments of silence" cases (*see* below). Clark stated firmly that the ruling did not have the effect of "affirmatively opposing or showing hostility to religion."

The second point is the distinction between devotional exercises and the teaching of religion, on the one hand, and teaching *about* religion, on the other. Clark's opinion addressed this issue as well:

> In addition, it might well be said that one's education is not complete without a study of comparative religion or the history of religion in its relationship to the advancement of civilization. It certainly may be said that the Bible is worthy of study for its literary and historic qualities. Nothing we have said here indicates that such study of the Bible or of religion, when presented objectively as part of a secular program of education, may not be effected consistently with the First Amendment.

This distinction made possible the teaching of religious studies courses in secondary schools and the development of religious studies programs in state-supported colleges and universities.

There have been other important cases involving devotional activities. Requiring the posting of the Ten Commandments in public school classrooms was held to violate the establishment clause (*Stone* v. *Graham*, 1980), as did state authorization of a "moment of silence" for "meditation or voluntary prayer" (*Wallace* v. *Jaffree*, 1985). More recently, the Court held that the practice of asking area clergy to offer prayers of invocation and benediction at the beginning and end of middle- and high school graduation ceremonies was unconstitutional, as well (*Lee* v. *Weisman*, 1992). In response to this decision, students in several high schools chose to have a student-led prayer at their graduation ceremonies. The Supreme Court has not yet heard a case dealing with this practice.

As you will learn in Chapter 7, the general public favors prayer and other devotional activities in public schools. This is reflected in movements for voluntary student prayers at graduation ceremonies, for example, and in things such as the "see you at the pole" movement, in which students gather around the school's flagpole for prayer. The Court's decisions disallowing organized prayer have not been overturned, however, because political elites—those who make the laws—and religious elites are both less favorable toward doing so than is the general public.

Creation and Evolution

Two important cases dealt with what is to be taught about how humankind began. This was the issue in the earlier Scopes trial, in Tennessee, as well. In 1968, the Court's ruling in *Epperson* v. *Arkansas* struck down a law that made it illegal "to teach the theory or doctrine that mankind ascended or descended from a lower order of animals" or to adopt or use a textbook that taught the theory of evolution. Following this ruling, Arkansas attempted to establish a "balanced treatment" plan, under which both evolution and the Genesis account of the divine creation of humankind would be taught. A federal district court ruled this "balanced treatment" approach unconstitutional on the grounds that "creationism" is a religious rather than a scientific doctrine. Thus, requiring that it be taught clearly violated the establishment clause. Nearly two decades after *Epperson,* the Supreme Court in *Edwards* v. *Aguillard* struck down the Louisiana Balanced Treatment for Creation-Science and Evolution-Science in Public Instruction Act. The Act required the teaching of both perspectives.

Equal Access

Two cases have dealt with the use of public secondary school facilities by religious groups. In each case, the concern was that allowing the use of these government facilities by religious groups was an establishment of religion. In both cases, the Court ruled that such use did not violate the establishment clause. In fact, to disallow use of a "limited public forum," such as a school building, to religious groups, was in itself not permissible. In 1984, the federal government passed the Equal Access Act, which required that public secondary schools which maintain a "limited public forum" and allow noncurricular student groups to meet on school property must allow equal access to such groups without regard to the "religious, philosophical, or other" content of their meetings. The constitutionality of the Act was upheld in *Board of Education* v. *Mergens*. In this case, which began in Nebraska, a student had asked permission to form a student Christian club that would meet to read and discuss the Bible and pray together. The school claimed that such a club would violate the establishment clause. The Appeals Court held that the school did maintain a "limited public forum" and consequently could not discriminate against a particular club because of its ideological content. On appeal, the Supreme Court upheld that decision. A similar case on the secondary school level is discussed in the following section. In *Lamb's Chapel* v. *Center Moriches Union School District* (1993) the Court held that a church using public school facilities to show a religiously oriented film did not violate the establishment clause.

The Equal Access Act and the Court's upholding of its constitutionality has ramifications beyond access of student *religious* groups to school facilities. It also means equal access for student groups that come together around social issues over which people are deeply divided, frequently along religious lines. It means, for example, that schools that permit noncurricular groups to meet on school premises must allow both the "Students for Traditional Family Values" and the "Student Gay Alliance" to meet. It means that "Students for Reproductive Choice" and "Student Right to Life" supporters must receive equal consideration.

Religious Activities and Post-Secondary Education

Since most of you reading this book are college or university students, we have chosen to treat cases involving post-secondary education separately.

Four significant cases have dealt with monetary aid to religiously-affiliated post-secondary schools. One concerned equal access for religious groups, and the rest concerned funding in one way or another.

Monetary Aid

In *Tilton* v. *Richardson* (1971) the Court upheld the 1963 Higher Education Facilities Act that provided grant money to religiously-affiliated colleges for the construction of buildings that would be used for secular purposes. Although the religious school did benefit, the Court held that the principal or primary effect of the Act was not to advance religion. Two years later, in *Hunt* v. *McNair*, the use of state-issued revenue bonds to help a religiously-sponsored college to borrow money was upheld, since the benefit was available to all institutions of higher education, regardless of affiliation. In 1976, the Court ruled that annual general purpose grants to religiously-affiliated colleges do not violate the establishment clause, since post-secondary schools are not as "permeated by religion" as religiously-affiliated primary and secondary schools *(Roemer* v. *Board of Public Works)*.

The most recent of the government funding cases came out of the Virginia courts. The University of Virginia routinely authorized payments from the Student Activities Fund to outside contractors for printing costs on a range of student publications. All of the materials included a disclaimer that they were independent of the university and that the university did not sponsor them. It withheld payment for the printing costs of *Wide Awake: A Christian Perspective at the University of Virginia* on the grounds that it "primarily promotes or manifests a particular belief in or about a deity [God] or ultimate reality" and was therefore prohibited by the university's guidelines. The students then charged that the university had violated their free speech rights.

The Fourth Circuit Court held that the university's action did indeed violate the students' freedom of speech, but that the violation was justified because funding the publication would have violated the establishment clause, since the university was state-funded. When *Rosenberger* v. *Rector and Visitors of the University of Virginia* (1995) reached the Supreme Court, the lower courts' findings were overturned and the university was told to fund the publication. The majority opinion, written by Justice Antonin Scalia, noted that the money was to be paid directly to a third-party printer, not to the religious organization itself. The Court also distinguished between the student activities fee money that was at issue in the case and tax monies, holding that the activity fees were not "public funds" in the same sense as are tax revenues. Further, to fund secular publications and not fund religious ones was found to discriminate against religion, and thus be in violation of the free exercise clause. It was also held to be a denial of free speech, unconstitutional discrimination on the basis of viewpoint, which was not excused by attempted compliance with the establishment clause. In addition, the Court held that funding all activities, without attempting to decide which were religious and which not, required less government entanglement with religion than if the university tried to decide between them.

It was also noted that the program was essentially neutral to religion. That neutrality was not violated when the university—as an agency of the government—followed neutral criteria and extended benefits to recipients whose views included both religious and secular.

Not all on the high court agreed (the decision was 5–4). Justice David Souter, after noting the strongly evangelistic nature of *Wide Awake*, was sharp in his dissent:

> Using public funds for the direct subsidization of preaching the word is categorically forbidden under the Establishment Clause. . . . The Court is ordering an instrumentality of the State to support religious evangelism with direct funding. This is a flat violation of the Establishment Clause.

Finally, in a case in some ways similar to *Zobrest*, the Court found that the establishment clause does not prohibit the provision of assistance (under a vocational rehabilitation program) to a blind student who was studying in a Christian college to become a full-time religious worker (*Witters v. Washington Department of Services for the Blind*, 1986). In this case, the money was paid directly to the student, rather than to the school.

Equal Access

The case of *Widmar v. Vincent*, decided in 1981, parallels the high school equal access cases, but on the university level. In this case, a state statute that prohibited the use of state university buildings "for purposes of religious worship" was ruled unconstitutional. Since the university did maintain an "open forum," in which various groups used its facilities, it could not exclude a group based on its content or its activities within the limits of the law. No state approval of any religious practice was implied, and a wide variety of religious and secular groups had the same privileges.

Other Establishment Clause Cases

There are a number of other situations in which questions regarding the possible establishment of religion are involved. Two of the most controversial are questions concerning taxation and holiday displays.

Taxation and Entanglement

One of the most far-reaching in its effects is *Walz* v. *Tax Commission* (1970). In *Walz*, the Court upheld the practice of allowing real estate tax exemptions for religious buildings against a challenge that to do so was an establishment of religion. The exemption was available to a wide range of not-for-profit groups, and this proved to be one part of the key to the Court's decision. Again, Chief Justice Warren E. Burger wrote for the Court:

> The legislative purpose of a property tax exemption is neither the advancement nor the inhibition of religion; it is neither sponsorship nor hostility. New York, in common with the other states, has determined that certain entities that exist in a harmonious relationship to the community at large, and that foster its "moral or mental improvement," should not be inhibited in their activities by property taxation or the hazard of loss of those properties for nonpayment of taxes. It has not singled out one particular church or religious group, or even churches as such; rather, it has granted exemption to all houses of religious worship within a broad class of property owned by non-profit, quasi-public corporations which include hospitals, libraries, playgrounds, scientific, professional, historical, and patriotic groups.

The other key in this case was the Court's decision that the elimination of the exemption would lead to much greater government entanglement with religion than did the exemption itself. The principle that a statute or practice must not lead to excessive government entanglement of religion was first articulated in *Walz*. While providing the exemption required a one-time declaration of an organization's not-for-profit standing, doing away with the exemption would give "rise to tax valuation of church property, tax liens, tax foreclosures, and the direct confrontations and conflicts that follow in the train of those legal processes." This would be altogether too much entanglement.

As have many people since the case was decided, Justice William O. Douglas disagreed with the ruling. The majority opinion distinguished between a subsidy, which grants funds, and an exemption, which does not collect funds. In his opinion, he stated succinctly: "Indeed I would suppose that in common understanding one of the best ways to 'establish' one or more religions is to subsidize them, which a tax exemption does. . . . A tax exemption is a subsidy."

On the other hand, the Court struck down a sales tax exemption for periodicals published or distributed by religious groups solely for the purpose of promoting their faith as having insufficient breadth to avoid violating the establishment clause (*Texas Monthly, Inc. v. Bullock*, 1989).

Other taxation questions have been decided as free exercise cases and will be discussed in Chapter 6.

Holiday Displays

Two relatively recent cases have dealt with the legality of Christmas displays. In *Lynch* v. *Donnelly*, the Court upheld the display of a nativity scene on city property as one part of a Christmas display that also included secular symbols. Justice Sandra Day O'Connor concurred with the majority opinion, but also discussed at length the framework in which the governmental use of religious symbols was to be analyzed. There can be absolutely no government endorsement of religion. Such endorsement "sends a message to nonadherents that they are outsiders, not full members of the political community, and an accompanying message to adherents that they are insiders, favored members of the political community."

Whether the display is a government "endorsement," then, depends upon the effect of the display more than on the particular symbols it contains. Specifically, O'Connor stated that the decision rests on "what viewers may fairly understand to be the purpose of the display." In this case, the display contained a welter of holiday symbols, both religious and secular. In a context that included such a diversity of symbols, she held that the setting "negates any message of endorsement" of the Christian belief about Christmas. While the four dissenting justices agreed with the principle, they reached the opposite conclusion, seeing the inclusion of the nativity scene as setting the "government's imprimatur of approval on the particular religious beliefs exemplified by the creche." The principle is important: governmental use of religious symbols is unconstitutional if it endorses religion, but acceptable if it does not, and the decision depends largely upon the context in which the religious symbols are displayed.

The second relevant case here is *County of Allegheny v. American Civil Liberties Union Greater Pittsburgh Chapter* (1989). The case dealt with two recurring Christmas displays. For many years there had been a nativity scene (crèche) placed on the staircase of the country courthouse. There had also been a Hanukkah menorah (the eight-branched candle holder used in Judaism) outside the city-county building, along with a Christmas tree and a sign honoring liberty. The Court ruled the first an unconstitutional endorsement of religion, but permitted the second.

Based on the context, there was nothing in the nativity scene display that detracted from its religious meaning, as there had been in the *Lynch* case. Further, its location increased the likelihood that a viewer would interpret it as a government endorsement:

> Furthermore, the creche sits on the Grand Staircase, the "main" and "most beautiful part" of the building that is the seat of county government. No viewer could reasonably think that it occupies this location without the support and approval of the government. Thus, . . . the county sends an unmistakable message that it supports and promotes the Christian praise to God that is the creche's religious message.

In the instance of the menorah and the Christmas tree, the judges thought differently. The menorah is certainly a religious symbol. But, like the Christmas tree, it was held to be "the primary visual symbol for a holiday that, like Christmas, has both religious and secular dimensions."

Endorsing both Christmas and Hanukkah as *religious* holidays would violate the Constitution every bit as much as underwriting one or the other. The Court held that the city was well within constitutional limits by acknowledging both as secular cultural holidays. This particular display, the Court ruled, "simply recognizes that both Christmas and Chanukah [an alternate spelling of Hanukkah] are part of the same winter-holiday season, which has attained a secular status in our society."

Summary and Conclusions

In this chapter, we focused on interpretations of the establishment clause in the First Amendment to the U.S. Constitution. We have seen that establishment clause cases have arisen around two primary issues:

- The use of tax monies or other public funds for support for religiously-sponsored organizations, usually schools. In general, the Court has held that the same aid must be available to all students and that it is best if the aid goes to the students or their parents, rather than to the school. Assistance in paying for personnel is more suspect than paying for textbooks and the like. Religious content per se has to be avoided.

- Support for religious activities by agencies of the government. Many of these cases have concerned devotional activities such as prayer and Bible reading in public schools. Others have dealt with how the beginning of humankind shall be taught. Equal access by religious groups to the use of public buildings has resulted in a number of cases. Still others have dealt with holiday displays on public property. Taxation cases have considered whether religiously-owned property should be taxable.

We have also noted that there is a range of interpretations concerning how strictly separation is to be taken:

- *Strict separation* holds that the government should offer no support at all to religion.
- *Strict neutrality* is similar, while allowing for greater flexibility and having neutrality rather than complete separation as its goal.
- *Accommodation* allows for government support for religion as long as there is no discrimination among religions.

It is difficult to attempt to wrap up the Supreme Court's findings in the establishment clause cases into one neat package. Certainly there can be differences of opinion on the overall effect of these findings, just as there are differences about specific cases. Nevertheless, the following conclusions seem both fair and accurate.

- With respect to government aid to religion, direct assistance clearly violates the establishment clause. At the same time, the fact that some indirect benefit may accrue to a religious organization from a particular policy or practice is not on the face of it grounds for holding that action to be unconstitutional. Nor are religious organizations to be barred from benefiting from programs from which other similar agencies benefit.

- Devotional exercises in public schools fall far outside the pale of what is constitutional. However, religious groups and individuals cannot be excluded from access to school facilities because they are religious. Further, the ban on religious exercises does not entail a parallel ban on teaching and studying about religion from an academic perspective.

- In general, the Supreme Court's decisions in establishment clause cases have maintained three basic underlying principles:

  1. Religion and government are to be kept separate, with government remaining neutral toward religion.

  2. Some relationship between the two is unavoidable, however.

  3. Within the boundaries laid out by the first principle, the Court's decisions have recognized and supported the important roles of religion in the lives of people in the United States, the role of religious organizations, and the presence of religion in the public life of the nation.

As you have seen in this chapter, the application of the seemingly simple principle of the establishment clause is anything but simple. In Chapter 6, we will consider the application of the free exercise clause and the working out of the meaning of that clause through Supreme Court decisions. The inclusion of both clauses in the First Amendment makes church-state jurisprudence even more complex.

Important Terms

Pure establishment case

Pure free exercise case

Mixed first amendment case

Strict separation

Strict neutrality

Accommodation

Review Questions

1. In what three places in the Constitution do we find religious liberty addressed? State each in your own words and tell what it means.

2. What is incorporation?

3. What five things have happened since the Bill of Rights was written that have affected its practical application?

4. With what two types of situations have establishment clauses typically dealt?

5. What three principles have guided the Court in interpreting the establishment clause?

6. State the three-part test articulated in *Lemon*.

7. What does the Equal Access Act provide for?

8. What general principles emerge from the cases reviewed in this chapter?

Discussion Questions

1. What does freedom of religion mean to you personally?

2. Which of the three principles you stated in question 5 above seems best to you? Why?

3. Think about each of the general principles listed in the Summary and Conclusions section. With which do you agree? Why? With which do you disagree? Why?

For Further Reading

Alley, Robert S. (Ed.). 1988. *The Supreme Court on Church and State*. New York: Oxford University Press.

Cases and judicial opinions, both majority and dissent, with very little commentary.

Drakeman, Donald L. 1991. *Church-State Constitutional Issues: Making Sense of the Establishment Clause. Contributions in Legal Studies, Number 62*. Paul L. Murphy, Series Editor. New York: Greenwood Press.

Thorough analysis of the issues with extensive case citations.

Eastland, Terry. 1993. *Religious Liberty in the Supreme Court: The Cases That Define the Debate Over Church and State*. Washington, D.C.: Ethics and Public Policy Center.

Cases and judicial opinions, with several analytic essays and some extracts from media responses to cases.

Levy, Leonard W. 1994. *The Establishment Clause: Religion and the First Amendment, Second Edition.* Chapel Hill: University of North Carolina Press.

A thorough historical survey by a notable establishment clause scholar.

Relevant World Wide Websites

Remember to visit our website for updates and additional links at: http://bsuvc.bsu.edu/~00amcorbett/relpol.htm

Two websites are particularly relevant for this chapter and Chapter 6. Further, each of these sites has links to other sites.

http://supct.law.cornell.edu/supct has general information on the U.S. Supreme Court, a set of links to all Court decisions since 1990 plus a database of three hundred they consider the "most important" pre-1990 cases, all searchable by several different categories. It also tells how to subscribe to an e-mail service that provides immediate updates on the Court's decisions.

http://w3.trib.com/FACT/ is a resource for people who want to learn more about any of the civil liberties guaranteed in the First Amendment, including specific information on religious liberty. It is frequently updated and includes an FAQ (frequently asked questions) section. This site has links to several of the documents mentioned in this chapter and in Chapter 6.

References

Abraham, Harry J. 1989. "The Status of the First Amendment's Religion Clauses: Some Reflections on Lines and Limits," in James E. Wood, Jr. (Ed.), *Readings on Church and State.* Waco, Texas: J.M. Dawson Institute of Church-State Studies.

Drakeman, Donald L. 1991. *Church-State Constitutional Issues: Making Sense of the Establishment Clause. Contributions in Legal Studies, Number 62.* Paul L. Murphy, Series Editor. New York: Greenwood Press.

Eastland, Terry. 1993. *Religious Liberty in the Supreme Court: The Cases That Define the Debate Over Church and State.* Washington, D.C.: Ethics and Public Policy Center.

Levy, Leonard W. 1994. *The Establishment Clause: Religion and the First Amendment, Second Edition.* Chapel Hill: University of North Carolina Press.

Mead, Sidney E. 1977. "Neither Church nor State: Reflections on James Madison's 'Line of Separation,'" in James E. Wood, Jr. (Ed.), *Readings on Church and State*. Waco, Texas: J.M. Dawson Institute of Church-State Studies.

Morgan, Richard E. 1972. *The Supreme Court and Religion*. New York: Free Press.

O'Brien, David M. 1991. *Constitutional Law and Politics, Volume Two: Civil Rights and Civil Liberties*. New York: W.W. Norton.

Weber, Paul J. 1990. "Neutrality and First Amendment Interpretation," in Paul J. Weber, ed., *Equal Separation: Understanding the Religion Clauses of the First Amendment. Contributions in Legal Studies, Number 58*. Paul L. Murphy, Series Editor. New York: Greenwood Press.

CHAPTER 6

The Free Exercise Clause

Suppose one believed that human sacrifices were a necessary part of religious worship, would it be seriously contended that the civil government under which he lived could not interfere to prevent a sacrifice? Or if a wife religiously believed it was her duty to burn herself upon the funeral pile [sic] of her dead husband, would it be beyond the power of the civil government to prevent her carrying her belief into practice?
—*Reynolds* v. *United States*, U.S. Supreme Court, 1879

It behooves us to recognize that protecting religious minorities will sometimes mean protecting and perpetuating practices we deem morally repugnant. . . . But if we are committed to the proposition that the claims of God are not subject to the authority of civil government but commended to the consciences of believers, then we will be forced to tolerate some claims that seem to us very wrong.
—Michael W. McConnell, "Taking Religious Freedom Seriously"

Overview

The overall question that guides this chapter is: *Under what circumstances are people free to practice their religious beliefs, and under what circumstances has it been held that they must refrain from such practices?* The two quotations above present very different leanings on the interpretation of the free exercise clause of the First Amendment to the U.S. Constitution. This chapter examines applications and controversies concerning the free exercise clause. To refresh your memory on the religious clauses of the First Amendment, let's state them again: *Congress shall make no law respecting an establishment of religion, or prohibiting the free exercise thereof.* As in the previous chapter, our focus is on interpretations of the clause by the Supreme Court, but we will also consider certain important legislation in this area (e.g., the Religious Freedom Restoration Act). The major questions we will consider are:

- How have approaches to interpreting the free exercise clause differed from approaches to interpreting the establishment clause?
- What distinctions has the Supreme Court made between religious beliefs and actions based on those beliefs? If people are free to hold any sort of religious beliefs, are they also free to act on those beliefs?
- What happens when an action of the government *inadvertently* restricts the religious freedom of some people? Is the action unconstitutional?
- How have the religious grounds for military draft exemption changed over time? And how is this related to what the Supreme Court defines as religion? For example, if the draft were brought back, could someone be exempted from military service on philosophical grounds rather than religious grounds?
- What important religious liberty cases have been brought to the Supreme Court by the Jehovah's Witnesses? Can a person be required to recite the Pledge of Allegiance if doing so violates the person's religious views? Do people have a right to distribute religious literature door to door even if there is a local ordinance against it?
- What important religious cases have been brought to the Supreme Court by Sabbatarians (those who observe Saturday as their Sabbath)? Are Sunday closing laws legal?
- What special religious freedom issues have developed out of the situation of Native Americans?
- How did the Religious Freedom Restoration Act come about and what is its significance? What is the significance of the Supreme Court's declaring the Act unconstitutional? What do its supporters say about it and what do its opponents say about it?
- How do the free exercise clause and the establishment clause sometimes conflict with one another?

Perspectives on Interpretation of the Free Exercise Clause

As we saw in Chapter 5, establishment cases are about setting limits on allowable direct or indirect government support for religion. Put differently, how far can the government legitimately go to encourage religion? Free exercise cases, on the other hand, deal with adjudicating whether or not certain actions done in the name of religion should be free from government interference.

Free exercise is often about making exceptions for smaller, lesser-understood and sometimes unpopular groups whose religious practices may be thought of as "unconventional" (Corbett, 1997). Examples include Jehovah's Witnesses whose door-to-door evangelism and distribution of tracts has sometimes come into conflict with local ordinances banning these activities, Native American Church members whose use of peyote runs afoul of antidrug laws, and religious pacifists who refused to be drafted into military service.

Interpretation of the free exercise clause of the First Amendment has developed differently from the interpretation of the establishment clause in at least three respects.

1. It has *not* led to "the somewhat tortuous devising of tests to which the Court had to resort for establishment clause purposes" (*Religion in the Constitution: A Delicate Balance*, 1983: 21). See, however, our discussion of the crucial "compelling interest test" later in this chapter.

2. Whereas the meaning of the establishment clause has been worked out largely through *judicial* means, the meaning of the free exercise clause has been interpreted through numerous *legislative* acts, as well as in Supreme Court decisions.

3. While the justices have frequently referred to the intentions of the founders of the nation and the framers of the Bill of Rights in establishment clause cases, there have been fewer such references in free exercise cases (Eastland, 1993: 7–8).

Analysts and commentators do not agree on how much free exercise of religion the clause has been construed to allow. Some view it as "an expansive interpretation that encompasses all sorts of religious belief, including the constitutionally protected right to have no religion," (*Religion in the Constitution: A Delicate Balance*, 1983: 21). Seen from this angle, people in the

United States—followers of majority religions, minority religions, or no religion at all—have a great deal of freedom to practice their religious beliefs, subject only to the distinction between belief and action described below.

Others, however, take a less positive view. Law professor Michael W. McConnell notes that the religion clauses of the First Amendment were intended to protect those whose practices seemed strange to the majority. Despite this intention, the religious clauses have often not been interpreted this way, with the result that the strong language of free exercise has not always translated into the degree of protection that the clauses should have offered (McConnell, 1993).

It is not our purpose here to adjudicate this difference of opinion. As we will see in our review of the relevant Supreme Court cases, the difference is partly one of time: the mood of the Court has differed at different times in the history of its interpretation of the free exercise clause. The difference is also undoubtedly one of perspective: what to one observer appears to be great latitude may seem to another restrictive.

In the Beginning:
Reynolds v. *United States*

The first clear-cut test of the free exercise clause to come before the Supreme Court was *Reynolds* v. *United States* (1878). George Reynolds was a member of the Church of Jesus Christ of Latter-day Saints (Mormons). For a brief period of time in the latter half of the 1800s, the Mormon Church supported the practice of polygamy, specifically polygyny—allowing a man to marry more than one wife. (The practice of polygamy is no longer condoned by the Mormon Church, and polygamous groups calling themselves "Mormon" are not sanctioned by either of the two major branches of the church.) Because this practice was clearly at odds with the dominant cultural pattern in the territories, Congress exercised its power to make laws for the territories and disallowed the practice of polygamy. Reynolds was convicted under this statute, and eventually his case made its way to the U.S. Supreme Court.

Belief and Action

The justices' decision in *Reynolds* set two important precedents. One is the distinction between religious *beliefs* and the *actions* that flow from those beliefs. The former are untouchable by the Court; the latter are not. Chief Justice Morrison Waite wrote the majority opinion, very conscious that his would be the first interpretation of the free exercise clause. In that opinion, he wrote: "Congress was deprived of all legislative power over mere *opinion,* but was left free to reach *actions* which were in violation of social duties or subversive of good order." In the opinion of the Court, the practice of multiple marriage certainly was "in violation of social duties and subversive of good order." Thus, the restriction of Reynolds' free exercise of his religion was justified, even mandated.

The principle was restated in *Cantwell* v. *Connecticut* (1940), although that particular case was decided in favor of free exercise. Justice Owen J. Roberts wrote for the Court that "the First Amendment . . . embraces two concepts, freedom to believe and freedom to act. The first is absolute but, in the nature of things, the second cannot be. Conduct remains subject to regulation for the protection of society."

Secular Regulation Rule

The other precedent solidified in *Reynolds* has come to be known as the *secular regulation rule.* It did not begin with the Court's finding in *Reynolds,* but that case focused it and set it firmly as a precedent. Simply, the secular regulation rule means that if a governmental action serves a valid secular purpose, it can be enforced against a free exercise claim, even though it puts a particular burden on the practice of religion.

This interpretation was restated in *Employment Division* v. *Smith* (1990), which we discuss below. In that case, Justice Antonin Scalia wrote for the Court. After noting that the exercise of religion includes actions as well as beliefs, Justice Scalia reasoned that the state would be violating the free exercise of religion clause if it banned religious acts for religious reasons. However, if prohibiting the exercise of religion was an incidental effect (not the purpose) of an otherwise valid law, then the First Amendment has not been violated. Justice Scalia stated that "We have never held that an individual's religious beliefs excuse him from compliance with an otherwise valid law prohibiting conduct that the State is free to regulate."

Currently, the distinction between belief and action still stands in the Court's decisions. The fate of the secular regulation rule has been more complex, and we will review it below.

Conscientious Objection and Religiously Motivated Action

Throughout American history, whenever the government has deemed it necessary to draft young men for military service, it has made provision for those who, by reason of conscience, could not participate. The evolution of what constitutes a sufficient basis for exemption reflects both the increasing religious pluralism of the United States and a dramatically broadening vision of the grounds for exemption—from membership in one of a few denominations to consideration of individual conscience, wholly apart from religion as most people think of religion.

World War I and the Selective Service Act of 1940

World War I necessitated the first conscription under the Selective Service Draft Act of 1917. This Act allowed exemption for those who were members of a "well-recognized sect or organization" that had strict pacifism as a part of its official doctrine. These were the "historic peace churches"— for example, the Society of Friends, Amish, Mennonites, and Seventh-day Adventists. Each held, as a central tenet of its faith, that Jesus' life and words as recorded in the New Testament prohibited Christians from fighting in wars for any reason. Because the churches themselves had standards for who was to be considered a member, deciding who was and who was not exempt seemed a relatively easy and clear-cut matter.

The ambiguity in this apparently clear situation was that there were members of other churches who were also pacifists, although their communities of faith did not hold pacifism as an official tenet. Methodism, for example, had a pacifist minority. The Selective Service Administration enlarged the interpretation of the 1917 Act so that it permitted exemption for members of *any* recognized church whose objections to participation in war were religiously grounded.

The Selective Service Act of 1940 incorporated that administrative decision. This Act exempted persons who "by reason of religious training and belief" were opposed to participation in war. Other reasons that were not clearly religious—personal moral grounds and philosophical objections, for example—were explicitly disallowed. Draft boards applied the rule inconsistently, resulting in a flurry of cases in federal district and circuit courts.

The Universal Military Training and Service Act

Mostly because of the uncertainties of interpretation and the unevenness of application in the 1940 Act, Congress passed a much more comprehensive measure in 1948. This Universal Military Training and Service Act extended the exemption to "anyone, who, because of religious training and belief . . . is conscientiously opposed to a combatant military service or to both combatant and non-combatant military service." Religious training and belief was further defined in the Congress as "an individual's belief in relation to a Supreme Being involving duties superior to those arising from any human relation, but. . . . not any essentially political, sociological, or philosophical views or merely a personal moral code" (cited in O'Brien, 1991: 740).

The term "Supreme Being" had been used in one of the earlier circuit court conscientious objector decisions to distinguish between "a conscientious social belief" or a "sincere devotion to a high moralistic philosophy" and *religiously* motivated objection (*Berman* v. *U.S.,* Ninth Circuit Court). In the pre-1960s religious milieu, belief in a Supreme Being was perhaps an adequate test of whether or not a pacifist's objection was truly "religious." After the flowering of religious pluralism that characterized the 1960s and beyond, the history of interpretation in this area shows that belief in a Supreme Being was no longer an adequate test of whether a pacifist's objection was truly "religious."

The Evolution of the Definition of Conscientious Objection

The first serious challenge came in 1965, as opposition to the Vietnam War increased among those whose reasons did not necessarily fit the terms laid down in the 1948 Act. Daniel Seeger was convicted when he refused induction after his application for conscientious objector standing was denied. He had placed quotation marks around the word "religious" on the application and acknowledged some degree of agnosticism (i.e., uncertainty, skepticism) regarding the existence of a Supreme Being. He was, he maintained, a believer in "goodness and virtue for their own sakes" (*United States* v. *Seeger,* 1965).

In its ruling in the *Seeger* case, the Supreme Court dramatically enlarged the scope of what constituted allowable grounds for exemption. The justices held that the meaning of the Act requires a "given belief that is sincere and meaningful and occupies a place in the life of its possessor parallel to that filled by the orthodox belief in God of one who clearly qualifies for the exemption." Further, "religious belief" was held to include "all sincere beliefs which are based upon a power or being, or upon a faith, to which all else is subordinate or upon which all else is ultimately dependent" (*United States v. Seeger,* 1965). With the inclusion of the phrase "or upon a faith," the Court augmented the meaning to include sincere nontheists (those whose religious belief does not involve a Supreme Being) as well as theists.

Five years later, Elliott Welsh II posed an even greater test for the Court's reading of the Act. Whereas Seeger had enclosed the word "religious" in quotation marks, Welsh crossed out the entire phrase "religious training and belief." His objection, he held, was based purely on his study of history and sociology. He was, as one commentator notes, "a considerably larger camel for the needle's eye" of the exemption clause (Morgan, 1972: 169).

In *Welsh,* the Court cited the "great weight" that they had declared needed to be given to a registrant's description of his belief as "religious," even if these beliefs did not come from the point of view of a particular recognized religion. They were considerably less willing to take Mr. Welsh's statement that his beliefs were not religious at face value:

> The Court's statement in *Seeger* that a registrant's characterization of his own belief as "religious" should carry great weight . . . does not imply that his declaration that his views are nonreligious should be treated similarly . . . [V]ery few registrants are fully aware of the broad scope of the word "religious" as used [in the Act], and, accordingly a registrant's statement that his beliefs are nonreligious is a highly unreliable guide for those charged with administering the exemption" (*Welsh v. United States,* 1970).

This further expansion of the admissible grounds for exemption had the effect of removing the distinction between religious and nonreligious grounds. The grounds for exemption became *conscience* rather than *religion.* This does avoid the potential establishment clause charge that religion is being preferred over nonreligion. It also, however, changes the interpretation dramatically. In an opinion that concurred in the result but arrived there by a different route, Justice John Harlan described the Court as having "performed a lobotomy and completely transformed the statute by reading out of it any distinction between religiously acquired beliefs" and those arising from other sources (*Welsh v. United States,* 1970).

The final Supreme Court decision on this subject that we will discuss is *Gillette v. United States* (1971). In all the cases we reviewed previously, the issue was conscientious, principled objection to *all* wars. *Gillette* raised a different issue, one that also stemmed from religious grounds. The issue in this case was whether one could legitimately claim that a *particular* war, rather than war in general, was unjust.

Gillette, a Catholic, claimed exemption from participation in the Vietnam War on the grounds that it had not been declared by Congress, the agency of the government authorized to declare war, and thus was unjust. Gillette's attorneys argued that the Act was unconstitutional as written. The only way to preserve its constitutionality was to extend its protection to "selective objectors" as well. Otherwise, its constitutionality was questionable under both the establishment clause and the free exercise clause. The Court held otherwise, and the requirement that a conscientious objector object to all wars in principle stood. This issue will in all likelihood rest unless and until there is another draft of people for military service.

Jehovah's Witnesses, Evangelism, and the Free Exercise of Religion

The challenge that conscientious objectors raised to the secular regulation rule was, in the eyes of some analysts, the lesser of two challenges brought against it. The "far more important" one came from the religious group popularly known as Jehovah's Witnesses (Morgan, 1972: 56).

The Witnesses and the Pledge of Allegiance

Jehovah's Witnesses—whose full, official name is the Watchtower Bible and Tract Society—is a Christian community of faith that began in the United States in the late 1800s. A very aggressive program of missionary activity—based largely on door-to-door evangelism and the distribution of religious tracts—is central to its belief and practice. Jehovah's Witnesses also emphasize the importance of giving honor to God alone. Thus, in order to avoid placing loyalty to their nation above loyalty to God (to whom they refer as Jehovah), they do not participate in "patriotic" exercises that many Americans take for granted, such as repeating the Pledge of Allegiance to the flag and singing the national anthem.

The *Gobitis* Case

Two early Witnesses cases involve a practice customary in the first half of the twentieth century. Very often, the school day for both elementary and secondary school students began with the class standing, facing the flag, and repeating the Pledge of Allegiance together. In 1940, William and Lillian Gobitis, ages ten and twelve, were expelled from their school when they refused to participate in this exercise because they were Jehovah's Witnesses. Their father sued, and both the federal district court and the federal appeals court upheld his claim based on the free exercise of his children's religion. The Supreme Court, however, ruled against the children's freedom to abstain from what their faith told them was idolatry.

Justice Felix Frankfurter wrote the opinion of the Court. He was well aware of the gravity of any situation in which claims of liberty and authority come into conflict. Further, "judicial conscience is put to its severest test" when "the liberty invoked is liberty of conscience, and the authority is the authority to safeguard the nation's fellowship" (*Minersville School District* v. *Gobitis,* 1940). Justice Frankfurter's reasoning in this case is complicated. He acknowledged that government may not interfere with the expression of religious belief. He then raised the question of whether "the constitutional guarantee compel[s] exemption from doing what society thinks necessary for the promotion of some great common end, or from a penalty for conduct which appears dangerous to the general good?" Citing both *Reynolds* and a later Latter-day Saints polygamy case, he restated the secular regulation rule:

> Conscientious scruples have not, in the course of the long struggle for religious toleration, relieved the individual from obedience to a general law not aimed at the promotion or restriction of religious beliefs. The mere possession of religious convictions which contradict the relevant concerns of a political society does not relieve the citizen from the discharge of political responsibility.

He then argues that the flag salute is required "in the interest of promoting national cohesion," and that a vital national interest is at stake since "[n]ational unity is the basis of national security." He recognizes that some measures to promote national unity may appear harsh, and that "others, no doubt, are foolish." These judgments, however, are not for the Court to make.

Both Justice Harlan F. Stone's dissent from the Court's opinion and a *Christian Century* editorial on the case reflect the uneasiness with that decision, which led to a different ruling three years later in *West Virginia Board of Education* v. *Barnette.* Justice Stone agreed that government may suppress religious practices that are dangerous to public health and safety, or are a threat to public morals. However, he simply did not see the Gobitis children's refusal to participate in the Pledge of Allegiance as such an activity.

"It is impossible not to view with respect an opinion written by the conspicuously liberal Justice Frankfurter and concurred in by so large a majority of the court," wrote the *Christian Century* editor. "Yet it is permissible to believe that the decision was not a wise one." The editorial distinguished sharply between loyalty to the nation, which is obviously important, and the flag salute, which it described as "an arbitrary piece of ritual which is one way of expressing and teaching loyalty." It acknowledged that, to Jehovah's Witnesses, the flag salute might well seem to be worshiping an image, even though in the judgment of the editor, this is "a foolish idea." After noting that there must be room for even foolish ideas, the editorial averred that "[w]illingness to salute the flag is no criterion of loyalty" (*Christian Century,* June 19, 1940, cited in Eastland, 1993: 37–38).

The *Barnette* Case

The issue had been raised squarely in *Gobitis:* was the secular regulation that children salute the flag in school a strong enough promoter of the national interest that it should overrule their religious liberty? The same issue arose three years later, in *West Virginia Board of Education* v. *Barnette* (1943). Because the grounds in *Barnette* were broader, it is not exactly a free exercise of religion case. Religion had supplied the motive for Barnette's pursuit of his rights through the judicial system. However, the Court held that the question of whether his religious views afforded protection from the law was relevant only if the law was itself constitutional. In *Barnette,* the Court held that it was not. Justice Robert H. Jackson wrote for the Court:

> If there is any fixed star in our constitutional constellation, it is that no official, high or petty, can prescribe what shall be orthodox in politics, nationalism, religion, or other matters of opinion or force citizens to confess by word or act their faith therein. If there are any circumstances which permit an exception, they do not now occur to us.

The case did, however, come to the Court as a free exercise case, and three of the concurring justices understood it at least partly in those terms.

Justices Hugo L. Black, William O. Douglas, and Frank Murphy each addressed the issue of whether religious refusal to participate in the Pledge of Allegiance to the flag was a threat to the nation, and concluded that it was not. Justice Frankfurter, who had written for the Court in *Gobitis*, predictably dissented in *Barnette*, citing similar grounds as he had previously. "Law is concerned with external behavior," he wrote, "and not with the inner life of man.... One may have the right to practice one's religion and at the same time owe the duty of formal obedience to laws that run counter to one's beliefs." *Barnette* has been widely interpreted as a reversal of the Court's earlier ruling, an interpretation that we think is valid.

Door-to-Door Evangelism and Literature Distribution

Jehovah's Witnesses were responsible for bringing several more cases before the Supreme Court in the 1940s and on into the 1970s. All had to do with the Witnesses' missionary activity, which has been unpopular with many non-Witnesses. The Witnesses believe that they are responsible for reaching as many people as they possibly can with their message. This leads many members to commit a great deal of time to door-to-door evangelism, as well as to other similar activities. At times, people put off by their approach have sought to have their activities curtailed by legal means. In those cases that have reached the Supreme Court, the Witnesses' right to do what they do has been upheld.

An increasing number of arrests of Witnesses in the 1930s led the group to reactivate its legal department, which had been inactive for some time. The legal department has leadership at the group's headquarters in Brooklyn, New York, and has a corps of attorneys, who are themselves Witnesses, throughout the United States (Manwaring, 1962: 27). Their spirited defense of their own position contributed greatly to lessening the impact of the secular regulation rule on non-Witnesses cases as well.

Perhaps the best known of the cases involving missionary activity is *Cantwell* v. *Connecticut* (1940), decided the same year as *Gobitis*. We discussed *Cantwell* in the preceding chapter regarding its role as the case in which the free exercise clause was first incorporated at the state level. Cantwell and his sons, all Witnesses, were arrested in New Haven, Connecticut, after they had solicited funds, an activity for which they had not obtained the required license. They were convicted under a state statute that forbade the solicitation of funds without a license on the grounds that the funds were for a religious or charitable group. This particular case is important because it was the first case in which the Supreme Court had invalidated on the grounds of religious liberty a statute enacted by a state government. This required expanding the protection of the First Amendment explicitly to actions of states. Justice Owen J. Roberts wrote the Court's opinion:

> We hold that the statute, as construed and applied to the appellants, deprives them of their liberty without due process of law in contravention of the Fourteenth Amendment. The fundamental concept of liberty embodied in that Amendment embraces the liberties guaranteed by the First Amendment. The First Amendment declares that Congress shall make no law respecting an establishment of religion or prohibiting the free exercise thereof. The Fourteenth Amendment has rendered the legislatures of the states as incompetent as Congress to enact such laws.

The Connecticut statute required that all persons obtain a license before soliciting funds. To do so, they had to apply to a state officer (the secretary of the public welfare council of the state), who was empowered to decide if the cause for which funds would be solicited was indeed a religious one. If he determined that it was not, approval to solicit was withheld. This was held to be an impermissible restriction on religion. "Such a censorship of religion as a means of determining its right to survive is a denial of liberty protected by the First Amendment and included in the liberty which is within the protection of the Fourteenth."

Because the Cantwells had, with their hearers' permission, played a recording that was very derogatory toward Catholics, they had also been charged with disturbing the peace. After noting that "the offense known as breach of the peace" covers a wide variety of conduct, the Court observed that the recording attacked the Catholic Church in a way "which naturally would offend not only persons of that persuasion, but all others who respect the honestly held religious faith of their fellows." Offense notwithstanding, the Court held that the Cantwells' communication, "considered in light of the constitutional guaranties, raised no such clear and present menace to public peace and order as to render him liable to conviction of the common law offense in question."

Other Witnesses Cases

Several other cases dealt with variations of the same issue. *Murdock* v. *Commonwealth of Pennsylvania* (1943) held that a license tax on canvassing and soliciting cannot be applied to the Witnesses, and in the same year, *Martin* v. *Struthers* overturned an ordinance banning them from door-to-door solicitation. In the same year, as well, the Court held that police may not stop the Witnesses from soliciting on Sundays *(Douglas v. City of Jeanette)* and overturned a statute banning handbill distribution *(Jamison v. Texas)*. The right of the Witnesses to distribute their literature in a private company town was upheld *(Marsh v. Alabama,* 1946), as was their right to use the public parks for religious purposes *(Niemotko v. Maryland,* 1951). In 1977, a Witness challenged New Hampshire's requirement that his car bear a license plate with the motto "Live Free or Die." His challenge was upheld and he was allowed to cover the offending slogan *(Wooley v. Maynard)*.

The Court's decisions in these cases were hailed by some as an impressive enlargement of religious freedom, not only for the Witnesses but for all religious people, particularly those whose actions were motivated by their adherence to an unpopular or little-understood minority faith. Others were not as enthusiastic. Writing in 1972, even before the passage of the American Indian Religious Freedom Act (1978) and the Religious Freedom Restoration Act (1993), both of which we discuss below, Richard Morgan cautioned:

> The Court has done ill to retreat from the secular regulation rule. . . .
> The free-exercise clause should not be expanded into a general protection of unorthodox (otherwise proscribable) behavior. . . . In a period of decline in traditional religions and rise of a welter of "fad faiths" it is extremely unwise to begin admitting exceptions to otherwise popular health, welfare, and criminal regulations (Morgan, 1972: 208).

Sabbatarians, Saturday Work Exemptions, and Title VII

Sabbatarians are people who observe Saturday as their Sabbath or religious day of rest. This includes not only Jews, but certain Christians, such as Seventh-day Adventists and most congregations of the Worldwide Church of God. Because of the predominance of traditional forms of the Christian faith in the history of the United States, laws were enacted and customs developed that either required or encouraged the closing of businesses on Sunday. This practice causes hardship for Sabbatarians, whose religion stipulates that they do not work on Saturday, or who close their place of business on Saturday—*their* Sabbath, as well as being required to close it on Sunday.

"Blue Laws"

Before we discuss the work exemption cases, we want to review a case concerning laws that require businesses to be closed on Sundays, at least until noon. In *Braunfield v. Brown* (1961), Orthodox Jews challenged these "blue laws" in the Supreme Court and lost. Other cases—*McGowan v. Maryland* and *Two-Guys from Harrison-Allentown* v. *McGinley* (both 1961)—had raised a similar issue from the perspective of the establishment clause. That is, was the government within its constitutional rights to mandate Sunday as a day of rest? In these two cases, the Supreme Court held that the setting aside of Sunday as a day of rest does not violate the establishment clause: while the origins of the practice were in the realm of religion, the custom serves a valid and necessary secular purpose.

Braunfield approached the issue from the perspective of the free exercise clause, alleging that it seriously impeded his free exercise of religion. A group of Orthodox Jewish businessmen charged that requiring them to close their business on Sunday imposed a financial hardship on them of such magnitude that it was a serious interference with their practice of their religion. Orthodox Judaism stipulates that no work be done on the Sabbath, from nightfall on Friday through nightfall on Saturday. Thus, the appellants had to close their business during that time, while businesses owned by their gentile counterparts remained open. In essence, the Jewish businessmen had two days during which they had to close their business, while gentiles had only one. The appellants alleged that the economic disadvantage was severe enough that they were compelled to choose between their livelihood and their faith.

Chief Justice Earl Warren announced the judgment, concurring with the lower court; no "opinion of the Court" was written. In his announcement, Warren cited *Reynolds* as well as several cases involving Jehovah's Witnesses and the distribution of religious literature. *Braunfield* was distinguished from the Witnesses cases. Warren noted that the laws struck down in those cases made a specific *religious* practice illegal. The Sunday closing laws, by contrast, did not do so, but rather, "simply regulate a secular activity." Justice Warren noted that the nation was made up of people of almost every conceivable religious preference, and that:

> Consequently, it cannot be expected, much less required, that legislators enact no law regulating conduct that may in some way result in an economic disadvantage to some religious sects and not to others because of the special practices of the various religions.

In essence, Warren's comments uphold the secular regulation rule in its specific application to economic activity.

Justice Potter Stewart dissented, defining the lower court's ruling as one that upheld a law that "compels an Orthodox Jew to choose between his religious faith and his economic survival." That "cruel choice" would be adjudicated again and again in subsequent cases dealing with Saturday employment and later on in cases involving Native Americans, the use of peyote as a sacrament, and the Religious Freedom Restoration Act (which we discuss below).

While *Braunfield* dealt with the effects of *not* working because of Sabbath observance, several subsequent cases dealt with the right to work *in spite of* Sabbath observance.

Sherbert and the Compelling Interest Test

Sherbert v. *Verner* (1963) is a crucial case, because in it the Supreme Court ruled for the first time that the free exercise clause of the First Amendment does require that persons be exempted from a secular regulation if that regulation impinges significantly on the free exercise of their religion. It also set a standard for judicial decision making in free exercise cases that is comparable to the role that *Lemon* (*see* Chapter 5) played for nonestablishment jurisprudence. Adell Sherbert was a Seventh-day Adventist who lost her job because she refused to work on Saturday, her Sabbath. When she could not find a job that did not require Saturday work, she filed for unemployment compensation, which she was denied on the grounds that she refused to accept "suitable work." In what one analyst calls "a critical turning-point for free-exercise jurisprudence" (Eastland, 1993: 169), the Supreme Court held in favor of Sherbert. The Court declared that the government must have a "compelling interest" in order to burden the free exercise of religion, not just the "rational basis" required by *Reynolds*.

Justice William J. Brennan, Jr., writing for the Court, found that the government had not demonstrated a sufficiently compelling interest to justify the imposition of a burden on Sherbert's free exercise of her religion, a hardship that he compared to "a fine imposed against the appellant for her Saturday worship." Justice Brennan understood this case to be quite different than that presented in *Braunfield;* he held that the state's interest in "providing one uniform day of rest for all workers" was sufficiently compelling to justify the limitation, and that the secular end could be reasonably met in no other way.

The standards that were laid down in *Sherbert* may be summarized this way: In order for a law or policy to be constitutional under the free exercise clause, the Court must first decide if that law or policy places a burden on a religious group or practice. If so, then the Court must decide whether the government has a compelling interest that would justify the infringement of religious liberty. If the compelling interest is there, then the government must demonstrate that its interests can be served in no other way than by limiting freedom of religion. This became the standard until 1990, when it was overturned in *Smith* (discussed below).

Justice John M. Harlan, joined by Justice Byron R. White, wrote a strong dissent, part of which prefigured later questions about the wisdom of the Court's ruling. The purpose of the unemployment benefit, he held, was to tide people over during times when *work was unavailable,* rather than when an individual voluntarily became *unavailable for work.* To mandate an exception for those whose unavailability stemmed from religious convictions meant giving benefit to religion over nonreligion.

Civil libertarians hailed the decision as a crucial step in protecting the interests of minority religions against a culturally-imposed "tyranny of the majority." One report, for example, pointed out that "it is not accidental" that workplace rules and customs "are generally compatible with majority practices and beliefs" even if those rules and customs are essentially secular in intent (*Religion in the Constitution,* 1983: 42).

Others have been less enthusiastic. Writing almost a decade later, one analyst of the role of religion in American law identified three potentially serious problem areas that result from the *Sherbert* decision: (1) There is an apparent conflict between this ruling and the establishment clause, which forbids favoring religion over nonreligion. (2) The finding potentially involves the Court in deciding what is and what is not a religion, in order to determine who is eligible for the exemption, again risking running afoul of the establishment clause. (3) Finally, decisions might have to be made on the basis of how many people seek to avail themselves of a particular exemption, an awkward situation at best (Morgan, 1972: 148–154). Later events, discussed below, illustrate that the matter of religiously-motivated exemptions from otherwise applicable secular laws was far from settled in the *Sherbert* case.

The Civil Rights Act of 1964 and Religious Discrimination in the Workplace

What is and is not permissible in workplace-related cases is not only a matter of case law. Title VII of the Civil Rights Act of 1964 makes discrimination against employees on the basis of religion unlawful, whether by an employer or by a labor union. The relevant section of the Act (701j) protects not only religious belief but practice, and avoids the issue of what makes something religious. It has usually been understood in light of the very broad interpretation of religion worked out as case law evolved in response to the question of conscientious objection to warfare. The Act requires that an employer accommodate employees' religious needs unless such accommodation would cause undue hardship to the employer.

This left room for confusion about what constituted "undue hardship," and the Equal Opportunity Employment Commission (EEOC), which is the federal agency responsible for enforcement of the Act, issued additional guidelines in 1978 that clarified requirements for both employers and employees. The Office of Federal Contract Compliance Programs in the Department of Labor has also issued guidelines on the application of Title VII in workplaces in which federal contracts are involved.

We note briefly four similar workplace cases. *Trans World Airlines* v. *Hardison* (1977) began the process of delineating the exact nature of the accommodations that an employer had to make. In *Thomas* v. *Review Board of Indiana Employment Security Division* (1981) the denial of unemployment benefits to a worker who terminated employment because of religious objections to working in the production of weapons was struck down. In *Hobbie* v. *Unemployment Appeals Commission of Florida* (1987), the Court held that it was irrelevant that the worker experienced a religious conversion after beginning work. Finally, in an expansion of the application of the exemption that echoed *Seeger*, the Court held that the denial of unemployment compensation to a person who refused Sabbath work even though the refusal was not based on religious reasons violated the free exercise clause (*Frazee* v. *Illinois Department of Employment Security*, 1989).

Religious Discrimination Compared with Racial or Gender Discrimination

The problem of religious discrimination in the workplace has both similarities with and differences from discrimination based on race or gender. Overt, intentional acts of discrimination are similar to intentional discrimination on religious grounds and are equally unlawful. Similarly as well, discrimination may be unforeseen and unintentional, but it is still unlawful, since employers are responsible for foreseeing what might reasonably happen as a result of a particular practice. This applies equally in all three situations. The particular religion of the claimant is irrelevant, as is the race or gender of the complainant in race and sex discrimination cases.

However, there are significant dissimilarities as well. In race and sex discrimination cases, the objective is to ensure equal treatment regardless of the defining characteristic. In religious discrimination cases, the appellants usually seek the right to be treated differently based upon their religious affiliation. The elimination of discrimination based on race or gender seeks to enhance equality, whereas the removal of that based on religion helps to preserve diversity. Race and gender discrimination often results from historical patterns of discrimination in the educational process, whereas this is not the situation with religious discrimination. Whereas legislation concerning race and gender discrimination deals with a finite, relatively small number of races and two genders, that dealing with religious discrimination must take into account an almost infinite variety of beliefs and practices. Finally, because the implementation of workplace practices that work to ensure religious liberty must be done in a way that does not violate the establishment clause, it is limited in ways that similar action to end race and gender discrimination is not (*Religion in the Constitution*, 1983: 41–42).

Religious Employers and the Law

We need to briefly mention cases dealing with religious *employers* rather than employees. Title VII forbids religious discrimination in employment. Does this mean that synagogues, churches, and seminaries (schools for the training of ministers and other church professionals) cannot limit their hiring to members of their own faith? No. Title VII was amended in 1972 to exclude religious organizations from the requirements of Title VII's ban on religious discrimination in all phases of workplace operation. This exemption applies only to the ban on discrimination based on religion; other provisions of Title VII that ban discrimination on the basis of race, color, sex, or national origin apply to religious employers as much as to secular employers.

Native Americans, Sacred Lands, and National Parks
Background

As a result of the history of the United States government's dealing with Native Americans, there are dimensions to constitutional questions about their free exercise of their native religions that are not present in the situations already discussed. Native Americans remain, to a degree, under the jurisdiction of the government, and not completely in control of their own affairs. This calls for a degree of government involvement in accommodating their free exercise of religion that in other circumstances would be an impermissible establishment of religion. It has only been in recent history that the government has taken the religions of the native peoples seriously. For most of the history of the United States, Native American religions have been regarded as "heathen" or "pagan," perhaps not even genuine religions, and, more often than not, actively suppressed. Usually, the Native Americans were seen only as the objects of religious conversion by Christian missionaries, a view actively supported by the government for many years.

Sam Gill, commenting on the treatment of Native Americans by the federal government writes that the European white-dominated government has always assumed that it knew better than the Native Americans what they themselves needed and wanted, even when they made their desires known clearly. At best, it has followed a paternalistic policy. At worst, it has moved entire tribes and killed people in the interest of advancing Christian American interests. Not until late in this century, with the passage of the American Indian Religious Freedom Act in 1978, were Native Americans guaranteed the same rights that others took for granted (Gill, 1988). Even then, the guarantee was not enforced.

The 1934 Indian Reorganization Act established the principle of governmental noninterference in Native American religious affairs, ending active persecution. Significant problems remained, however, with otherwise neutral laws that heavily burdened Native practices. Such laws included those establishing museums' rights to keep and display Native American artifacts and laws concerning public access to and use of government lands that are sacred to Native Americans.

Native American religions hold that the land itself is sacred; rocks, rivers, trees, and specific places occupy in their thought a place equivalent to that of churches, mosques, and synagogues in Christianity, Islam, and Judaism. This means that forbidding access to them, or allowing tourist access to them, has the same impact on Native American religion that forbidding access to a church, synagogue, or mosque, or allowing indiscriminate tourist access to it would have on Christians, Jews, or Muslims.

The American Indian Religious Freedom Act

Existing legislation and case law should have been adequate to deal with the special situation of Native American religions, but it was not. In 1978, President Jimmy Carter signed the American Indian Religious Freedom Act. In part, the Act states that

> it shall be the policy of the United States to protect and preserve for American Indians their inherent right of freedom to believe, express, and exercise the traditional religions of the American Indian, Eskimo, Aleut, and Native Hawaiians, including but not limited to access to sites, use and possession of sacred objects and the freedom of worship through ceremonials and traditional rites.

The wording of the Act seems clear enough; its application proved otherwise. For example, in *Lyng* v. *Northwest Indian Cemetery Protective Association* (1988) the Supreme Court held that roads could be constructed and timber harvested in areas under the jurisdiction of the National Park Service that had traditionally been used by several Native American tribes for religious ceremonies. This commercial use of the land was a desecration of it from the Native American point of view. The Court did not dispute that logging activity "could have devastating effects on traditional Indian religious practices." It did, however, hold that the government's carrying out public policy simply could not be contingent on "measuring the effects of a governmental action on a religious objector's spiritual development." Essentially, the ruling in *Lyng* was that the governmental interests involved simply outweighed the Native Americans' free exercise claims.

Lyng made clear that the American Indian Religious Freedom Act was not an absolute guarantee of Native American religious freedom, even in cases in which public health and safety interests were not at stake.

Native Americans, Peyote, *Woody,* and *Smith*
Background

The traditional religious practices of Native Americans come into play again in a landmark case that led directly to the passage of the Religious Freedom Restoration Act in 1993. The background is provided by a California State Supreme Court case. The Native American Church blends elements of Christianity with the traditional peyote way of the Native Americans. Peyote is a cactus that has psychotropic (consciousness-altering) properties, and is central to the rituals of the Native American Church, much as the use of wine in the sacrament of communion is central to the worship of many Christian churches. Peyote is also an illegal drug.

In cases involving the use of peyote by members of the Native American Church, the members have often been charged with illegal use, transportation or simply possession of the drug. Native Americans then argue that the drug is essential to the practice of their religion, and thus protected by the First Amendment. The issue becomes one of balancing the government interest in regulating drug traffic and use against this free exercise claim. Several cases have been heard in lower courts with varying results. We will discuss only one of these.

In *People* v. *Woody* (1964), a California court convicted members of the Native American Church who were using peyote in a ritual context on possession of narcotics charges. The Native Americans appealed to the California Supreme Court, which reversed the decision. The issue was whether the government's legitimate interest in restricting the use of illegal drugs was sufficiently compelling to justify abridging the Native Americans' religious liberty. The Court rejected the state's assertion that it needed to be able to regulate the ritual use of peyote because of peyote's "deleterious effects upon the Indian community and . . . the infringement such practice would place upon the enforcement of narcotics laws. Justice Tobriner wrote for the majority:

> We have weighed the competing values represented in the case on the symbolic scale of constitutionality. On one side we have placed the weight of freedom of religion as it is protected by the First Amendment; on the other, the weight of the state's "compelling interest." Since the use of peyote incorporates the essence of the religious expression, the first weight is heavy. Yet the use of peyote represents only slight danger to the state and to the enforcement of its laws; the second weight is relatively light. The scale tips in favor of the constitutional protection.

Oregon v. *Smith* and the Reversal of the Compelling Interest Test

The case of *Employment Division, Department of Human Resources of Oregon* v. *Smith* came before the United States Supreme Court in 1990. The case was similar in that it involved the ritual use of peyote by members of the Native American Church. It involved two members of the church who were denied unemployment compensation after they were fired from their jobs because of their ritual use of peyote. What makes this case more complex is that the job from which the two church members were fired was that of drug rehabilitation counselors. Citing a number of the earlier Sabbatarian cases, the two men claimed that the state could not make the availability of unemployment benefits contingent on their abstaining from the central sacrament of their religion. When the case made its way to the Oregon Supreme Court, that body held that the petitioners were indeed entitled to benefits. The state of Oregon took the case to the United States Supreme Court. The Court first sent the case back to Oregon, so that Oregon could decide whether the ceremonial use of peyote did in fact violate the state's controlled substance laws (on which the two parties had not agreed).

The Oregon court found that the petitioners' religious use of peyote did violate the law, which explicitly made "no exception for the sacramental use" of the substance. This, the court concluded, made the law itself unconstitutional because it violated the free exercise clause. Thus, the petitioners were still entitled to benefits.

In *Smith*, the United States Supreme Court held that the denial *was* justified, that Oregon's drug laws could be applied to Native American Church members. We will look at Justice Antonin Scalia's opinion of the Court in some detail, as well as at Justice Sandra Day O'Connor's concurrence with different reasoning, and Justice Harry A. Blackmun's strongly worded dissent.

Justice Scalia for the Court

Justice Scalia's opinion can be summarized as follows: Alfred Smith and Galen Black—the two Native Americans—contended that requiring them to obey an otherwise constitutional law as a condition of receiving unemployment benefits prohibited the free exercise of their religion in a constitutionally unacceptable way. Scalia held that the Court had "never held that an individual's religious beliefs excuse him from compliance with an otherwise valid law prohibiting conduct that the State is free to regulate." He cited jurisprudence to support his point, including citations to both *Reynolds* and *Gobitis,* discussed above. Smith and Black had based a part of their argument on three Sabbatarian employment benefit cases—*Sherbert, Thomas,* and *Hobbie.* In these cases, it was held that the government had to show a "compelling government interest" if it were to limit freedom of religion. It also had to act in a way that restricted religious freedom as little as possible—the "least restrictive means" test.

Scalia held that these two tests were not applicable to the *Smith* case. To apply them would result in the "constitutional anomaly" of a private right to ignore generally applicable laws.

He noted that the states were free to enact exemptions from drug laws for the benefit of members of the Native American Church and that several states had done so. This, however, is not the same as saying that such exemptions are constitutionally required.

In the *Gobitis* case, the test of the constitutionality of the government's action in requiring participation in the flag salute exercise was that it be a "reasonable exercise" of the state's power. In effect, Scalia held that this was what was required in *Smith* as well, rather than the more stringent tests used in *Sherbert*.

A Concurring Opinion

Justice Sandra Day O'Connor concurred in the opinion, but followed a different line of reasoning. In her opinion, the compelling interest test used in *Sherbert* should apply equally in *Smith*. There was no question that the criminal prohibition of the use of peyote imposed a severe hardship on the respondents' free exercise of religion. There was also no dispute that the state of Oregon had a significant interest in prohibiting the possession and use of controlled substances. The question was whether or not the state's interest was compelling. In O'Connor's mind, it was. She held that the uniform application of the statute was essential to accomplish its goal. "Because the health effects caused by the use of controlled substances exist regardless of the motivation of the user, the use of such substances, even for religious purposes, violates the very purpose of the laws that prohibit them. . . . Under such circumstances, the free exercise clause does not require the State to accommodate respondents' religiously motivated conduct."

Dissent and Response

Justices Blackmun, Brennan, and Marshall dissented. In their view, the religious use of peyote by members of the Native American Church was a vastly different matter than its use by the general public. "The carefully circumscribed ritual context in which respondents use peyote is far removed from the irresponsible and unrestricted recreational use of unlawful drugs. . . . Far from promoting the lawless and irresponsible use of drugs, Native American Church members' spiritual code exemplifies the values that Oregon's drug laws are presumably intended to foster."

The response to *Smith* was immediate and intense. The Court had eliminated the rigorous compelling interest test and replaced it with the much less exacting rational basis standard. A sixty-eight-member coalition formed to begin work toward the passage of a bill that would restore protection for freedom of religion. This coalition included people from nearly every religious and political viewpoint. They sought to restore what had been taken away by judiciary decision through an act of Congress. The coalition's membership ranged from the consensus or "mainline" religions through the nonconventional religions. Never in the course of American religious history had such a widely disparate group come together around a single issue. Mainline leaders were as concerned about the long-term effects of *Smith* as were leaders of nonconventional religions that were more likely to bear the weight of the results. The general feeling was that a loss of religious freedom for any group meant the potential loss of freedom for all.

The Religious Freedom Restoration Act

President Bill Clinton signed the Religious Freedom Restoration Act (RFRA) into law in 1993. It recognized that otherwise neutral laws may interfere with the free exercise of religion as surely as laws specifically intended to do so. It recognized the compelling interest test as stated in *Sherbert* as "a workable test for striking sensible balances between religious liberty and competing government interests," and restored this test as the one to be used in all such cases. Specifically, it requires that government meet two conditions if an otherwise neutral law infringes on religious liberty. Section 3, which spells out the core of the Act, states that

> Government shall not substantially burden a person's exercise of religion, even if the burden results from a rule of general applicability, except as provided in subsection (b). . . .
>   (b) . . . Government may substantially burden a person's exercise of religion only if it demonstrates the application of the burden to the person—(1) is in furtherance of a compelling governmental interest; and (2) is the least restrictive means of furthering that compelling governmental interest.

In other words, if the government acts in a way that exacts hardship on the free exercise of religion, it must have a very good reason for doing so, and then must proceed in a way that has the least possible impact.

The passage of the Act was hailed by many civil libertarians and religious liberty advocates as an essential restoration of an indispensable freedom (*see*, e.g., Wood, 1993, and Boston, 1994). Religious people—even those whose religions were little known and less understood, and perhaps mistrusted by the majority—could feel safe again, confident that their freedom of religion was secure. Others were not so certain. Some analysts contended that the compelling interest test was too rigorous and too absolute, without sufficient flexibility to work in the variety of cases on which the Court may have to decide (Saison, 1995). Others charged that the Act itself was an unconstitutional establishment of religion, because it protected religiously motivated conduct in situations in which the same conduct was not protected if it did not have religious motivation (Eisgruber, 1994).

Challenge and Reversal

The 1993 case *Church of the Lukumi* v. *Hialeah*, although a free exercise case, did not serve to test the strength of the Act. In that case, the city of Hialeah, Florida, had enacted a law prohibiting animal sacrifice, which is a central part of worship in the Santería religion. The law was struck down as unconstitutional because it was clearly directed specifically at the church. Since the law was not one of general applicability, it did not come under the provisions of the Act.

The Act was declared unconstitutional in the Supreme Court case of *City of Boerne, Texas* v. *Flores* (1997). St. Peter Catholic Church in Boerne is now too small to allow its congregation to worship. The church requested permission from the city to expand its building. Their request was denied because the church is located in a historic landmark district of the city. The church sued the city under the Religious Freedom Restoration Act.

The city's response charged that the Act itself was unconstitutional, and hence was not binding. Lawyers for the city alleged that by allowing an action based on religion that would not be permissible on other grounds, the Act violated the nonestablishment provision of the First Amendment.

As in the original passage of the Religious Freedom Restoration Act, a broad coalition of supporters came together and filed a friend-of-the-court brief stating that Congress did act with proper authority in passing the Act and urging the Court to uphold its constitutionality.

Justice Kennedy wrote the opinion of the Court, which held that in enacting the legislation, Congress had exceeded its legal powers. Although Congress does have the power, under the Fourteenth Amendment, to enforce guarantees of due process by legislation, the Act was held to have overstepped the boundaries of that power. Kennedy wrote that the "RFRA cannot be considered remedial, preventive legislation, if those terms are to have any meaning. RFRA is so out of proportion to a supposed remedial or preventive object that it cannot be understood as responsive to, or designed to prevent, unconstitutional behavior. It appears, instead, to attempt a substantive change in constitutional protections." It is this "substantive change" that goes beyond the power of Congress to enact. Kennedy also dismissed the argument that the application of otherwise neutral laws imposes an unfair burden on religion. "It is a reality of the modern regulatory state," he wrote in this regard, "that numerous state laws . . . impose a substantial burden on a large class of individuals. When the exercise of religion has been burdened in an incidental way by a law of general application, it does not follow that the persons affected have been burdened more than other citizens, let alone burdened because of their religious beliefs." He was very clear in his statement that the precedent of the Court, not legislation enacted by Congress, "must control" the understanding and application of the Constitution.

Justice Stevens' concurring opinion points out that the RFRA, in its effort to enhance the protection provided by the free exercise clause, violated the establishment clause: "If the historic landmark on the hill in Boerne happened to be a museum or an art gallery owned by an atheist, it would not be eligible for an exemption. . . . [The] statute has provided the Church with a legal weapon that no atheist or agnostic can obtain. This governmental preference for religion, as opposed to irreligion, is forbidden by the First Amendment."

Dissenting opinion focused on doubts about the soundness of the *Smith* decision itself, and called on the Court to reexamine that case rather than invalidating the RFRA. Since it was *Smith* that led to the passage of the RFRA, the place to begin when the question is reopened is there, not with the RFRA itself.

Negative reaction from supporters of the RFRA was swift and pointed. The First Amendment Center called it "a major blow to organized religion." Oliver Thomas, an attorney for the National Council of Churches, called it "a sad day. Every religious person in America," he continued, "will be affected by this decision, they just don't know it yet. Eventually every religion in America will suffer as a result." J. Brent Walker of the Baptist Joint Committee said that the "decision opens the door to . . . intrusive forms of government control of people of faith and houses of worship" (cited on the First Amendment Center's website). Supporters of the legislation vowed to resume their battle to reinstate the protections lost in *Smith*.

On one level, this was not a case primarily about freedom of religion but about the separation of powers of government. On this point, the majority of justices seemed to have no trouble agreeing that Congress had exceeded its boundaries. On another level, however, it *was* about freedom of religion. Kennedy's majority opinion devoted quite a lot of space to a discussion of the differences between the RFRA and the Voting Rights Act. Unlike the situation the Voting Rights Act was intended to remedy, the historical evidence does not support that there have been "modern instances of generally applicable laws passed because of religious bigotry." Burdens to religion from the application of generally applicable laws have been incidental and unintentional, rather than deliberate. Kennedy's statement about the realities of the modern regulatory state, quoted above, appears to dismiss these unintentional burdens as unimportant because they are not deliberate. To this extent, the case is about freedom of religion. The decision appears to us to leave the situation where it was in 1990 following *Smith*: the government must demonstrate that its interest in interfering with religious freedom must have a *rational basis;* it need not demonstrate a *compelling interest*. So far, it is too early to tell what the practical results of the decision will be.

Attempts at Legislative Augmentation of the Role of Religion

Two different constitutional amendments were initiated in the 104th Congress to augment the role of religion in American public life. Both stemmed from their proponents' perception that the government continues to discriminate against religion in favor of secularity. Representative Ernest J. Istook (Oklahoma, Republican) introduced a "religious liberties amendment." A "religious equality amendment" was sponsored by Representative Henry Hyde (Illinois, Republican) and Senator Orin Hatch (Utah, Republican). Representative Istook's bill specifically authorized official, school-sponsored prayer in public schools. The Hyde-Hatch version stated that neither federal nor state governments

> shall deny benefits to or otherwise discriminate against any private person or group on account of religious expression, belief, or identity; nor shall the prohibition on laws respecting an establishment of religion be construed to require such discrimination.

Neither amendment passed, but both indicate the types of proposals that we can reasonably expect to continue.

The National Association of Evangelicals—a mainstream evangelical ecumenical association—and the Christian Legal Society both supported these bills. They believe they are necessary to correct a long history of Supreme Court misreadings of the establishment clause in a way that has severely restricted free exercise. The bills are opposed by a coalition of religious and civil liberties groups—including the historically liberal National Council of Churches of Christ in the USA, another ecumenical organization—who believe that they violate the establishment clause because they permit, if not require, government funding of religion.

The 105th Congress will probably see the introduction of a number of amendments which their proponents hope will allow for conservative religion to play a greater role in public life. For example, the school prayer amendment (also called the religious equality amendment) that did not do well in the 104th Congress will be reintroduced in the 105th.

The Religious Freedom Restoration Act itself sought to reverse by legislative implementation what had been done judicially in the *Smith* case. These proposals that follow after it also seek to undo what the Supreme Court's interpretation of the First Amendment has done.

Establishment and Free Exercise: Conflicting or Complementary?
Tension Between the Clauses

As we pointed out in Chapter 5, the establishment clause and the free exercise clause of the First Amendment sometimes seem to conflict with one another. This issue was raised by Justice Potter Stewart in his dissent to the Court's finding in *Sherbert*. He stated that "there are many situations where legitimate claims under the free exercise clause will run into head-on collision with the Court's sterile and insensitive construction of the establishment clause."

The problem has arisen largely around the issue of exempting religiously motivated action from otherwise applicable laws (as in *Sherbert* and *Smith*, for example). The establishment clause prohibits the government from preferring religious motivations over others, while the *Sherbert* interpretation of the free exercise clause appears to require special exemption for religiously motivated actions. The paradox is this: "If the government applies its laws neutrally, it will prohibit some people from practicing their religion. If the government exempts those with religious objections, it will discriminate against those with non-religious objections" (Sherry, 1992: 124).

Some legal scholars see this as a problem, while others regard it as part of the genius of the system. Some believe that the Court cannot, and perhaps should not, reconcile the two clauses. On this view, doing so would defeat their purpose. Decisions should be based very closely on the facts of each case and seek to preserve the value of the clause that is the most applicable (e.g., Davis, 1996; Neuborne, 1993). The dynamic tension between the clauses must be left intact.

Others call for a harmonization of the two clauses. Free exercise is held to protect freedom of belief and practice by the prevention of penalties. The establishment clause likewise protects religious liberty by preventing individual choices from being circumscribed or pressured by governmental pressure (Sherry, 1992; Marshall, 1991; McConnell, 1990).

According to one scholar, however, all attempts at reconciling the conflict thus far have either simply recreated the paradox or devalued one of the two clauses. Which clause one would rather see devalued is a matter of personal preference, but one or the other will have to be, if a true reconciliation is to happen (Sherry, 1992: 130).

Other analysts believe that interpretations which devalue neither clause but yet resolve the paradox are indeed possible. The establishment clause and the free exercise clause together are "a single religion clause whose establishment and free-exercise provisions serve one central value—the freedom of religion" (Glendon, 1993: 477). The job of the Court in upcoming cases will be to find an interpretation that allows the clauses to function together (Glendon, 1993: 481). It must "develop an interpretation of the two religious clauses that makes the free-exercise clause and the establishment clause consistent and complementary rather than antagonistic toward each other" (McConnell, 1993: 506).

One proposal for doing so comes from Michael McConnell of the University of Chicago. He develops three criteria: (1) A law or policy is unconstitutional if its purpose or likely effect is to increase religious uniformity either by inhibiting the religious practice of the person or group challenging the law (free exercise clause) or by forcing or inducing a contrary religious practice (establishment clause); (2) A law or policy is unconstitutional if its enforcement interferes with the independence of a religious body in matters of religious significance to that body; (3) Violation of either of these principles will be permitted only if it is the least restrictive means for (a) protecting the private rights of others, or (b) ensuring that the benefits and burdens of public life are equitably shared (McConnell, 1993: 506). Whether or not this is a workable proposal will be decided by its actual applicability in the Court's decisions.

An Illustrative Case

The case of *Board of Education of the Kiryas Joel Village School District* v. *Grumet* illustrates the complexity of this issue (Levy, 1994). The Satmar Jews are a Hasidic Jewish group that is distinctive from the great majority of American Jews in that they try to remain as isolated as possible. All of their children attended private, religious schools except for those for whom special education was necessary. (The Court in *Aguilar* v. *Felton* in 1985 had ruled that public school teachers could not be paid to teach in religious schools, since doing so violated the establishment clause.) When the children were forced to attend public schools in order to meet their special education needs, they were ridiculed by other children because they were "different." The Village then received permission to form a school district of its own, so that public school teachers could teach the necessary special education classes. Learning-disabled Hasidic children from outside the district also attended this school. The New York State Supreme Court then ruled that creating a public school district whose boundaries were the same as those of the Hasidic enclave was unconstitutional because it created a symbolic union of government and religion, thus violating the establishment clause. The United States Supreme Court later held that the state law that had created the special school district was, indeed, unconstitutional, by a vote of 6 to 3.

If the question is framed in terms of the state's creating a special school district for a religious group, in effect "religiously gerrymandering" a district (Levy, 1996: 252), then the action is clearly unconstitutional. However, if the question is seen as one of whether a state may create a school district whose boundaries happen to coincide with those of a particular village, in order to teach the learning-disabled children of that village, who happen to follow the religious practices of the small Satmar group, then the school district looks more like an accommodation of a minority religion, particularly since cultural isolation is itself a major tenet of Satmar belief.

Summary and Conclusions

The overall question that has guided this chapter is: Under what circumstances are people free to practice their religion, and under what circumstances must they refrain from doing so?

Near the end of the nineteenth century, the *Reynolds* case led to a distinction between religious belief and action based on that belief. Beliefs are beyond the reach of any government intervention, but actions are subject to the law. The "secular regulation rule" meant that a government action that serves a valid secular purpose is constitutional even if it burdens the free exercise of religion.

We have reviewed issues around religion and refusal to participate in war, and have seen that the definition of "conscientious objection" has been broadened (and the impact of the secular regulation rule lessened) so that it is now a matter of freedom of conscience rather than freedom of religion.

We then reviewed a number of cases concerning the door-to-door evangelistic activities and tract distribution of Jehovah's Witnesses. Court decisions in these cases have expanded freedom of religious practice, not only for the Witnesses but for all of us.

Religious issues in the workplace, including the "blue laws" that restrict Sunday business hours and Sabbatarians who refuse to work on Saturday, ultimately gave rise to the important *compelling interest test.* With this test, the Court held that a valid secular regulation that burdens free exercise is unconstitutional unless the government has a compelling interest in the regulation, strong enough to justify the free exercise burden (*Sherbert,* 1963). This test became the standard until it was overruled in *Smith* in 1990.

Unlike the situation with respect to the establishment clause, legislation, as well as jurisprudence, has played and continues to play a significant role in the development of free exercise law. This is apparent in the special case of Native American religious freedom, and one outcome of the *Smith* case was the passage of the Religious Freedom Restoration Act in 1993.

Finally, in this chapter, we looked at the tension between the two religious liberty clauses themselves. Compliance with the requirements of one clause may lead to violation of the other. While some scholars see this as a dynamic balance that should be maintained, others see it as a problem to be resolved.

What conclusions can we draw from all of this? The answer to the question with which we began is far from clear, and cannot, in principle, have a final answer. Religious liberty litigation and legislation arise out of changing circumstances and, therefore, will themselves continue to change.

The same question that was raised in the *Sherbert* case—did allowing for Sherbert's free exercise violate the establishment clause?—was raised repeatedly about the Religious Freedom Restoration Act. Legislative bids to revise the role of religion in public life—such as the religious equality and religious liberty amendments—are held by their supporters to be necessary to guarantee freedom of religion. Their opponents charge that they amount to an establishment of religion. As we saw in Part I, the issue of the role of religion in public life has been a part of our national discourse since before the nation was founded. It is an issue that will be a lively part of the American scene for the foreseeable future.

The expansion of individual religious liberty is part of a larger expansion of individualism that began, as we saw in Chapter 4, in the decade of the 1960s. There is some indication that the mood of the country may be moving in the other direction. After sketching out a number of "cultural indicators" that show a nation in deep trouble, Frohnen (1996: 3) notes that the situation in which we find ourselves "is in part the result of our desire to be 'freed' from social constraints. Americans as a people are passionately fond of liberty in all its forms." We might see jurisprudence and legislation in the next several years that tends in the opposite direction. Whatever happens, the relationship of religion to American public life will remain a fascinating area to watch.

In these last two chapters, we have examined judicial and legislative actions concerning religion and government, and we have found substantial divisions among the opinions of justices and legislators. In Chapter 7, we will see that the general public is also divided and ambiguous in its opinions on these issues.

Important Terms

Free exercise clause	Sabbatarian
Secular regulation rule	American Indian Religious Freedom Act
Conscientious objection	Religious Freedom Restoration Act
Jehovah's Witnesses	

Review Questions

1. In what three ways has free exercise clause interpretation developed differently from the interpretation of the establishment clause?
2. What is the significance of the *Reynolds* case?
3. What is the secular regulation rule? How much influence does it now have on free exercise cases?
4. Trace the evolution of what constitutes grounds for exemption from military service.
5. In what ways have Jehovah's Witnesses challenged the secular regulation rule?
6. What does Title VII mandate regarding freedom of religion?
7. What are the similarities and differences between workplace cases involving religious discrimination and those involving gender or racial discrimination?
8. What is the Native American Church?
9. What is the American Indian Religious Freedom Act?
10. What was the *Smith* case about and what is its larger significance?
11. What was the Religious Freedom Restoration Act? Why was it declared to be unconstitutional?

Discussion Questions

1. To what extent should employers be required to accommodate their employees' religious practices? Similarly, to what extent should professors be required to accommodate their students' religious practices?
2. To what extent should people be exempt from compliance with otherwise neutral laws on the basis of religion?
3. Do you think that the two religion clauses of the First Amendment are complementary or conflicting? What are the reasons for your answer?
4. Was the RFRA unconstitutional? Why do you answer as you do?

For Further Reading

In addition to the suggestions below, the Eastland and Alley books cited in Chapter 5 are also relevant for this chapter.

Flowers, Ronald B. 1994. *That Godless Court? Supreme Court Decisions on Church-State Relationships.* Louisville, Kentucky: Westminster/John Knox Press.

> Discussion of cases intended to demonstrate that the Court upholds an essentially secular view of the nation.

Flowers, Ronald B., and Robert L. Miller. 1987. *Toward Benevolent Neutrality: Church, State, and the Supreme Court.* Waco, Texas: Markham Press Fund.

> Argument for the proposal that the Court's decisions have in general supported a "benevolent neutrality" regarding religion.

Frankel, Marvin E. 1994. *Faith and Freedom.* New York: Hill and Wang.

> Discussion of cases and a plea for freedom of religious expression.

Kramnick, Isaac, and R. Laurence Moore. 1996. *The Godless Constitution: The Case Against Religious Correctness.* New York: W.W. Norton.

> Argument for maintaining what the authors understand as the constitutional principle of secularity against the incursion of "religious correctness."

Relevant World Wide Websites

Remember to visit our websites for updates and additional links at:
http://bsuvc.bsu.edu/~00amcorbett/relpol.htm

The two websites that were germane to Chapter 5 are relevant for this chapter as well:

http://supct.law.cornell.edu/supct General information on the U.S. Supreme Court, a set of links to all Court decisions since 1990 plus a database of three hundred they consider the "most important" pre-1990 cases, all searchable by several different categories. It also tells you how to subscribe to an e-mail service that provides immediate updates on the Court's decisions.

http://w3.trib.com/FACT/ A resource for people who want to learn more about any of the civil liberties guaranteed in the First Amendment, including specific information on religious liberty. Frequently updated and includes an FAQ (frequently asked questions) section. This site has links to several of the documents mentioned in this chapter and in Chapter 5.

The following site has information about the Religious Freedom Restoration Act:

http://www.religious_freedom.org/rfratop.html/

References

Boston, Rob. 1993. "Happy Birthday, RFRA (Religious Freedom Restoration Act)." *Church and State* 47: 8–11.

Corbett, Julia M. 1997. *Religion in America.* Upper Saddle River, New Jersey: Prentice Hall.

Eastland, Terry. 1993. "Introduction." Pp. 1–10 in Terry Eastland (Ed.), *Religious Liberty in the Supreme Court: The Cases That Define the Debate Over Church and State.* Washington, D.C.: Ethics and Public Policy Center.

Eisgruber, Christopher L. 1994. "Why the Religious Freedom Restoration Act Is Unconstitutional." *New York University Law Review* 69: 437–476.

Frohnen, Bruce. 1996. *The New Communitarians and the Crisis of Modern Liberalism.* Lawrence: University Press of Kansas.

Gill, Sam. 1988. "Native American Religions." Pp. 137–151 in Charles H. Lippy and Peter W. Williams (Eds.), *The Encyclopedia of the American Religious Experience: Studies of Traditions and Movements.* New York: Charles Scribner's Sons.

Glendon, Mary Ann. 1993. "Religion and the Court: A New Beginning?" Pp. 471–481 in Terry Eastland (Ed.), *Religious Liberty in the Supreme Court: The Cases That Define the Debate Over Church and State.* Washington, D.C.: Ethics and Public Policy Center.

Levy, Leonard W. 1994. *The Establishment Clause, Second Edition.* Chapel Hill: University of North Carolina Press.

Manwaring, David. 1962. *Render unto Caesar: The Flag-Salute Controversy.* Chicago: University of Chicago Press.

Marshall, William P. 1991. "In Defense of *Smith* and Free Exercise Revisionism." *University of Chicago Law Review* 58: 308–328.

McConnell, Michael W. 1990. "Free Exercise Revisionism and the *Smith* Decision." *University of Chicago Law Review* 57: 1109–1153.

McConnell, Michael W. 1993. "Taking Religious Freedom Seriously." Pp. 497–508 in Terry Eastland (Ed.), *Religious Liberty in the Supreme Court: The Cases That Define the Debate Over Church and State.* Washington, D.C.: Ethics and Public Policy Center.

Morgan, Richard E. 1972. *The Supreme Court and Religion.* New York: Free Press.

O'Brien, David M. 1991. *Constitutional Law and Politics, Volume Two: Civil Rights and Civil Liberties.* New York: W.W. Norton.

Religion in the Constitution: A Delicate Balance. 1983. United States Commission on Civil Rights Clearinghouse Publication No. 80.

Saison, Tania. 1995. "Restoring Obscurity: The Shortcomings of the Religious Freedom Restoration Act." *Columbia Journal of Law and Social Problems* 28: 653–690.

Sherry, Suzanna. 1992. "*Lee* v. *Weisman:* Paradox Redux." Pp. 123–153 in Dennis J. Hutchinson, David A. Strauss, and Geoffrey R. Stone (Eds.), *1992: The Supreme Court Review.* Chicago: University of Chicago Press.

Wood, Jr., James E. 1993. "The Restoration of the Free Exercise Clause (Religious Freedom Restoration Act)." *Church and State* 35: 715–722.

PART III

Religion and Public Opinion

CHAPTER 7

Public Opinion About Religion and Politics

Please tell me if you agree or disagree with the statement, "God is the moral guiding force of American democracy."

55% Agree   35% Disagree   10% Undecided

Do you think it is appropriate for religious leaders to talk about their political beliefs as part of their religious activities?

35% Appropriate   61% Not appropriate   4% No opinion

—*Public Perspective*

Overview

Where do Americans stand on mixing religion and politics? The contradictory nature of the survey results above is a preview of the ambiguity that characterizes public attitudes about church-state relations and the proper role of religion in politics. In the two preceding chapters, we saw that over time there has been considerable ambiguity in the Supreme Court's interpretations of proper and improper connections between church and state. We will see that the public holds a mix of ambiguous and sometimes seemingly contradictory views about the proper links between religion and politics. In this chapter, we will examine public attitudes relevant to the establishment clause and the free exercise clause of the First Amendment. We will also look at the views of various elites in American society, including religious and political elites. The major questions to guide our analysis in this chapter are:

- What are the public's views on general, abstract principles concerning religious establishment issues and religious free exercise issues? For example, do people support the principle of separation of church and state or do they support a view in which the government aids religion in some way?
- What are the public's views on more specific, concrete situations involving religious establishment issues and religious free exercise issues? For example, should the government provide financial aid to religious schools? Do religious groups have a right to get involved in the political process? Where does the public stand concerning religious freedom for those who are not religious?
- In what ways can establishment issues and religious free exercise issues become intertwined in the attitudes of people? For example, is school prayer seen by some as an establishment issue and by others as a religious free exercise issue?
- What kinds of views do people hold with regard to the specific area of prayer and religious observances in the public schools?
- If public support for school prayer is so high, why has the effort to amend the Constitution to restore school prayer failed so far?
- What kinds of views do political and religious elites in the United States hold toward religion and politics and the proper mix of the two?

The Public's Abstract Views on Church-State Relations

We know of no public opinion research that has asked people directly: *Do you favor or oppose separation of church and state?* Based on the information that we have, we can speculate that a majority of the public, if asked, would say that they do favor separation of church and state. However, as we shall see in this chapter, the majority also supports church-state connections in a variety of situations such as prayer in public schools.

The most valuable research on public attitudes toward church-state relations is based on a series of surveys commissioned by the Williamsburg Charter Foundation. The 1987 Williamsburg Charter Foundation study (reported in Wilcox et al., 1992; Wilcox, 1993; and Jelen and Wilcox, 1995) includes a national sample of 1,889 adults and a sample of 863 elites from seven groups. Four of the elite samples were from secular groups: 155 academics, 202 business leaders, 106 government leaders, and 100 media leaders. The other three elite samples consisted of religious leaders: 101 Protestant ministers, 100 Catholic priests, and 99 Jewish rabbis. The most comprehensive report of results from these surveys is Ted Jelen and Clyde Wilcox's *Public Attitudes Toward Church and State* (1995). In addition to using the Williamsburg Charter Foundation surveys, Jelen and Wilcox also added two additional studies: a survey of a sample of residents in Washington, D.C., and a series of in-depth interviews and focus groups.

The Public's Abstract Attitudes Toward Religious Establishment

The Williamsburg Charter surveys contained two *abstract* questions concerning *religious establishment*. These two questions and the percentages of respondents selecting each option are as follows (Jelen and Wilcox, 1995: 59, 161, 165):

Which of these statements comes closest to your opinion?

46% "The government should not provide any support to any religions."

54% "The government should support all religions equally."

Which of these statements comes closest to your opinion?

38% "The government should take *special steps* to protect the *Judeo-Christian heritage*."

62% "There should be a high *wall of separation* between church and state."

Each of these two questions has a *separationist* position (separation of church and state) and an *accommodationist* position (the government should take a favorable view toward religion). When these two positions are combined, there are four possible groups with the following results (Wilcox et al., 1992: 265, 271; Jelen and Wilcox, 1995: 60).

- The *separationists* are the 36 percent who took the separationist view on both questions—the government should not help religion and there should be a high wall of separation.
- The *accommodationists* are the 33 percent who took the accommodationist view on both questions—help all religions equally but protect the Judeo-Christian heritage.

- The *nonpreferentialists* are the 21 percent who took the view that the government should help all religions equally while also saying that there should be a high wall of separation between church and state.
- The *Christian preferentialists* are the 9 percent who said that the government should not provide any support to religion but should take special steps to protect the Judeo-Christian heritage.

It appears that there are contradictions in some of these positions. How, for example, can one say that the government should support all religions equally and also say that the government should take special steps to protect the Judeo-Christian heritage? How can one say that the government should not provide any support for religion and also say that the government should take special steps to protect the Judeo-Christian heritage? Let's note several possibilities that could explain inconsistencies here. First, the questions themselves are limited. For example, the first question requires the respondent to choose between no government help for religion and the government helping all religions equally. This question does not allow for other possibilities, such as the person who wants the government to help *particular* religions but not other religions. Second, some people are simply inconsistent in their attitudes, perhaps because they responded to the questions separately without thinking about the implications that one view has for another view. Most of us have at least some degree of inconsistency in our religious or political views. Third, Jelen and Wilcox (1995: 65) suggest that some respondents might interpret the word *support* in the first question in terms of *financial* support, and some who oppose financial support might nevertheless favor other forms of linkages between church and state. Fourth, Jelen and Wilcox (1995: 62) also suggest that some people were expressing *nonattitudes*—they didn't have any real opinions but were simply selecting whatever choice they thought was the socially accepted choice, the "right" choice.

Thus, in terms of abstract principles regarding the establishment issue, there is substantial ambiguity in public attitudes. Further, there is no consensus on these matters.

The Public's Abstract Attitudes Toward Religious Free Exercise

The Williamsburg Charter survey did not include questions dealing with abstract principles regarding the free exercise clause. However,

Jelen and Wilcox (1995: 115) did include two abstract free exercise questions in their Washington sample. The first question asked whether "people have the right to practice their religion as they see fit, even if their practices seem strange to most Americans." Since support for free exercise of religion was almost unanimous (96 percent) for this question, we can speculate that if a sample of the American public were asked this question, there would be very strong majority support for free exercise of religion.

The second question asked whether "it is important for people to obey the law, even if it means limiting their religious freedom." Only 21 percent disagreed with this statement. We can speculate that a substantial majority of the American public would agree with the idea that people should obey the law even if a law limited their religious freedom. However, we are dealing with an *abstract* principle here; let's now examine public attitudes about *specific* situations involving the establishment and free exercise clauses.

The Public's Concrete Views on Church-State Relations

Establishment Issues

While 62 percent of the respondents in the Williamsburg Charter survey said that they supported the abstract idea of a high wall of separation between church and state, we will see that the public supports an accommodationist view on at least some specific, concrete issues such as prayer and religious observances in public schools. Various studies (e.g., Jelen and Wilcox, 1995; Elifson and Hadaway, 1985; Woodrum and Hoban, 1992) show that many people favor an accommodationist view on specific issues, and this is especially true among conservative Christians (Tamney and Johnson, 1987). This disparity between abstract principles and more specific situations is mirrored in research on support for democratic principles that shows high support for general, abstract principles but lower support for specific applications of such principles (Prothro and Grigg, 1960; McClosky, 1964).

The Williamsburg Charter survey contained a number of questions about specific, concrete matters related to religious establishment. Analysis by Wilcox (1993) and Jelen and Wilcox (1995) shows that the church-state establishment attitudes of people—as indicated by their responses to thirteen specific questions—are clustered into three attitude dimensions centered on:

- public displays of Judeo-Christian religious symbols (e.g., public display of manger scene at Christmas)
- using public schools in religious socialization
- using tax dollars to support religion.

Table 7.1, compiled from information in Jelen and Wilcox (1995), presents results from some of these specific questions. The percentages in the table are those who took the *accommodationist* position on each question. For most of these questions, a strong majority took the accommodationist position. For example, 93 percent think it's OK for the government to pay for military chaplains, 86 percent think it's OK for city governments to put up manger scenes at Christmas, and 72 percent think

TABLE 7.1

Percentages of the Public Taking the Accommodationist Position on Concrete Religious Establishment Issues

Statement/Question	Percentages Taking the Accommodationist Position
	%
It's good for Congress to start sessions with a public prayer.	72
It's good for sporting events at public high schools to begin with a public prayer.	64
It's OK for a city government to put up a manger scene on government property for Christmas.	86
It's OK for a city government to put up candles on government property for a Jewish religious celebration.	84
Many grade schools and high schools around the country are run by various churches and religious groups. Do you think the government should provide *financial aid* to these schools?	45
Public schools should allow student religious groups to hold voluntary meetings in school classrooms when classes are not in session.	74
The government should require that Judeo-Christian values be emphasized in public schools.	37
Churches should have to pay taxes on all their property.	46
Do you think it's OK for the government to pay for chaplains for the military?	93
[If respondents answered yes above, they were asked the following question.] Do you think it's OK for the government to pay for some Buddhist chaplains for the military?	64

Source: Based on the 1987 Williamsburg Charter Foundation survey of the general public reported in Jelen and Wilcox (1995: 78, 163–164).

it's good for Congress to start sessions with a public prayer.

On the other hand, there was a *separationist* majority on some issues. A majority opposed financial aid to schools run by religious groups, a majority rejected the idea that the government should require that Judeo-Christian values be emphasized in public schools, and a majority agreed that churches should have to pay taxes on their property.

Thus, a large majority of the public supports church-state accommodation in many concrete religious establishment situations—especially when the state support of religion is primarily symbolic (e.g., prayers in public schools) rather than financial. On the other hand, the majority rejects accommodation in some situations. We can speculate that the majority is most likely to reject accommodation in three situations:

- when it involves substantial financial aid to religion
- when it *requires* religious teaching or observances in public settings
- when accommodation favors one religious group over another.

Jelen and Wilcox (1995: 80) emphasize that *support for religious accommodation in concrete situations is high even among those who took the separationist position on both the abstract issues discussed earlier*—those who said that the government should not provide any support for religion and that there should be a high wall of separation between church and state. Among the separationists, for example, 92 percent did not object to the government paying for chaplains in the military, 81 percent did not object to a manger scene on city property at Christmas, and 81 percent did not object to the use of school classrooms by student religious groups when classes are not in session.

Thus, for many *concrete* establishment situations, a majority of *abstract* separationists take an accommodationist position rather than a separationist position. What accounts for such inconsistency? Again, the inconsistency might be due to the same types of factors discussed earlier (respondents simply don't think of the issues together, limitations on possible alternatives in the questions, etc.). However, Jelen and Wilcox (1995: 82) also point out that for many of these situations the survey respondents might be interpreting the situation as one involving the *free exercise of religion* rather than as an *establishment issue*. Thus, the mix of public attitudes reflects the tension between the free exercise clause and the establishment clause that we discussed in Chapter 6.

Accommodationists—those who took the accommodationist position on both abstract issues—are also not completely consistent when it comes to concrete situations. Some accommodationists took the separationist position on each of the concrete issues. Among the accom-modationists, for example, 45 percent rejected the idea that the govern-ment should require teaching of Judeo-Christian values in public schools, and 48 percent would tax all church property. Oddly enough, on the issue concerning use of school classrooms by student religious groups, there were somewhat more accommodationists (21 percent) than separa-tionists (19 percent) who took the separationist position.

While such results imply inconsistencies in people's attitudes toward es-tablishment issues, they also imply that survey researchers need to ask people more questions in order to obtain a clearer mapping of attitudes in this area. The focus groups used by Jelen and Wilcox (1995) help delve into these mat-ters further. The discussions in these focus groups indicated that many people took the accommodationist position on the concrete establishment is-sues (such as prayer in public schools) because they regarded it as a consen-sual government accommodation to religion that would not offend anybody. Jelen and Wilcox (1995: 83) report a very interesting finding: when the mod-erator or someone else in the group pointed out that a practice such as school prayer might offend some people, some people who had favored the practice would immediately back away from the accommodationist position. Thus, at least some of the inconsistency between the abstract establishment views of people and their concrete establishment views can be explained by whether the person believes that accommodation would offend other people.

Free Exercise Issues
Communitarians versus Libertarians

While Wilcox and Jelen (1995) view establishment issues along a *separat-ionist-accommodationist* dimension, they utilize Reichley's (1985) *com-munitarian-libertarian* distinction to examine views about religious free exercise. Both views would allow people to hold whatever religious *beliefs* they want to, but the two views are different in terms of the *behavior* that would be allowed on the basis of these religious beliefs.

- The *communitarian* view permits people to act on the basis of their religious views so long as the behavior does not offend the majority's religious or moral views within the community. It is ac-ceptable for public policy to limit the behavior of religious minori-ties whose unconventional religious practices run counter to com-munity norms.

- The *libertarian* view permits a much broader range of behavior based on religious beliefs. This view would allow all religious practices that do not violate other basic human rights.

Levels of Support for Religious Free Exercise

The Williamsburg Charter Foundation surveys contained questions about religious free exercise, and some of these are presented in Table 7.2 along with the percentages supporting free exercise. Based on these results (and from other results not included here), we can identify three levels of support for religious free exercise.

First, in some situations a strong majority supports the free exercise of religion. This includes situations in which religious leaders try to close pornographic bookstores, public support of political candidates by religious leaders, rejection of the view that there is no place in America for the Moslem religion, approval of the idea that Jewish groups can give money to politicians

---

TABLE 7.2

Percentages of the Public Supporting
Religious Free Exercise in Various Situations

Question/Statement	Percentages Supporting the Free Exercise Position
	%
There should be laws against the practice of Satan worship.	35
Followers of the Reverend Sun Myung Moon should not be allowed to print a daily newspaper in Washington, D.C.	56
Religious groups should have a legal right to get involved in politics.	68
There is no place in America for the Moslem religion.	71
It should be against the law for unusual religious cults to try to convert teenagers.	24
It's OK for the Right to Life movement to use religion in the debate about abortion.	56
It's OK for Jewish groups to give money to politicians who support Israel.	61
Do you think it is proper for religious leaders to publicly support political candidates who are running for office?	64
Do you think it is proper for religious leaders to try to close pornographic bookstores?	66

Source: Based on the 1987 Williamsburg Charter Foundation survey of the general public reported in Jelen and Wilcox (1995: 117, 162–165).

who support Israel, and affirmation of the right of religious groups to get involved in politics. Note, however, that even in situations in which a strong majority supports religious free exercise, there is a substantial minority that does not. For example, 71 percent reject the idea that there is no place in America for the Moslem religion, but that leaves 29 percent who do not.

Second, in some situations there is majority support for religious free exercise but the level of support is not greatly above 50 percent. For example, 56 percent agreed that it was acceptable for the Right to Life movement to use religion in the debate about abortion.

Third, in some situations only a minority supports religious free exercise. Only 35 percent rejected the notion that there should be laws against Satan worship, and only 24 percent rejected the idea that it should be illegal for cults to try to convert teenagers. Some of the more controversial free-exercise issues involve unconventional religious groups that are labeled "cults." Because the term cult has such a negative connotation, many people react very negatively to any group that is labeled a cult. Jelen and Wilcox's (1995: 120) discussions with focus groups showed that people have difficulty in drawing a distinction between a church and a cult, but nevertheless they strongly opposed cults.

In results from the 1991 National Opinion Research Center General Social Survey (NORC GSS), 65 percent agreed that religious leaders should not try to influence how people vote in elections, and 54 percent agreed that religious leaders should not try to influence government decisions. Similarly, an NBC/ *Wall Street Journal* survey showed that only 41 percent thought it was appropriate for religious groups to advance their beliefs by being involved in politics and working to affect policy, and only 40 percent thought it was appropriate for political leaders to talk about their religious beliefs as part of their political campaigns (*Public Perspective* September/October, 1994: 93). Gallup and Castelli (1989: 230) reported that when asked whether churches should keep out of political matters or express their views on day-to-day social and political questions, only 37 percent said that churches should express their views. On the other hand, a more recent survey by the Pew Research Center (1996) showed substantial increases in public support for church involvement in politics. In contrast with results from a 1965 Gallup Poll showing that 53 percent felt that churches should stay out of political matters, the Pew Research Center found that in 1996 a majority of 54 percent thought that the churches should express their views on political and social issues. Thus, there does seem to be a trend toward greater support for church involvement in politics.

While we cannot develop one single generalization that will explain all situations in which support for religious free exercise is low, it is apparent that many of these situations involve groups that many people consider to be harmful. Jelen and Wilcox (1995: 123–124) suggest that the public supports free exercise for those groups it does not consider dangerous and opposes free exercise for groups it considers possibly harmful. This pattern is similar to public attitudes toward political tolerance for different groups in society: many people decide whether to tolerate a group (e.g., whether the group should be allowed to give a public speech) on the basis of whether they like the group or not (Lawrence, 1976; Corbett, 1980; Sullivan et al., 1979).

Another way of looking at the low level of support for religious free exercise in many situations is to say that many Americans hold the communitarian view rather than the libertarian view of religious free exercise. For these people, Jelen and Wilcox (1995: 140) suggest that religious freedom might be regarded in terms of its instrumental value in increasing social cohesion and public morality; if the religious freedom of certain religious groups does not increase social cohesion or public morality, then the religious freedom of such groups is not particularly valuable.

Support for Religious Freedom for the Nonreligious

To what extent is the public supportive of the rights of those who are not religious? Table 7.3 presents results from several survey questions, three

---

TABLE 7.3

Public Attitudes Toward the Rights of Those Who Are Not Religious

There are always some people whose ideas are considered bad or dangerous by other people. For instance, somebody who is against all churches and religion. If such a person wanted to make a speech in your community against churches and religion, should he be allowed to speak, or not? (1990–1994 NORC GSS)

No	27%	Yes	73%

Should such a person be allowed to teach in a college or university, or not? (1990–1994 NORC GSS)

No	46%	Yes	54%

If some people in your community suggested that a book he wrote against churches and religion should be taken out of your public library, would you favor removing this book, or not? (1990–1994 NORC GSS)

Oppose	71%	Favor	29%

[How much do you agree or disagree?] Politicians who do not believe in God are unfit for public office. (1991 NORC GSS)

Strongly agree	15%	Agree	15%		Neither	28%
Disagree	31%	Strongly disagree	11%			

Source: National Opinion Research Center General Social Surveys for the years indicated.

of which concern a hypothetical person who is against all churches and religion. While there was little support for the rights of such a person during the 1950s (Stouffer, 1955), these results and others (Nunn et al., 1978; Corbett, 1982, 1991) show that tolerance of those who oppose churches and religion has greatly increased. For example, only 27 percent would not allow such a person to give a speech in their community, and only 29 percent would favor removing a book by such a person from the public library. In a 1991 NORC GSS question not shown, 66 percent responded that books and films that attack religion should be allowed, while only 34 percent would legally prohibit such books and films.

On the question of whether politicians who do not believe in God are unfit for public office, there were more people on the tolerant side (42 percent) than there were who believed that atheists are unfit for public office (30 percent). On the other hand, in the Williamsburg Charter public survey, only 33 percent said they were willing to vote for an atheist for president (Jelen and Wilcox, 1995: 45), and another survey found that only 23 percent would vote for a candidate who does not believe in God (*Public Perspective* September/October, 1994: 97). However, only 6 percent thought that atheists were a threat to democracy, and only 2 percent thought that atheists had too much influence and power (Jelen and Wilcox, 1995: 45). Overall, these results suggest a higher level of acceptance of atheists than one might have expected.

Free Exercise Views versus Establishment Views

Jelen and Wilcox (1995: 113) emphasize that free exercise issues and establishment issues sometimes get intertwined, and one person might view a particular situation as if it were an establishment issue while another person views the same issue as if it were a religious free exercise issue (although most people in the general public might not even think in terms of a distinction between the two or use this kind of terminology). For example, opponents of organized prayer in public schools act as if this were an establishment issue whereas proponents of school prayer act as if it were a free exercise issue. Further, Jelen and Wilcox (1995: 149) report that those who were most supportive of religious accommodation for Christian groups tended to be the least supportive of religious free exercise for non-Christian religious minorities. In general, however, there were not very strong connections between people's attitudes on establishment issues and their views on free exercise issues.

Jelen and Wilcox (1995: 25) propose a four-group typology resulting from the two primary positions on establishment issues (separationist or accommodationist) combined with the two primary positions on free exercise issues (communitarian or libertarian). Using a technique called cluster analysis, Jelen and Wilcox (1995: 150) found that respondents in their Washington, D.C. sample were roughly equally divided into these four groups, thus establishing the usefulness of the typology. Let's examine the four types of groups.

Religious Nonpreferentialists: Libertarian Accommodationists

Religious nonpreferentialists "favor allowing religion a place in the public square and favor allowing all religious groups to participate" (Jelen and Wilcox: 1995: 150). This group supported religious free exercise for both Christian and non-Christian groups—including such practices as Hare Krishnas soliciting money at airports, conscientious objection to war, the refusal of children to pledge allegiance to the flag if such a practice violated their religious beliefs, and Christian Scientists withholding medical treatment from their children. This group also gave strong support to the abstract right to practice religion.

Religious nonpreferentialists also gave broad support to religious accommodation. For example, they supported public displays of religious symbols, funding for chaplains (including Buddhist chaplains) in the military, and allowing student religious organizations to use public school property for meetings.

In terms of religious composition, this group consisted primarily of well-educated, white Catholics and very liberal black pentecostals. Thus, Jelen and Wilcox (1995: 151) note that the ". . . group of respondents who most clearly regarded religious accommodation as a component of religious free exercise were not evangelical Protestants but rather those who have been the historical victims of discrimination."

Christian Preferentialists: Communitarian Accommodationists

Christian preferentialists strongly favored religious accommodation, but they opposed accommodation for non-Christian groups or even liberal Christian groups. They supported government help for religion, government protection of the Judeo-Christian heritage, school prayer, requiring that schools teach Judeo-Christian values and creationism, public displays of religious symbols, and so on (Jelen and Wilcox, 1995: 151). However, they opposed non-mainstream religious practices such as conscientious objection to war, allowing children to refuse to pledge allegiance to the flag, allowing Native Americans to use peyote in religious ceremonies, and civil disobedience based on religious values. They also tended to believe that non-Christian immigrants should convert to Christianity.

This group consisted primarily of orthodox Protestants who held orthodox religious identities, said they were born again, and believed that the Bible was literally true (Jelen and Wilcox, 1995: 151). It appears that many members of this group feel that religious accommodation and religious free exercise should be based on the preferences of the majority Judeo-Christian heritage—or perhaps simply the Christian heritage.

Religious Minimalists: Communitarian Separationists

Religious minimalists support separation of church and state and oppose religious free exercise. This group took separationist views on the establishment issues and opposed free exercise by all kinds of groups. For example, they strongly opposed allowing student religious groups to use school property for meetings. They also opposed fundamentalist ministers preaching on college campuses, Jews missing work on Jewish holidays, cults recruiting teenage members, and Hare Krishnas soliciting money at airports (Jelen and Wilcox, 1995: 153).

You might expect that this group was primarily secular, but that is not the case. In fact, this group ranked second among the four groups in terms of frequency of attendance at religious services, in orthodox religious identities, and in belief that the Bible is literally true (Jelen and Wilcox, 1995: 153). They were also somewhat more likely to be Baptist and pentecostal. It appears that this group believes that Christians should be separated from the sinfulness of the secular world (Jelen, 1987) and that the mixing of church and state will have a corrupting influence on religion. Thus, we see that strong opposition to mixing church and state can come from people who are very religious.

Religious Free-Marketeers: Libertarian Separationists

Religious free-marketeers believe in strict separation of church and state, but they are very supportive of religious free exercise except when it appears to violate the principle of separation of church and state. This group would allow all kinds of religious groups to compete freely for adherents. Its abstract separationist view is indicated in its opposition to government aid to religion, its opposition to government support for the

Judeo-Christian heritage, and its support for a high wall of separation between church and state (Jelen and Wilcox, 1995: 152). Its concrete separationist view is indicated in its opposition to public displays of religious symbols, funding for military chaplains, teaching creationism in public schools, and public school prayers. Their support for religious free exercise was indicated in their support for allowing Native Americans to use peyote in religious ceremonies, their support for allowing fundamentalist ministers to preach on college campuses, their opposition to laws against cults and Satanism, and their opposition to requiring that non-Christian immigrants convert to Christianity.

Jelen and Wilcox (1995: 153) describe this group as especially well educated, disproportionately Jewish, and quite secular. They had very low church attendance and low doctrinal orthodoxy. Jelen and Wilcox (1995: 153) point out that cultural conservative elites have often suggested that secular, well-educated Americans are hostile to religion. However, the results show that this secular group is very supportive of religious free exercise in situations that do not seem to involve religious establishment issues. This secular group extends its support for religious free exercise to conservative Christian groups as well.

Thus, we have irony here. The most secular group is one of the most supportive of religious free exercise, whereas one of the two most religiously orthodox groups (the religious minimalists) were among the least supportive of religious free exercise. Based on their analysis of attitudes, Jelen and Wilcox (1995: 154) report a very important finding: "[O]ur data lead us to reject firmly the hypothesis that people who seek to minimize the public role of religion are either irreligious or antireligious and that those who are secular are hostile to religion."

A Case in Point:
Public Attitudes About Prayer and Religious Observance in Public Schools

In order to demonstrate further the mix of attitudes held by the public concerning linkages between religion and politics, let's further examine the controversial area of prayer and religious observances in public schools. Survey results in Table 7.4 (page 234) show that the majority favors prayer in public schools; thus, the majority takes the accommodationist view here. A 60 percent majority disagrees with the Supreme Court's rulings about reading the Lord's Prayer or Bible verses in public

TABLE 7.4

Public Attitudes Toward Prayer in the Public Schools

The United States Supreme Court has ruled that no state or local government may require the reading of the Lord's Prayer or Bible verses in public schools. What are your views on this—do you approve or disapprove of the court ruling? (combined 1990–1994 NORC GSS)

Approve   40%   Disapprove   60%

In your opinion, should there be daily prayers in all public schools? (1991 NORC GSS)
Yes   64%   No   36%

Which of these three statements comes closest to your feelings about prayers in the public schools? (1986 NORC GSS)
The Lord's Prayer or some Bible verse should be read daily.   29%
There should be a moment for silent prayer or meditation daily.   53%
No prayer or other religious observances should be held in the public schools.   18%

An amendment to the U.S. Constitution has been proposed that would permit prayers to be spoken in the public schools. Do you favor or oppose this amendment? (1994 Phi Delta Kappa-Gallup International Institute Poll)
Favor   71%   Oppose   25%   No opinion   4%

If prayer were to be allowed in the public schools, do you think all children should be required to participate in them, or not? (Gallup International Institute Poll)
Should be required   18%   Should not   81%   No opinion   1%

Again, suppose prayer were allowed in the public schools in this community. In addition to Christian prayer, would you favor or oppose allowing spoken Jewish, Muslim or Hindu prayer by students who hold these faiths? (Gallup International Institute Poll)
Favor   73%   Oppose   20%   No opinion   7%

Sources: National Opinion Research Center General Social Surveys for the years indicated. The Gallup Poll results are in *Emerging Trends,* September 1995: 2–3, and *Gallup Poll Monthly,* July 1995: 15.

schools. A majority of 64 percent thinks that there should (definitely or probably) be daily prayers in all public schools. A majority of 53 percent believes that there should be a moment for silent prayer or meditation daily, and another 29 percent favor reading the Lord's Prayer or some Bible verse daily. Further, 71 percent favor a constitutional amendment to permit prayer in public schools. Let's note, however, results from two other questions not shown. First, only 46 percent *strongly* favored a constitutional amendment to permit prayers in public schools. Second, only 29 percent said *yes* when asked whether this was the kind of issue for which it was worth changing the Constitution (*Emerging Trends,* September 1995: 1).

While support for school prayer is very high in the general public, only a small minority of 18 percent would *require* all children to participate in prayer in public schools. This supports the contention that many people see prayer in the public schools as a *free exercise* issue rather than as an *establishment* issue. Returning to the constitutional amendment question, the wording of the question asked about an amendment that would *permit* prayers in public schools rather than *requiring* prayers. The last set of results in Table 7.4 also supports the contention that many people view this as a free exercise issue rather than as a means of establishing particular religious doctrines in the public schools. If there were prayers in public schools, only a small minority of 20 percent would oppose Jewish, Muslim, or Hindu prayers by children who hold these faiths.

Opponents of school prayer and other religious observances in public schools usually base their arguments on the establishment clause of the First Amendment, and they also view school prayers as an imposition on the religious freedom of those whose religious or nonreligious views are violated by the particular religious views being expressed. These survey results suggest that most people in the general public look at this matter, rightly or wrongly, in terms of *exercising religious freedom* rather than *establishing any particular religious views or imposing views on an unwilling audience.* This idea is also supported by the fact that the majority favors silent prayer over spoken prayer. Further, 74 percent believe that only a small percentage of parents would be offended by school prayer, and 55 percent said that school prayer should not be permitted if it offended a large percentage of parents (*Gallup Poll Monthly,* July 1995: 16).

However, the results in Table 7.4 also show that there is a minority that would *require* prayer and opposes anything but Christian prayer. In another question not shown, while 81 percent said that prayers in public schools should reflect all major religions, 13 percent of the respondents said that prayers in public schools should be basically Christian, reflecting Christian values and beliefs (*Gallup Poll Monthly,* July 1995: 15). Thus, a minority does want to use public schools for required religious observances that would include only Christian beliefs.

While prayer and other religious activities organized by teachers or other authorities in public schools have been found to be unconstitutional, certain aspects of religious studies are permitted in public schools. Three out of four Americans would not object to each of four types of permitted activities: teaching about the religions of the world in comparative religion studies, making facilities available after school hours for use by student religious groups, offering elective courses in Bible studies, and using the Bible in literature, history, and social studies classes (*Emerging Trends*, September 1995: 4).

If support for prayer in public schools is so strong and so many people favor a constitutional amendment to provide school prayer, why hasn't a constitutional amendment been proposed by Congress? In order for Congress to propose an amendment to the Constitution, a two-thirds vote in favor of the amendment is required in both houses of Congress. Then the proposed amendment must be ratified by three fourths of the states. While prayer amendment bills have been brought to a vote in Congress, none has received the necessary two-thirds support in both houses of Congress. The reasons for this are more related to elite views than public views. So, let's now examine elite views.

Elite Views on Church and State

There are many kinds of elites in society—political elites, religious elites, business elites, social elites, media elites, and so on. Unlike surveys of the general public, we have no representative sample of *all* elites in the United States. However, we do have some information about several types of elites (based on samples that might not be as representative as we would like), and we will examine that information in this section.

Beginning primarily with Samuel Stouffer's (1955) study of the general public and a sample of community leaders during the 1950s, research has shown that political elites and the general public differ from each other in terms of certain political attitudes. In general, political elites tend to support basic democratic principles more than the general public does (Stouffer, 1955; McClosky, 1964; Nunn et al., 1978; McClosky and Brill, 1983). On this basis, we might expect that political elites would be more supportive of separation of church and state and would also be more supportive of religious free exercise. Thus, in terms of Jelen and Wicox's typology, we might expect that political elites would be more likely to be religious free-marketeers than the general public is.

Much—if not all—of the difference between political elites and the general public occurs simply because political elites have higher education than the general public does. Jelen and Wilcox (1995: 68, 130) demonstrated that in the general public those with higher education are more likely to support separation of church and state and they are more likely to support religious free exercise. On this basis, we might expect that other types of elites would also differ from the general public in the same ways that political elites do. On the other hand, religious elites might differ from other kinds of elites.

Elite Attitudes Toward Prayer in Public Schools

We demonstrated earlier that a high majority of the American public favored prayer in public schools and that over 70 percent favored a constitutional amendment to bring this about. We also noted that there had not been sufficient support (two thirds in each house) in Congress to pass a bill formally proposing a school prayer amendment. There are several reasons for this. First, as indicated earlier, many who favor such a constitutional amendment do not feel strongly about it—and some who favor a prayer amendment back off from that position when asked whether this is an issue for which it is worth changing the Constitution. Second, there are different proposals for bringing about prayer in public schools and it is difficult for proponents of school prayer to agree on one particular proposal. Third, Elifson and Hadaway (1985: 328) suggest that the characteristics of those who are most likely to favor school prayer (southerners, the less educated, and those with lower income) might make this majority too silent to be heard by the more educated, higher-income elites in Congress. Fourth, as we shall see, elites are not unified in support of prayer in public schools.

Political Elites and School Prayer

Support for school prayer is higher among some religious groups than among others. For example, the 1991 NORC GSS asked the following question: "In your opinion, should there be daily prayers in all public schools?" In a different question, people were asked their religious preference and we have grouped people into nones (no religion), Jews, Catholics, mainline Protestants, and evangelical Protestants—this classification will be explained more fully in the next chapter. The *yes* response was given to the prayer question by:

- 22 percent of those who indicated no religion
- 3 percent of Jews
- 62 percent of Catholics
- 61 percent of mainline Protestants
- 80 percent of evangelical Protestants

Overall, while 80 percent of evangelical Protestants wanted school prayer, only 55 percent of the rest of the respondents did. This is very relevant *if* political elites are less likely to be evangelical Protestants than the general public is.

Table 7.5 shows the religious affiliations of U.S. senators and representatives of the 104th Congress in 1995. The table is set up so that the largest group (Catholics) is listed first, the second largest group is second, and so on. With 28 percent of the senators and representatives, Catholics are the largest religious group in Congress, but this is only slightly higher than the percentage of Catholics in the general population. Baptists (13 percent) are the second largest group, but they are actually "underrepresented" in Congress—about 20 percent of the general public is Baptist. Among Protestant denominations in the 1991 NORC GSS, Baptists showed the strongest support (84 percent) for school prayer. Methodists constitute 11 percent of Congress and this is very close to their percentage in the public. Episcopalians, Presbyterians, and Jews are "overrepresented" in Congress. While 10 percent of Congress is Presbyterian, only 5 percent of the public is. While 9 percent of Congress is Episcopalian, only 2 percent of the public is. While 6 percent of Congress is Jewish, only a little more than 2 percent of the public is.

In general, the religious composition of Congress is not drastically different from the general public. However, the important pattern here is that religious affiliations that are more likely to include evangelical Protestants are "underrepresented" in Congress. This, in turn, means that support in Congress for school prayer is less likely than in the general public.

Further, members of Congress might give disproportionate attention to those who are most crucial to their efforts to get reelected. Green and Guth (1989) examined attitudes about school prayer among a very important group of political activists: major contributors to political party, ideological and interest-group political action committees (PACs). Their results showed that political contributors were sharply divided over a proposed school prayer amendment and that opponents slightly outnumbered proponents. Only right-wing PACs overwhelmingly supported a school prayer amendment. Further, only 4 percent of the contributors listed school prayer as one of the most important problems facing the country and 60 percent of those who listed it were opposed to it (Green and Guth, 1989: 45).

Green and Guth (1989: 53) conclude that the broad but relatively shallow support for school prayer among the general public has a much

TABLE 7.5

Religious Affiliations of U.S. Senators and Representatives:
104th Congress, 1995

Religious Affiliation	Senators	Representatives	Total	Percentage
				%
Catholic	21	127	148	28
Baptist	10	59	69	13
Methodist	11	48	59	11
Presbyterian	10	46	56	10
Episcopalian	14	35	49	9
Jewish	9	25	34	6
Protestant— unspecified	2	25	27	5
Lutheran	5	15	20	4
Mormon	3	10	13	2
Christian	—	12	12	2
Congregationalist	5	2	7	1
United Church of Christ	2	5	7	1
Christian Scientist	—	5	5	<1
Unitarian	3	2	5	<1
Unspecified	1	4	5	<1
African Methodist	—	4	4	<1
Greek Orthodox	2	2	4	<1
Assembly of God	1	2	3	<1
Seventh-day Adventist	—	2	2	<1
Christian Missionary Alliance	—	1	1	<1
Disciples of Christ	—	1	1	<1
Eastern Orthodox	1	—	1	<1
Nazarene	—	1	1	<1
Pan-African Orthodox Christian	—	1	1	<1
United Brethren in Christ	—	1	1	<1

Source: Compiled from information in *Congressional Quarterly Weekly Report,* February 18, 1995, pp. 541–549.

narrower base among political contributors and that it is central only to the New Christian Right's agenda. What accounts for this? Green and Guth's (1989: 45) analysis showed that support for school prayer among political contributors was related to the same factors that it was in the general public, and that in comparison with the public, political contributors had higher education, higher income, higher status jobs, and were less likely to be conservative Protestants.

To emphasize this point about the link between education and attitude toward school prayer in the general public, let's note that in the 1991 NORC GSS an overwhelming majority (76 percent) of those with twelve years of school or less favored daily prayers in school compared to only a minority (42 percent) of those who had four or more years of college. Thus, the higher education of elites could have a substantial impact on their attitudes toward school prayer.

As a further indication of the lack of unity among political elites for school prayer, studies of delegates to the national political party conventions have demonstrated that support for school prayer among these political elites is not so high as it is in the general public. For example, Plissner and Mitofsky's (1988) study of 1988 delegates found that a bare majority of 51 percent of Republican delegates favored school prayer while 65 percent of Democratic delegates opposed it.

Religious Elites and School Prayer

We have seen that members of Congress and political contributors do not match the profile of those in the general public who are most likely to support school prayer. This lack of unity among political elites for school prayer is also reflected in the views of religious elites. For example, while some religiously conservative Protestant leaders have supported a prayer amendment, the National Council of Churches has opposed it. A study of 178 Catholic and Protestant religious leaders in the United States found that they overwhelmingly believed that clergy should take a stand on public issues and that religious leaders should be the most influential group in American society (Lerner et al., 1989: 58). Analysis of their responses to questions showed that these religious leaders were much more liberal and Democratic than the general public is. However, there were many very sharp religious and political differences among these clergy; they were not at all unified on political, religious, or social issues—or on the proper role of the church in dealing with such issues. While Lerner et al. (1989) did not ask these religious leaders their views on school prayer, the sharp divisions on many other issues lead us to speculate that these religious leaders would be far from unified on the question of prayer in school.

Guth et al. (1991) surveyed almost five thousand ministers from seven Protestant denominations representing a high proportion of the nation's white Protestants and representing several distinct traditions (e.g., the pentecostal Assemblies of God, the theologically conservative Southern Baptist Convention, and mainline churches such as the Presbyterian Church). This study demonstrated substantial theological and political divisions among the clergy. For a theological example, 97 percent of the Assemblies of God ministers strongly agreed that Jesus is the only way to salvation, whereas only 22 percent of the Disciples of Christ ministers strongly agreed. For a political example, 58 percent of the Assemblies of God ministers were Republicans, compared to only 15 percent of the Disciples of Christ ministers. Other studies (e.g., Quinley, 1974; Jelen, 1993) have also shown substantial political differences among the clergy.

Given both theological and political cleavages among the Protestant clergy, it is no surprise that there is substantial disagreement among these ministers concerning school prayer. Some groups of ministers (e.g., Assemblies of God and Southern Baptist Convention) were mostly in favor of school prayer whereas some (e.g., Disciples of Christ and Presbyterian Church) were mostly opposed to school prayer (Guth et al., 1991: 81).

Elite Views on Abstract Establishment Issues

The Williamsburg Charter Foundation study included seven types of elites. Four were secular: academic, business, government, and media elites. The other three consisted of Protestant ministers, Catholic priests, and Jewish rabbis. Recall that two questions were used to measure abstract separationist-accommodationist views. In the first question, respondents selected from the *no help* position (the government should not provide any support to any religions) or the *help all* position (the government should support all religions equally). In the second question, respondents selected from the *protect* position (the government should take *special steps* to protect the *Judeo-Christian heritage*) or the *high wall* position (there should be a high *wall of separation* between church and state). These two items were then combined to form a typology ranging from the most separationist position (no help/high wall) to the most accommodationist position (help all/protect).

Based on Wilcox et al. (1992: 271), Figure 7.1 presents the percentages of the public and each of the seven types of elites who took the most separationist abstract position (the government should not provide any support to religion and there should be a high wall of separation between church and state). While only 36 percent of the public took this separationist position, *a majority of all secular elites were separationists.* Among academic elites, 86 percent took the separationist position. Approximately two-thirds of the other secular elites took the separationist position. Among secular elites, media elites were the least separationist (63 percent) although elite journalists tend to be much more secular than the general public is (Lichter et al., 1986). Thus, secular elites are much more separationist *in the abstract* than the general public.

Among the religious elites, Jewish rabbis were overwhelmingly (77 percent) separationist, perhaps because they would expect that any reli-

---

FIGURE 7.1

Percentages of the Public and Seven Types of Secular and
Religious Elites Taking the Most Separatist Abstract
Church-State Position: Williamsburg Charter Study

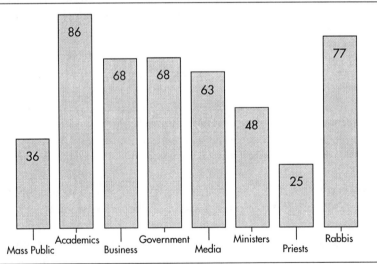

Source: Based on results from the Williamsburg Charter surveys of the public, secular elites, and religious elites presented in Clyde Wilcox et al. (1992: 271). The results presented here are the percentages of each group that took the no help/high wall position: the government should not provide any support to religions and there should be a high wall of separation between church and state.

gious accommodation would favor the dominant Protestant and Catholic views. Further, approximately half (48 percent) of the Protestant ministers took the separationist position, and only 22 percent of them took the most accommodationist position (help all religions equally/protect the Judeo-Christian heritage). Further, when Jelen and Wilcox (1995: 99) separate Protestant ministers into mainline and evangelical groups, they find that a majority (60 percent) of mainline ministers take the most separationist position as contrasted with only 37 percent of the evangelical ministers. Thus, we see again that there is deep division among Protestant ministers concerning church-state relations.

Catholic priests are the only elite group that was less separationist than the general public. Only 25 percent of Catholic priests took this separationist position whereas 47 percent of them took the most accommodationist position (help all religions equally/protect the Judeo-Christian heritage). In sum, among religious elites, Jewish rabbis overwhelmingly favor separation of church and state, Protestant ministers are divided but more likely to take this position than any of the other three possible combinations, and Catholic priests are more supportive of religious accommodation than the public or any other of these elite groups.

Elite Views on Concrete Establishment Issues

Recall that the Williamsburg Charter Foundation surveys contained a number of questions that concerned more specific, concrete establishment issues (e.g., school prayer, allowing manger scenes on public property at Christmas). Let's examine the views of secular elites on these issues first and then look at the views of religious elites.

Secular Elite Views

The views of academic elites constituted a distinct pattern whereas the views of the other three secular elite groups were fairly similar to one another (Jelen and Wilcox, 1995: 101). Thus, we will discuss the academic elites first and then generalize about the other three secular groups combined.

Academic elites were the most supportive of separation of church and state in concrete situations. They were much more likely than the general public or any of the other elite groups (although Jewish rabbis were a close second) to support separationism. For example, at least three out of four academic elites opposed each of the following: prayer in Congress, prayer at high school sports events, government funds for religious schools, a moment of silence in public schools, and the government requiring the teaching of Judeo-Christian values. On the other hand, academic elites took accommodationist positions on four of the thirteen concrete establishment issues, but these particular situations might be interpreted to involve the issue of religious free exercise rather than establishment issues: they favored government funding of military chaplains (in both questions about Christian chaplains and Buddhist chaplains), opposed taxing church property, favored teaching both evolution and creationism in school, and favored allowing student religious groups to use school property for meetings. These results and others we will discuss later in the chapter show that academic elites are very supportive of both separation of church and state and religious free exercise.

Jelen and Wilcox (1995: 100) show that the other secular elites (business, government, and media) were fairly similar to one another except that the media elites were the most separationist of these three groups. A majority of these government, business, and media elites took the separationist position only on four issues; they were especially opposed to accommodationism in funding for religious schools and in the government requiring the teaching of Judeo-Christian values. Unlike the academic elites, for the thirteen concrete establishment questions, a majority of these secular elites took the accommodationist position on nine issues (or eight for the media elites). In sum, while these business, media, and government elites were much more supportive of separation of church and state *in the abstract* than the general public was, they are not much more separationist that the public in these *concrete* establishment situations. Only academic elites (and media elites to a lesser degree) are substantially more separationist than the public is in concrete religious establishment situations.

Religious Elite Views

The Jewish rabbis were very similar to the academic elites in terms of their high support for separation of church and state on most of the thirteen concrete establishment issues. They took the accommodationist position on only a few issues such as favoring government funding for chaplains (Christian and Buddhist) and opposing taxing church property (Jelen and Wilcox, 1995: 100). Interestingly, only two elite groups opposed city governments displaying candles on government property for a Jewish religious celebration: the academic elites (60 percent opposed) and the Jewish rabbis (83 percent opposed).

By contrast, a majority of Catholic priests and Protestant ministers took the accommodationist position on most concrete establishment issues. Catholic priests took the accommodationist position on all but one of the thirteen issues, and Protestant ministers were accommodationist on all except three issues. Jelen and Wilcox (1995: 102–103) also compared mainline Protestant ministers with evangelical Protestant ministers and found that mainline ministers were more separationist than evangelical ministers on every issue.

Elite Views on Concrete Religious Free Exercise Issues

We saw earlier that the public supports religious free exercise for groups that it does not consider to be potentially harmful. For seventeen questions used by Jelen and Wilcox (1995: 117) to indicate religious free exercise, a majority of the public supported free exercise on nine issues and opposed it on eight issues. For the seventeen issues, the average percentage of the public supporting religious free exercise was 49 percent. Thus, on average, about half of the public took the free exercise position on each issue. Based on information in Jelen and Wilcox (1995: 133–134) we computed similar information for each of the seven types of elites in order to make some comparisons.

While a majority of the public supported religious free exercise in nine of the seventeen issues, the number of issues on which elite groups gave majority support to free exercise ranged from fourteen to seventeen. Business elites were the least supportive of religious free exercise, but a majority of them opposed religious free exercise for only three of the seventeen questions (opposition to Hare Krishnas soliciting money at airports, agreement that religious groups should stay out of politics, and disagreement with the idea that religious groups should be able to hide illegal immigrants). Thus, even the least supportive of the elites were much more supportive of religious free exercise than the general public was.

The extent to which elite groups gave majority support to religious free exercise varied from one question to another. For example, 100 percent of the academic elites and the media elites rejected the notion that there is no place in America for the Moslem religion. On the other hand, the majority support was at a minimum (51 percent) among Catholic priests who barely rejected the notion that Hare Krishnas should be prohibited from soliciting money at airports.

Figure 7.2 shows the average percentage of the public and each elite group supporting religious free exercise for the seventeen questions. As indicated before, on average 49 percent of the public took the free exercise position on each question. Figure 7.2 makes it clear that all the elite groups are much more supportive of religious free exercise than the general public is. Again, the elite group that is least supportive of free exercise is the business group and yet it is substantially more supportive of free exercise than the public is. The most supportive group is the academic elites group, which averaged 80 percent for each of the seventeen questions.

Looking at the results this way, we can see that academic elites are the most supportive of religious free exercise, business elites are the least supportive (but not by much), and there is little difference among government elites, media elites, ministers, priests, and rabbis. Given that elites have more power in society, this suggests that religious free exercise will in practice probably be closer to the more expansive views of the elites than to the more restricted views of the general public.

FIGURE 7.2

Average Percentages of Public and Seven Elite Groups Supporting Religious Free Exercise on Each of Seventeen Questions

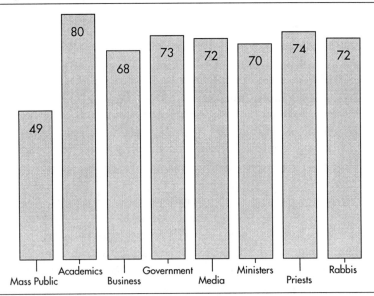

Source: Computed from results from the Williamsburg Charter surveys of the public, secular elites, and religious elites presented in Jelen and Wilcox (1995: 133–134).

Summary and Conclusions

We have examined public and elite attitudes toward church-state relations in the U.S., focusing on attitudes that are relevant to religious establishment and free exercise issues. Let's first reiterate some of the major findings concerning the abstract views of the public on religious establishment.

- About a third are religious *separationists,* about a third are religious *accommodationists,* about a fifth are religious *nonpreferentialists* who believe the government should help all religions equally but also believe in a high wall of separation between church and state, and about one tenth are *Christian preferentialists* who don't want the government to help all religions equally but do want the government to protect the Judeo-Christian heritage.
- People hold apparently contradictory views on establishment issues; such contradictions might be explained in various ways (e.g., by survey question inadequacies, people thinking of different issues in isolation from one another, particular interpretations of the issues).
- In terms of abstract principles, it appears that public support for religious free exercise is very high.

We next examined the public's views on more specific, concrete issues dealing with politics and religion. Some of the major findings are listed below.

- A majority of the public takes an accommodationist view on many specific, concrete establishment issues (especially when state support of religion is primarily symbolic rather than financial).
- A majority takes the separationist view in some situations—especially when the issue concerns financial aid to religion, requiring religious teaching or observances in public institutions, or favoring one religious group over another.
- The views of people on religious free exercise can usefully be distinguished as communitarian (people can act on their religious beliefs so long as it doesn't offend the majority within the community) or libertarian (people can act on their religious beliefs so long as they do not violate the rights of other people).

- In some situations a bare majority to a strong majority supports the free exercise of religion. This includes such matters as allowing religious groups to take part in politics, using religious themes in political discourse in some situations, and tolerance of at least some degree of religious diversity.

- In other situations, a majority does not support religious free exercise. This is especially the case when religious groups are involved that the general public considers to be harmful in some way (e.g., "cults"). It appears that public attitudes in many such situations are communitarian rather than libertarian.

- Most people support the rights of those who are not religious, but a substantial minority of the public does not.

- When establishment views are combined with religious free exercise views, four major combinations result: *religious nonpreferentialists* (accommodationists who support religious free exercise); *Christian preferentialists* (accommodationists who limit the accommodation to Christian groups—or perhaps just orthodox Christian groups—and take a communitarian view on religious free exercise); *religious minimalists* (support separation of church and state and oppose religious free exercise); and *religious free-marketeers* (support separation of church and state but also support religious free exercise).

We examined public attitudes about prayer in public schools in order to demonstrate the mix of attitudes that the public holds. Let's list some of our major findings.

- A majority of the American public favors prayer in public schools and a constitutional amendment to bring this about.

- Most people are not convinced that it is worth changing the Constitution in order to bring about prayer in public schools.

- The great majority of people would not *require* that school children take part in prayer.

- We can speculate that most supporters of school prayer think of it as if it were a religious free exercise issue rather than an establishment issue, whereas most opponents think of it as an establishment issue.

In order to understand more fully the role of religion in American politics, we examined the views of political and religious elites. Below are some of our major findings.

- The kinds of people in the general public who most support school prayer tend to be somewhat underrepresented in Congress, among PAC contributors to political candidates, and among delegates to political party conventions; thus, support for school prayer is lower among political elites than it is in the general public.

- Religious elites are not unified in terms of either religious or political views, and they are sharply divided on the issue of school prayer.

- Both secular and religious elites are more separationist than the public is on *abstract* establishment issues.

- With the exception of academic elites, the secular elites were not much more separationist than the general public on *concrete* establishment issues.

- While Jewish rabbis gave high support to separation of church and state, Protestant ministers (especially evangelicals) and Catholic priests took the accommodationist position on most concrete establishment issues.

- Although academic elites were the most supportive of religious free exercise and business elites were the least supportive, all elite groups—both religious and secular—gave higher support to religious free exercise than the public did; this suggests that religious free exercise in practice will probably mirror the views of elites more than the general public in most situations.

Overall, we conclude that the American public has a mix of attitudes toward church-state relations. People support separationism more in the abstract than in specific situations, and their level of support for religious free exercise depends to a great extent on the nature of the group involved. To a very great extent, Americans are communitarian: they will support religious freedom for various viewpoints provided that this doesn't conflict substantially with community norms. At the same time, elites are usually more likely than the public is to support separation of church and state, and they are much more likely to support religious free exercise.

In this chapter we have seen that there are differences among people in terms of their views of church-state relations. In the next chapter, we will examine the ways in which differences in the religious attitudes of people are linked to differences in the political views that people hold concerning such matters as political tolerance, racism, social welfare programs, pornography, capital punishment, and other issues.

Important Terms

Religious separationism

Religious accommodationism

Religious communitarianism

Religious libertarianism

Religious minimalists

Religious free-marketeers

Religious nonpreferentialists

Christian preferentialists

Review Questions

1. Describe the patterns of attitudes that the public has toward prayer and other religious observances in the public schools.

2. Sometimes different people might interpret a particular church-state issue in different terms—some might see the issue as an establishment issue and some might see it as a free exercise issue. Using the school prayer issue as an example, what effects does this difference in perception have on public attitudes?

3. In terms of abstract views concerning religious establishment issues, describe each of the following views: separationists, accommodationists, nonpreferentialists, and Christian preferentialists. Which two of these four groups are the biggest in the American public?

4. In terms of concrete views concerning religious establishment issues, describe the kinds of situations in which the public supports an accommodationist position and the kinds of situations in which the public supports a separationist position.

5. In terms of religious free exercise issues, describe the kinds of situations in which the public is likely to take a communitarian view and the kinds of situations in which the public is likely to take a libertarian view. Include in this an explanation of what seems to account for whether the public will allow religious free exercise by a particular group.

6. Describe the public's patterns of tolerance or intolerance toward those who are not religious.

7. In terms of Jelen and Wilcox's typology formed by combining the separationist- accommodationist dimension with the libertarian-communitarian dimension, describe the four types that result: religious nonpreferentialists, Christian preferentialists, religious

minimalists, and religious free-marketeers. In terms of education, religious views, etc., what kinds of people are most typical of each of these four groups?

8. Given that support for school prayer is so high in the general public, why hasn't there been a constitutional amendment to bring this about?

9. If you have not included this in your answer above, indicate what kind of religious group is most likely to be "underrepresented" in Congress (aside from those with no religion) and what effects this has on the chances of passing a constitutional amendment to bring about school prayer.

10. Overall, how do elite *abstract* views on establishment differ from the general public's views? Which secular elites are the most separationist? Which religious elites are the most separationist?

11. Describe the general pattern of elite views on *concrete* establishment issues. Which elites are the most separationist? How do the elites compare to the general public?

12. Describe the patterns of elite views on religious free exercise issues. How do they compare to the public?

Discussion Questions

1. We have seen that the majority favors prayer and other religious observances in the public schools. Are these the kinds of issues in which the majority should prevail or are they the kinds of issues in which it is more important to protect the rights of minorities? Why or why not?

2. We have seen that there is substantial inconsistency between the public's views on abstract establishment issues and their views on more specific, concrete establishment issues. What could be done to reduce this inconsistency so that people's abstract views and concrete views are more in accord with each other?

3. We have seen that political leaders support religious free exercise more than the general public does. Is this a matter in which political leaders should follow the views of the public or should they use their own judgment on this particular type of issue? Why?

4. We have seen that there are divisions among religious elites concerning church-state issues. When the views of religious leaders on church-state matters (such as prayer in public schools or funding for schools run by religious groups) are publicized, which kinds of views are more likely to receive attention?

For Further Reading

Castelli, Jim. 1988. *A Plea for Common Sense: Resolving the Clash between Religion and Politics.* New York: Harper and Row.

This book includes substantial discussion of public attitudes toward church and state and also analyzes the overall church-state issue.

Jelen, Ted G., and Clyde Wilcox. *Public Attitudes Toward Church and State.* Armonk, New York: M.E. Sharpe.

This excellent work, to which we have referred frequently in this chapter, is the best overall treatment of public attitudes on church-state relations.

Wilcox, Clyde, Joseph Ferrara, John O'Donnell, Mary Bendyna, Shaun Geehan, and Rod Taylor. 1992. "Public Attitudes Toward Church-State Issues: Elite-Mass Differences." *Journal of Church and State* 34: 259–277.

This article, based on the Williamsburg Charter Foundation studies, provides further information on elite-mass differences in attitudes toward church-state relations.

Relevant World Wide Websites

Remember to visit our website for updates and additional links at:
http://bsuvc.bsu.edu/~00amcorbett/relpol.htm

The following websites provide information from public opinion surveys, including questions about politics, questions about religion, and some questions about the proper connections between politics and religion:

http://www.soc.qc.edu/QC_Software/GSS.html General Social Survey Resources at Queens College

http://www.gallup.com Gallup Poll Organization

http://www.princeton.edu/~abelson/ Princeton Survey Research Center

http://www.people-press.org Pew Research Center for the People and the Press http://www.irss.unc.edu/data_archive IRSS Public Opinion Poll Question Database

Some examples of organizations that are close to the *accommodationist* view of religion and politics are:
The Christian Coalition http://cc.org/
The American Family Association http://www.afa.net
The Rutherford Institute http://www.rutherford.org/

Some examples of organizations that are close to the *separationist* view of religion and politics are:
Americans United for the Separation of Church and State http://www.au.org/
People for the American Way http://www.pfaw.org/
American Civil Liberties Union http://www.aclu.org/

References

Castelli, Jim. 1988. *A Plea for Common Sense: Resolving the Clash between Religion and Politics*. New York: Harper and Row.

Corbett, Michael. 1980. "Education and Contextual Tolerance: Group-Relatedness and Consistency Reconsidered." *American Politics Quarterly* 8: 345–360.

Corbett, Michael. 1982. *Political Tolerance in America: Freedom and Equality in Public Attitudes*. New York: Longman.

Corbett, Michael. 1991. *American Public Opinion: Trends, Processes, and Patterns*. New York: Longman.

Elifson, Kirk W., and C. Kirk Hadaway. 1985. "Prayer in Public Schools: When Church and State Collide." *Public Opinion Quarterly* 49: 317–329.

Gallup, George, Jr., and Jim Castelli. 1989. *The People's Religion: American Faith in the 90's*. New York: MacMillan.

Green, John C., and James L. Guth. 1989. "The Missing Link: Political Activists and Support for School Prayer." *Public Opinion Quarterly* 53: 41–57.

Guth, James L., John C. Green, Corwin E. Smidt, and Margaret M. Poloma. 1991. "Pulpits and Politics: The Protestant Clergy in the 1988 Presidential Election." Pp. 73–93 in James L. Guth and John C. Green (Eds.), *The Bible and the Ballot Box: Religion and Politics in the 1988 Election*. Boulder, Colorado: Westview Press.

Jelen, Ted G. 1987. "The Effects of Religious Separatism on White Protestants in the 1984 Presidential Election." *Sociological Analysis* 48: 30–45.

Jelen, Ted G. 1993. *The Political World of the Clergy*. New York: Praeger.

Jelen, Ted G., and Clyde Wilcox. 1995. *Public Attitudes Toward Church and State*. Armonk, New York: M.E. Sharpe.

Lawrence, David G. 1976. "Procedural Norms and Tolerance: A Reassessment." *American Political Science Review* 70: 80–100.

Lerner, Robert, Stanley Rothman, and Robert Lichter. 1989. "Christian Religious Elites." *Public Opinion* March/April: 54–58.

Lichter, Robert, Stanley Rothman, and Linda Lichter. 1986. *The Media Elite*. Bethesda, Maryland: Adler and Adler.

McClosky, Herbert. 1964. "Consensus and Ideology in American Politics." *American Political Science Review* 58: 361–382.

McClosky, Herbert, and Alida Brill. 1983. *Dimensions of Tolerance*. New York: Russell Sage Foundation.

Nunn, Clyde Z., Harry J. Crockett, Jr., and J. Allen Williams, Jr. 1978. *Tolerance for Nonconformity*. San Francisco: Jossey-Bass.

The Pew Research Center for The People & The Press. 1996. "The Diminishing Divide . . . American Churches, American Politics." Presented on the World Wide Web at http://www.people-press.org/relgrpt.htm.

Plissner, Martin, and Warren Mitofsky. 1988. "The Making of the Delegates, 1968–1988." *Public Opinion* September/October: 45–47.

Prothro, James W., and Charles M. Grigg. 1960. "Fundamental Principles of Democracy: Bases of Agreement and Disagreement." *Journal of Politics* 22: 276–294.

Quinley, Harold E. 1974. *The Prophetic Clergy: Social Activism among Protestant Ministers*. New York: Wiley.

Reichley, A. James. 1985. *Religion in American Public Life*. Washington, D.C.: Brookings Institution.

Stouffer, Samuel. 1955. *Communism, Conformity, and Civil Liberties*. New York: Doubleday.

Sullivan, John L., James Piereson, and George E. Marcus. 1979. "An Alternative Conceptualization of Political Tolerance: Illusory Increases 1950s-1970s." *American Political Science Review* 73: 781–794.

Tamney, Joseph B., and Stephen D. Johnson. 1987. "Church-State Relations in the Eighties: Public Opinion in Middletown." *Sociological Analysis* 48: 1–16.

Wilcox, Clyde. 1993. "The Dimensionality of Public Attitudes Toward Church-State Establishment Issues." *Journal for the Scientific Study of Religion* 32: 169–176.

Wilcox, Clyde, Joseph Ferrara, John O'Donnell, Mary Bendyna, Shaun Geehan, and Rod Taylor. 1992. "Public Attitudes Toward Church-State Issues: Elite-Mass Differences." *Journal of Church and State* 34: 259–277.

Woodrum, Eric, and Thomas Hoban. 1992. "Support for Prayer in School and Creationism." *Sociological Analysis* 53: 309–321.

CHAPTER 8

Religious Orientations and Political Orientations Among White Americans

Biblical Literalism and Tolerance of Communists

Results from the 1994 National Opinion Research Center General Social Survey indicate that a speech by a Communist would be allowed by:

51% of those who believe that the Bible is "the actual word of God and is to be taken literally, word for word."

76% of those who believe the Bible is "the inspired word of God but not everything in it should be taken literally, word for word."

85% of those who believe the Bible is "an ancient book of fables, legends, history, and moral precepts recorded by men."

Overview

The results above show that the religious beliefs of people can be strongly related to their political beliefs. In this case, people who take the literalist view of the Bible are—as a group—less politically tolerant toward Communists. In the previous chapter, we explored the attitudes of people toward the proper mix of religion and politics. In this chapter, we will demonstrate that the kinds of political views that people hold are connected to their religious views to some extent.

In this chapter, we will look at religious-political links among whites only—the next chapter will be devoted to religious-political links among black Americans. We need to do separate analyses for whites and blacks because of substantial differences between blacks and whites in terms of both religious and political orientations, and the unique ways in which religion and politics interact among black Americans (Hall and Ferree, 1986; Combs and Welch, 1982; Welch and Foster, 1987).

We cannot examine all possible links between political orientations and religious orientations in one chapter. Instead, we will focus on the ways in which certain political orientations are related to religious identifications, biblical literalism, and religious commitment. The major questions that structure the analysis in this chapter are:

- Why is it that the political views of people are often related to their religious views?
- Why aren't the links between religious views and political views even stronger than they are?
- In what ways are religious identifications, biblical literalism, and religious commitment each related to the following political orientations?

    1. Political identifications (political party and ideology) and voting preferences

    2. Economic issues (specifically support for social welfare)

    3. Noneconomic issue areas such as racial and sexual equality, political tolerance, and the social issues (e.g., pornography, abortion, euthanasia, prayer in public schools)

Sources and Limitations of Links Between Religion and Politics
Why Are Religious and Political Orientations Linked?

Let's look at three explanations for religious-political links: the *substantive* explanation, the *compositional* explanation, and the *subcultural* explanation.

Substantive Explanation

The substantive explanation means that certain religious beliefs are translated directly into political beliefs. For example, if a person's religion includes the belief that it is never justified to take the life of another person, then this religious belief might be translated directly into certain political beliefs concerning political issues such as capital punishment, war, and euthanasia.

Compositional Explanation

The compositional explanation concerns the ways in which differences in socio-economic characteristics of religious groups can affect their political views. Socio-economic composition—in terms of such characteristics as education, income, region, and race—can vary from one religious group to another, and this can lead to political differences among different religious groups. For example, Jews are more politically tolerant than Protestants and Catholics. Part of the reason for this might be that Jews have higher levels of education than Protestants and Catholics, and people with higher education tend to be more politically tolerant. To take another example, Presbyterians and Episcopalians are somewhat less supportive of social welfare programs than other Protestants; to some extent, this conservatism on economic matters might be due to the higher-than-average income of Presbyterians and Episcopalians. Thus, the socio-economic composition of religious groups might affect political orientations, and we need to keep this in mind when examining links between religious orientations and political orientations.

Given the compositional explanation, we need to be cautious in interpreting relationships between religious orientations and political orientations: if we find that a religious orientation is related to a political orientation, this does not mean that the religious orientation *causes* the political orientation—although we can speculate about reasons why the religious orientation might affect the political orientation. It is possible that other factors might affect *both* the religious orientation and the political orientation. For example, suppose people who hold a certain religious belief support government programs to help the poor. This does not mean that the religious belief *caused* these people to support government programs to help the poor. It is possible that some other factor affected both their religious beliefs and their attitudes toward the government helping the poor. For example, it might be that people with low incomes tend to hold certain kinds of religious beliefs and certain kinds of beliefs toward governmental programs to help the poor. Thus, in the analysis in this chapter, we will try to make sense of relationships between religious orientations and political orientations, but we need to keep in mind that the existence of a relationship does not mean that the religious orientation *caused* the political orientation, or vice versa.

Subcultural Explanation

The subcultural explanation is based on the idea that members of a particular religious group can share common cultural patterns in addition to their religious beliefs. Such patterns could result from the particular historical circumstances in which a religious group existed at some time. The cultural patterns of a religious group could lead to particular political preferences. For example, during an earlier time in the United States, the Democratic Party recruited many Catholic immigrants due greatly to its appeal to relatively poor immigrants—which ties in with the compositional explanation discussed above. However, this preference for the Democratic Party has persisted among many Catholics even though Catholics are no longer worse off economically than Protestants. Further, Catholics are more liberal than Protestants on certain political issues even when we take levels of income and education into account. Thus, the compositional explanation does not currently explain why Catholics are more liberal than Protestants. Similarly, the high level of political tolerance among Jews could only be partly explained by their higher education level—the high political tolerance of Jews is probably also due to their history as a persecuted minority. Thus, some links between religion and politics among religious groups might not be due to either religious beliefs or compositional differences (e.g., differences in education or income). Such links might be due to subcultural patterns arising out of the historical circumstances of the group.

Why Aren't Religious-Political Links Stronger?

Linkages between political orientations and religious orientations are often weak—and sometimes there is no link between religion and politics where you might expect one. Why aren't the links between political orientations and religious orientations stronger than they are? Let's look at four explanations.

Belief Superficiality

When people hold a belief deeply, it will probably affect the other beliefs they hold. Conversely, when people hold a belief in a shallow, superficial way, this belief is not likely to affect their other beliefs. The more superficial a particular political or religious belief is to a person, the less likely this particular belief is to be related to other political or religious beliefs.

Some religious and political orientations of some people are fairly superficial. One reason is that people sometimes "inherit" religious or political orientations within a particular environment, and orientations attained in this way might not have great depth. As an example, consider any particular denomination. While some people chose that particular denomination because of their religious beliefs, some members of that denomination did not choose it on the basis of religious beliefs. Instead, they chose that denomination because their parents or friends were members of that denomination or for various other reasons that did not concern religious beliefs directly. For these people, we would not necessarily expect their denominational preference to affect other kinds of beliefs they hold.

Similarly, people can hold political orientations superficially. For example, when people are asked to identify themselves as liberals, moderates, or conservatives, over 90 percent will classify themselves. However, these identifications are not much related to views on specific political issues (Levitin and Miller, 1979; Corbett, 1991). Although people classify themselves as liberals, moderates, or conservatives, most people do not have a good understanding of these terms (Luttbeg and Gant, 1985). Consequently, links between such self-classifications and other orientations (political or religious) are often weak.

Compartmentalization of Beliefs

Beliefs might be kept mentally separate from one another—they simply aren't thought of together. People can compartmentalize their religious beliefs so that no linkage is established between them and the political realm. For them, whether consciously or unconsciously, religion exists in one realm and politics exists in a separate realm. Thus, religious beliefs do not affect political beliefs, and vice versa.

Belief Translation Difficulties

If someone holds a religious belief that has implications for political beliefs, there might still be difficulty in "translating" this religious belief into its political implications. There might be ambiguity, or it might be necessary to take circumstances into consideration. Or people might have to weigh the priorities of different religious values: if one religious value leads to one political implication, but another religious value leads to a different political implication, which value should prevail? For example, suppose someone's religious beliefs prohibit taking part in a war. Are there situations in which someone who holds this belief might feel that war is justified? There can also be all kinds of problems in interpretation. As a result, people who share a particular religious orientation might draw different political implications from it, and this results in weaker links between religious and political orientations.

Cross-Pressures on Beliefs

In the United States, many factors influence the political beliefs of people. For many people, religious orientations are simply one influence among a number of factors such as educational background, economic situation, regional subculture, racial subculture, psychological traits, and so on. Some influences might push a person in one political direction, and other influences might push the person a different direction. Thus, the person is "cross-pressured." For some people, religious beliefs are the primary influence on political beliefs; for some, religious beliefs have little or no influence; for others, it depends on the situation.

Political and Religious Orientations Used Here
NORC GSS Surveys

In this chapter we will describe research findings concerning political and religious linkages, and we will demonstrate some linkages using data from the National Opinion Research Center General Social Surveys. Almost every year since 1972, the NORC GSS has surveyed adults in the United States on their opinions concerning various topics including political and religious matters. Here we will combine the 1990–1994 NORC GSS surveys to provide a large data base containing information from 6,244 white survey respondents.

We do not assume that you are familiar with statistical terminology and we won't use statistical jargon here. We will simply note that the statistical relationships we will describe are *statistically significant* at the .05 level or better. This means we can be confident that the relationships found in these NORC GSS samples do apply to the general population in the United States.

Let's briefly look at the political and religious orientations that we will use in demonstrating certain linkages. (See the Appendix for a fuller description of the survey questions.)

Political Orientations

Political Identifications and Voting Preferences

We will examine three identifications and preferences: political party identification, liberalism-conservatism self-classification, and presidential voting preferences for the 1988 and 1992 elections.

Support for Social Welfare

The NORC GSS contains four questions that concern whether the government should redistribute wealth through taxing and spending policies, help poor people, help solve the problems in society, and help people with medical bills. These four questions were combined into a composite measure of support for social welfare which ranges from 0 (lowest support) to 18 (highest support).

Racial and Sexual Equality

We combined three racial equality questions (concerning neighborhood segregation, racial discrimination in selling houses, and laws against inter-racial marriage) into one composite measure of support for racial equality. Respondents' scores range from 0 (they did not support racial equality on any of the three questions) to 3 (support for racial equality on all three questions). Similarly, we used four questions concerning sexual equality (women should run homes while men run the country, should a woman have a job if her husband can support her, willingness to vote for a woman for president, and whether women are emotionally suited for politics). We combined these questions into a composite measure of support for sexual equality which ranges from 0 to 4.

Political Tolerance

We define political tolerance as willingness to allow freedom of expression to others. The NORC GSS contains fifteen questions to measure political tolerance similar to the method used by Samuel Stouffer (1955). The fifteen questions consist of three questions (concerning a public speech, teaching in college, and removing a book from the library) asked about each of five hypothetical persons (a Communist, a militarist, a racist, a homosexual, and a person who is against all churches and religion). The composite measure of political tolerance for each respondent ranges from 0 to 15 depending on how many tolerant responses the person gave.

Social Issues

Social issues concern changes or disruption in traditional values and social patterns. This includes crime-related issues, abortion, sex education in public schools, pornography, homosexuality, religious observances in the schools, euthanasia, and other issues dealing with possible changes in traditional ideas about morality. We will examine religious linkages to such social issues individually. On the matter of abortion, however, there are seven questions in the NORC GSS that each ask about a different situation. We developed a composite measure of support for allowing abortions by adding up the number of situations (out of seven) in which the respondent said an abortion should be allowed.

Religious Orientations
Religious Identifications

The NORC GSS asks people: "What is your religious preference? Is it Protestant, Catholic, Jewish, some other religion, or no religion?" Here we will exclude those who indicated *some other religion* because this category is small (only 3% of white respondents chose this category) and it consists of a mixture of various preferences (Hindu, Muslim, Buddhist, and others).

It is not meaningful to analyze all Protestants as a single group; there are great variations in religious attitudes and political attitudes among Protestants. Thus, we might examine differences among Protestant denominations. However, a detailed comparison of political differences among many specific denominations would be unwieldy. As a result, researchers have developed various methods of grouping Protestant denominations into a fairly small set of categories. Researchers have classified Protestants as either mainline or evangelical (e.g., Kellstedt and Green, 1993; Jelen and Wilcox, 1990), liberal or conservative (e.g., Kiecolt and Nelsen, 1988), mainline or conservative (e.g., Johnson, 1994), fundamentalist versus evangelical versus charismatic/pentecostal versus moderate to liberal (Wilcox et al., 1993), liberal versus moderate versus fundamentalist (Smith, 1990), and so on.

We will classify Protestants as either *mainline* or *evangelical* basically using the classification scheme developed by Ted Jelen and Clyde Wilcox (1990). The evangelical category includes such groups as Southern Baptists, evangelical Methodists, members of the Missouri Synod

Lutheran Church, and Holiness Nazarene. The mainline category includes such groups as United Methodists, Episcopalians, and most Presbyterians.

Thus, using this classification scheme for Protestants, we will compare the political views of five religious identification groups: nones (9.5 percent of the white survey respondents), Jews (2.6 percent), Catholics (28.1 percent), mainline Protestants (26.9 percent), and evangelical Protestants (33.0 percent).

Biblical Literalism

A NORC GSS question asked people which of three statements came closest to their view of the Bible. We are classifying people religiously as:

- *biblical literalist*—if they chose "The Bible is the actual word of God and is to be taken literally, word for word."
- *conservative*—if they chose "The Bible is the inspired word of God, but not everything in it should be taken literally, word for word."
- *liberal*—if they chose "The Bible is an ancient book of fables, legends, history, and moral precepts recorded by men."

Religious Commitment

We will use three questions to indicate the extent to which people are committed to religion in the more traditional sense. These questions concern frequency of attendance at religious services, frequency of praying, and strength of their religious preference. Using these questions, we computed a composite religious commitment measure, and then we categorized people into roughly the highest third in religious commitment, the middle third, and the lowest third.

Political Attitudes and Religious Identifications

We will first examine the ways in which the five religious identifications (nones, Jews, Catholics, mainline Protestants, and evangelical Protestants) are linked to voting choices, political party identifications, and ideological identifications. Then we will look at linkages between these religious identifications and specific political issues.

"Nones"

The category "nones" consists of those who selected the *no religion* response when asked whether they were Protestant, Catholic, Jewish, some other religion, or no religion. However, we cannot assume that everyone in this category is either an atheist or an agnostic; when we look at the answers of the nones to some other questions, we find that some of them say that they believe in God and we find that some of them attend church with some degree of regularity. (Conversely, a small percentage of those who classified themselves as Protestants, Catholics, or Jews indicated that they did not believe in God and that they never attend church.) Thus, it appears that some people selected the *no religion* category even though they did have a religion of some sort—perhaps an unorthodox religion that didn't quite fit into any of the other categories. In order to make this category somewhat more internally consistent, in the analysis for this chapter we have eliminated those nones who attend church at least once a month (3.3 percent of the nones).

Some analysts (e.g., Condran and Tamney, 1985; Tamney et al., 1989) have classified nones into different types in order to explain how or why people become nones; here, however, we will not attempt to analyze different types of nones. Although small, this group has been growing in recent times. In 1957, only 2.7 percent were nones (Condran and Tamney, 1985: 415). In 1972 when the NORC GSS was first done, 5.2 percent of the respondents selected the *no religion* category. In 1994, the percentage had grown to 9.2 percent.

Political Identifications and Voting Behavior of Nones

Of the five religious groupings of white respondents, the nones provided the second-highest level of support for Democratic presidential candidates in 1988 (51 percent for Dukakis) and 1992 (54 percent for Clinton). Table 8.1 shows that nones voted less Democratically than Jews did, but substantially more Democratically than Catholics did. On the other hand, perhaps in line with their religious independence, fully 50 percent of nones are Independents rather than Democrats (32 percent) or Republicans (18 percent). While nones are not strongly committed to the Democratic label, they are more likely than any other of these religious groups to label themselves as liberals (47 percent).

Views of Nones on Political Issues

Table 8.2 shows that nones are the most economically liberal of the five groups. However, differences among the five groups on the support for

TABLE 8.1

Voting Choices, Party Identifications, and Ideological
Identifications by Religious Identifications

	Nones	Jews	Catholics	Mainline Protestants	Evangelical Protestants
	%	%	%	%	%
1988 presidential vote					
Dukakis	51	72	35	25	24
Bush	49	28	65	74	76
1992 presidential vote					
Clinton	54	71	40	37	32
Bush	20	21	39	42	52
Perot	27	8	21	21	16
Political party identification					
Democrat	32	58	36	28	28
Independent	50	25	34	30	34
Republican	18	17	30	42	38
Ideological identification					
liberal	47	46	25	24	18
moderate	32	34	41	36	39
conservative	21	20	34	40	43

social welfare measure are not great. Nones are either the most liberal or the second most liberal (second to Jews) on all other issues in the table. For example, nones are the most politically tolerant, the most supportive of suicide for a terminally ill person, the second most supportive of the Supreme Court's ruling against prayer and religious observances in the public schools, and the second most supportive of allowing abortion.

Why are nones so liberal? We can only speculate on this. Perhaps the lack of commitment to religion or orthodox religion reflects skepticism about anyone claiming to possess absolute truth and this leads to tolerance for diversity. Perhaps nones politically react against those who clothe their political ideas in religious language. Perhaps the somewhat above average education level of nones leads them to liberalism on noneconomic issues.

TABLE 8.2

Views on Political Issues by Religious Identifications

	Nones	Jews	Catholics	Mainline Protestants	Evangelical Protestants
average support for social welfare score	10.0	9.1	9.8	8.9	9.2
average political tolerance score	12.7	12.1	10.7	10.1	8.9
average support for sexual equality score	3.6	3.8	3.5	3.4	3.2
average support for racial equality score	2.4	2.6	2.3	2.2	2.0
average support for abortion score	5.9	6.5	4.3	4.8	4.1
	%	%	%	%	%
percent allowing an abortion for a single woman	74	94	44	51	38
percent supporting Supreme Court's prayer decision	68	86	43	40	30
percent allowing birth control methods for teenagers	79	81	60	56	50
percent opposed to making divorce harder to get	69	73	47	45	39
percent favoring legalizing marijuana	38	36	20	17	20
percent approving suicide by terminally ill person	80	73	62	65	58
percent opposed to capital punishment	24	27	20	17	15
percent favoring a permit to buy a gun	80	97	85	80	75
percent opposed to outlawing pornography	82	84	65	55	49

Some analysts have used the term "secular voter" to refer to those with no religious affiliation and also those who appear to be only nominally religious—those who do not, for example, take part in religious activities such as attending church. This secular group would constitute a much larger group than the nones, depending on just how one defined it. For example, while about 15 percent of the respondents in the NORC survey said that they never attend church, about 38 percent attend only once or twice a year or less. Analysis by Kellstedt and Green (1993) and Kellstedt et al. (1994) indicates that this group is growing and that it is moving solidly into the Democratic coalition. The liberalism of these secular voters in the Democratic Party provides the counterpoint to the conservatism of evangelical Protestants in the Republican Party.

Jews
Jewish Political Identifications and Voting Behavior

For the five religious groups considered, Jews are by far the most Democratic in voting and in political party identifications. In 1988 and 1992, over 70 percent of Jews voted for the Democratic candidate, and 58 percent of Jews are Democrats whereas only 17 percent are Republicans. Despite the strong identification of Jews with the Democratic Party, Menendez (1977: 113) points out that Jews voted Republican in presidential elections from the time of Abraham Lincoln up through Taft. Beginning with Woodrow Wilson in 1912, Jews began to shift votes to the Democratic candidates. This support for the Democratic Party was solidified by Franklin Roosevelt's commitment to liberal values and his resistance to Hitler (Menendez, 1977: 114).

Jewish Views on Political Issues

Jews match the nones in identifying as liberals. Table 8.2 shows that Jews are slightly more conservative than most of the other groups on social welfare issues. However, on all noneconomic issues (sexual equality, racial equality, political tolerance, abortion, pornography, etc.) in the table, Jews are either the most liberal or second-most liberal—with nones being more liberal than Jews on some issues. Thus, Jews are substantially more liberal on noneconomic issues than Catholics, mainline Protestants, and evangelical Protestants.

Obviously, not all Jews are liberal. Sigelman (1991: 201) argues that political differences abound within the Jewish community. For example,

Orthodox Jews are conservative on many political issues; however, only about 10 percent of American Jews are Orthodox (Cohen, 1989; Kosmin and Lachman, 1993). Also, in recent times, there has been a neo-conservative movement among some Jewish intellectuals such as Irving Kristol and Daniel Bell. These neo-conservatives have argued, among other things, that the economic interests of Jews and society are not served well by liberalism and the Democratic Party. While the neo-conservative movement has not attracted large numbers of Jews, the existence of the movement does indicate that some Jewish elites are not as hostile to conservatism as they once were (Lerner et al., 1989: 331).

Thus, on noneconomic issues, Jews are generally more liberal than Protestants or Catholics. This liberalism includes such matters as freedom of expression, racial equality, sexual equality, and the social issues. Various studies (e.g., Nunn et al., 1978; Corbett, 1982) have demonstrated that Jews are more politically tolerant than Protestants and Catholics. However, Sullivan et al. (1982) argue that Jews are not more tolerant of their "least-liked group" than Protestants or Catholics are. Sullivan et al. asked people to identify the group in society they liked the least; then the researchers measured the respondents' political tolerance toward that "least-liked group." It is likely that the great majority of Jews chose a Nazi group as their least-liked group, and it is not surprising that Jews might not have higher than average levels of tolerance when it comes to a Nazi group. However, this kind of least-liked group situation is not adequate to measure the full range of political tolerance. In the NORC GSS surveys, Jews were more tolerant than Protestants or Catholics toward all five hypothetical persons (atheist, Communist, homosexual, militarist, and racist), and this list includes people of the political right and the political left.

Explanations for Jewish Liberalism

At least some of the explanation for Jewish liberalism is due to the historical background of Jews as a persecuted minority. This has led to Jewish support for equality and freedom for minority groups in general. In addition to their historical background, however, Jews also have higher than average levels of education; people with higher education tend to be more liberal on noneconomic issues (Corbett, 1991). For the 1990–1994 NORC surveys, Jews had an average of 15.6 years of school; nones had 13.7 years; Catholics (13.3 years) and mainline Protestants (13.4 years) were similar to each other; and evangelical Protestants had the lowest—12.4 years.

Lerner et al. (1989: 346) reviewed several explanations of greater liberalism among Jews. First, there is the explanation offered by writers such as Fuchs (1956), who says that Jewish liberalism is derived from traditional religion based on universalism, cosmopolitanism, and concern for social justice. Lerner et al. (1989) reject this explanation by citing research (e.g., Rothman and Lichter, 1982) which demonstrates that liberalism is lower among Jews who are more religious.

The second explanation reviewed by Lerner et al. (1989) was formulated by Lipset (1981). This is the status inconsistency explanation. Basically the idea is that, although Jews have upper-class attributes of higher income and education, they have been objects of prejudice and discrimination by the larger society; there is a status inconsistency in the socioeconomic attributes of Jews and their status in society. In order to reduce this strain, Jews want to eliminate prejudice and discrimination in general. Lerner et al. (1989) reject this explanation on the grounds that Jews have continued to be liberal despite the tremendous decrease in anti-Semitism that has occurred in American society.

Lerner et al. (1989) propose a third explanation based on political socialization. Lerner et al. argue that certain kinds of political attitudes have been passed down from one generation to the next. Centuries of marginality, of being on the outside of society, gave rise to certain kinds of political views among Jews. These political views, which basically supported aid for the downtrodden, persisted even after Jews were no longer shut out of the main society.

Catholics

Political Identifications and Voting Behavior of Catholics

Let's look at the results for Catholics in Table 8.1 from three angles. First, contrary to the popular belief—based on past voting patterns—that Catholics are heavily Democratic, these results show that Catholic voters are now volatile in presidential elections. Kosmin and Lachman (1993: 200) state that " . . . the historic and overwhelming support for Democrats has largely disappeared from the nation's Catholic population." Kenski and Lockwood (1991: 186) refer to Catholics as a critical swing vote in presidential elections, and they echo the conclusions of Gallup and Castelli (1987: 191) that no Democrat can be elected president without heavy Catholic support and that neither Democrats nor Republicans can take the Catholic vote for granted. In 1988, 65 percent voted Republican. In 1992, however, Catholics gave approximately equal proportions of their votes to Clinton (40 percent) and Bush (39 percent) and gave 21 percent to Perot. While Catholics still vote more Democratic than Protestants do, they vote substantially less Democratic than nones and Jews do.

Second, in terms of political party identifications, Catholics are only somewhat more Democratic (36 percent) than they are Independent (34 percent) or Republican (30 percent). This is a change from earlier times when Catholics were heavily Democratic. In the 1972 NORC GSS survey, for example, 54 percent of white Catholics were Democrats, 30 percent were Independents, and only 16 percent were Republicans.

Third, in terms of ideological identification, Catholics are in the middle of the five groups. They are more likely to classify themselves as liberal than Protestants are but less likely than nones or Jews are. Catholics are more likely to classify themselves as moderate (41 percent) than any other group is.

Views of Catholics on Political Issues

Turning to specific issues in Table 8.2, we find three patterns. First, as indicated by their average support for social welfare score of 9.8, Catholics are more liberal on economic issues than any of the other groups except nones. Second, Catholics take their most conservative stance on abortion. Catholics are more conservative than any group except evangelical Protestants on abortion issues. Third, the general pattern for Catholics on most other issues is a middle position between the relatively liberal position of nones and Jews on the left and the relatively conservative position of both Protestant groups on the right.

Changes in Catholic Political Loyalties

Traditionally, Catholics have been heavily Democratic and this support reached its peak in 1960 when John F. Kennedy was elected as the first Catholic president. In earlier times, Catholics—especially recent immigrants from Ireland—were attracted to the Democratic Party because of its recruitment efforts among immigrants and because it advocated programs that would help people who were relatively poor. These party identifications were handed down from one generation to the next, even though Catholics and Protestants are roughly equal now in economic terms.

The proportion of Democrats among Catholics has declined over the last twenty years or so and the erosion is continuing (Abramson et al., 1990; Reichley, 1985; Kenski and Lockwood, 1991). This erosion in Democratic strength among Catholics has occurred because of the

changed economic circumstances of Catholics from an earlier time, because of Republican Party attempts to attract Catholics (primarily on the
basis of abortion issues and some other social issues and economic issues), and because of decreasing effectiveness in transmission of party
identification from one generation to the next. Leege (1996) has demonstrated that the increased Republicanism among Catholics comes primarily from young Catholic men who do not attend church regularly. Further, Leege (1996: 15) argues that the issues that concern these young
Catholic men are crime, affirmative action, rights for racial minorities,
immigration, and the use of tax money to benefit such people.

If such trends continue, differences in political behavior between
Protestants—at least mainline Protestants—and Catholics might disap-
pear in the future. When we examine party identifications of under-thirty
respondents, we find that young Catholics are more Republican than
older Catholics; we also find that the differences in party identifications
between young Catholics and mainline Protestants are not as large as the
differences among older Catholics and mainline Protestants.

Mainline Protestants

Political Identifications and Voting Behavior of Mainline Protestants

Table 8.1 shows the traditional Republican leaning of mainline Protestants. In 1988, 74 percent of mainline Protestants voted for Bush—a level
of Republican support matched only by the evangelical Protestants. In
1992, mainline Protestants gave a plurality (42 percent) of their votes to
Bush, a smaller percentage (37 percent) to Clinton, and a substantial minority (21 percent) to Perot. While mainline Protestants are second to
evangelical Protestants in voting for Republican presidential candidates,
they are the most Republican in terms of party identifications (42 percent
Republican, 30 percent Independent, and 28 percent Democrat). Mainline Protestants are also second only to evangelical Protestants in labeling
themselves as conservatives; 40 percent are conservatives, 36 percent are
moderates, and 24 percent are liberals.

Views of Mainline Protestants on Political Issues

In terms of economic issues, mainline Protestants are the most conservative group, and this is one of the main reasons they have supported the
Republican Party for a long time. On most other issues in Table 8.2,
mainline Protestants are the second most conservative group—a bit more

conservative than Catholics and a bit less conservative than evangelical Protestants.

The greater conservatism of Protestants in general might be due to certain concepts such as the idea of the "Protestant work ethic" (work hard, save your money, and get ahead). Part of the conservatism might also have to do with the fact that Protestants as a group have been the majority—rather than a minority—in the United States; thus, some Protestants might not be as sensitive to ideas concerning minorities as the other religious groups are. Another part of the explanation is that Protestants are somewhat different from other groups in terms of socio-economic composition. Two compositional differences are important here. First, Protestants have lower average education levels than nones, Jews, and Catholics—and people with lower education tend to be more conservative on noneconomic issues. Second, Protestants have a higher proportion of their identifiers in the South than other religious groups do; among whites in the NORC GSS surveys, 42 percent of Protestants are from the South, compared with only 20 percent of non-Protestants. This is relevant because the South tends to be more conservative on a wide range of noneconomic political issues (Corbett, 1991).

Weakening of Mainline Protestant Political Loyalties

While mainline Protestants have for a long time been the core of the Republican Party, this situation is changing. Kellstedt et al. (1994) make two points about this. First, mainline Protestants are not as numerous as they were. Over the last few decades mainline Protestant churches have been losing adherents to the evangelical Protestant churches at a fast rate. Thus, at this point, there are fewer mainline Protestants than there are evangelical Protestants. Second, perhaps in reaction against some of the views of the New Christian Right in the Republican Party, mainline Protestants are less Republican than they have been in the past. Arguing that new political party coalitions are in the making, Kellstedt et al. (1994: 322) point out that while Catholics were becoming less Democratic, mainline Protestants were becoming less Republican. Lopatto (1985) compared data for presidential elections from 1960 to 1980 and mapped these trends earlier. However, the further weakening of Republican identifications among mainline Protestants can even be seen in the 1990–1994 combined NORC GSS sample we have been using. The percentages of mainline Protestants identifying as Republicans by year are:

- 47 percent in 1990
- 43 percent in 1991
- 42 percent in 1993
- 38 percent in 1994

As mainline Protestants have become less Republican, they have become more likely to identify themselves as Democrats or Independents. Green and Guth (1991: 219) discuss another factor that could contribute to the weakening of mainline Protestant ties to the Republican Party: mainline Protestant religious leaders have moved to the left and toward the Democratic Party, reviving some of the liberal activism of the Social Gospel era.

Evangelical Protestants

Political Identifications and Voting Behavior of Evangelical Protestants

Table 8.1 shows that evangelical Protestants have become the strongest base of support for Republican presidential candidates. In 1988, 76 percent of evangelical Protestants voted for Bush, and they were the only one of the five religious groups to give a majority of their votes to Bush in 1992. On the other hand, while evangelical Protestants are more likely than mainline Protestants to vote Republican, they are not yet as likely to label themselves as Republicans, perhaps because in the not too distant past many of these evangelicals were voting for Democratic presidential candidates. In terms of ideological identifications, evangelical Protestants have the highest percentage of conservatives (43 percent) and the lowest percentage of liberals (18 percent).

Views of Evangelical Protestants on Political Issues

Table 8.2 shows that evangelical Protestants are more liberal than either mainline Protestants or Jews on the support for social welfare score. Aside from this, however, evangelical Protestants are the most conservative (or tied for most conservative) on all other issues in the table. Research (e.g., Wilcox, 1992) has generally shown evangelicals to be substantially more conservative on social issues than other groups are. Evangelical Protestants are less politically tolerant, less supportive of sexual or racial equality, more opposed to abortion, more supportive of making divorces harder to obtain, more opposed to gun permits, more opposed to pornography, and so on. The conservatism of evangelical Protestants over a wide range of noneconomic issues has been demonstrated by many studies; for example, Guth et al. (1995) found that evangelicals were less supportive of protecting the environment.

Changes in Political Loyalties Among Evangelical Protestants

Evangelical Protestants, especially in the South, voted Democratic until relatively recent times. The loosening of the connection between evangelical Protestants probably began in 1960 when a Catholic, John F. Kennedy, was the Democratic nominee for president. As the Democratic Party became more associated with racial equality in the middle and late 1960s, some southern Democrats split off from the party and began voting for Republicans. Further, during the social turmoil of the 1960s—civil rights demonstrations, antiwar demonstrations, the renewal of the sexual equality movement, urban riots, the murders of John Kennedy, Robert Kennedy, and Martin Luther King, Jr.—the emphasis switched from economic issues to social issues. While economic issues are more salient for mainline Protestants, the social issues continue to be the focus of evangelical Protestants (Kellstedt and Green, 1993: 63). The conservatism of the Republican Party on social issues (e.g., abortion, prayer in schools, gay rights, pornography, euthanasia) was more in line with the traditional views of evangelical Protestants on such matters.

Still, the migration of evangelical Protestants from Democratic voting to Republican voting took time and it was temporarily interrupted by the strong support given to a Democratic southern evangelical, Jimmy Carter, in 1976. Kellstedt et al. (1994: 311) concluded that the really abrupt change occurred in the 1984 presidential election when evangelical Protestants voted overwhelmingly for Ronald Reagan; by the 1992 election evangelical Protestants were a core voting bloc within the Republican Party. Several analysts (e.g., Wilcox, 1989; Smidt and Kellstedt, 1992) have also noted another change: evangelical Protestants have historically been less likely to vote than mainline Protestants, but voting turnout is increasing steadily as evangelical Protestants have become more active in the political process in other ways. This increase in political activity—in addition to their increase in number of adherents in the population—further increases the power of evangelical Protestants within the Republican Party.

Biblical Literalism and Political Orientations
Biblical Literalism, Political Identifications, and Voting

We classified people as *biblical literalists* if they take a literal view of the Bible, *conservatives* if they believe the Bible was inspired by God but is not literally true word for word, and *liberals* if they view the Bible as a human product. This biblical literalism question has been used as a measure of religious fundamentalism (e.g., Tamney et al., 1989) and as an indicator of religious belief or religious orthodoxy dimensions (e.g., Jelen, 1991; Kellstedt and Smidt, 1993; Guth and Green, 1989). Following Kellstedt and Smidt (1993), we are using biblical literalism as one important indicator of doctrinal beliefs, but this is a simplification of some complex conceptual and measurement issues related to doctrinal beliefs. In the 1990–1994 NORC GSS pooled data file, we have the following distribution:

- 30 percent are biblical literalists
- 54 percent are conservatives
- 16 percent are liberals

The majority (53 percent) of literalists are evangelical Protestants and another 26 percent are mainline Protestants, but 19 percent are Catholic. A majority of mainline Protestants are conservatives (59 percent), while 28 percent are literalists and only 12 percent are liberals. Almost half (48 percent) of evangelical Protestants are literalists, 45 percent are conservatives, and only 8 percent are liberals. More than two thirds of Catholics are conservative, with the remaining third split between literalists (19 percent) and liberals (13 percent). Jews are split between the conservative (44 percent) and liberal (48 percent) groups. Among nones, 56 percent are liberal, 36 percent are conservative, and 8 percent are literalists. Some of these results indicate slack in the way people answer questions about their religious views—considering that 8 percent of those who selected the *no religion* category (even after excluding those who attend church at least once a month) take a literalist view of the Bible while 8 percent of evangelical Protestants take the liberal view that the Bible is just the creation of humans.

Table 8.3 shows that biblical literalists were the most Republican and biblical liberals were the least Republican in voting in both 1988 and 1992 presidential elections. However, there is not any substantial difference be-

TABLE 8.3

Voting Choices, Party Identifications, and
Ideological Identifications by Views of the Bible

	Biblical Literalists	Biblical Conservatives	Biblical Liberals
	%	%	%
1988 presidential vote			
Dukakis	26	29	44
Bush	74	71	56
1992 presidential vote			
Clinton	35	36	55
Bush	51	43	23
Perot	15	21	22
Political party identification			
Democrat	32	29	36
Independent	34	34	40
Republican	34	37	24
Ideological identification			
liberal	17	26	42
moderate	40	39	31
conservative	43	36	26

tween the literalist group and the conservative group. The most striking pattern here is that biblical liberals are so much more likely to vote Democratic. With regard to political party identifications, we see that biblical liberals are the most Democratic followed by biblical literalists. Although biblical literalists are the most likely group to vote Republican, they are more likely to call themselves Democrats than biblical conservatives are. In terms of political party identifications, biblical liberals are most likely to be political liberals, biblical literalists are (by a narrow margin) more likely to call themselves political conservatives, and biblical conservatives are (by a narrow margin) more likely to call themselves political moderates.

The patterns in Table 8.3 are not strong: biblical literalism does not help much in explaining presidential voting and political party identifications. However, the connection between biblical literalism and these political orientations is actually stronger than it first appears. One problem that muddies the relationship is that we are not distinguishing among the different religious identification groups (nones, Jews, Catholics, mainline Protestants, evangelical Protestants). By lumping all these groups together, we might cover up some patterns that exist. Another problem is that we have not taken account of demographic variables (education, region, etc.) that are related to both biblical literalism and political orientations and might serve to hide patterns that actually exist. Kellstedt and Smidt (1993) do an extensive analysis of the relationship between biblical literalism and these political orientations (plus views on abortion) within the Catholic group, the mainline Protestant group, and the evangelical Protestant group while statistically controlling for the effects of education, age, gender, and region. They find that view of the Bible is an important predictor of presidential voting among Protestants, but not among Catholics. Further, view of the Bible was strongly related to views about abortion. Overall, patterns between biblical literalism and political orientations were much stronger among evangelical Protestants than the other groups.

In addition to the results in tables in this chapter, we have also performed all the analysis while controlling for education level. In general, this has not produced any dramatic results and we have not complicated the discussion by reporting these results. However, there is a general pattern when we control for the effects of education: *overall, relationships among religious variables and political variables are stronger among those with greater education.* In this particular situation, education level affects the results for biblical literalists substantially but does not seem to have a great effect on the results for biblical conservatives and liberals. That is, the higher the education level of biblical literalists, the more different they are from biblical conservatives and liberals. For example, consider the following:

- Among those with twelve years of school or less, 28 percent of biblical literalists are Republican.
- Among those with more than twelve years of school, 50 percent of biblical literalists are Republican.

Thus, while biblical literalism does not at first seem to be a strong predictor of political identifications, it is more important when we take other factors into consideration as well.

Biblical Literalism and Political Issues

When we turn to political issues, there are clear patterns. Table 8.4 shows that biblical literalists are more liberal on economic issues than biblical conservatives and liberals. This is in line with some other studies that have shown that biblical literalists are more likely to support economic restructuring (e.g.,Tamney et al., 1989). However, aside from economic liberalism, the political conservatism of biblical literalists on noneconomic issues is very clear. Biblical literalists are substantially less politically tolerant. As an aside, we note that Nunn et al. (1978) found that political tolerance was lower among those who were most certain that the devil exists. Biblical literalists are also less supportive of sexual and racial equality, more opposed to abortion, more opposed to the Supreme Court's prayer decision, more opposed to suicide by a terminally ill person, and more opposed to pornography. For example, while the great majority (76 percent) of biblical liberals and 50 percent of biblical conserva-

TABLE 8.4

Views on Political Issues by Views of the Bible

	Biblical Literalists	Biblical Conservatives	Biblical Liberals
average support for social welfare score	10.2	9.3	9.4
average political tolerance score	7.5	11.0	12.2
average support for sexual equality score	3.0	3.5	3.6
average support for racial equality score	1.9	2.3	2.3
average support for abortion score	3.3	4.7	6.0
	%	%	%
percent allowing an abortion for a single woman	27	50	76
percent supporting Supreme Court's prayer decision	23	45	64
percent allowing birth control methods for teenagers	44	60	77
percent opposed to making divorce harder to get	38	46	65
percent favoring legalizing marijuana	17	21	34
percent approving suicide by terminally ill person	48	68	80
percent opposed to capital punishment	18	17	23
percent favoring a permit to buy a gun	78	80	90
percent opposed to outlawing pornography	39	60	79

tives would allow an abortion for a woman who is single, only 27 percent of biblical literalists would allow an abortion in this situation.

Research by Guth et al. (1995) indicates that biblical literalists are less supportive of protecting the environment. Guth et al. (1995: 367) restate the argument that literalists ". . . take seriously the anthropocentric view of Creation in the Genesis account—that the world was created for humans to use, or even exploit." We might add that it appears—on the basis of everyday observations—that there is a lack of support for protecting the environment among those who believe that the end of the world is coming soon.

The biblical literalists' greater economic liberalism is perhaps explained partly by the fact that their income is lower than that of biblical conservatives and liberals, and their much greater conservatism on social issues is explained partly by the fact that their education levels are lower than the other two groups. In the sample we have been using, 33 percent of the biblical literalists had a family income of $15,000 or less—compared to 18 percent of the conservatives and 19 percent of the liberals. At the other end, only 15 percent of biblical literalists had a family income of at least $50,000 while 29 percent of conservatives and 35 percent of liberals did. In terms of education, biblical literalists averaged 11.7 years, biblical conservatives averaged 13.7 years, and biblical liberals averaged 14.2 years.

Further, biblical literalists are more likely to be from the South than the other groups are; 45 percent of the biblical literalists were from the South, compared to 29 percent of the conservatives and 27 percent of the liberals. The regional subculture of the South tends toward conservatism on noneconomic political issues. Also, biblical literalists are somewhat more likely to be female and to be older; these characteristics can be relevant for political conservatism, especially on such social issues as pornography. What happens when we examine relationships between biblical literalism and political issue stands while controlling for such demographic characteristics? In general, the relationships remain. Such relationships are somewhat stronger in the South but they exist outside the South as well. There is little difference between males and females in terms of relationships between biblical literalism and views on political issues generally. The relationships also do not vary greatly by age category, income category, or education level.

When we say that these demographic characteristics do not greatly affect the relationships between biblical literalism and political conservatism, this does not mean that the overall results are the same regardless of education level, income, etc. Instead, we are saying that the *relationship,* the *pattern* between biblical literalism and political conservatism, is pretty much the same even when we control for the effects of demographic characteristics. The relationship might be more pronounced for certain demographic categories (e.g., southerners, high education respondents, etc.), but the fundamental pattern is still there.

As an example, let's look at the relationship between biblical literalism and political tolerance while controlling for the effects of education. For present purposes, let's just group people into two education levels: those who completed twelve or fewer years and those who completed more than twelve years of school. Figure 8.1 shows that all three religious groups with more than twelve years of school are more politically tolerant than those with less than twelve years of school. For both education lev-

FIGURE 8.1

Political Tolerance by Biblical Literalism by Education Level

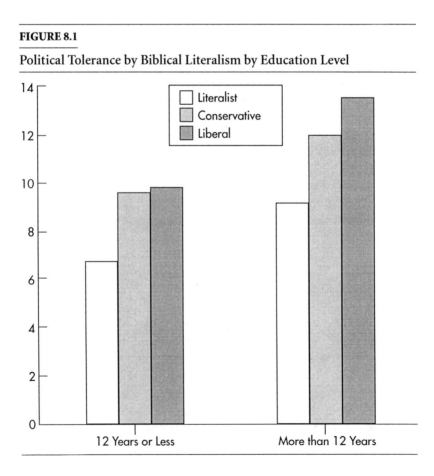

els, however, the relationship between biblical literalism and political tolerance follows the same pattern: biblical literalists are the least tolerant, conservatives are in the middle, and liberals are the most tolerant. As indicated earlier, this pattern and many other relationships are more pronounced among those with higher education.

Let's emphasize a point: the relationships between religious orientations and political orientations are tendencies—they are not ironclad, perfect patterns. For example, we have seen that evangelical Protestants and biblical literalists tend to be conservative on social issues and that people who are evangelical Protestants are very likely to be biblical literalists. We might then make the mistake of overgeneralizing about the political views of evangelical Protestants or biblical literalists. Figure 8.2 presents the distribution of views of people who are

FIGURE 8.2

Evangelical Protestants'/Biblical Literalists' Views on the Supreme Court Ruling on Prayer in Public Schools

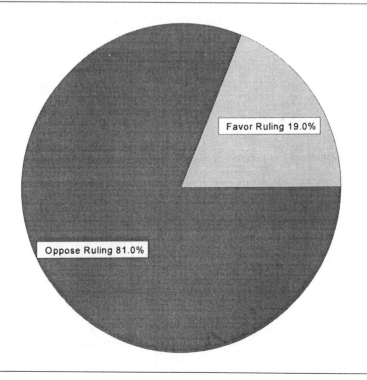

Favor Ruling 19.0%

Oppose Ruling 81.0%

both evangelical Protestants and biblical literalists on an issue that is quite salient to many people of such persuasion—the Supreme Court's ruling on prayer in public schools. As might be expected, these people are very strongly opposed to the court ruling. However, note that 19 percent of these evangelical Protestant/biblical literalist respondents approved of the ruling. Thus, we must be careful not to overgeneralize about the political views of any religious group. While biblical literalists tend to be more conservative on social issues than other groups, we could nevertheless project that there are millions of biblical literalists in this country who take liberal positions on issues such as sexual equality, racial equality, sex education in the public schools, or euthanasia.

Religious Commitment and Political Orientations

The Meaning and Measurement of Religious Commitment

To what extent do people make a commitment to their particular religion? Is the religion important to them? In their classic work, Stark and Glock (1968) identified four dimensions of religious commitment: belief, practice, knowledge, and experience. In practice, scholars doing research in this area have usually used several indicators of religious commitment such as frequency of praying, church attendance, Bible reading, or measures of subjective salience which more directly question respondents about how important religion is to them.

Given that many of the religious-political patterns that we have found are not very dramatic, what might lead to stronger linkages between religion and politics among individuals? Research has shown that certain aspects of religious commitment are important either as predictors of political attitudes or as variables which accentuate relationships between other religious variables (e.g., religious identifications) and political attitudes (Guth and Green, 1993). Wilcox (1987: 274) argues that religious variables ". . . may exert strong influence on the attitudes and behaviors of those for whom religious beliefs are highly *salient*." [emphasis added] The question of salience here means: How important is religion to the person? Guth and Green (1993) suggest that salience might be the core concept on which we should focus our efforts in looking for linkages between religious orientations and political orientations, and they find that those for whom religion is most salient are usually more politically conservative.

Similarly, a number of studies (e.g., Wilcox, 1992; Kellstedt, 1989) have found that relationships between religious variables and political variables are affected by another aspect of religious commitment—frequency of attendance at religious services. Churches can serve as political communities that give members cues about political issues (Wald et al., 1988, 1993; Jelen, 1992; Welch et al., 1993). In order for members to receive cues, of course, they must attend the religious services. Thus, those who attend religious services most often will be more in tune with the political messages flowing from this religious context. Another aspect of religious commitment, devotionalism (as indicated by such things as frequency of praying and Bible reading) has also been shown to affect political attitudes (Leege et al., 1993)—in a politically conservative direction generally.

Given the questions available in the NORC GSS, we measured religious commitment by combining frequency of praying, frequency of attendance at religious services, and strength of religious preference. Based on this composite measure, we then divided the distribution of people roughly into thirds: low religious commitment (31 percent of the sample), medium religious commitment (39 percent), or high religious commitment (30 percent). For present purposes, this measure will do fine; however, some scholars are working on developing better measures of religious commitment (Kellstedt, 1993).

Keep in mind that this measure indicates religious commitment in a very traditional sense. People who hold nontraditional religious beliefs might be very committed to their religious views without traditional indications such as praying or attending religious services.

Since this measure indicates *traditional* religious commitment, it is probably related to biblical literalism. At the same time, if biblical literalism and religious commitment are too closely linked, then we are being redundant in this analysis. Figure 8.3 shows that religious commitment and biblical literalism are related, but they are not related so strongly that we are dealing with the same concept with two different names. For example, among those who are high in religious commitment, 46 percent are biblical literalists but a majority of 51 percent are biblical conservatives.

Two other points make it necessary to analyze biblical literalism and

FIGURE 8.3

Biblical Literalism Group Composition
of Religious Commitment Groups

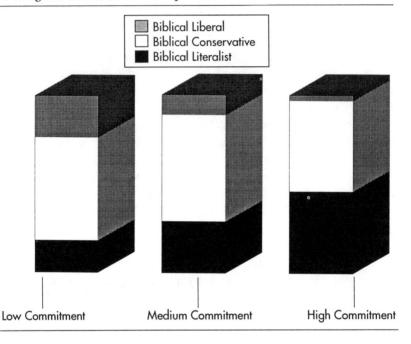

	Biblical Liberal
	Biblical Conservative
	Biblical Literalist

Low Commitment   Medium Commitment   High Commitment

religious commitment separately. First, these two variables are related in different ways to certain other political variables that we are not discussing here. For example, biblical literalists are less likely to vote than other groups are; however, those who have high religious commitment are more likely to vote than those who have lower religious commitment. Second, there are differences in the ways in which biblical literalism and religious commitment are related to demographic characteristics—and this can make a difference in how each is related to political orientations. Biblical literalism is strongly related to income, education, sex, age, and region. While both biblical literalism and religious commitment share a link to age (older people have higher religious commitment) and sex (women have higher religious commitment), religious commitment is not related to income at all and it is not much related to education or region.

Religious Commitment, Political Identifications, and Voting Preferences

As Table 8.5 shows, low and medium religious commitment groups do not differ much in presidential voting, but those with high religious commitment were more likely than others to vote Republican in 1988 and 1992. In fact, Bush received 57 percent of the votes among the high commitment group—compared to only 35 percent and 38 percent among the low and medium commitment groups, respectively. Perot made his strongest showing among those with low religious commitment and Clinton's support was about evenly divided between the low and medium commitment groups. Religious commitment is not much related to political party identifications—the high religious commitment group is the most Republican of the three and the low religious commitment group is the most Independent of the three, but these patterns are not dramatic.

TABLE 8.5

Voting Choices, Party Identifications, and Ideological Identifications by Religious Commitment

	Religious Commitment		
	Low	Medium	High
	%	%	%
1988 presidential vote			
Dukakis	29	33	19
Bush	71	67	81
1992 presidential vote			
Clinton	41	43	29
Bush	35	38	57
Perot	24	19	14
Political party identification			
Democrat	30	33	29
Independent	39	33	30
Republican	31	34	41
Ideological identification			
liberal	30	25	16
moderate	40	40	32
conservative	31	35	52

Religious commitment is somewhat more strongly related to liberalism-conservatism self-identifications. There is not much difference in liberalism-conservatism self-classifications between the low and medium religious commitment groups: in both cases, 40 percent are moderates and the remaining 60 percent split roughly equally between liberals and conservatives. However, the majority (52 percent) of those with high religious commitment are political conservatives while only 16 percent are political liberals. Thus, there is a tendency for those with high religious commitment to think of themselves as politically conservative, to identify themselves as Republicans, and to vote for Republican presidential candidates.

Political Issues by Religious Commitment

Table 8.6 shows that religious commitment is not much related to support for social welfare. The high commitment group scored 8.9 (out of 14 possible) while the other two groups each scored 9.6. Thus, those with

TABLE 8.6

Views on Political Issues by Religious Commitment

| | Religious Commitment | | |
	Low	Medium	High
average support for social welfare score	9.6	9.6	8.9
average political tolerance score	11.1	10.3	8.8
average support for sexual equality score	3.6	3.4	3.2
average support for racial equality score	no significant difference among groups		
average support for abortion score	5.2	4.9	2.8
	%	%	%
percent allowing an abortion for a single woman	59	53	20
percent supporting Supreme Court's prayer decision	51	41	27
percent allowing birth control methods for teenagers	66	61	37
percent opposed to making divorce harder to get	59	44	29
percent favoring legalizing marijuana	24	23	15
percent approving suicide by terminally ill person	75	68	45
percent opposed to capital punishment	13	16	24
percent favoring a permit to buy a gun	no significant difference among groups		
percent opposed to outlawing pornography	72	57	34

higher religious commitment are slightly more conservative on social welfare issues, but there is no important pattern here.

In line with Guth and Green (1993) and Kellstedt (1993), there is a pattern linking religious commitment to political conservatism on social issues. Those with greater religious commitment are less politically tolerant and less supportive of sexual equality; however, religious commitment is not related at all to support for racial equality. The relationship between religious commitment and lower support for sexual equality does not exist among people in the under-thirty age bracket. Further, while this link exists among both males and females, it is somewhat stronger among females than among males. Thus, this link between religious commitment and a lack of support for sexual equality exists primarily among older females. Younger women, regardless of level of religious commitment, are more supportive of sexual equality than older women are. Therefore, as time goes by, this relationship might fade away.

There is a very strong connection between religious commitment and abortion attitudes: the greater the religious commitment, the greater the opposition to allowing abortion. For example, while majorities (59 percent and 53 percent respectively) of those with low religious commitment or medium religious commitment would allow an abortion by a woman who is single, only 20 percent of those with high religious commitment would allow the abortion. Religious commitment is a better predictor of abortion attitudes than either biblical literalism or religious identifications.

Those with higher religious commitment are also more opposed to the Supreme Court prayer ruling, more opposed to birth control devices for teenagers, more supportive of making it more difficult to obtain a divorce, more opposed to suicide by a terminally ill patient, and more opposed to pornography. On the liberal side, however, those with higher religious commitment are more opposed to capital punishment than the other two groups are.

Summary and Conclusions

In this chapter we explored relationships between religious orientations and political orientations among white Americans. We discussed reasons for expecting such relationships (the substantive explanation, the compositional explanation, and the subcultural explanation), and we outlined reasons why such relationships are not stronger than they are (belief superficiality, compartmentalization of beliefs, belief translation difficulties, and cross-pressures on beliefs). Using pooled data from the 1990–1994 NORC GSS surveys, we examined relationships between a series of political variables and three religious variables: religious identifications, biblical literalism, and religious commitment. All three types of religious variables are important predictors of political identifications and attitudes.

In comparing the political orientations of religious identification groups (nones, Jews, Catholics, mainline Protestants, and evangelical Protestants), we found certain patterns:

- Nones and Jews occupy the liberal end of the political continuum.
- Nones and Jews are the most Democratic. Nones are second only to Jews in voting for Democratic presidential candidates. However, in line with their religious independence, nones are more likely to be Independents whereas Jews are the most Democratic group.
- Nones are a bit more liberal than the other groups on economic issues while Jews are about average now, but differences among the five groups on economic issues are not great.
- Nones and Jews are much more liberal than other groups on noneconomic political issues. Both support political tolerance, sexual equality, racial equality, and liberalism on social issues (abortion, school prayer, pornography, euthanasia, and so on).
- In contrast to their past as staunch Democrats, Catholics are now in the middle and can best be thought of as a swing group in elections. Catholics are now split in roughly equal proportions among Democrats, Independents, and Republicans.
- In ideology, a plurality of Catholics are moderates and there are more conservatives than liberals.
- Catholics are still above average in liberalism on economic issues.
- On noneconomic issues, Catholics are moderates—except that Catholics are somewhat more conservative on abortion issues.
- Mainline Protestants and evangelical Protestants occupy the conservative end of the political spectrum.
- Evangelical Protestants have replaced mainline Protestants as the strongest and biggest core of the Republican Party. Both groups

are more likely to identify themselves as Republicans than anything else and both are more likely to identify themselves as conservatives than anything else.

- Mainline Protestants are the most conservative group on economic issues, whereas evangelical Protestants are about average.

- Mainline Protestants tend to be more concerned about economic
issues, whereas evangelical Protestants are more concerned about
the social issues.

- While both groups of Protestants are conservative on noneconomic issues, evangelical Protestants are the most conservative—
especially on social issues such as abortion, school prayer, pornography, and euthanasia.

Turning to biblical literalism, we have seen that there are certain patterns between the political views of people and how they interpret the
Bible.

- Biblical literalists were the most Republican and biblical liberals
were the most Democratic in presidential voting in both 1988 and
1992. Biblical liberals are also the most likely to be Democrats,
followed by biblical literalists.

- There is also a weak pattern for political self-classification as liberal, moderate, or conservative to correspond with the biblical
liberal, conservative, and literalist categories respectively.

- While biblical literalism does not at first appear to be strongly related to political identifications, it is more important when we
control for other factors such as education.

- Biblical literalists are somewhat more liberal on economic issues
than the other two groups are.

- On noneconomic issues, biblical literalists are the most politically
conservative, religious conservatives are in the middle, and religious liberals are the most politically liberal. Thus, biblical literalists are less politically tolerant, less supportive of sexual or racial
equality, more opposed to abortion, more opposed to pornography, and so on.

- While the compositional explanation (especially the lower average education and income levels and higher probability of resid-
ing in the South) helps to explain political conservatism among

biblical literalists, it does not completely explain their greater conservatism.

We also found that the political orientations of people were related to their levels of religious commitment.

- Those with high religious commitment were more likely to vote Republican in 1988 and 1992.
- Religious commitment is not much related to political party identification, but high religious commitment is somewhat associated with Republican identification.
- Those who are high in religious commitment are more likely to call themselves conservatives.
- Religious commitment is not much related to social welfare issues.
- For noneconomic issues (especially the social issues), those who have high religious commitment are the most conservative politically, those who have medium religious commitment are in the middle, and those who have low religious commitment are the most politically liberal.

Overall, there are some definite patterns between religious orientations and political orientation among white Americans. These patterns are strongest for the noneconomic political issue areas (political tolerance, racial and sexual equality, and the social issues). For such issues, we can come to an overall conclusion: political conservatism and religious conservatism often go hand in hand. Such issues have become more salient to the general public than economic issues since the late 1960s, and these are the types of issues (especially the social issues) which might tie in more directly with specific religious beliefs. It appears that religious orientations will remain important factors in influencing political behavior and attitudes concerning noneconomic political issues. At the same time, we have not seen a corresponding connection between religious liberalism and political liberalism on economic issues such as governmental assistance to the poor.

In the next chapter, we will see that religion and politics have been very much intertwined among black Americans, especially since the civil rights movement. However, the role of religion in politics among black Americans has been different than it has been for white Americans.

Important Terms

Socio-economic composition of groups
Cross-pressures
Social issues

Social welfare issues
Religious commitment
Status inconsistency

Review Questions

1. What are the three basic explanations of why the religious orientations of people can be related to their political orientations?
2. What are the four major reasons why the links between religious orientations and political orientations are not stronger than they are?
3. Why are Jews more likely than Protestants to be Democrats?
4. Why have Jews traditionally been more liberal than Protestants or Catholics?
5. Describe the political identifications and voting preferences of the nones—the basically atheist or agnostic group.
6. In terms of stands on political issues, describe the major patterns of differences and similarities among mainline Protestants, evangelical Protestants, Catholics, Jews, and nones.
7. In terms of socio-economic characteristics, what kinds of people are generally more likely to be biblical literalists?
8. How is biblical literalism related to political party preference, liberalism-conservatism self-identification, and voting preference?
9. Describe the major pattern of relationships that exist between biblical literalism and the noneconomic political issue areas (political tolerance, racial equality, etc.).
10. To what extent are the relationships between biblical literalism and stands on noneconomic political issues due to the compositional explanation?
11. Describe the links between religious commitment and political party preference, liberalism-conservatism identification, and voting preference.
12. Describe the major pattern of relationships between religious commitment and the noneconomic political issue areas. To what extent is this pattern due to compositional effects?

Discussion Questions

1. Why is it that the religious attitudes of Americans are not more strongly related to their attitudes concerning social welfare issues?

2. Imagine a society in which there are two religious groups and two political groups. Suppose that you could predict what political group a person was in simply by knowing which religious group that person was in. Would this strong link between religious orientation and political orientation be helpful or harmful for the operation of a democracy? Why or why not?

3. In this chapter, we have viewed religious attitudes as an influence on political attitudes. Can the process work in the other direction? Can the political attitudes that people hold influence the kinds of religious views they adopt?

4. Can you think of any situations in which two people who hold the same religious orientations have very different views on political matters? How can the same religious belief lead to different political beliefs?

For Further Reading

Fowler, Robert Booth. (1985) *Religion and Politics in America*. Metuchen, New Jersey: American Theological Library Association.

Chapter 3 provides a general discussion of voting behavior of religious groups and puts this into historical context.

Guth, James L., and John C. Green (Eds.). 1991. *The Bible and the Ballot Box: Religion and Politics in the 1988 Election*. Boulder, Colorado: Westview Press.

Part 4 *(Religion and the Electorate in 1988)* in this excellent volume is especially relevant for relating religious attitudes to voting behavior.

Jelen, Ted G. 1989. *Religion and Political Behavior in the United States*. New York: Praeger.

This edited volume contains a number of excellent articles linking religious attitudes to political attitudes. Part 2 *(Religion and Politics Among the Mass Public)* is especially relevant here.

Kosmin, Barry A., and Seymour P. Lachman. 1993. *One Nation Under God: Religion in Contemporary America*. New York: Harmony Books.

Chapter 5 ("The Politics of Religion and the Religion of Politics") of this book—which is based on a tremendously large sample of Americans—discusses linkages between religious orientations and political orientations.

Leege, David C., and Lyman A. Kellstedt (Eds.). 1993. *Rediscovering the Religious Factor in American Politics.* Armonk, New York: M.E. Sharpe. This is an excellent collection of articles written especially for the book by eminent scholars of religion and politics.

Relevant World Wide Websites

Remember to visit our website for updates and additional links at:
http://bsuvc.bsu.edu/~00amcorbett/relpol.htm

The website for the Religion and Politics section of the American Political Science Association is
http://www.gac.edu/Academics/poli-sci/relpol/r&p.html

The public opinion websites listed in the previous chapter are also relevant here. These websites provide information public opinion surveys, including questions about politics, questions about religion, and some questions about proper connections between politics and religion. You can use such information to explore relationships between political and religious attitudes further.

http://www.soc.qc.edu/QC_Software/GSS.html General Social Survey Resources at Queens College
http://www.gallup.com Gallup Poll Organization
http://www.princeton.edu/~abelson/ Princeton Survey Research Center
http://www.people-press.org Pew Research Center for the People and the Press
http://www.irss.unc.edu/data_archive IRSS Public Opinion Poll Question Database

References

Abramson, Paul R., John H. Aldrich, and David W. Rohde. 1990. *Change and Continuity in the 1988 Elections.* Washington, D.C.: Congressional Quarterly.

Cohen, Steven M. 1989. *The Dimensions of American Jewish Liberalism.* New York: American Jewish Committee.

Combs, Michael, and Susan Welch. 1982. "Blacks, Whites, and Attitudes Toward Abortion." *Public Opinion Quarterly* 46: 510–520.

Condran, John G., and Joseph B. Tamney. 1985. "Religious 'Nones': 1957 to 1982."

Sociological Analysis 46: 415–423.

Corbett, Michael. 1982. *Political Tolerance in America: Freedom and Equality in Public Attitudes.* New York: Longman.

Corbett, Michael. 1991. *American Public Opinion: Trends, Processes, and Patterns.* New York: Longman.

Fuchs, Lawrence H. 1956. *The Political Behavior of American Jews.* New York: Free Press.

Gallup, George, Jr., and Jim Castelli. 1987. *The American Catholic People.* New York: Doubleday.

Green, John C., and James l. Guth. 1991. "The Bible and the Ballot Box: The Shape of Things to Come." Pp. 207–225 in James L. Guth and John C. Green (Eds.), *The Bible and the Ballot Box: Religion and Politics in the 1988 Election.* Boulder, Colorado: Westview Press.

Guth, James L., and John C. Green. 1989. "God and the GOP: Religion among Republican Activists." Pp. 223–241 in Ted G. Jelen (Ed.), *Religion and Political Behavior in the United States.* New York: Praeger.

Guth, James L., and John C. Green. 1993. "Salience: The Core Concept?" Pp. 155–174 in David C. Leege and Lyman A. Kellstedt (Eds.), *Rediscovering the Religious Factor in American Politics.* Armonk, New York: M.E. Sharpe.

Guth, James L., John C. Green, Lyman A. Kellstedt, and Corwin E. Smidt. 1995. "Faith and the Environment: Religious Beliefs and Attitudes on Environmental Policy." *American Journal of Political Science* 39: 364–382.

Hall, Elaine J., and Myra Marx Ferree. 1986. "Race Differences in Abortion Attitudes." *Public Opinion Quarterly* 50: 193–207.

Jelen, Ted G. 1991. *The Political Mobilization of Religious Beliefs.* New York: Praeger.

Jelen, Ted G. 1992. "Political Christianity: A Contextual Analysis." *American Journal of Political Science* 36: 692–714.

Jelen, Ted G., and Clyde Wilcox. 1990. "Denominational Preference and the Dimensions of Political Tolerance." *Sociological Analysis* 51: 69–81.

Johnson, Stephen D. 1994. "What Relates to Vote for Three Religious Categories?" *Sociology of Religion* 55: 263–276.

Kellstedt, Lyman. 1989. "Evangelicals and Political Realignment." Pp. 99–117 in Corwin E. Smidt (Ed.), *Contemporary Evangelical Political Involvement.* Lanham, Maryland: University Press of America.

Kellstedt, Lyman. 1993. "Religion, the Neglected Variable: Agenda for Future Research on Religion and Political Behavior." Pp. 273–303 in David C. Leege and Lyman A. Kellstedt (Eds.), *Rediscovering the Religious Factor in American Politics.* Armonk, New York: M.E. Sharpe.

Kellstedt, Lyman, and John C. Green. 1993. "Knowing God's Many People: Denominational Preference and Political Behavior." Pp. 53–71 in David C. Leege and Lyman A. Kellstedt (Eds.), *Rediscovering the Religious Factor in American Politics.* Armonk, New York: M.E. Sharpe.

Kellstedt, Lyman, and Corwin Smidt. 1993. "Doctrinal Beliefs and Political Behavior: Views of the Bible." Pp. 177–198 in David C. Leege and Lyman A. Kellstedt (Eds.), *Rediscovering the Religious Factor in American Politics.* Armonk, New York: M.E. Sharpe.

Kellstedt, Lyman A., John C. Green, James L. Guth, and Corwin E. Smidt. 1994. "Religious Voting Blocs in the 1992 Election: The Year of the Evangelical?" *Sociology of Religion* 55: 307–326.

Kenski, Henry C., and William Lockwood. 1991. "Catholic Voting Behavior in 1988:

A Critical Swing Vote." Pp. 173–187 in James L. Guth and John C. Green (Eds.), *The Bible and the Ballot Box: Religion and Politics in the 1988 Election.* Boulder, Colorado: Westview Press.

Kiecolt, K. Jill, and Hart M. Nelsen. 1988. "The Structuring of Political Attitudes Among Liberal and Conservative Protestants." *Journal for the Scientific Study of Religion* 27: 48–59.

Kosmin, Barry A., and Seymour P. Lachman. 1993. *One Nation Under God: Religion in Contemporary America.* New York: Harmony Books.

Leege, David C. 1996. "The Catholic Vote in '96: Can It Be Found in Church?" *Commonweal* September 27, 1996: 11–18.

Leege, David C., Kenneth D. Wald, and Lyman A. Kellstedt. 1993. "The Public Dimensions of Private Devotionalism." Pp. 139–156 in David C. Leege and Lyman A. Kellstedt (Eds.), *Rediscovering the Religious Factor in American Politics.* Armonk, New York: M.E. Sharpe.

Lerner, Robert, Althea K. Nagai, and Stanley Rothman. 1989. "Marginality and Liberalism Among Jewish Elites." *Public Opinion Quarterly* 53: 330–352.

Levitin, Teresa E., and Warren E. Miller. 1979. "Ideological Interpretations of Presidential Elections." *American Political Science Review* 73: 751–771.

Lipset, Seymour Martin. 1981. *Political Man. Expanded Edition.* Baltimore: Johns Hopkins University Press.

Lopatto, Paul. 1985. *Religion and the Presidential Election.* New York: Praeger.

Luttbeg, Norman R., and Michael M. Gant. 1985. "The Failure of Liberal/ Conservative Ideology as a Cognitive Structure." *Public Opinion Quarterly* 49: 80–93.

Menendez, Albert J. 1977. *Religion at the Polls.* Philadelphia: Westminster.

Nunn, Clyde Z., Harry J. Crockett, Jr., and J. Allen Williams, Jr. 1978. *Tolerance for Nonconformity.* San Francisco: Jossey-Bass.

Reichley, A. James. 1985. *Religion in American Public Life.* Washington, D.C.: Brookings Institution.

Rothman, Stanley, and S. Robert Lichter. 1982. *Roots of Radicalism: Jews, Christians, and the New Left.* New York: Oxford University Press.

Sigelman, Lee. 1991. "Jews and the 1988 Election: More of the Same?" Pp. 188–203 in James L. Guth and John C. Green (Eds.), *The Bible and the Ballot Box: Religion and Politics in the 1988 Election.* Boulder, Colorado: Westview Press.

Smidt, Corwin, and Paul Kellstedt. 1992. "Evangelicals in the Post-Reagan Era: An Analysis of Evangelical Voters in the 1988 Presidential Election." *Journal for the Scientific Study of Religion* 31: 330–338.

Smith, Tom W. 1990. "Classifying Protestant Denominations." *Review of Religious Research* 31: 225–245.

Stark, Rodney, and Charles Y. Glock. 1968. *American Piety: The Nature of Religious Commitment.* Berkeley: University of California Press.

Stouffer, Samuel. 1955. *Communism, Conformity, and Civil Liberties.* New York: Doubleday.

Sullivan, John L., James E. Piereson, and George E. Marcus. 1982. *Political Tolerance and American Democracy.* Chicago: University of Chicago Press.

Tamney, Joseph B., Shawn Powell, and Stephen Johnson. 1989. "Innovation Theory and Religious Nones." *Journal for the Scientific Study of Religion* 28: 216–229.

Tamney, Joseph B., Ronald Burton, and Stephen D. Johnson. 1989. "Fundamentalism and Economic Restructuring." Pp. 67–82 in Ted G. Jelen (Ed.), *Religion and Political Behavior in the United States.* New York: Praeger.

Wald, Kenneth D., Dennis E. Owen, and Samuel S. Hill, Jr. 1988. "Churches as Political Communities." *American Political Science Review* 82: 531–548.

Wald, Kenneth D., Lyman A. Kellstedt, and David C. Leege. 1993. "Church Involvement and Political Behavior." Pp. 121–138 in David C. Leege and Lyman A. Kellstedt (Eds.), *Rediscovering the Religious Factor in American Politics.* Armonk, New York: M.E. Sharpe.

Welch, Michael R., David C. Leege, Kenneth D. Wald, and Lyman A. Kellstedt. 1993. "Are the Sheep Hearing the Shepherds? Cue Perceptions, Congregational Responses, and Political Communication Processes." Pp. 235–254 in David C. Leege and Lyman A. Kellstedt (Eds.), *Rediscovering the Religious Factor in American Politics.* Armonk, New York: M.E. Sharpe.

Welch, Susan, and Lorn Foster. 1987. "Class and Conservatism in the Black Community." *American Politics Quarterly* 15: 445–470.

Wilcox, Clyde. 1987. "Religious Orientations and Political Attitudes: Variations Within the New Christian Right." *American Politics Quarterly* 15: 274–296.

Wilcox, Clyde. 1989. "The New Christian Right and the Mobilization of the Evangelicals." Pp. 139–156 in Ted G. Jelen (Ed.), *Religion and Political Behavior in the United States.* New York: Praeger.

Wilcox, Clyde. 1992. *God's Warriors: The Christian Right in Twentieth-Century America.* Baltimore: Johns Hopkins University Press.

Wilcox, Clyde, Ted G. Jelen, and David C. Leege. 1993. "Religious Group Identifications: Toward a Cognitive Theory of Religious Mobilization." Pp. 72–99 in David C. Leege and Lyman A. Kellstedt (Eds.), *Rediscovering the Religious Factor in American Politics.* Armonk, New York: M.E. Sharpe.

CHAPTER 9

Religion and Politics Among Black Americans

Primarily, the Black Church has a responsibility to be involved in the total liberation of black personhood and to help empower the black community.

—An anonymous black minister quoted in
The Black Church in the African American Experience

Any religion that professes to be concerned with the souls of men and is not concerned with the slums that damn them, the economic conditions that strangle them, and the social conditions that cripple them is a dry-as-dust religion.

—Rev. Martin Luther King, Jr., *Stride Toward Freedom*

Overview

The Black Church and religion have played a unique role among black Americans, a role that was not necessary among most white Americans. The historical background of black Americans—and the crucial fact of slavery—led to a role for black churches and religion that has survived in large part up until the present. The combination of historical experiences and the continuing effects of those experiences today (e.g., lower income and education among black Americans) has led to differences between black Americans and white Americans in terms of religious views, political views, and the ways in which religious views and political views are connected to one another.

In this chapter we will examine the historical development of the Black Church and show how it became the central institution in the black community from its beginnings through the civil rights period and on up through the present. Then we will demonstrate patterns of religious and political differences between black and white Americans. Lastly, we will examine the ways in which religious views are related to political views among black Americans. The major questions that guide our analysis are:

- What does the term "Black Church" mean?

- How did Christianity develop among slaves in the United States and what purposes did it serve for slavemasters and for slaves?

- How did churches become the central institution in the black community and how did they serve as training grounds for political activities?

- What role did the Black Church play in the civil rights movement?

- What role does the Black Church play in politics in the black community today and what factors are decreasing this role?

- What are the major challengers to the traditional Black Church?

- Does religion among black Americans serve as an *inspiration* for political involvement or an *opiate* that undercuts motivation to improve the situation of people?

- What patterns of differences are there between black and white Americans in religious views and political views?

- Among black Americans, how are religious identifications, biblical literalism, and religious commitment related to the political identifications, voting preferences, and views on specific political issues?

Historical Development of the Black Church

In order to understand religion and politics among black Americans, it is crucial to understand the role of the Black Church. We are using the term as Lincoln and Mamiya (1990: 1) have used it: "as a kind of sociological and theological shorthand reference to the pluralism of black Christian churches in the United States."

The Black Church has been the central institution in most black communities. Some scholars (Lincoln and Mamiya, 1990; Roof and McKinney, 1987) estimate that over 80 percent of black Christians are in seven predominantly black denominations: the African Methodist Episcopal Church; the African Methodist Episcopal Zion Church; the Christian Methodist Episcopal Church; the National Baptist Convention, U.S.A., Incorporated; the National Baptist Convention of America, Unincorporated; the Progressive National Baptist Convention; and the Church of God in Christ. Black Christians are primarily Baptists and Methodists. Although there are differences among blacks and among black churches, there is an underlying pattern that describes the development of the Black Church and gives it its unique character.

Let's look at how the Black Church evolved from the time of slavery up through the civil rights movement. In this examination, we will draw heavily from the work of Lincoln and Mamiya's (1990) impressive work, *The Black Church in the African American Experience*.

Black Religion During Slavery

When black people were brought to this country as slaves, they brought their African culture with them. However, there is debate over how much of this culture survived the slave experience and white efforts to convert slaves to Christianity. Whites were at first ambivalent about converting slaves, especially since an English common law tradition held that baptism made slaves free. In reaction, many colonies passed laws that permitted slaves to be converted and baptized without freeing them (Scherer, 1975). By the time of the Civil War, most slaves had been converted to Christianity, primarily by Baptist and Methodist missionaries. However, many whites viewed conversion of slaves to Christianity in terms of an instrumental purpose: to make better slaves. Religion was used as a means to teach slaves to be obedient and docile not only to God but also to their masters in this world (Raboteau, 1978).

While it might appear that this "slave religion" was an entirely negative thing that only served the purposes of the slavemasters, Lincoln and Mamiya (1990) make several points that provide a more positive slant to this religious experience among slaves. First, slaves developed their own type of Christianity that somewhat reflected their African past and the situation in which they found themselves. While whites initiated Christianity among slaves, they did not completely control its development. Slaves ordinarily attended white churches but sat in a separate section. However, they also exercised some freedom in their religious lives and met secretly to develop their own songs, religious rituals, and religious leaders. This underground slave religion was termed the "invisible institution" by Frazier (1963).

Second, Lincoln and Mamiya (1990: 201) point out that religion among black people was the only institutional area that was allowed to develop to any substantial degree. Aside from religion and the family, slaves were not allowed to develop other political, economic, educational, or social institutions. As a result, the Black Church took on many roles that its white counterpart did not. Thus, the Black Church became the central institution in black communities, and over time it became the focus for dealing with social, economic, and political problems in the black community. Lincoln and Mamiya (1990: 8) eloquently state: "The Black Church has no challenger as the cultural womb of the black community." Thus, the role of religion during slavery had lasting effects on the role of the Black Church in later times.

Third, slave religion served a survival function for blacks. There is a debate—to which we will return later in this chapter—about whether black religion focuses too much on otherworldly themes and undercuts efforts to improve the conditions of blacks in this world. This kind of criticism might be applied to Christianity among the slaves—it promised them rewards in the next life but required that they serve their masters in this life. However, Lincoln and Mamiya (1990: 201) and some other scholars (e.g., Wilmore, 1983; Berry and Blassingame, 1982) have argued that in the face of oppressive dehumanization, religion contributed to the survival of slaves by preventing their total dehumanization and by giving them some feeling of self-worth. Further, survival itself became a political act because it kept open the possibility that it would lead to future leaders who would be able to overcome oppression. Lincoln and Mamiya refer to this theme as the *survival tradition*.

Fourth, even during slavery, black religion also developed a *liberation tradition* that persisted and expanded later. Lincoln and Mamiya (1990: 4) emphasize strongly that this emphasis on freedom has persisted in the religion of black Americans from slavery to the present, but freedom has meant different things at different times. During slavery, freedom emphasized liberation from bondage; the three largest slave revolts in American history were led by black ministers (Lincoln and Mamiya, 1990: 203). After emancipation, freedom meant the freedom to be educated, the freedom to be employed, and the freedom to move from one place to another. In the twentieth century, ". . . freedom means social, political, and economic justice" (Lincoln and Mamiya, 1990: 4).

Black Religion from Reconstruction to the Great Urban Migration

After the Civil War, the Civil Rights Act of 1867 allowed black Americans to participate in the political process for about ten years—until the failure of Reconstruction. During that brief time a number of black Americans were elected to public office. Many who were elected were members of the clergy, and many black clergy were active in state and local political activities. The Black Church began to function as a political organization and was so politically influential that political factions attempted to persuade black voters through the church—especially by working through black ministers.

This brief era of public political participation ended after Reconstruction. Lincoln and Mamiya (1990: 205) cite several factors that led to the complete disenfranchisement of black voters in the South: the removal of protection provided by federal troops, unrestrained Ku Klux Klan activities, economic discrimination, restrictive black codes, electoral obstacles such as poll taxes, and the legitimation of Jim Crow segregation by the Supreme Court in the "separate but equal" doctrine in the *Plessy* v. *Ferguson* decision in 1896.

From the end of Reconstruction to the passage of the Voting Rights Act of 1965, the Black Church became the primary arena for black political activity. While blacks were excluded from mainstream politics, they engaged in "surrogate politics" within the church by electing church leaders, selecting pastors, trustees, deacons, and so on. This surrogate politics in the Black Church "became an intensive training ground of political experience with all of the triumphs and disappointments of which the political process is capable" (Lincoln and Mamiya, 1990: 206). Further, the political astuteness that was developed in church politics could be transferred to the public political arena if there was an opportunity.

The church became a place where talented black men could achieve some degree of success and respect. In order to achieve high levels of leadership in the Black Church, the minister had to have great political ability and also have strong bureaucratic and leadership skills. Black ministers were usually the most educated people in the black community and they often served as liaisons between the black community and the dominant white culture. The black clergy who derived their livelihood from the church were not as economically vulnerable as others, and they were expected to take a stand—they were expected to speak out about political and social issues, especially racial discrimination.

Black Religion from the Great Urban Migration to the Civil Rights Period

In the twentieth century, with the decline of family farms in the South, millions of black Americans moved from the black belt in the South to take jobs in urban areas of the industrial North. This led to growth of established churches in northern cities, and it also led to a proliferation of many small *storefront churches*—small churches that were often set up in a rented storefront. However, despite these changes, the Black Church continued to be the central institution in the black community in both the South and the North.

During the early part of the twentieth century, political organization among blacks took a different turn with the development of secular, broad-based civil rights organizations such as the National Association for the Advancement of Colored People (established in 1909) and the Urban League (established in 1911). However, while these political organizations were not religious in nature, they drew their primary support from the Black Church and the black clergy. Thus, while organizations such as the Urban League and the NAACP were separate from the Black Church, they did not diminish the role of the Black Church as the central political institution in the black community.

The Great Depression had a strong impact on black communities, and "the devastating economic conditions which gripped the black communities pushed many black churches into a conservative political stance, and many of the new storefront churches withdrew into a revivalistic sectarianism" (Lincoln and Mamiya, 1990: 209). While much political activity was centered on the church during the Depression, it was also a time when many black clergy emphasized the *otherworldly* theme rather than pushing for action to alleviate the conditions of blacks in this world.

Up until the beginning of the major thrust of the civil rights movement in the 1950s, many black clergy who tried to improve the conditions of blacks did so in a low-key, behind the scenes, nonconfrontational way (Lincoln and Mamiya, 1990: 210), although there were exceptions, such as Adam Clayton Powell's civil rights protests in Harlem. They attempted, for example, to negotiate with white employers for jobs for black workers. The retreat of some black clergy into an otherworldly stance and the relatively low-key approach of many other black clergy led Lincoln and Mamiya (1990: 211) to describe the interwar period as a relatively quietistic time for black church leadership. That changed dramatically with the civil rights period.

Black Religion in the Civil Rights Period

We usually think of the civil rights period as the 1960s, but there were many significant events that occurred during the 1950s. While some important civil rights activities took place even earlier, many scholars mark the 1954 decision of the Supreme Court in *Brown* v. *the Board of Education of Topeka, Kansas* as the major beginning point of the civil rights period. In this famous case, the Supreme Court demolished the "separate but equal" rule of the 1896 *Plessy* v. *Ferguson* case, ruled that racial segregation in public schools was unconstitutional, and ordered that schools desegregate quickly.

Another very important event occurred one day in December, 1955, in Montgomery, Alabama. Rosa Parks, a tired black domestic worker returning home from work, took a seat on a bus in the front section—the "white section." When the bus driver later told her to move to the back of the bus, she refused. For this, Rosa Parks was arrested and put in jail. In response, black leaders in Montgomery—most of whom were ministers—organized the Montgomery bus boycott. Blacks refused to ride the city buses and, after about a year, were successful in desegregating the city's transportation system. This basic scenario was repeated in some other southern cities. Further, this successful boycott provided a model and an inspiration for many civil rights protests (marches, boycotts, sit-ins, freedom rides, etc.) that came later, especially during the early 1960s.

Black churches were the centers for coordinating the boycott activities, and the black clergy involved in this boycott selected a young Baptist minister, Dr. Martin Luther King, Jr. to lead the boycott. King's leadership in this boycott ultimately led to his leadership of the civil rights movement in general. In 1957, King founded the Southern Christian Leadership Conference (SCLC), which became one of the leading civil rights organizations especially during the early and mid-1960s. Lincoln and Mamiya (1990: 211) refer to the SCLC as the political arm of the Black Church. Black churches also provided help for other civil rights organizations such as the Student Nonviolent Coordinating Committee (SNCC) and the Congress of Racial Equality (CORE).

Based on his study of Jesus and Mohandas Gandhi, King advocated nonviolent protest. This included civil disobedience: deliberately breaking laws that were unjust. In the 1940s, sociologist Gunnar Myrdal (1944) had formulated a problem that provided the title of his book: *An American Dilemma: The Negro Problem and Modern Democracy*. Myrdal said that white Americans give strong support to democratic ideals such as equality, but they do not apply these ideals to black Americans. Myrdal predicted that white Americans would resolve this dilemma one way or another—they would either abandon the ideals or they would begin to apply them to blacks. King's strategy was to confront the conscience of American whites—to force whites to see the contradiction between the high ideals that they held on the one hand and the non-application of these ideals to blacks on the other hand. King wanted reconciliation with whites, but it had to be a reconciliation that gave blacks the same rights as whites.

While in jail for participating in protest activities, King (1963) wrote his famous "Letter from Birmingham Jail" that provided the rationale for the civil rights movement and for civil disobedience. In doing so, King distinguished between a *just law* (which people had a moral responsibility to obey) and an *unjust law* (which people had a moral responsibility to disobey). A just law is in accord with moral law or the law of God and an unjust law is not. Laws that legalize racial inequality are unjust, especially when a minority was not allowed to vote or to have any say about the passage of such laws. The civil rights movement openly defied laws that legitimized racial discrimination and segregation—laws that came tumbling down during the middle and latter part of the 1960s as new laws (e.g., the 1964 Civil Rights Act and the 1965 Voting Rights Act) demolished the legal basis for racial discrimination and segregation.

Black and white Americans of many religious persuasions—and secular orientations as well—supported civil rights. However, the Black Church was the core of the civil rights movement (Morris, 1984). Hundreds of black clergy and their congregations supported the efforts for civil rights. Black churches provided meeting places, information centers, and the activists for civil rights demonstrations. From their pulpits, black clergy provided the inspiration and guidance. Let's also note that many whites were involved in the civil rights movement and many of them were ministers as well.

Black churches paid a heavy price for their role in the civil rights movement. White racists opposed to civil rights also understood the importance of black churches in supporting the movement, and several hundred black churches were attacked, bombed, or burned during the civil rights years (Lincoln and Mamiya, 1990: 212)—and there was another rash of destruction of black churches more recently during 1996.

The Black Church in Politics Today

While the role of the Black Church today does not match its pivotal role during the civil rights period, it has continued to be very important in politics and it is still the central institution in the black community. The centrality of the Black Church in politics is demonstrated very well by its role in Jesse Jackson's 1984 and 1988 campaigns for the Democratic nomination for president.

Jesse Jackson was one of the talented black ministers who gained national attention in working with Martin Luther King, Jr. in the civil rights movement. Additionally, Jackson gained recognition for creating Operation Push (People United to Save Humanity), a program that was designed primarily to motivate black teenagers to get an education and succeed economically. In his 1984 campaign, Jackson developed the idea of a *Rainbow Coalition* of different races and groups working together to solve various problems (e.g., racial inequality and poverty).

Black churches and black ministers played a crucial role in Jackson's campaign. Jackson told ABC's *Nightline* program that Mondale had big labor, Reagan had big business, but that he had "Big Church" (cited in Castelli, 1988: 58). Jackson frequently spoke in black churches, obtained support and endorsements from many black ministers, and raised a great deal of money for his campaign from black congregations. In the 1984 campaign, Jackson was more controversial among blacks than he was later; he had many critics among blacks and he was viewed by many as a publicity seeker. However, Hertzke (1991: 12) argues that by 1988 "Jackson was the undisputed leader of black America." In this role, Jackson continued to use black churches and ministers as crucial resources in his 1988 campaign. Although black Americans who went to the polls voted overwhelmingly for Jackson, those who attended church where ministers preached politics and endorsed candidates were more likely to support Jackson and to actually vote in the primaries (Wilcox, 1991: 167).

The continuing importance of the Black Church is indicated by several factors. First, black churches continue to serve as forums for candidates and ministers continue to give endorsements for candidates. Second, while it is becoming less common, some black ministers still hold elected or appointed public offices. However, most elected or appointed black public officials these days are more likely to be from such areas as business, law, or administrative backgrounds. Third, black Americans still give overwhelming endorsement of the role of their churches and ministers in politics. Most black Americans in a study by Hanes (1985) indicated that black churches and black ministers were the major influences in their thinking. Another study done in 1979–1980 found that 82 percent of blacks believed that the church had helped the condition of blacks in America, 12 percent believed the church had made no difference, and 5 percent believed that the church had hurt blacks (Taylor et al., 1987: 129).

At the same time, certain factors are decreasing the cultural unity within the black community. Based loosely on the work of Lincoln and Mamiya (1990: 383–384), let's summarize some of these factors. First, increasing secularization in the black community reduces the influence of religion and the black churches. Second, with the breakdown of segregation and the expansion of opportunities for black Americans, black society is becoming more differentiated and pluralistic, and this reduces cultural unity. The growth of opportunities for blacks has created a more complex, more heterogeneous black community. Third, the role of the minister in the community has been diminished by the growth of competing elites in the black community such as lawyers and other professionals. Black ministers were once the most educated members of their communities, but this is no longer necessarily true. Fourth, the increasing separation of the black community into two primary class divisions (a coping sector and a crisis sector) has reduced cultural unity. The coping sector consists of middle-income working-class people and middle-class people, whereas the crisis sector consists of the working poor and the dependent poor. Fifth, while the Black Church has been the predominant and central institution in terms of both religion and politics within the black community, there are religious-political challenges to the Black Church, and these challenges have no doubt decreased the degree of cultural unity. There has not been complete unity within the Black Church and some blacks have rejected the traditional Black Church completely. Let's examine some challenges to the Black Church.

Religious-Political Challenges to the Black Church

Chidester (1988) argues that three major religious-political strategies were pursued by black Americans to deal with racial inequality: separation, integration, and liberation. We have examined the integration strategy as pursued by Martin Luther King, Jr. and supported by most others in the Black Church. Before looking at the other two options, let's emphasize two points. First, not everyone in the Black Church supported integration; some wanted the church to tend to the religious needs of people and stay out of *thisworldly* affairs. Second, the kind of integration strategy pursued by Martin Luther King, Jr. lost influence in the latter part of the 1960s as more militant leaders such as Stokely Carmichael rejected the nonviolent, moderate approach of King and substituted a more aggressive strategy with the slogan "Black Power."

How much room for challenges is there outside the Black Church? We have viewed the Black Church in terms of Protestants, and they constitute about 82 percent of the black community. About 9 percent of black Americans are Catholic, less than 1 percent are Jewish, about 5 percent have no religion, and about 4 percent are in the *other* category. Thus, there is not much room for challenges from outside the Black Church, but we will look at two that have received substantial attention from either the general public or black religious intellectuals: black liberation theology and Islam.

Black Liberation Theology

The theme of liberation has permeated black Christianity since slaves were converted. However, black liberation theology is a different approach. Whereas the traditional liberation theme was based on traditional Christian theology (which has been developed primarily by whites), black liberation theology is a Christian theology developed systematically from a black perspective. For example, some black liberation theologians argue that God is black—either metaphorically black (e.g., James Cone, 1969) or literally black (e.g., Albert Cleage, Jr., 1968).

There are many different black liberation theologians (e.g., James Cone, Albert Cleage, Jr., James Deotis Roberts) and they do not agree on everything. However, there are several themes on which most black liberation theologians agree. The controlling theme of black liberation theology is the idea that Jesus is the liberator of the poor and oppressed (Corbett, 1997: 225). While this liberation orientation might contain some otherworldly hope and it might have some hope for a future in which oppression and pain no longer exist, the crucial focus of this liberation is *liberation now*, liberation in this world, liberation as sociopolitical and economic justice.

In black liberation theology, God is on the side of the oppressed and opposes oppressors. God wants justice and equality in this world, and black people can help bring this about. Instead of focusing on otherworldly concerns, black theology emphasizes determined, aggressive political action to bring about justice and equality in this world.

The best-known proponent of black liberation theology is James Cone, whose first major work in this area was *Black Theology and Black Power* (1969). Cone argued that religious authority arises out of the experience of oppression and that people come to know Christ through oppression. Because Jesus is the liberator of the oppressed and blacks are the oppressed, then God must be black (metaphorically). Any theology that does not stand for the liberation of the oppressed is simply wrong—or even anti-Christian. Christianity must be viewed and interpreted in terms of the liberation of black people. White people had Christianity all wrong or else they could not have oppressed others. Whites, however, can liberate themselves from their own oppressive structures by joining in the liberation of blacks.

Cone (1969) charged that black churches were corrupted by adoption of the otherworldly orientation of white churches. White missionaries taught blacks to be obedient and compliant in this world and promised them rewards in the other world. His orientation is very much thisworldly, he advocates action by blacks to achieve goals in this life, and (unlike Martin Luther King, Jr.) he does not in principle reject violence as a means to achieve these goals.

There are differences among black liberation theologians on important matters such as the ultimate goal in the relationship between white oppressors and the black oppressed. Some (e.g., Albert Cleage, Jr., 1972) advocate black nationalism—a black nation within the United States. Others (e.g., James Deotis Roberts, 1974) advocate reconciliation between whites and blacks.

How much influence has black liberation theology had among black ministers? It is difficult to answer such a question, but it appears that the Black Church has not changed dramatically as a result of black liberation theology. Lincoln and Mamiya (1990: 179) indicate that black liberation theology has only a limited influence on the ministers in their national survey of black ministers. They asked ministers: "Have you been influenced by any of the authors and thinkers of black liberation theology (e.g., James Cone, Gayraud Wilmore . . .)"? Only about one third of the black ministers indicated any influence from black liberation theology. However, given that younger and more educated black ministers were more likely to say that they had been influenced by black liberation theology, this leaves open the possibility that it might be more influential in the future.

Islam

Based on their sample of more than 100,000 Americans, Kosmin and Lachman (1993: 135) estimate that 1 to 2 percent of the black population are Muslims (followers of the religion of Islam). Overall, Kosmin and Lachman estimate that there are 1.5 million Muslims in the United States and that 40 percent of this group are black Americans.

In general, Islam has attracted black males more than females. In black Christian churches, the majority of the members are female, but the reverse is true for Islam. Islam is a patriarchal religion and this is probably part of its appeal to black males, Kosmin and Lachman (1993: 136) suggest, because it increases their self-respect. Lincoln and Mamiya (1990: 391) suggest that Muslims project a more macho image. At the same time, however, remember that Islam requires people to live a self-disciplined, modest life and avoid evils such as drinking, gambling, and illicit sex. Lincoln and Mamiya also suggest that black males are more involved in Islam because Muslims have worked with black males in prisons and on the streets in order to convert them.

The Nation of Islam—Black Muslims

In terms of the religious-political linkage, the most important strand of Muslim development in the United States is the Nation of Islam group—the Black Muslims. The Nation of Islam was founded in 1933 in Detroit by Wali Fard, who advocated an unusual version of Islam that was often in conflict with traditional Islam. The movement was led by Elijah Muhammad (born Elijah Poole) from 1934 until his death in 1975. Elijah Muhammad taught that Christianity was a slave religion designed to exploit blacks by their white masters. Islam was the true religion for blacks, and blacks should separate themselves from whites rather than integrating with white society—the "white devils."

The Black Muslims advocated a separate nation for blacks within the United States. At the personal level, the group emphasized self-help and self-discipline for blacks. It demanded changes in self-defeating ghetto lifestyles and greater stability in work habits and family life. The Black Muslims prohibited drinking alcohol, gambling, illegal drugs, and sexual license, and required respect for women (within a patriarchal family structure). While these values were in accord with traditional Islam, many of the Nation of Islam teachings were not (e.g., the emphasis on separation from whites).

Malcolm X

The Nation of Islam was small and obscure until Malcolm X became Elijah Muhammad's national representative in the 1950s and established mosques in many major cities. Born Malcolm Little, the son of a Baptist minister who was killed by a white mob, Malcolm later rejected the name Little and took the X as his last name to stand for his missing African name. Malcolm Little became a criminal during his teenage years, and he was in prison when he converted to Islam—Black Muslims have been very active in converting and working with black prisoners. After his conversion, Malcolm X began a program of educating himself in prison. When he was released in 1952, he began working with the Black Muslims and quickly gained prominence in the movement.

By the early 1960s, the Black Muslims had become well known and Malcolm X had become the chief symbol of the group, although Elijah Muhammad was still the leader of the group. It was during this time that the Black Muslims made the term *black power* a household word. Malcolm X continued with the themes of black self-help, self-discipline, integrity, and separation from whites. He wanted black unity, he wanted blacks to have control over their own institutions, and he preferred that blacks have their own separate nation.

Conflict with Elijah Muhammad developed in 1963 when Elijah Muhammad chastised Malcolm X for making the public comment that Kennedy's assassination was the "chickens coming home to roost." In 1964, Malcolm X formed his own organization, Muslim Mosque, Incorporated. Later that year, he traveled to the Islamic holy city of Mecca on a pilgrimage, and he came back from that pilgrimage with a different perspective. The new Malcolm X adopted a much more traditional Islamic view (rather than the modified view that Black Muslims had adopted) and this entailed a softening of his views toward the inherent evilness of whites. While Malcolm X still condemned white racism, he began to emphasize the need to humanize all people. In addition to his religious organization (Muslim Mosque), Malcolm X formed a secular, nonsectarian organization (Organization of Afro-American Unity) that admitted people of any race. However, before he could develop his new views very much, Malcolm X was murdered in 1965 by men who were alleged to be Black Muslims.

The American Muslim Mission

What happened to the Nation of Islam after Malcolm X left? It continued its course until 1975 when Elijah Muhammad died. At that point, the group ultimately went in two directions. The larger part of the group followed Elijah Muhammad's son Wallace (changed to Warith later) Deen Muhammad, who steered his followers away from the Nation of Islam into a new group that was eventually called the American Muslim Mission. This group adopted traditional Islamic beliefs, abandoned the beliefs that were peculiar to Black Muslims, and rejected racial separation and racial hatred. In the American Muslim Mission, a racially integrated organization, there were no black Muslims or white Muslims—just Muslims.

These Muslims who followed Wallace Deen Muhammad are politically different in many ways from the Black Church and the differences are apparent in their weekly newspaper, *The Muslim Journal*. This newspaper advocates conservative ideas such as the free market, self-discipline, and hard work to get ahead; and it endorsed the Republican candidate, George Bush, for president in the 1988 election (Kosmin and Lachman, 1993: 137). Thus, this Muslim group among black Americans represents a substantial departure from the Black Church in both religion and politics.

Minister Louis Farrakhan and the Nation of Islam

Thus, following Malcolm X's departure from the Nation of Islam and his embrace of a more traditional Islamic view, the greater part of the remaining Nation of Islam did the same thing. However, the other part did not, and the Nation of Islam still exists. It is led by Minister Louis Farrakhan, and estimates of the number of people in this group vary from 10,000 (Castelli, 1988) to 20,000 (Lincoln and Mamiya, 1990) to 30,000 (Kosmin and Lachman, 1993). Farrakhan has continued to advocate the views of Elijah Muhammad—including the view of whites as the devil and the idea of racial separation. However, he has probably gained the most public attention for his anti-Semitism—such as his statement that Jews were members of a "gutter religion."

In his 1984 campaign for president, Jesse Jackson came into conflict with American Jews partly because of his reference to New York as "Hymietown" and partly because of his refusal to disassociate himself from Farrakhan. Farrakhan created a very disciplined security organization and he supplied bodyguards for Jesse Jackson during part of the 1984 campaign. While Farrakhan's following is not very large, he has received a great deal of attention, and his potential influence was reflected in his success in organizing the Million Man March in Washington, D.C., in 1995.

Black Religion: Opiate or Inspiration?

What effects do religious orientations have on black political *involvement*? Earlier we looked at the role of the Black Church as the center of political activity in the black community. Despite this role, some have argued that religion serves—as Karl Marx put it—as an *opiate* for black Americans. When religion has an *otherworldly* focus, it emphasizes heaven and eternal life after death; this is sometimes called a "pie-in-the-sky" view of religion. When religion has a *thisworldly* focus, it emphasizes political and social action to improve this world; this is basically the *social gospel orientation.*

Some critics have argued that the otherworldly focus of religion gives black Americans comfort in this life by promising them a better life in the other world, but it undercuts any motivation to undertake political and social actions to improve the situation of blacks in this life. By contrast, some analysts have concluded that religious involvement among black Americans inspires political involvement. Let's label these two conflicting views of religion among blacks as the *opiate view* and the *inspiration view* and examine them briefly.

The Opiate View

One of the best-known statements of the opiate view of the effects of religion among black Americans is by E. Franklin Frazier (1963), although this view has been presented by others more recently (e.g., Adolph Reed, 1986). Frazier argued that the authoritarian control of the church over blacks kept them from developing themselves and kept them from learning democratic processes. In fact, he argued that the Black Church and black religion were responsible for the backwardness of American blacks. The Black Church and black religion kept black Americans subservient, meek, and ignorant. With increasing secularization—especially in urban areas—some blacks were able to escape the influence of the church and take action to improve the situation of blacks. The otherworldly focus of black churches kept blacks from taking political and social action in this world to improve their situation.

The first significant research to test this opiate view was Gary Marx's (1967, 1969) survey of over a thousand black Americans in urban areas. Marx developed a measure of religiosity by combining items concerning religious orthodoxy, attendance at religious services, and the subjective importance of religion. He measured civil rights militancy by asking respondents several questions about their attitudes toward civil rights demonstrations, the pace of civil rights progress, and willing to take part in a civil rights demonstration. His findings showed that blacks who had higher religiosity were less militant in terms of civil rights—and this was true even when controlling for demographic variables (e.g., age, region, education) that might affect the linkage between religiosity and militancy. However, some blacks who had high religiosity were militant, and Marx (1969) analyzed the type of religious orientations within this group; in general, this study supported the idea that an otherworldly reli-

gious orientation inhibited civil rights activism, while a thisworldly religious orientation increased civil rights activism.

Johnson's (1986) thorough review of other major studies that attempted to replicate or re-analyze Marx's study draws two important
conclusions. First, blacks with no religious commitment had the highest
civil activism. Second, high civil activism is also found among blacks who
are members of mainline black churches that have a social gospel orientation. Different black churches have had different views on political involvement by blacks, and several studies have shown substantial differences among black ministers. For example, Johnstone's (1969) study of
fifty-nine black ministers in Detroit classified them as *militants* (organiz-
ers and activists in the civil rights movement), *traditionalists* (those who
wanted the church to focus on the gospel and stay out of politics), and
moderates (who were in between the other two groups). While Johnstone
studied ministers only, the views of these ministers about political involvement can be reflected by entire congregations—either because the
members of the congregation are influenced by the ministers or because
members originally chose the church because they agreed with its orientation. Thus, religious commitment among blacks in a church with an
otherworldly focus might very well inhibit political involvement.

The Inspiration View

The inspiration view sees black churches and religion as providing an inspiration for political involvement among black Americans. Religion is
seen as a resource to spur political involvement. For example, religious
commitment such as church attendance might foster group identity and
black consciousness, and this could motivate black Americans to take
part in political activities that would improve their situation. Church attendance also exposes members of the congregation to the liberation
theme of black ministers. Wilcox and Gomez (1990) argue that black
churches mold black pride and black identification; this comes about
through exposure to sermons by preachers seeking to build black consciousness. It is also possible that religious commitment might enhance
self-esteem, and this in turn can provide the confidence needed for political involvement.

Lincoln and Mamiya's (1990) study of 1,894 black clergy in 1983
showed very high support for political involvement. For example, 91 percent supported protest marches on civil issues and 92 percent said that
churches should express their views on day-to-day social and political

questions. In response to the issue of why blacks don't participate in politics more than they do, Lincoln and Mamiya (1990: 213) argue that blacks are alienated from the political system because of past frustrations. They further argue that black churches actually help to overcome this alienation from electoral politics.

Several studies are relevant to certain ideas involved in the inspiration view, and we will list some major findings here:

1. Blacks with higher religious and church involvement have higher political participation (Wilcox and Gomez, 1990; Harris, 1994; Kellstedt and Noll, 1990; Wilcox, 1991; Peterson, 1992). Figure 9.1 demonstrates this using the 1990–1994 NORC GSS file; in both

FIGURE 9.1

Voting Participation in the 1988 and 1992 Presidential Elections by Level of Religious Commitment: Black Americans Only

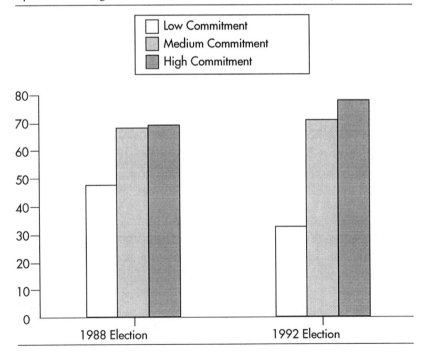

1988 and 1992, black Americans with lower religious commitment were less likely to vote.

2. Some research shows that higher religious involvement leads to higher political interest and political efficacy (Harris, 1994).

3. Wilcox and Gomez (1990) found that blacks (especially older, less-educated blacks) with higher religious involvement were more likely to be satisfied with the status quo—even though blacks with higher religious involvement were more likely to participate in politics. On the one hand, this supports the opiate view, but on the other hand, it supports the inspiration view.

4. Wilcox and Gomez (1990) did not find any connection between religious involvement and attitudes toward collective action.

5. While religious involvement does appear to affect political attitudes and behavior, the impact is not very strong. Wilcox and Gomez (1990: 283) refer to the effects of religious involvement on political attitudes and behavior as "fairly modest."

Overall, the results of these studies lean more toward the inspiration view than toward the opiate view of the role of black religion and churches in fostering political involvement. However, there is also indication that the otherworldly orientation among blacks can undercut motivation to bring about changes in this world that would improve the situation of black Americans.

Race Differences in Religious and Political Attitudes

The historical background of black Americans and the unique role of the Black Church as the center of the black community (including politics) have no doubt had important effects on the ways in which religious and political attitudes are linked to one another among black Americans. Before examining such relationships, however, we want to demonstrate that there are substantial differences in both religious and political attitudes between black Americans and white Americans. These differences are very likely due in large part to the different historical backgrounds of black and white Americans. Because of these religious and political differences, the patterns concerning religious/political linkages among whites that we saw in the previous chapter are not necessarily the same for black

Americans—although some of the patterns are the same. After examining differences between whites and blacks in religious and political views, we will return to the question of how these two types of views are linked to one another among black Americans.

Religious Differences

Table 9.1 (based on the 1990–1994 combined NORC GSS data described in the previous chapter) shows that there are substantial religious differ-

TABLE 9.1

Religious Differences Between Blacks and Whites

	White Respondents	Black Respondents
Religious group identifications		
nones	9%	6%
Jews	3%	<1%
Catholics	28%	10%
mainline Protestants	27%	22%
evangelical Protestants	33%	61%
number of respondents	5,740	802
Biblical literalism groups		
biblical literalists	30%	54%
biblical conservatives	54%	37%
biblical liberals	16%	10%
number of respondents	4,062	594
Religious commitment categories based on white respondents[a]		
low (scores 1–6)	31%	12%
medium (scores 7–12)	39%	47%
high (scores 13–16)	30%	41%
number of respondents	2,813	442

[a]In the previous chapter, white respondents were placed into one of three categories that each represented roughly one third of the white respondents. Each person had a religious commitment score that ranged from 1 to 16. Those with scores 1–6 are in the low category, those with scores of 7–12 are in the middle, and those with scores of 13–16 are in the high category. The results for black respondents in this table show how they would be distributed using this same scoring procedure.

ences between whites and blacks in terms of all three religious variables used in the previous chapter. First, in terms of religious identifications, black are overwhelmingly (83 percent) Protestant, and a majority (61 percent) are evangelical Protestants. Blacks are less likely than whites are to be nones (6 percent), Jews (only .2 percent), or Catholics (10 percent).

Second, a majority (54 percent) of blacks—compared to 30 percent of whites—take the literalist view of the Bible.

Third, blacks score higher on religious commitment than whites do. In the previous chapter, we described a religious commitment score based on frequency of attendance at religious services, frequency of praying, and strength of religious preference. Each person could score from 1 to 16 on this measure of religious commitment. However, for ease of presentation we divided white respondents into three groups that each contained roughly a third of the respondents. Those who had a score of 1 to 6 were in the low commitment category, those with scores of 7 to 12 were in the medium category, and those with scores over 12 were in the high religious commitment category. Using these same categories for blacks, Table 9.1 shows that 41 percent are in the high religious commitment category, 47 percent are in the medium category, and only 12 percent are in the low commitment category. Thus, blacks have higher religious commitment than whites. This is in accord with much research (e.g., Wilcox, 1991; Taylor et al., 1987; Corbett, 1997; Gallup and Castelli, 1989) showing blacks to be highly religious in certain ways: attending religious services, praying, participating in other religious activities, Bible reading, strength of religious preference, becoming members of a church, ranking God as important in their lives, and ranking religion as an important part of life. Alluding to the Gallup International organization surveys on religious beliefs in twenty-three nations, Gallup and Castelli (1989: 122) concluded that "American blacks are, by some measures, the most religious people in the world."

Political Differences
Democratic Identification and Voting Among Black Americans

In accord with past research (e.g., Wilcox, 1991), Table 9.2 demonstrates that there are substantial political differences between black and white Americans. First, blacks vote overwhelmingly Democratic in presidential elections. While George Bush received an unusually high percentage (26 percent) of votes from blacks in his 1988 landslide victory, black voters

TABLE 9.2

Political Differences Between Blacks and Whites

	White Respondents	Black Respondents
1988 presidential voting		
Dukakis	31%	74%
Bush	69%	26%
number of respondents	2,407	281
1992 presidential voting		
Clinton	39%	92%
Bush	41%	5%
Perot	20%	3%
number of respondents	2,614	361
Political party identification		
Democrat	31%	68%
Independent	35%	24%
Republican	34%	7%
number of respondents	6,123	907
Ideological identification		
liberal	25%	36%
moderate	38%	37%
conservative	37%	27%
number of respondents	6,042	867

returned to a more typical pattern in 1992 and gave 92 percent of their votes to Bill Clinton. Before the 1930s, black voters were Republican—because Abraham Lincoln freed the slaves and because the Democratic Party in the South prevented most blacks from voting for a long time after Reconstruction ended. However, because of the appeal of Democratic economic programs to help the poor during the Great Depression, black voters have been overwhelming Democratic since Franklin Roosevelt's New Deal coalition was formed in the 1930s.

The attraction of black voters to the Democratic Party was strengthened by the success of a Democratic president, Lyndon Johnson, in obtaining passage of the 1964 Civil Rights Act—a tremendous victory for outlawing racial discrimination. While many Republicans in Congress supported this legislation, the key point is that the Democratic candidate,

Lyndon Johnson, pushed for the passage of the Civil Rights Act while the Republican candidate, Barry Goldwater, opposed it. Other legislation (e.g., the 1965 Voting Rights Act) passed during the mid-1960s further increased the attraction of blacks to the Democratic Party. Today, black voters are by far the most loyal group of Democratic voters.

Table 9.2 shows that more than two thirds (68 percent) of black Americans identify themselves as Democrats—as compared to 31 percent of whites—and only 7 percent identify with the Republican Party. Further, of the 24 percent that call themselves Independents, 11 percent lean toward the Democratic Party, 10 percent are straight Independents, and 4 percent lean toward the Republican Party.

Political Liberalism and Conservatism Among Black Americans

In terms of ideological identifications, Table 9.2 shows that blacks are more likely than whites to call themselves liberals (36 percent vs. 25 percent) and less likely than whites to call themselves conservatives (27 percent vs. 37 percent). Do these self-classifications mean much in terms of specific political issues? There are substantial patterns of differences between black and white Americans for many specific political issues. Using the political issues discussed in the previous chapter, we can summarize some patterns.

First, blacks are more liberal on economic issues than whites—even when we control for income differences between whites and blacks (Welch and Foster, 1987). Blacks are more supportive of social welfare programs to help the poor and disadvantaged because they are more likely to be poor or to have friends or relatives who need help.

Second, blacks are more supportive of racial equality than whites, but there is no substantial pattern of differences between whites and blacks concerning sexual equality.

Third, blacks are somewhat less politically tolerant than whites. This somewhat lower tolerance among blacks is probably due to their lower education levels and to less exposure to social diversity.

Fourth, blacks are less willing to allow abortion than whites. In the past, the difference between blacks and whites on the abortion issue was larger—to a great extent because of religious differences between whites and blacks—but the difference has been fading (Wilcox, 1990). For the seven abortion questions asked in the NORC GSS, the typical situation is that blacks and whites differ by about 3 to 4 percent. For example, 47 percent of whites versus 44 percent of blacks would allow an abortion for a woman who did not want to have any more children.

Fifth, for the social issues, blacks are more liberal than whites on some issues and more conservative than whites on others. Blacks are more conservative than whites on the Supreme Court's school prayer decision and the euthanasia issue. However, blacks are more liberal than whites on the question of whether divorce should be more difficult to obtain, the pornography issue, gun control laws, and capital punishment. On some issues (e.g., sex education in public schools and the legalization of marijuana) there is no difference between whites and blacks.

Overall, blacks are more politically liberal than whites on many issues, especially economic issues. At the same time, blacks are generally more conservative on religious matters. Kosmin and Lachman (1993: 205) refer to this situation among blacks as "the apparent paradox of theological conservatism and political liberalism." Blacks and whites are also different in terms of attitudes toward church-state relations; blacks are less supportive of the separation of church and state in terms of abstract principles and some concrete applications such as prayer in public schools (Jelen and Wilcox, 1995). In the 1990–1994 NORC GSS data, for example, 71 percent of black respondents said that there should definitely be daily prayers in all public schools—as contrasted with 34 percent of white respondents.

We have compared black and white Americans in terms of both religious views and political views. Now, let's look at the linkages between religion and politics among blacks.

Links Between Religious and Political Attitudes Among Black Americans

We will focus the following discussion around the three religious variables used previously: religious group identification, biblical literalism, and religious commitment.

Religious Group Identification
Lack of Linkages to Political Identifications and Voting

In the following analysis, we will exclude Jews because there were only two black Jews in the 1990–1994 NORC GSS file. Our analysis of the other religious group identification (nones, Catholics, mainline Protestants, and evangelical Protestants) among black Americans showed that these identifications had no impact on voting in either the 1988 or the

1992 presidential elections. Black Americans voted overwhelmingly Democratic regardless of their religious views. Religious identification also had no impact of ideological identification (liberal, moderate, or conservative). In terms of political party identification, the only noteworthy pattern is that a majority (52 percent) of the nones are Independents whereas more than two thirds of other black Americans are Democrats.

Thus, in accord with previous research showing no denominational differences in the connection between religion and politics among blacks (e.g., Wilcox and Gomez, 1990), *our analysis indicates that the religious groups identifications used here have little impact on black Americans in terms of voting, ideological identification, or political party identification.* Kellstedt and Noll (1990: 366) concluded that while religion is associated with increased political activity among blacks, it is race that explains partisanship and voting.

Lack of Impact on Most Political Issues

These religious identifications also have virtually no impact on the views of black Americans on almost all the specific political issues included in the previous analysis. For example, unlike the situation among white Americans, religious identifications do not affect the views of black Americans on sexual equality, social welfare programs, abortion, pornography, euthanasia, and many other issues. There are, however, exceptions here and there. For example, like the situation for whites, the nones among blacks are more politically tolerant and the evangelical Protestants are less politically tolerant than the others. Similarly, as might be expected, the nones are less likely to favor prayer in public schools. Another difference is indicated in the percentages who oppose capital punishment: 52 percent of mainline Protestants, 43 percent of evangelical Protestants, 33 percent of Catholics, and 31 percent of the nones. Overall, these religious group identifications that have so much impact on the political views of whites have only scattered effects on the political views of black Americans.

Biblical Literalism
Links to Political Identifications but Not to Presidential Voting

Biblical literalism had no impact on presidential voting among black voters in either 1988 or 1992. However, it is connected to both political party identification and ideological identification. While only 7 to 8 percent of blacks in any biblical literalism category are Republicans, the distribution of Democratic and Independent identifications varies according to views of the Bible. Biblical literalists are more likely (73 percent) to be Democrats than biblical conservatives (67 percent) or biblical liberals (54 percent). Thus, the more literalist black Americans are in their interpretation of the Bible, the more Democratic they are, and vice versa. On the other hand, biblical literalism is negatively related to a liberal self-identification: 44 percent of biblical liberals identify themselves as political liberals, 36 percent of biblical conservatives are political liberals, and 30 percent of biblical literalists are political liberals.

Thus, biblical literalists are more likely to be Democrats but less likely to be liberals. This seeming paradox can probably be explained this way. Blacks who are more orthodox in the religious views are probably also more orthodox politically in the sense that they stick more closely with the traditional Democratic identification. On the other hand, blacks who are more orthodox religiously are probably more conservative on many social issues and therefore they would be less likely to call themselves liberals. If this is the case, then we would expect that biblical literalism would be linked to views on specific political issues.

Biblical Literalism and Views on Specific Political Issues

Wilcox (1992: 69) concluded that religious variables affect black political views on social issues in much the same way that they affect white political views. Biblical literalism here is related to some political issues among blacks, but it is not related to others. For example, biblical literalism is not related to social welfare issues, sex education, gun control, or capital punishment. On the other hand, the degree of biblical literalism is associated with political conservatism concerning many social issues such as sexual equality, abortion, school prayer, birth control devices for teenagers, euthanasia, and pornography. For social issues such as these, the usual pattern is that biblical literalists are the most politically conservative, biblical conservatives are in the middle, and biblical liberals are the most politically liberal. We have presented results for four social issues in Figure 9.2 to demonstrate the general patterns.

Religious Commitment
Links to Political Identifications and Presidential Voting

Because of the relatively small number of black Americans in the low religious commitment category, our analysis does not show any statistically significant differences in voting behavior among the low, medium, and high religious commitment groups. The only pattern in the results was that those with low religious commitment were less Democratic than the other two groups in their voting in both 1988 and 1992. Similarly, while 73 percent of those in the medium and high religious commitment categories identify with the Democratic Party, only 51 percent of those with low religious commitment are Democrats. Thus, among blacks, religious commitment and loyalty to the Democratic Party often go hand in hand. Similar to the situation with regard to biblical literalism, however, those with higher religious commitment are less likely to label themselves as liberals—probably because they are more conservative on social issues. While 48 percent of those with low religious commitment are liberals, 34 percent of those in the medium category are liberals, and only 28 percent of those in the high religious commitment are liberals.

FIGURE 9.2

Percentages of Each Biblical Literalism Group Taking the
Liberal Position on Four Issues: Black Americans Only

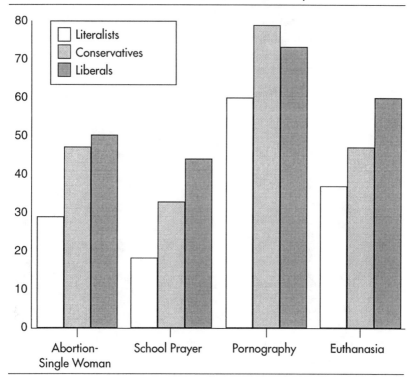

Religious Commitment and Views on Specific Political Issues

Among whites, high religious commitment is associated with political conservatism on many social issues. The same is often true for blacks, but there
is a mixed pattern. Degree of religious commitment is not at all related to
certain issues such as sexual equality, political tolerance, sex education, gun
control, and capital punishment. Other research has demonstrated that,
unlike the situation for whites, religious involvement among blacks is not
associated with less support for gender equality or even of equal protection
of homosexuals (Wilcox, 1991: 163). However, black Americans with
higher religious commitment are more politically conservative on some
social issues such as abortion, prayer in public schools, birth control
devices for teenagers, euthanasia, and pornography. Figure 9.3 demon-

FIGURE 9.3

Percentages of Each Religious Commitment Group Taking a
Liberal Position on Each of Four Issues: Black Americans Only

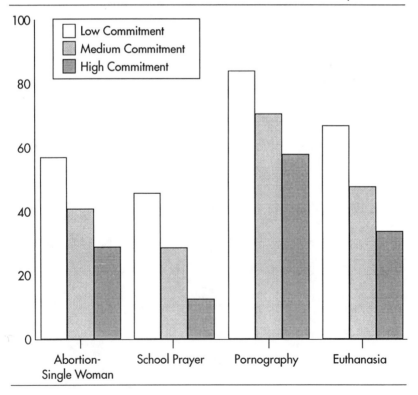

strates some of these patterns. Thus, as indicated by previous research (e.g., Cook and Wilcox, 1990), religious commitment among blacks affects some social issues but not others.

Black Americans with high religious commitment are also less supportive of social welfare programs. The high religious commitment group had an average support for social welfare score of 11.9, the medium group had an average score of 13.1, and the low religious commitment group had an average score of 13.5. This is the same general pattern as for whites, but the difference here is not substantial, and blacks with high religious commitment are much more liberal on economic issues than whites who have high religious commitment.

We have seen that black and white Americans differ in terms of religious orientations, political orientations, and often in terms of the ways in which religious and political orientations are linked together. It is easy to see why black Americans are politically liberal on many issues—especially economic issues. Hundreds of years of slavery and oppression have heaped disadvantages on black Americans that lead to lower income, worse job opportunities, worse living conditions, and continuing prejudice and discrimination against blacks.

Summary and Conclusions

The Black Church and religion among blacks have played a crucial role in religion, politics, and connections between religion and politics among black Americans. During slavery, slaves were converted to Christianity, but they converted Christianity to their own perspective that emphasized *liberation*. Religion and liberation became intertwined in slave religion and this theme has continued, although the meaning of liberation has changed over time. Religion also served a survival function for slaves by preventing their complete dehumanization and by giving them some feeling of self-worth. The Black Church was the only institution that was allowed to develop, and it took on many different roles as a result.

After the Civil War, black Americans were allowed to participate in politics for a while. During this time, the Black Church continued to be the central institution in the black community and it became the center of political activities. After Reconstruction was abandoned, blacks were prevented from taking part in politics, but the church became an arena for *surrogate politics*. By taking part in church politics, black leaders developed skills that could be transferred to the broader political arena when the opportunity came. Black ministers became the leaders of the community and those who were in a position to do so were expected to speak out about political and social issues, especially racial discrimination.

During the 1950s, some of the major events of the coming civil rights movement occurred and the Black Church took on a central role which it maintained throughout the civil rights era of the 1950s and 1960s. Martin Luther King, Jr. pursued a strategy of nonviolent confrontation in order to convince white Americans to extend to blacks the same freedoms they claimed for themselves. Black churches were at the center of the civil rights movement and provided resources and activists. While the Black Church is still at the center of politics in the black community, certain factors are decreasing the cultural unity within the black community.

Black liberation theology is a Christian theology developed systematically from a black perspective. The controlling theme is the idea of Jesus as the liberator of the poor and oppressed. Since blacks are the oppressed and God is on their side, black liberation theologians argue that God is black (either metaphorically or literally). Black liberation theology emphasizes aggressive political and social action in this world to bring about justice and equality.

In terms of the Islamic challenge to the Black Church, the most notable strand of Muslim development is the Nation of Islam group—the Black Muslims—which adopted a modified version of traditional Islamic religion. The Black Muslims emphasized self-help and self-discipline for blacks, rejected whites as the devil, and pushed for a separate black nation within the United States. This group was inconspicuous until Malcolm X took a prominent role in it during the 1950s. In the 1960s, however, Malcolm X left the Nation of Islam and formed his own organizations. Further, after a pilgrimage to Mecca, he changed his religious views toward more traditional Islamic religious views and he softened his stand toward whites and integration.

After the death of Elijah Muhammad in 1975, his son led almost all of the members of the Nation of Islam into a new, racially integrated organization that followed traditional Islam and rejected teachings of the Black Muslims that were not in accord with traditional Islam. The remnants of the Nation of Islam still exist, led by Louis Farrakhan, who still advocates the basic ideas of Elijah Muhammad.

We examined two views on the effects of religion among blacks on their political involvement. The *opiate* view says that the otherworldly view of religion (as opposed to a thisworldly view) leads blacks to focus on heaven and eternal life after death and ignore activities on this earth that could improve the situation of blacks. The *inspiration* view says that religion serves as a resource that helps to motivate blacks to involve themselves in political activities to improve the condition of blacks. Religious involvement among blacks does serve to increase political involvement to some extent, but the otherworldly orientation of some ministers and churches can lead to an acceptance of the status quo.

Differences in historical backgrounds have led to substantial differences between black and white Americans in religious orientations, political orientations, and the kinds of linkages that exist between religious and political orientations. Blacks are overwhelmingly Protestant—mostly evangelical—more likely to be biblical literalists, and have higher religious commitment than whites. Black Americans vote overwhelmingly Democratic and identify themselves as Democrats much more than whites do. Blacks are more likely to be liberals, and this is reflected in many political issues, especially economic issues. However, on some of the social issues (e.g., abortion, prayer in public schools), blacks are more conservative than whites.

Unlike whites, religious group identifications have little impact on the political orientations of blacks except for the greater political conservatism of black evangelical Protestants on some social issues. Among blacks, biblical literalism has no impact on presidential voting. However, biblical literalists are more likely to be Democrats but less likely to call themselves liberals. Similar to the situation among whites, biblical literalism among blacks is linked to political conservatism on many of the social issues. Voting behavior is not linked to religious commitment among blacks, but blacks with high religious commitment are more likely to be Democrats—but less likely to call themselves liberals. Among blacks, religious commitment is not related to many political attitudes, but it is associated with conservatism on certain social issues such as abortion, prayer in public schools, euthanasia, and pornography.

Thus, the Black Church and religion have served to support the black community in terms of both religious and political concerns. The historical experiences of black Americans have led to certain patterns of religious views and certain patterns of political views that are not the same as those among white Americans. Aside from its otherworldly function, religion among black Americans has also served as a continuing source of inspiration for liberation—liberation from slavery, liberation from racial discrimination, liberation from poverty, liberation from all social ills.

Important Terms

Black Church

Survival tradition

Liberation tradition

Invisible institution

Surrogate politics

Just law

Black liberation theology

Black Muslims

Nation of Islam

Opiate view of religion

Inspiration view of religion

Otherworldly focus of religion

Thisworldly focus of religion

Review Questions

1. How did the Black Church become the central institution in the black community?

2. Describe the survival tradition of religion for blacks during slavery.

3. Describe the liberation tradition of religion for blacks during slavery.

4. How did surrogate politics within the Black Church help black leaders develop?

5. Describe the role of the Black Church in the civil rights movement.

6. Describe the civil rights views of Martin Luther King, Jr. and explain how these views related to his religious views.

7. How did Jesse Jackson use black churches in his 1984 and 1988 campaigns?

8. What factors are decreasing the cultural unity within the black community and thus reducing the role of black churches?

9. What is black liberation theology and how is it different from traditional Christianity in terms of religious and political orientations?

10. What kinds of views are held by the Black Muslims—the members of the Nation of Islam?

11. How did the views of Malcolm X change over time?

12. What happened to the Nation of Islam when Elijah Muhammad

died in 1975? Describe the religious and political views of the two groups that emerged.

13. Compare and contrast the opiate view of religion and the inspiration view of religion. Which view is supported more by studies?

14. What are some of the major ways in which black and white Americans are different in terms of religious orientations?

15. What are some of the major ways in which black and white Americans are different in terms of political orientations?

16. Why is it that religious group identifications are not much related to voting behavior among black Americans?

17. Among black Americans, how are biblical literalism and religious commitment each related to:

- voting behavior
- political party identification
- ideological identification
- views on social welfare issues
- views on social issues (e.g., school prayer, abortion, pornography)

Discussion Questions

1. How can the same religion support two opposing viewpoints? For example, how could Christianity be interpreted to support slavery and also be interpreted to stand for liberation? How is it that the leaders of the civil rights movement and their opposition both claimed that God was on their side?

2. How could the Republican Party use religious themes and the social issues in an effort to attract black voters?

3. Is black liberation theology less useful or more useful to black Americans than traditional Christianity?

4. What effects would there be for the American political system if the great majority of black Americans converted to Islam?

5. When it comes to improving the world, is religion an opiate or an inspiration?

6. Should religious institutions focus on otherworldly themes, thisworldly themes, or a combination of both?

For Further Reading

Chidester, David. 1988. *Patterns of Power: Religion and Politics in American Culture.* Englewood Cliffs, New Jersey: Prentice-Hall.

> Chapter 5 ("Black Americans") contains an incisive analysis of the historical linkage between religion and politics among black Americans.

Cone, James H., and Gayraud S. Wilmore. 1993. *Black Theology: A Documentary History.* Maryknoll, New York: Orbis.

> If you're interested in black liberation theology, this two-volume work contains an excellent collection of writings by key black liberation theologians.

King, Martin Luther, Jr. 1963. *Why We Can't Wait.* New York: Harper and Row.

> This work by Martin Luther King, Jr. contains a series of writings—including "Letter from Birmingham Jail"—explaining the rationale, strategy, and goals of the civil rights movement.

Lincoln, C. Eric, and Lawrence H. Mamiya. 1990. *The Black Church in the African American Experience.* Durham, North Carolina: Duke University Press.

> This is an excellent and comprehensive examination of the role and development of the Black Church from the time of slavery up to recent times.

Relevant World Wide Websites

Remember to visit our website for updates and additional links at:
http://bsuvc.bsu.edu/~00amcorbett/relpol.htm

The NAACP (National Association for the Advancement of Colored People) website is:
http://www.naacp.org/

The National Urban League website is at:
http://www.nul.org/

The following website contains materials concerning the civil rights movement:
http://www.ghgcorp.com/hollaway/civil/intro.htm

For information on a major black church in the United States, see the following website devoted to the African Methodist Episcopal Church:
http://www.voicenet.com/~jfisher/ame.html

The Nation of Islam website can be found at:
http://www.noi.org/

For information about Martin Luther King, Jr., a good place to start is:
http://www-leland.stanford.edu/group/King/

Information on Malcolm X can be found at:
http://members.aol.com/jcobain/malcolmx.htm

References

Berry, Mary, and John Blassingame. 1982. *Long Memory: The Black Experience in America*. New York: Oxford University Press.

Castelli, Jim. 1988. *A Plea for Common Sense: Resolving the Clash between Religion and Politics*. New York: Harper and Row.

Chidester, David. 1988. *Patterns of Power: Religion and Politics in American Culture*. Englewood Cliffs, New Jersey: Prentice-Hall.

Cleage, Albert B., Jr. 1969. *The Black Messiah*. New York: Sheed and Ward.

Cleage, Albert B., Jr. 1972. *Black Christian Nationalism: New Directions for the Black Church*. New York: William Morrow.

Cone, James H. 1969. *Black Theology and Black Power*. New York: Seabury.

Cook, Elizabeth Adell, and Clyde Wilcox. 1990. "Religious Orientations and Political Attitudes among Blacks in the District of Columbia." *Polity* 22: 527–544.

Corbett, Julia Mitchell. 1997. *Religion in America, Third Edition*. Upper Saddle River, New Jersey: Prentice Hall.

Frazier, E. Franklin. 1963. *The Negro Church in America*. New York: Alfred A. Knopf.

Gallup, George, Jr., and Jim Castelli. 1989. *The People's Religion: American Faith in the 90's*. New York: MacMillan.

Hanes, Walton, Jr. 1985. *Invisible Politics: Black Political Behavior*. Albany: State University of New York Press.

Jelen, Ted G., and Clyde Wilcox. 1995. *Public Attitudes Toward Church and State*. Armonk, New York: M.E. Sharpe.

Johnson, Stephen D. 1986. "The Role of the Black Church in Black Civil Rights Movement." Pp. 307–324 in Stephen D. Johnson and Joseph B. Tamney (Eds.), *The Political Role of Religion in the United States*. Boulder, Colorado: Westview Press.

Johnstone, Ronald L. 1969. "Negro Preachers Take Sides." *Review of Religious Research* 11: 81–89.

Kellstedt, Lyman A., and Mark A. Noll. 1990. "Religion, Voting for President, and Party Identification: 1948–1984." Pp. 355–379 in Mark A. Noll (Ed.), *Religion and American Politics: From the Colonial Period to the 1980s*. New York: Oxford University Press.

King, Martin Luther, Jr. 1958. *Stride Toward Freedom*. New York: Ballantine Books.

King, Martin Luther, Jr. 1963. "Letter from Birmingham Jail." In *Why We Can't Wait*. New York: Harper and Row.

Kosmin, Barry A., and Seymour P. Lachman. 1993. *One Nation Under God: Religion in Contemporary America*. New York: Harmony Books.

Lincoln, C. Eric, and Lawrence H. Mamiya. 1990. *The Black Church in the African American Experience.* Durham, North Carolina: Duke University Press.

Marx, Gary. 1967. *Protest and Prejudice.* New York: Harper and Row.

Marx, Gary. 1969. "Religion: Opiate or Inspiration of Civil Rights Militancy Among Negroes?" *American Sociological Review* 32: 64–72.

Morris, Aldon D. 1984. *The Origins of the Civil Rights Movement.* New York: Free Press.

Myrdal, Gunnar. 1944. *An American Dilemma: The Negro Problem and American Democracy.* New York: Harper and Row.

Peterson, Steven A. 1992. "Church Participation and Political Participation: The Spillover Effect." *American Politics Quarterly* 20: 123–139.

Raboteau, Albert. 1978. *Slave Religion: The "Invisible Institution" in the Antebellum South.* New York: Oxford University Press.

Reed, Adolph, Jr. 1986. *The Jesse Jackson Phenomenon: The Crisis of Purpose in Afro-American Politics.* New Haven: Yale University Press.

Roberts, James Deotis. 1974. *A Black Political Theology.* Philadelphia: Westminster Press.

Roof, Wade Clark, and William McKinney. 1987. *American Mainline Religion: Its Changing Shape and Future.* New Brunswick, New Jersey: Rutgers University Press.

Scherer, Lester B. 1975. *Slavery and the Churches in Early America, 1619–1819.* Grand Rapids, Michigan: Eerdmans.

Taylor, Robert Joseph, Michael C. Thornton, and Linda M. Chatters. 1987. "Black Americans' Perceptions of the Sociohistorical Role of the Church." *Journal of Black Studies* 18: 123– 138.

Welch, Susan, and Lorn Foster. 1987. "Class and Conservatism in the Black Community." *American Politics Quarterly* 15: 445–470.

Wilcox, Clyde. 1990. "Race Differences in Abortion Attitudes." *Public Opinion Quarterly* 54: 248–255.

Wilcox, Clyde. 1991. "Religion and Electoral Politics Among Black Americans in 1988." Pp. 159–172 in James L. Guth and John C. Green (Eds.), *The Bible and the Ballot Box: Religion and Politics in the 1988 Election.* Boulder, Colorado: Westview Press.

Wilcox, Clyde. 1992. *God's Warriors: The Christian Right in Twentieth-Century America.* Baltimore: Johns Hopkins University Press.

Wilcox, Clyde, and Leopoldo Gomez. 1990. "Religion, Group Identification, and Politics among American Blacks." *Sociological Analysis* 51: 271–285.

Wilmore, Gayraud. 1983. *Black Religion and Black Radicalism: An Interpretation of the Religious History of Afro-American People, Second Edition.* Maryknoll, New York: Orbis.

PART IV

Effects of Religious Influences in Politics

CHAPTER 10

Religious Groups as Political Interest Groups

When the vast majority of interest groups are advocating public policies which will benefit them, it is important that we have strong groups that advocate on behalf of others. Furthermore, amid the self-interest of policymaking and the battles over legislative and regulatory details, it is important that we have groups articulating a political program founded on ethical and religious convictions.

—Robert Zwier, "An Organizational Perspective on Religious Interest Groups"

Overview

Organized religious interest groups seek to influence public policy in Washington and at the state and local levels in much the same ways that other interest groups do. At the same time, there are some important unique features in the operations of religious interest groups. In this chapter, we will examine the methods, goals, and types of religious interest groups—primarily at the national political level. We will see that, in line with the religious pluralism in the United States, there is substantial diversity in the goals that religious interest groups seek and the means by which they seek those goals. The major questions to guide this examination are:

- With what kinds of issues have religious interest groups been involved?
- What strategies do interest groups use to pursue their goals and to what extent do religious interest groups use these same strategies?

- What types of religious interest groups are there and what are the relative strengths and limitations of different types?
- How do religious interest groups lobby public officials and how well do they do it?
- To what extent are the leaders of religious interest groups representative of the views of their members? What kinds of religious interest groups have more of a problem in this regard than others do?
- What are some lobbying groups? How do they pursue their goals? How effective are they? What advantages and disadvantages do they have?
- How has the New Christian Right's political strategy evolved over the years?

Increasing Diversity of Religious Interest Groups

An interest group is a group of people who share some interest or set of interests and pursue their interests through the political system (Corbett, 1991: 292). As we have seen in previous chapters, religious interest groups have been involved in many U.S. political issues, such as the civil rights movement, abortion, pornography, religious observances in the schools, international human rights, certain foreign policy issues (aid to Israel, apartheid in South Africa, aid to the Contras in Nicaragua), caring for the homeless and the hungry, nuclear weapons policy, aid to religious schools, textbook selection in local schools, Internal Revenue Service policies, public displays of religious symbols, and welfare policies.

Perhaps because of the increasing emphasis on social issues (prayer in public schools, abortion, gay rights, pornography, euthanasia, etc.) in the United States, the number of religious lobbying groups has greatly increased. Hertzke (1988: 5) noted that in 1950 there were only sixteen religious lobbying groups in Washington, but there were five times that many by 1985. Further, as a reflection of the increasing diversity and pluralism of religion in the United States, Hertzke (1988: 5) observes that the diversity of religious lobbying groups has increased and their religious agendas have become broader.

Hertzke (1989b: 127) sees great ideological diversity among the religious lobbyists, but highlights the two ideological poles. The liberal end consists of what Hertzke calls the *peace and justice* cluster: liberal mainline Protestants (Methodists, Presbyterians, Lutherans, Episcopalians, the United Church of Christ), the peace churches (Mennonites, Friends, Brethren), the black churches, some Catholic groups (Network, Maryknoll), and Jewish groups. On the conservative end are those groups emphasizing traditional moral values (e.g., the Christian Coalition, Concerned Women for America, and Focus on the Family), some evangelical Protestant groups, and Catholic anti-abortion groups. In between the liberal end and the conservative end are groups such as the U.S. Catholic Conference and Evangelicals for Social Action that combine conservative views on abortion with liberal views on economic and foreign policy goals. Hofrenning (1995: 85) provides a slightly different classification but is in essential agreement with the discussion above.

Strategies of Interest Groups

Religious interest groups employ many of the same strategies as other kinds of interest groups. However, they are also unique in certain ways. The basic goal of any interest group is to shape public policy in some area. This might involve the passage of laws, preventing the passage of laws, overturning past policies, the interpretation of policies, the enforcement or nonenforcement of policies, proposals for constitutional amendments, or any other situation in which policies are considered, formulated, interpreted, or executed. How do interest groups pursue their goals? Depending on the nature of the interest group (size, resources, goals, etc.), an interest group can engage in one or more types of activities. We will discuss some of these activities below.

Referendum Voting

In recent times many states have presented voters with ballot propositions concerning issues of concern to different religious groups: state lotteries, capital punishment, gay rights, smoking, tax issues, abortion, liquor sales, and so on. In such situations, the members of a religious interest group might try to mobilize those who share their views and persuade those who are undecided. Interest groups can be successful in referendum voting, but Magleby (1989) argues that those interest groups who *oppose* a ballot proposition have an advantage over others because they can raise doubts about the need, implementation, and impact of the proposed policy.

Shaping Public Opinion

A religious interest group might try to persuade the general public to support its views in order to achieve its public policy goals. The interest group might try to shape public opinion through media campaigns, individual efforts such as writing letters to the editors of newspapers or magazines, calls to call-in radio shows, or mass mailings. If the public is persuaded, then public officials should be amenable to the interest group's policy goals. While this sounds reasonable, there are at least two problems here.

The first problem is that it is extremely difficult for any interest group to shape public opinion. Most interest groups lack the resources to carry on a sustained campaign to shape public opinion. Even when such campaigns are undertaken, most people ignore them. Also, the effort might backfire and people might become more negative toward the interest group (Key, 1961; Page et al., 1987). This is demonstrated by the fact that in the 1984 elections, candidates in some states tried to distance themselves from public support by certain conservative religious interest groups, and it is demonstrated by the fact that some members of the Christian Coalition who run for public office run as "stealth candidates" who keep silent about their association with the group.

The second problem is that even when public opinion supports a particular measure, this does not guarantee that public officials will act in accord with public opinion. For example, as we discussed in an earlier chapter, a substantial majority of the public supports prayer in the public schools, but this has not been enacted into public policy.

We also need to keep in mind that the religious values within a society affect the public policies that are enacted. For example, several studies of states have shown a connection between public policies and the religious composition or culture of the states (e.g., Hutcheson and Taylor, 1973; Fairbanks, 1977; and several studies included in Segers and Byrnes, 1995).

Grassroots Efforts

Grassroots efforts are attempts by interest groups to generate a large number of communications from the constituents of a public official to persuade the public official to take some action (such as voting for or against a particular bill). This includes personal visits, letters, telegrams, telephone calls, fax messages, and e-mail. Some religious interest groups have become extremely adept at generating quick and massive grassroots pressure on public officials, while other religious interest groups have little or no capability in this area.

During earlier times, most religious interest groups did not feel a need to generate grassroots pressures on policymakers. However, especially since the political thrusts of New Christian Right groups beginning basically in the 1970s, grassroots efforts have become more important. Hertzke (1988: 46) argues that members of Congress today are more sensitive to constituent pressure than they used to be, even if it is apparent that the "spontaneous" grassroots groundswell has been generated by a Washington lobbyist.

Grassroots efforts are also important in raising money for religious interest groups. Direct-mail appeals to members of a group are used to raise money for the group to use in achieving its political goals. Berry (1984: 84) argues that the key to success in direct-mail solicitation is to make the reader scared or angry about something. A direct-mail specialist quoted by Berry stated that you've got to have a "devil"—a person or group that is visibly and actively working against the soliciting group's interests. For example, a Moral Majority fundraising letter given to one of us by a student several years ago contains a "survey" and an appeal for funds—a typical combination for many direct-mail solicitations. Here is an example of the questions: "Do you believe that smut peddlers should be protected by the U.S. Constitution, so that they can openly sell pornographic materials to your children?" In his appeal, Falwell says:

> We have been silent too long. We have let the liberals and the socialists and the gay rights advocates and the left-wing politicians run our nation. If you will stand with me . . . I'll go right into the Halls of Congress and fight for decent, God-fearing laws.

On the liberal side, a 1996 letter from People for the American Way (a group that was originally organized to counter the Moral Majority) charges: "The Christian Coalition and other political religious extremists are creating a dangerous political and social climate in our country."

Media Efforts

Religious interest groups might use mass media to articulate their political views in the hope that this will affect public policy—either by affecting policymakers directly or inspiring their members or the general public to contact policymakers. Such efforts range from writing letters to newspaper editors to the production of publications or broadcasts. Sometimes such media efforts consist of publishing political articles in magazines whose primary purpose is religion. For example, Fairbanks (1989) traces the political messages in three leading evangelical periodicals *(Christianity Today, Christian Herald,* and *Eternity)*. The Christian Coalition has a much more elaborate media organization (a magazine, a mass-mailing list, a sophisticated fax system, a website, etc.) that is more explicitly political and aimed at grassroots mobilization; further, Pat Robertson can flash a telephone number on the screen of his *700 Club* program and inspire many telephone calls to the White House or Congress on some matter.

Seeking Public Office

Members of a religious interest group might seek elective or appointed public offices in order to further the goals of their group. Seeking public elective office is seldom a good strategy for any interest group. In order to win elections, a candidate must usually have a broad base of support, and candidates who are viewed as representatives of an interest group will have difficulty in getting elected. Interest groups might have a better chance of getting members *appointed* to public offices. However, members of *religious* interest groups will have special problems in seeking public office because of the American public's leeriness in mixing religion and politics. Thus, when Pat Robertson sought the Republican nomination for president in 1988, instead of focusing on his position as a religious leader, he portrayed himself as a successful businessman.

Electoral Campaign Efforts

While it is not usually very fruitful for members of an interest group to run for public office, many interest groups put substantial efforts and resources into the campaigns of other candidates. Ideally, in a particular election an interest group would like for its favored candidate to win the election, have everyone perceive the efforts of the interest group as crucial in the victory, and create the impression that the efforts of the interest group will prevail in future elections as well.

In practice, elections can be a tricky business for interest groups. First, a particular interest group is seldom in a position to determine the outcome of an election. Second, the participation of an interest group might backfire (e.g., "My opponent is a puppet for special interest groups"). Third, many interest groups concentrate their resources on candidates who are already favored to win or who have at least a moderately good chance of winning, and they give only token help to candidates they are fairly sure will lose. For this reason, incumbents usually have an advantage in obtaining campaign contributions from interest groups (Sabato, 1984). Fourth, however, sometimes interest groups give campaign contributions to candidates that don't support the views of the interest group in order to soften their opposition.

While some interest groups try mightily to determine who wins an election, most interest groups harbor few delusions about having a substantial impact on the results of the election. Rather, their electoral efforts are more focused on what happens *after* the election. The goal of campaign contributions and other efforts by an interest group is said to be *access* to the public official. That is, members of the group—or their lobbyist—will be able to discuss their views directly with the public official and receive an attentive hearing.

Langbein (1986) showed that the amount of time a U.S. representative spends in the office with interest group representatives is related to the amount of PAC (political action committee) campaign contributions to the representative. Thus, campaign contributions do buy access. Schlozman and Tierney (1986: 164) emphasize the importance of access. There is no assurance that all viewpoints on an issue will be represented in the legislative process, and a public official who only hears one side of an issue is likely to be persuaded by that side.

Do campaign contributions influence the voting behavior of public officials? Keep in mind that interest groups are most likely to give campaign contributions to candidates who already support their viewpoint. If a pro-choice candidate receives contributions from pro-choice groups, gets elected, and takes a pro-choice stand on bills concerning abortion, this does not mean that campaign contributions influenced the representative's vote on bills. Thus, studies of effects of campaign contributions on voting decisions of public officials have to take other factors into consideration, such as the political ideology and party affiliation of the public official. Several studies have done this, and their basic conclusion is that campaign contributions do seem to predispose representatives to vote favorably on the interests of a group in certain situations: situations in which the issue is not very visible to the public and the issue does not seem to be very important to the representative, the representative's party, or the representative's constituency (Jacobson, 1985; Jones and Keiser, 1987; Ginsberg, 1982).

However, religious interest groups are not usually dealing with the relatively invisible issues on which campaign contributions seem to have the most effect, and few of them form PAC organizations. The two primary sources of substantial financial support for candidates are black churches that raise campaign funds for favored candidates, and New Christian Right groups that campaign for favored candidates through devices such as very selective voter registration drives and the massive distribution of scorecards or other literature that shows some candidates in a favorable light and some in an unfavorable light.

In the 1980 elections, several New Christian Right groups (especially Jerry Falwell's Moral Majority) supported Ronald Reagan; they also targeted a number of liberal U.S. senators for defeat, and most of them were defeated. Thus, the Moral Majority and other conservative groups in this effort appeared to be effective. However, these senators probably would have lost anyway; these were liberal Democratic senators in fairly conservative Republican states (e.g., Senator Bayh from Indiana) in a year in which the Republican presidential candidate was winning big. After 1980, efforts by New Christian Right groups to defeat liberal Democrats have often failed, although New Christian Right groups such as the Christian Coalition apparently had a very substantial role in the Republican landslide in the 1994 congressional elections.

Lobbying

Lobbying refers to direct personal efforts to persuade public officials to support a particular view on some public issue. Lobbying by religious groups has gone on for some time in the United States, but in recent times it has increased substantially. We will give substantial attention to this lobbying by religious groups later in the chapter.

Court Cases

Sometimes interest groups pursue goals through litigation. Some groups such as the National Association for the Advancement of Colored People (NAACP) and the American Civil Liberties Union (ACLU) pursue their goals primarily through legal action or the threat of legal action. Jehovah's Witnesses are not usually involved in politics at all, but they have instigated several important court cases (*see* Chapter 6) concerning the free exercise clause of the First Amendment. When groups resort to the courts to achieve their policy goals, it is often because their policy goals are unpopular and have little chance of success in the legislative process.

Religious interest groups of various persuasions do battle in the courts over religious issues, especially issues involving religious observances in public schools. On the liberal side—favoring separation of church and state—we find such groups as the ACLU, People for the American Way, the Baptist Joint Committee, and the American Jewish Committee (along with several other liberal Jewish groups). On the conservative side—favoring greater accommodation between church and state—we find such groups as the Rutherford Institute, the Christian Legal Society, and the American Center for Law and Justice, which was created by Pat Robertson.

Protest

Interest groups might engage in protest in order to affect public policy. In an earlier chapter we described the role of churches in civil rights protests, which included marches, demonstrations, boycotts, freedom rides, and some acts of civil disobedience. In more recent times, there have been many demonstrations against abortion clinics. Religious interest groups sometimes boycott the sponsors of television shows that the group finds to be offensive. Religious interest groups sometimes picket stores that sell pornographic materials. Sometimes religious groups hold marches or demonstrations to protest violent crime, discrimination, nuclear weapons, hunger, or some other matter.

Types of Religious Interest Groups
Church-Based Groups versus Individual Membership Groups

Weber (1982, 1986) divided religious interest groups into three types: *church-based groups* (e.g., the Methodists, the Presbyterians, the Baptist Joint Committee), *individual membership groups* (e.g., Bread for the World, Evangelicals for Social Action), and *coalition groups* (e.g., Washington Inter-religious Staff Council). Zwier (1994) interviewed representatives of a number of religious interest groups in Washington, D.C. in order to investigate differences between church-based groups and individual membership groups. Based on Zwier (1994: 98–100), we will summarize some important distinctions between these two types of religious interest groups.

1. While church-based groups were usually established to monitor government actions affecting the churches, individual membership groups were usually established to influence public policy through lobbying or mobilizing members to contact government officials.
2. For church-based groups, the Washington office is part of the church hierarchy, whereas individual membership groups are not usually subunits of larger organizations.
3. The Washington staff of church-based groups are often church bureaucrats and over half come from pastorates or other church positions. For individual membership groups, the staffs have more diverse backgrounds.
4. Political activity is not the primary goal of the churches and so church-based groups have to compete within their church organizations for resources and attention. By contrast, individual membership groups consists of people who usually joined the organization because of its political goals.

Strengths and Limitations of Each

Having identified differences between the two types of religious interest groups, Zwier (1994: 101) then asks whether such differences lead to differences in activities, strengths, and limitations. First, Zwier finds that the Washington staffs have two very different authority relationships. Church-based groups have greater organizational restrictions than individual membership groups; they have to clear their activities with leaders in their church organizations. However, church-based groups do not have to pay much attention to the views of their members (the members of their church congregations). For mainline liberal churches, this has led to situations in which religious lobbyists were taking liberal positions on some issues on which their members were conservative (Hadden, 1969; Adams, 1970; Reichley, 1985; Hertzke, 1988).

On the other hand, while individual membership groups are less constrained by organizational authorities, they are more subject to their members. Individual membership groups must have a supportive following, and they cannot afford to lose that following by ignoring the views of their members.

Zwier (1994: 111–114) discusses the relative strengths and limitations of church-based groups versus individual membership groups. We will summarize his major points.

Strengths of Church-Based Groups

1. Church-based groups have a positive public image which gives them legitimacy as political actors.
2. Churches often have large resources for their advocacy.
3. Churches represent large numbers of voters.
4. Churches have the potential for access to public officials who are members of that church.
5. Churches have potential strength because of their many local organizations.
6. Church-based groups have longer experience in Washington than individual membership groups do.

Limitations on Church-Based Groups

1. Many people oppose the involvement of churches in political activities.
2. Many people did not join their churches for political reasons and the political activities of the church might not be important to them.
3. The hierarchical organization of church-based groups reduces their speed and flexibility.
4. The Washington lobbyists of church-based groups typically have little training in policy analysis and lobbying.
5. The church-based groups tend to deal with too many issues rather than focusing on a few.
6. Because many church representatives see their role as witnessing rather than winning legislative battles, this reduces their impact.

Strengths of Individual Membership Groups

1. Individual membership groups have a more politically active constituency than the church-based groups do.
2. Because of their organizational structure, individual membership

groups can act more quickly and more flexibly than church groups.

Limitations on Individual Membership Groups

1. Individual membership groups have a greater need to achieve victories to sustain their membership and the need for victories in the present might detract from important long-term efforts.

2. Individual membership groups, depending on their geographic dispersal, might have difficulty in obtaining access to the most appropriate public officials.

Lobbying by Religious Interest Groups
Legal Limitations on Political Activities of Religious Interest Groups

One past limitation on religious involvement in politics was a prohibition against members of the clergy holding public office. Two states, Maryland and Tennessee, still banned the clergy from holding office until the bans were ruled unconstitutional in the 1970s (Kelley, 1991).

Churches and religious organizations have a substantial legal limitation on their activities. Under section 501(c)(3) of the Internal Revenue Code, religious groups and other public service organizations are tax exempt. Further, such organizations can receive tax deductible contributions, and this is extremely important for their support (Davis, 1991: 104). In order for organizations to receive such benefits, they must be nonprofit, and there are two important additional requirements. First, the organization cannot devote a "substantial" part of its activities to attempts to influence legislation. Second, such organizations are prohibited from "participation" or "intervention" in political campaigns on behalf of any candidate for public office. These two requirements are called the *lobbying clause* and the *electioneering clause*.

These requirements have resulted in court cases (Davis, 1991; Gaffney, 1991; Kelley, 1991). Some argue that such requirements ought to be ruled unconstitutional. While such requirements do limit the political activities of religious groups, the vagueness of the requirements leaves a great deal of room for political activity by religious groups. The IRS and the courts have been liberal in interpreting how much activity religious organizations can carry out. In fact, Davis (1991) argues that most violations of these requirements are overlooked entirely. Further, religious organizations have developed ways to work within the letter of the law and still achieve their political goals. For example, a religious organization might distribute "report cards" or "scorecards" about candidates in an election. Even though these reports do not explicitly endorse any candidate, they make it very obvious who the "good" candidates are. On the other hand, in 1996, the government brought charges against the Christian Coalition for violating the provisions concerning political activities by tax-exempt groups, and the Christian Coalition might have to give up its tax-exempt status.

General Strategies of Lobbying

Hertzke (1988: 49) groups the strategies of lobbyists into two categories: *home district pressure* (which does not depend on direct access to the legislator) and *classic insider strategies* (which are based on direct access to the legislator). Although most religious lobbyists use both strategies simultaneously, different religious interest groups have different advantages and disadvantages in the two areas, and it apparently is becoming more and more important that a group have substantial capabilities in both strategies in order to succeed.

Home District Pressure

Home district pressures are designed to bring influence on the legislator from the legislator's district. Hertzke (1988:49) describes four methods of exerting home district pressure.

First, *mass constituency mobilization* consists of strategies aimed at generating a groundswell of constituent support (through letters, telephone calls, etc.) for some policy and making it appear that there are many, many people in the legislator's district who are passionately concerned about the policy. Schlozman and Tierney (1986: 184) note that public officials are not particularly concerned with an amorphous perception of the views of the general public; rather, what influences them is "the understanding that there is a narrower group of citizens who care intensely about a policy matter and are likely to act on their views." The New Christian Right has become expert in mobilizing grassroots pressure, but this strategy is also used by liberal religious groups to a more limited extent.

Second, *elite mobilization* consists of efforts to bring pressure through elite constituents in the legislator's district. Lobbying organizations keep lists of key contacts in the legislator's district who can be alerted to contact their representative quickly about some policy issue. Whereas conservative religious groups have mastered mass mobilization better than other religious groups have, liberal religious groups often have the advantage in elite mobilization.

Third, *direct electoral mobilization* consists of attempts to influence who wins in elections. Religious interest groups can do this though registering voters, distributing materials on the candidates' views, making endorsements, contributing campaign money, providing campaign workers, and making sure that supportive voters get to the poll on election day.

Fourth, *media strategies* consists of attempts to use the media strategically by staging dramatic events. Hertzke (1988: 68) uses the example of famous athletes testifying in favor of school prayer while, on the other side, religious leaders in full clerical garb hold a press conference on the Capitol steps to explain why they oppose prayer in public schools. Such tactics are designed to influence the media in order to arouse attentive constituents within the public so that they will persuade members of Congress.

Classic Insider Strategies: The Detail Work

Grassroots mobilization might mold the congressional agenda, create a favorable environment, or predispose legislators to respect the power of an interest group, but the "detail work" of lobbyists is necessary to forge the precise language or outcomes of bills (Hertzke, 1988). Hertzke emphasizes that there is a big difference between insider lobbying and token lobbying. When a religious interest group focuses just on making its views known to legislators, this is not really insider lobbying. Insider lobbying requires activities crafted for specific policy goals: drafting the language of bills, providing possible amendments, creation of coalitions, negotiating with opponents, and providing information and arguments to congressional members.

Hertzke (1988: 70) argues that most religious lobbyists are not particularly good at the insider strategy because of several reasons. First, most religious lobbies have small staffs. Second, many religious groups lack focus; they are involved in so many issues that it's difficult for them to concentrate their efforts on issues where they might be more effective. Third, many religious lobbyists are not very assertive in obtaining access to legislators or in using that access aggressively when they get it. Fourth, some religious groups lack experience in lobbying. Fifth, given the nature of religious issues and the strength of the views of religious lobbying groups, it might be difficult for them to think strategically and compromise—qualities that are usually necessary in order to have an impact in the legislative process. Zwier (1989: 185) gives a description that is very important in explaining some of the behavior of religious interest groups:

> [M]any of these groups are in Washington not so much to pass or defeat legislation but to make a statement. Their foremost concern is not with the results of the policy process (although they would rather win than lose) but with how the process is conducted and with the nature of the debate. Success is defined in terms of whether the moral aspects of public issues have been included in the discussion.

On the other hand, Hertzke (1988: 79) notes that religious lobbying groups have had "episodic" effectiveness on the insider detail work, and he suggests that religious lobbyists have done their best insider work on church-state issues. Hertzke provides several examples of situations in which religious lobbyists have been effective in detail work: Jewish groups such as the American Jewish Committee have been very skillful at insider work in general and particularly on issues concerning support for Israel; the Seventh-day Adventists helped write the Equal Employment Opportunity Commission guidelines in 1964 and 1972 because of their concern about their members losing jobs because of their Saturday worship; the National Association of Evangelicals worked on the Social Security Bill in 1983 on matters relating to taxes and auxiliaries (such as nursing homes) of religious institutions; the Concerned Women for America wrote an antipornography bill; and Bread for the World had an impact on the Food for Peace international aid program and famine relief bills.

Coalitions

In order to study the coalition strategies of religious interest groups, Zwier (1989) interviewed thirty-eight representatives of religious groups with offices in Washington. He found that religious interest groups frequently worked in coalitions because these groups tend to have small staffs and limited budgets. Another reason is their common identity and shared values.

Zwier (1989) and Hofrenning (1995) have emphasized that religious interest groups don't fit traditional interest groups theory well in certain respects. One difference is that traditional interest group theory tends to focus on the material interests of groups. Although religious groups do get involved in material issues that affect them (such as tax policies for nonprofit organizations), material benefits are not usually the primary consideration of religious interest groups. Zwier (1989) also notes that, contrary to traditional interest group theory, many of these religious interest groups were interested in the *process* of cooperation at least as much as the *results*. Another interesting finding is that religious interest groups tended to form coalitions with other religious groups that held similar *political* perspectives rather than seeking coalitions with religious groups that held similar *theological* views.

Overall, most religious interest groups appeared ready to join in a coalition on a particular political issue with just about any other group that shared their views on that issue. However, there were exceptions to this. If you were a lobbyist working on a piece of legislation, it would be advantageous for you to have a number of religious groups in your coalition. The leaders of religious interest groups realize that they are sometimes used for purposes of adding legitimacy to a coalition, and they might be reluctant to join the coalition. Further, some religious groups such as the Seventh-day Adventists are particular about choosing coalition partners; for example, their representative indicated that they would be reluctant to form an alliance with the Church of Scientology or the ACLU even if they were in agreement on the political issue involved (Zwier, 1989: 177).

An interesting example of a coalition is reflected in a handout entitled *Religion in the Public Schools: A Joint Statement of Current Law.* As its title indicates, this statement puts forth interpretations of current law on religion in the public schools on such matters as student prayers, teaching about religion, equal access, religious holidays, and so on. This joint statement was released on April 13, 1995, in Washington, D.C., and was endorsed by a wide variety of groups such as the ACLU, American Jewish Committee, Baptist Joint Committee, Christian Legal Society, National Association of Evangelicals, American Humanist Association, Christian Science Church, National Sikh Center, and the American Muslim Council.

An even broader coalition was involved in the Religious Freedom Restoration Act of 1993 (discussed in Chapter 6). Support ranged from secular groups such as the ACLU to fundamentalist Protestants, and it included mainline Protestants, evangelical Protestants, Jewish groups, Catholics, members of Native American religions, and Muslim groups.

While religious interest groups often form temporary coalitions around some particular issue, Zwier (1989: 178) notes that there are some relatively permanent coalitions of religious interest groups, such as WISC (Washington Interreligious Staff Council). When it was established in 1968, WISC included only churches within the National Council of Churches, but it has expanded to include about thirty-five religious groups. WISC includes liberal Protestants, Catholics, and Jewish groups but does not include the more religiously conservative groups. WISC utilizes task forces to combine and share their resources for political issues on which they share a common view. Rather than having a number of different religious groups working individually to pursue the same goal, these religious groups pool their resources in order to be more effective. However, Zwier also notes that, aside from any legislative goals, participants in religious interest group coalitions indicated that they benefited from the communal association itself; they learned from each other and enjoyed each other's company.

Distinctiveness of Religious Lobbying

What do religious lobbyists represent? Aside from the usual view that lobbyists represent *the views of the members* of their interest groups, Hertzke (1988: 101) describes three kinds of representation that are relatively distinct for religious lobbyists.

First, most religious lobbyists represent *church institutions*. Church organizations do have tangible institutional interests because they own property, employ people, have tax exemptions, operate schools, colleges, universities, and other enterprises. As institutions, church organizations have a variety of material interests to protect.

Second, religious lobbyists represent *theological traditions and biblical values*. While most religious lobbyists avoid using religious language when they are lobbying, these religious values provide the motivation and parameters for the goals sought in the legislative process. By contrast, many other types of interest groups ordinarily seek material benefits for their members.

Third, religious lobbyists might represent *world church organizations* rather than just U.S. church organizations. Many churches are international organizations that engage in such activities as running relief agencies, missionary programs, and development programs. Church organizations that have international activities include the Catholic Church, the National Council of Churches, the Baptists, the Seventh-day Adventists, the National Association of Evangelicals, and others. Given an international connection, this affects the perspectives and goals of a religious lobbying group, especially on issues involving foreign policy. For example, several church lobbying groups have been strongly involved in human rights issues and policies toward Central America.

Lobbying Co-religionists in Public Office

Can lobbyists count on the support of public officials who share their religious views? In an earlier chapter, we discussed the religious preferences of members of Congress and argued that the particular distribution of religious preferences might partly account for the fact that Congress has never achieved sufficient support for the passage of a prayer amendment proposal. Do the religious beliefs of members of Congress affect their decisions? In general, research indicates that religious affiliation does not seem to have a dramatic effect on the voting decisions of members of Congress except on the issue of abortion (Page et al., 1984). On the abortion issue, religious views do seem to affect voting behavior, especially among Catholics (Hanna, 1979).

However, Hanna (1979) and Benson and Williams (1986) also studied members of Congress in terms of religious *beliefs* rather than general religious *preference,* and both studies found substantial relationships between the religious beliefs of members of Congress and their voting on bills. Members who identify with a particular religion might differ from one another in terms of this approach. For example, Hanna distinguishes a variety of ways that different Catholic traditions and philosophies could affect the political views of Catholic members of Congress. Hanna suggests that two of these traditions seem to dominate. The first emphasizes strict codes of conduct, rules, guidelines, and a rigid, puritanical devotion to duty and order. The other emphasizes Christian love, compassion, and concern for humanity, especially the poor and the helpless. When examined in such terms, the religious beliefs of public officials apparently do have an impact on their political decisions.

Access

To what extent do religious interest groups achieve access to public officials? Hertzke (1989a) indicated that the extent to which congressional members grant serious access to religious lobbyists depends to a great extent on their own ideological and religious views. Congressional members tend to filter out the views of religious groups with whom they disagree. In reference to New Christian Right groups, for example, the congressional members interviewed by Hertzke appeared to be very biased for or against such groups and to base access on whether or not they agreed or disagreed with the group. Most policymakers grant greater access to those with whom they agree. Because of this, lobbyists usually lobby policymakers who sympathize with their goals and avoid those who are opposed to their goals. When it comes to religious lobbying, however, this usual pattern might not hold. Berry (1977: 218) argued that public interest groups (which included religious groups) were more likely than other groups to lobby their opponents.

Hertzke (1989a) argued that Jewish groups have been very successful in achieving access in Congress and in the White House. Part of the reason for this is their ethnic and religious link to strategic foreign policy concerns. However, Hertzke also attributes this success to the quality of their leadership and the educated and politicized nature of their constituents. Hertzke argues that the example of Jewish lobbying means that excellent lobbying on the part of other religious groups could, under the right conditions, overcome the filtering biases of policymakers. With some notable exceptions, religious groups usually are not very aggressive and they are not very skillful in the detail work of lobbying.

Note that the degree of access of a particular religious interest group will ebb and flow depending on the political composition of Congress at any given time. For example, when Republicans gained control of Congress in 1994, access increased for conservative religious groups and decreased for liberal religious groups. Similarly, access to the White House will depend to a great extent on who the president is. For example, Hertzke (1989a: 264) noted that the Reagan White House appointed a Protestant, a Catholic, and a Jew to establish and maintain contacts with religious constituencies. However, the Protestant coordinator was an evangelical sympathetic to the New Religious Right, the Catholic was a Right to Life Catholic, and the Jew was a neo-conservative. Thus, the access for religious groups was funneled through a conservative filter. Conversely, access during the Clinton administration is probably greater for more liberal religious interest groups. Further, Baptist groups (e.g., the Baptist Joint Committee) probably have an advantage in obtaining access to Clinton—a Baptist.

Effectiveness of Religious Lobbying

In his study of religious lobbyists in Washington, Zwier (1994) investigated two models of what religious groups are supposed to do in the political arena. The *witnessing* model "calls for the group to be a faithful witness, speaking truth to power, regardless of the policy impact the group has" (Zwier, 1994: 110). The *winning* model calls for the group to have a substantial impact on the outcome of the policy process.

Among the religious lobbyists in this study, 44 percent saw their role primarily in terms of witnessing, 28 percent saw their role as winning, and the rest were unable to choose (Zwier, 1994: 110). Thus, winning is not necessarily the most important goal of religious interest groups. This focus is confirmed by Hofrenning (1995), who views religious lobbyists as having a prophetic role that emphasizes the faithful articulation of religious values rather than winning specific legislative goals. Further, there is a very important pattern in Zwier's results: Almost three fourths of the witnessing groups were church-based groups, while nearly two thirds of the winning groups were individual membership groups. Thus, church-based groups are more focused on witnessing while individual membership groups focus more on winning policy victories.

What are the requirements for effective lobbying? Berry (1984: 119–123) developed several rules which we will summarize as follows: First and foremost, lobbyists must have credibility. Policymakers must be able to depend on the honesty and integrity of the lobbyist. It is likely that most religious lobbyists are seen by policymakers as having honesty and integrity. Second, lobbyists must separate factual information from rhetoric and platitudes. Lobbyists must have a great deal of knowledge in their policy area, and they must be able to provide information that policymakers need. Third, they shouldn't burn their bridges—lobbyists who do not have the support of a policymaker on a particular issue should not antagonize that policymaker and cut off chances of cooperation in the future. Fourth, lobbyists must be able to compromise—which can be more difficult at times for religious interest groups dealing with moral values than it is for interest groups seeking material benefits. Fifth, lobbyists should create a dependency on the part of the policymaker so that the policymaker depends on the lobbyist as a trusted source of information.

Hertzke (1988: 47) indicates that lobbyists will be most successful when their expertise is backed up by constituency support. Thus, good lobbyists will be able to generate grassroots support to back up their efforts. Some religious interest groups do this very well, some are less skillful, and some have virtually no capability in this area.

Hertzke (1988: 47) also indicates that cohesiveness within a religious interest group is important in determining its effectiveness. For example, when Jewish lobbying groups discuss issues of church-state relations with policymakers, the policymakers know that there is cohesive stand among Jews on such issues. On the other hand, when liberal mainline Protestant church groups discuss church-state issues with policymakers, the policymakers are aware that there can be substantial differences between the views of church leaders and their followers. The degree of cohesiveness among the members of a religious group will also, of course, have an impact on the ability of the group's lobbyist to generate grassroots support for some position.

Representativeness of Religious Leaders
The Gap Between Mainline Protestant Clergy and Church Members

Beginning with Ebersole's (1951) *Church Lobbying in the Nation's Capital,* a series of studies showed that church lobbyists in Washington promoted the views of church leaders rather than church members generally. This theme was emphasized by Hadden's (1969) *The Gathering Storm in the Churches,* in which Hadden demonstrated that the enthusiasm for the civil rights movement by liberal clergy was not shared by the more conservative majority of members in their churches. Using data from his own study of Protestant clergy and data from Glock and Stark's (1965) study of laity, Hadden (1969: 68) concluded that "Protestantism is divided within and among denominations on the most basic issues of theological doctrine." Foreshadowing the decline in membership of mainline Protestant churches in the coming years, Hadden (1969: 5) warned that the "Protestant churches are involved in a deep and entangling crisis which in the years ahead may seriously disrupt or alter the very nature of the church."

This theme of a gap between the liberalism of the mainline Protestant clergy and the conservatism of their congregations continued in Adams' (1970) *The Growing Church Lobby in Washington*, Reichley's (1985) *Religion in American Public Life*, and Hertzke's (1988) *Representing God in Washington*. Recall that in Chapter 7 we presented a variety of evidence to demonstrate that religious leaders are often more liberal than the general public.

Delegate Role versus Trustee Role of Church Leaders

It has been argued that the leaders of *any* organization dominate the organization in order to achieve their own goals rather than the organization's goals; this is Michels' (1962) "iron law of oligarchy." Drawing upon Pitkin's (1967) work, *The Concept of Representation*, Hertzke (1988: 97) distinguishes between two types of roles for representatives: the *trustee* role and the *delegate* role. The trustee role is the position that a representative must use his or her own judgment and reasoning in making policy rather than simply doing what the constituents want. The delegate role is the position that the representative must do what the constituents want.

Arguments can be made for either of these two representation roles. It can be argued, for example, that the leaders of mainline Protestant groups are actually taking the correct positions for their churches on issues and that the real problem is that they have not educated their congregations properly on the issues. Key (1961: 525) argued that attachment to the goals of a group varies with the degree of involvement in the group: top leaders express the group position in its purest form, a lower level of group activists basically support the official position, and below that members subscribe to the leaders' positions in varying degrees depending on their own level of involvement. Elliott Corbett, chief Washington lobbyist for the United Methodist Church, argued that where moral issues are involved, the church must exercise leadership and cannot afford to wait for its members to agree (Reichley, 1985: 254). However, in terms of effectiveness of lobbying efforts, Hertzke (1988) argues that "representative" lobbying (the delegate role) will be much more effective than "oligarchic" lobbying (the trustee role).

Increased Representativeness of Religious Lobbyists

Hertzke (1988: 44) notes two important trends that have increased the representativeness of religious interest groups. First, increases in the number and diversity of lobby groups have made them more representative of the pluralism of religious beliefs and practices in the general public. Second, religious lobbyists are now more likely to feel that they must generate constituent pressure on members of Congress, and this requires that religious leaders and their followers must be more in accord with one another.

Similar to Weber (1982, 1986), Hertzke (1988) distinguishes between two organizational types of religious interest groups: 1) the church denomination, in which lobbying is incidental to other activities; and 2) the direct-mail organization, in which members join for specifically political reasons. Drawing upon Hirschman's (1970) work, Hertzke argues that a key feature of the direct-mail organization which distinguishes them from the denominational organizations is the *ease of exit*. If, for example, a member of the Christian Coalition becomes dissatisfied with what the leadership is doing and wants to "exit" the organization, it is quite easy to do so; the person simply doesn't send any more contributions. However, it is not as easy for a member of the Presbyterian Church to leave the local congregation because of disagreement with what Presbyterian leaders in Washington are doing. Thus, direct-mail organizations must pay closer attention to the views of their members than the denominational organizations do.

Hertzke's (1988) examination of the extent of representativeness of religious interest groups leads him to three conclusions, which we will summarize. First, for just about any religious group, there will sometimes be disparity between the views of the lobbying group and the views of the members. For example, the Lutheran Council is in accord with the views of its members on environmental spending, but it is not in accord with its members on school prayer.

Second, the emphases of religious lobbies and their effectiveness in mobilizing constituent are strongly linked to the degree of member support. For example, while various mainline Protestant churches support abortion rights, the Episcopal Church leads the lobby effort because of its strong member support on this issue. Similarly, religiously conservative Protestant lobbying groups will place their emphasis on the social issues because this is where they receive the greatest support from their members.

Third, the *collective* impact of religious lobbying works reasonably well to represent broader public sentiment. *Collective representation* concerns how well all representatives as a group represent all the constituencies as a group. Rather than asking how well each individual religious lobbyist represents his or her particular members, we would ask how well all the religious lobbyists in Washington as a group represent the religious and political views of the American public as a whole. Hertzke argues that while the religious lobbying representation in Washington is not perfectly reflective of the general public, religious lobbying does work reasonably well in achieving collective representation. There is great diversity among religious lobbyists in terms of ideology, theology, and organization, and they represent views on a wide variety of issues of broad public concern.

Jewish Interest Groups

There is a variety of Jewish lobbying organizations even though there is usually agreement among most of them on a wide range of issues. The major Jewish groups (including the American Jewish Committee, B'nai B'rith's Anti-Defamation League, the American Jewish Congress, and the Union of American Hebrew Congregations) are all liberal. Altogether, the Jewish lobby is not large, but it is effective, especially with regard to issues concerning Israel and church-state relations. Each Jewish organization has its own lobbying staff, and Hyman Bookbinder of the American Jewish Committee has become legendary as the model of an effective religious lobbyist. Also, while the American Civil Liberties Union is a secular organization, Jews constitute a substantial proportion of its membership.

Jews constitute less than 3 percent of the American population, but they have influence and access to policymakers disproportionate to their size. There are several reasons for this. First, Jews have higher than average income and education, and this—coupled with impressive achievements in many areas in society—has led to greater influence. Second, Jews have been very active in American politics. *The Washington Lobby* (1987: 80) quotes Thomas A. Dine, executive director of the American Israel Public Affairs Committee (AIPAC): "Two thousand years of painful experiences have forced us into round-the-clock political activity." Third, the geographic concentration of many Jews in politically crucial states (e.g., New York) has meant that the national political party organizations could not ignore Jewish voters. Fourth, Hertzke (1989a: 274) argued that Jewish groups have been successful in achieving access in Congress and in the White House because of the quality of their leadership and because they actively and energetically seek access.

Not all Jews or Jewish organizations are liberal. In Chapter 8, we discussed the emergence of a small politically neo-conservative movement among some Jewish intellectuals. These neo-conservatives have argued, among other things, that the *economic* interests of Jews and society are not served well by liberalism (Lerner et al., 1989). In terms of noneconomic issues (such as the social issues), Orthodox and Hasidic Jews tend to share the views of conservative Protestants. The Rabbinical Council is the national organization for Orthodox Jews, who constitute only about 10 percent of the Jewish community. While Reform Jews, Conservative Jews, and secular Jews (who have a Jewish background but are not religious) tend to be politically liberal, Orthodox Jews are more politically conservative on at least some issues.

Jewish lobbying organizations are not always liberal. For example, Jewish organizations have been critical of affirmative action programs because they view such programs in terms of quotas, and quotas have been used in the past to limit the number of Jews in some occupations and types of opportunities (such as college admissions).

Jewish organizations have been very dedicated in protecting Israel, although there have been differences of opinion on specific policies. The pro-Israel lobby is spearheaded by AIPAC, which *The Washington Lobby* (1987: 79) calls "one of the more effective lobbying organizations in Washington." Most Jewish lobbying organizations have a variety of political goals, but AIPAC's only goal is the security of Israel. The leaders of most other major Jewish lobbying organizations are on its executive committee. AIPAC lobbies policymakers, distributes records of how policymakers vote on issues related to Israel, keeps its members informed on policy matters related to Israel, and influences campaign contributions to policymakers.

Domestically, Jewish organizations have strongly supported strict separation of church and state, liberal social and economic policies, and civil liberties. In coalitions with other groups, they have supported such liberal causes as women's rights, racial equality, abortion rights for women, and assistance to the poor.

In terms of strategy, Jewish lobbying organizations seem to be at their best in the detail work of insider lobbying. They are also good at inspiring key people to contact the policymakers of a particular district, and they can generate substantial grassroots pressure on issues concerning Israel.

Mainline Protestant Groups

Most mainline denominations (e.g., Methodists, Episcopalians, Presbyterians, Lutherans, American Baptists) have their own representatives in Washington. The National Council of Churches is the fundamental coalition of a number of liberal Protestant groups. There are some membership groups such as Bread for the World (a religious coalition which works on hunger problems in the world). Most major mainline Protestant church lobbies are members of two coalition groups, Interfaith-Impact (a coalition of Protestants, Catholics, Jews, Muslims, and others) and WISC (Washington Interreligious Staff Council). Through these coalitions, member groups are able to share some resources (e.g., mailing lists) and coordinate activities to achieve common goals. There are other coalition groups such as the Religious Coalition for Abortion Rights (a coalition of liberal Protestant and Jewish groups). Mainline Protestant lobbies also form coalitions with other religious groups and secular groups (e.g., the American Civil Liberties Union) on an ad hoc basis, depending on the issue involved.

Let's consider the representation of black religious groups in Washington. In an earlier chapter we discussed the local role of black churches in politics. At the national level, aside from representation by such groups as the National Association for the Advancement of Colored People (NAACP), the Urban League, and the Southern Christian Leadership Conference, there are Washington offices for several of the black Baptist or Methodist denominations (the Progressive National Baptist Convention, the Christian Methodist Episcopal Church, the African Methodist Episcopal Zion Church, the National Baptist Convention USA, etc.) The civil rights goals of black Americans have been sought in coalitions with other religious groups such as the National Council of Churches and secular groups such as the ACLU. Overall, the majority views of black Americans on civil rights issues and economic issues are ordinarily represented in conjunction with mainline Protestant groups, Jewish groups, and Catholic groups. However, Hertzke (1988) argues that the conservative views of blacks on some social issues (e.g., abortion, prayer in schools) are represented by some Protestant groups that are religiously and politically conservative.

Taking their original impetus from the this worldly, social reformist, ethics-oriented foundation of the Social Gospel movement, mainline Protestant leaders have been active in a variety of political issues and causes. Their participation in the civil rights movement has been regarded by some as the high point of mainline political activism (Jelen, 1993: 72). Mainline Protestant leaders have also worked for abortion rights, for sexual equality, for affirmative action, for separation of church and state on such issues as school prayer, against apartheid in South Africa, against U.S. policies in El Salvador and Nicaragua, and for programs for the hungry and the homeless. There has also been a substantial degree of pacifism (especially from the historic peace churches—Quakers, Mennonites, and Brethren) and opposition to nuclear weapons (and other weapons of mass destruction) among many mainline Protestant leaders. There has also been an active movement by various groups who base their efforts to protect the environment on Christianity (Kearns, 1996). In short, the theologically liberal mainline Protestant groups have generally supported liberal positions on a wide range of issues.

After their heyday of political and social activism during the 1960s, mainline Protestant leaders retreated somewhat from political activity. The leadership had been criticized because of the gap between their views and the views of their church members. Further, mainline churches began to lose many members to evangelical churches, and mainline Protestants are now less numerous than evangelical Protestants.

Jelen (1993: 72–73) notes three important characteristics of mainline Protestant political involvement. First, the Protestant mainline has emphasized the importance of structural or institutional factors—as opposed to individual behavior—in accounting for social problems. Large, impersonal forces (e.g., the economic system) cause human problems and must be fixed in order to alleviate the root causes of such problems as crime, poverty, and the breakup of the family. Second, mainline Protestant politics is associated with the liberal (and sometimes further left) side of the political spectrum. Third, mainline Protestant politics has been conducted almost completely at the level of religious elites. Thus, mainline leaders have engaged in direct lobbying of congressional members, but have not made frequent attempts to mobilize grassroots support for their positions. Similarly, they have not attempted to mobilize their members to vote for particular candidates in elections.

With some exceptions, mainline Protestant church lobbying groups have simply not been very successful at mobilizing church members even when they have tried. Hertzke (1988: 56) argues that the liberal church lobbies *collectively* have been able to mobilize respectable constituent opinion on only hunger and peace issues—and the term "collectively" here means the mainline Protestant churches in coalitions with other liberal Catholic and Jewish groups. Hertzke notes that the weakness of mainline Protestants at the constituency level is indicated by the small size of their mailing lists. Typically, one of the mainline denominations has a mailing list of about two thousand names—which is tiny compared to the mailing list of the Christian Coalition, which claims over 1.75 million members.

One problem in mainline mobilization is that church leaders are often more liberal on political issues (e.g., civil rights, prayer in public schools, abortion) than their congregations are. This can also be a problem in direct lobbying efforts by church groups.

Overall, it appears that the political influence of mainline Protestant groups has declined. Some (e.g., Hertzke, 1991) have attributed this to the concern of political leaders with being pure and politically correct rather than thinking about tough choices and tradeoffs. Similarly, Zwier (1994) argues that many church representatives see their role as witnessing their beliefs rather than winning legislative battles.

Catholic Groups

The Second Vatican Council, an assembly of all the world's Catholic bishops, began in 1962 and continued until 1965. We usually refer to this event as *Vatican II*. One of the most important results of Vatican II is summarized well by Hanna (1989: 76):

> The council stressed that the church as an institution and Catholics in general had a positive obligation to involve themselves in the problems of the world; it issued a series of documents that denounced various political, social, and economic ills—poverty, illiteracy, political repression—as morally wrong under Christian doctrine; and it urged Catholics to work to alleviate them.

The National Conference of Catholic Bishops (NCCB) is the organization through which Catholic bishops in the United States attempt to shape public policy through such activities as their pastoral letters against nuclear weapons, against abortion, for assistance to the poor, and others. The bishops work through their professional staff organization in Washington, the United States Catholic Conference (USCC), which includes both lay and religious scholars and a staff of lobbyists. Since the NCCB began in 1967, the bishops have issued more than 150 statements on public issues (Gelm, 1994: 59). The bishops also lobby members of Congress and sometimes file *amicus curiae* ("friend of the court") briefs in court cases to present their views. The bishops have been especially active on issues and court cases concerning abortion (Segers, 1990: 10).

With its network of local churches, the Catholic lobbying group has a strong base for generating grassroots pressure on congressional members on some issues at least. For example, Libby (1986) reported that during the conflicts in El Salvador and Nicaragua, the USCC generated a large volume of mail from U.S. Catholics to congressional members against U.S. policy in Central America. This particular situation also demonstrates that the Catholic lobby sometimes represents more than a domestic constituency.

On economic issues the bishops have taken a liberal position and supported assistance for the poor. On foreign policy, the bishops have pushed for peace-and-justice positions. For example, the bishops criticized United States policy in El Salvador and Nicaragua—arguing essentially that instead of using aid for military purposes, the United States should use foreign aid and negotiation as tools in these countries to resolve structural problems that resulted in rebellion in both. The bishops have also argued against nuclear weapons as a strategy of deterrence. The bishops have also condemned capital punishment, urged amnesty for Vietnam draft resisters, and supported a grape boycott to help César Chavez's efforts for farm workers (Hanna, 1989). Thus, on many kinds of issues, the bishops have taken either liberal positions or peace-and-justice positions. However, on the social issues (e.g., abortion, religious observances in public schools, gay rights) the bishops have taken conservative positions similar to those taken by conservative Protestants. Further, it appears that the bishops have now given abortion the highest priority among public issues (Gelm, 1994).

While the bishops take liberal positions on some issues and conservative positions on other issues, the seeming contradiction is resolved through the metaphor of "the seamless garment" of concern for life (or "consistent life ethic") as put forth by Catholic intellectuals such as the late Cardinal Bernardin of Chicago. This seamless garment is pro-life in many ways, not just an anti-abortion stand. It opposes abortion, capital punishment, euthanasia. It also opposes nuclear weapons and war. Unlike some conservative Protestants, however, the seamless garment view also supports bettering the lives of the poor and the downtrodden.

Gelm (1994) surveyed 150 of the approximately 300 U.S. bishops (some active and some retired) and found that most of the bishops believed that they should be politically active. However, at the same time, the bishops were very pessimistic about influencing the views of Catholics in the general population. Gelm also found political diversity among the bishops. They are conservative on social issues and liberal on economic and foreign policy issues. For some examples, 97 percent favored intensified efforts to eliminate poverty, 89 percent opposed increasing defense spending, 92 percent favored greater efforts to control pollution, and 96 percent favored greater abortion restrictions. However, the bishops were less cohesive on some of the social issues. For example, they were split 51 percent to 49 percent on the issue of less lenient treatment of criminals.

Unlike the decentralized Protestant community, the bishops are unified publicly. Nevertheless, the Catholic lobbying effort is not completely hierarchical; there are actually many different Catholic organizations. For example, Network, the "nuns' lobby," was also spawned by Vatican II. Based on the idea that action on behalf of justice was the same as preaching the gospel, some nuns abandoned their habits and began serving as social workers among the poor. Because of the structural problems in society that lead to poverty, the nuns started their Washington lobby in order to work for structural changes that would reduce poverty. Network is also active on peace and foreign policy issues because of its association with the Maryknoll nuns who do mission work on behalf of the poor in Central America and in other parts of the world (Hertzke, 1988).

Other Catholic religious organizations include the Campaign for Human Development, the Jesuit Social Ministries, the Catholic League for Religious and Civil Rights, the National Catholic Action Coalition, and other groups. O'Hara's (1990) analysis of Catholic-based lobbying groups resulted in a list of thirty-one groups with a wide range of viewpoints—and eleven of the thirty-one groups indicated specific policy disagreements with the official positions of the Catholic church. These Catholic lobbying organizations range from the very conservative (e.g., Catholic Center) to the very liberal (e.g., Dignity, Inc., which argues for gay rights and ministry to homosexuals).

An important group that is disproportionately—but not completely—Catholic is the National Right to Life Committee, which opposes abortion. Although anti-abortion forces would like to make abortion illegal, they have also fought smaller battles to make it more difficult for women to obtain abortions—such as working against public funding for abortions and working for various restrictions (e.g., requiring a twenty-four-hour waiting period, mandatory counseling about alternatives to abortion, and requiring that teenage girls obtain their parent's consent). Anti-abortion forces are opposed by some within their own ranks (e.g., Catholics for Free Choice) and by some other religious groups (e.g., the Religious Council for Abortion Rights). While the bishops and several Catholic or primarily Catholic organizations have been publicly unified in their opposition to abortion, recall from an earlier chapter that Catholics in the general public are not much different from Protestants in their attitudes toward abortion, and most people would allow abortion in health-related, rape, or incest situations.

Overall, Catholic lobbying groups have worked through various methods, including the detail work of insider lobbying and the strategy of generating grassroots pressures on congressional members. In their efforts, Catholic lobbyists have formed coalitions with liberal religious groups on some issues (e.g., peace issues, economic issues) and they have worked with conservative Protestants on some issues (e.g., abortion, aid to religious schools).

Conservative Protestant Groups: Evangelicals and the New Christian Right

Theologically conservative Christians are not a monolithic group in terms of either religion or politics. One way of looking at differences among theologically conservative Protestant groups is to classify them as evangelicals or fundamentalists—although there are other groups such as pentecostals and charismatics that stand outside this rough classification scheme. While fundamentalists are usually thought of as a subgroup of evangelicals, they are distinguished by their militant emphasis on correct belief—as opposed to evangelicalism's emphasis on communicating the Christian Gospel to everyone. Reverend Billy Graham is a good example of an evangelical and Reverend Jerry Falwell is a good example of a fundamentalist.

Beginning basically with such groups as Jerry Falwell's Moral Majority in the 1970s, a series of politically and religiously conservative groups has constituted what has variously been called the New Religious Right, the New Right, the New Religious and Political Right, or the New Christian Right. We will use the term New Christian Right (often called the NCR) here because this appears to be the most accepted current usage among religion-and-politics scholars. In addition to fundamentalists, some nonfundamentalist evangelicals are members of New Christian Right organizations—and some evangelicals are strongly opposed to the NCR. We will take a very brief look at the relatively low-key evangelical lobbying efforts first and then focus greater attention on the dramatic emergence of the New Christian Right.

Evangelical Groups

Hertzke (1988: 214–215) lists the following as examples of evangelical groups in Washington: the Baptist Joint Committee for Public Affairs, the National Association of Evangelicals, Evangelicals for Social Action, the General Conference of Seventh-day Adventists, the Christian Legal Society, the African Methodist Episcopal Church, and Sojourners Fellowship. Evangelical lobbying groups are sometimes aligned with liberal causes and sometimes aligned with conservative causes.

Several evangelical lobbying groups are concerned with religious establishment or religious free exercise issues. Some groups (e.g., the Seventh-day Adventists) have been more concerned with perceived threats to religious freedom from the right and have often aligned themselves with liberal religious groups. These groups favor separation of church and state, and so we could say that they are mostly concerned with the religious establishment clause (although some groups such as the Baptist Joint Committee are equally concerned with both establishment issues and free exercise issues). On the other hand, Hertzke (1988) notes that groups such as the Christian Legal Society and the National Association of Evangelicals have become more concerned with perceived threats to religious freedom from the left, from secular leaders whom they believe want to restrict religious freedom (especially for evangelicals) through a misuse of the establishment clause. Thus, these groups are more concerned with the religious free exercise clause.

Evangelicals for Social Action is a membership group that combines a conservative social agenda (e.g., opposition to abortion and pornography) with a moderately liberal economic and foreign policy agenda (Hertzke, 1988: 41). The group works with liberals on issues concerning hunger, poverty, peace, and racism but they also support traditional social values. Their goal is "a holistic discipleship which actively pursues peace, justice, and liberty in society according to biblical principles" (Smidt et al., 1994: 138).

Evangelical religious interest groups have used a variety of techniques ranging from endorsing candidates in elections to traditional lobbying methods. Somewhat akin to the Catholic lobby, evangelicals have espoused both liberal causes (on economic conditions and peace issues) and conservative causes (on social issues). They have sometimes worked in coalitions with liberal religious groups and they have sometimes worked in coalitions of conservative religious groups.

The New Christian Right (NCR)

The New Christian Right has waged battles against abortion, pornography, communism, secular humanism, atheism, welfare, distribution of condoms to teenagers, and gay rights. It has also waged battles for strong national defense, home schooling, aid to religious schools, school voucher plans, parental rights to discipline children, teaching creationism in public schools, and religious observances in public schools.

The New Christian Right became known in the late 1970s and especially in the 1980 election because of the activities of such groups as the Moral Majority, Christian Voice, and Religious Roundtable. In the 1980 election, the New Christian Right worked for the election of Ronald Reagan and for the defeat of six liberal Democratic senators. The NCR also worked for the election or the defeat of other candidates at various levels of office. Not only did Reagan get elected, but five of the six liberal Democratic senators were defeated, thus shifting control of the U.S. Senate to the Republican Party. For a while, New Christian Right groups, especially the Moral Majority, claimed credit for the election outcomes. However, later analysis (e.g., Pierard, 1983) suggested that Reagan's election was due more to dissatisfaction with Carter than anything else and that the liberal Democratic senators (who were mostly from fairly conservative Republican states such as Indiana, Idaho, and Iowa) would have lost anyway in an election in which the Republican presidential candidate won by a landslide. Zwier's (1984) examination of NCR activities in the 1980 election and 1982 election (in which the Democratic Party gained seats in the House and the New Christian Right was seen as being counterproductive) concludes that the NCR did not actually affect the elections very much in either year.

The role of New Christian Right groups in elections did not receive much public attention for a while after the 1982 elections. In the 1992 Republican convention, several convention speeches by New Christian Right leaders focused dramatically on the social issues and contained very heated rhetoric (e.g., Pat Buchanan's statement that America was in the midst of a "cultural war"). The uncompromising rhetoric of the NCR at the Republican convention was probably one of several factors that led to George Bush's defeat in 1992. Despite this, however, the NCR was very active in the 1994 congressional elections. Green's (1995) overview of NCR activities indicated that it provided substantial numbers of campaign workers and millions of voter guides—the Christian Coalition claimed that it distributed 33 million voter guides. Not only was the NCR active in 1994, but it apparently was a contributing factor in the Republican capture of both houses of Congress, Republican control of a majority of governorships, and major gains at the state and local levels (Green, 1995). The Christian Coalition and other New Christian Right groups were also very active in the 1996 elections (Rozell and Wilcox, 1997).

Although there are exceptions (such as the Christian Life Commission within the Southern Baptist Conference), the New Christian Right is characterized more by individual membership groups than church-based groups. Today the biggest of the NCR membership groups are the Christian Coalition (started by Pat Robertson and organized by its first executive director, Ralph Reed), Focus on the Family (founded by James Dobson), the Family Research Council (headed by Gary Bauer), and Concerned Women for America (founded by Beverly LaHaye). These groups pursue similar objectives, and they have symbolized their overall programs in terms of support for traditional "family values." Additionally, there are other groups that pursue more limited objectives or have smaller memberships. For example, the American Family Association is a large group that focuses primarily on what it sees as antifamily values in the mass media and uses boycotts to achieve its objectives. Another example is the Eagle Forum (headed by Phyllis Schlafly), which is a smaller group that focuses its efforts on education issues. Another group that is small in comparison with, say, the Christian Coalition is the Traditional Values Coalition which takes traditional viewpoints on a variety of morality issues.

While the family values theme of NCR groups might encompass their views on many social issues, it appears to be stretching the theme quite a bit to encompass some of their other positions. For example, the Christian Coalition's webpage in March, 1996, described a series of "contract with the American family issues" that included support for a balanced budget amendment, support for term limits for members of Congress, support for "reforming the legal system to discourage frivolous lawsuits," support for placing a limit of $250,000 on "pain and suffering" awards in health care liability lawsuits, and support for a line-item veto. Support for some of these measures is probably simply support for the more traditional Republican agenda as a way of increasing the link between the Republican Party and the New Christian Right.

The New Christian Right is not completely unified. This was demonstrated in 1988 when Pat Robertson sought the Republican nomination for president. He was not able to mobilize all the NCR voters for himself, and Jerry Falwell supported George Bush. Similarly, in 1996 Pat Buchanan was not able to mobilize the NCR for his effort to obtain the Republican presidential nomination. Further, there is not complete agreement among the members of the NCR about some of the issues. For example, NCR leaders such as Jerry Falwell and Pat Robertson have expressed strong support for Israel, but it is not likely that all their followers support Israel. Further, there are some theological differences among NCR groups that can make it difficult for them to achieve complete unity.

To a great extent, the New Christian Right had its roots in televangelism (televised religious programming). Jerry Falwell used his mailing list of donors from his *Old Time Gospel Hour* as an initial base from which to form the Moral Majority. For a while, Jim Bakker and Jimmy Swaggart were influential televangelists who also intermixed political views in their programming, but both were disgraced by scandals before the end of the 1980s. Pat Robertson's *700 Club* (an evangelical talk show), the flagship program of Robertson's Christian Broadcasting Network (CBN), provided the base for his 1988 attempt to run for president. In turn, the mailing list from his 1988 campaign provided the initial mailing list for the formation of the Christian Coalition (Reed, 1994). Note that for both the Moral Majority and the Christian Coalition, there is a common beginning point in televangelism, but this is not saying that the televangelism itself produced the New Christian Right movement; in fact, Johnston's (1989) analysis (based on data gathered in 1983) indicated that televangelism had little impact on the *political* behavior of viewers. In addition to its televangelism base, the NCR has been very active in radio programming, especially the large number of Christian radio stations.

It is ironic that a movement espousing traditional values is at the same time so technologically sophisticated. The Christian Coalition, for example, uses massive mailing lists, fax facilities, e-mail facilities, and a very sophisticated website. Given such capabilities and their mass membership base, the New Christian Right has great ability to mobilize constituency opinion—and generate a huge volume of mail, e-mail, and faxes to policymakers.

The Christian Coalition is currently the largest New Christian Right organization. In 1989, Pat Robertson selected Ralph Reed to be the executive director of the Christian Coalition, but Robertson was the president. Under Reed, the Christian Coalition concentrated on three things: gaining national members, developing state chapters, and mobilizing sympathetic voters (Hertzke, 1993). The very talented Ralph Reed oriented the Christian Coalition toward winning through a slow but steady process of long-term development. He criticized the defunct Moral Majority for being primarily a direct-mail organization and focusing too much on Falwell (Hertzke, 1993: 182). Thus, he built the Christian Coalition into an organization that by 1994 claimed more than 1.5 million members, had a Washington lobbying organization, forty-eight state chapters, and 1,400 local chapters (Green, 1995: 8). It has grown even more since 1994. In 1997, Reed resigned as executive director of the Christian Coalition in order to pursue other goals, and he was replaced by Randy Tate, a former U.S. representative from Washington State. However, Pat Robertson also made himself chairman of the board and appointed Donald Hodel as president.

Despite its size, the New Christian Right by itself is not big enough to win the goals it wants. Therefore, the NCR must form coalitions with other groups. The Christian Coalition made a very substantial effort to broaden its appeal. Rozell and Wilcox (1995: 257) quote the Christian Coalition training manual as listing the following groups that are potential allies: anti-tax, pro-business, educational reform, pro-family and pro-life, veterans, right-to-work, gun owners, home educators, antipornography, and others. On the basis of agreement concerning social issues such as abortion, pornography, and gay rights, the Christian Coalition has reached out to make connections with Catholics, Orthodox Jews, and black evangelical Protestants. For example, in 1996 Ralph Reed, William Bennett, and Rabbi Yechiel Eckstein (an Orthodox Jewish leader who has worked to strengthen relations between evangelical Protestants and Jews) together established a Center for Judeo-Christian Values in America. Further, the chief lobbyist for the Christian Coalition is Jewish, and Pat Robertson has expressed strong support for Israel.

As indicated by the spotlight on NCR leaders at the 1992 Republican convention and its lower-key role in the 1996 Republican convention, the New Christian Right has worked with—and become an important part of—the Republican Party. This, however, has caused quite a strain within the Republican Party (Hertzke, 1988, 1993; Guth and Green, 1989; Penning, 1994; Oldfield, 1996b). The traditional Republican Party emphasized *economic* conservatism, but the New Christian Right is primarily interested in *social* conservatism. This conflict between the two types of conservatism—and the traditional Republican belief that religious groups should stay out of politics—was exemplified by Barry Goldwater's blistering attack on Jerry Falwell and others who criticized him for supporting Sandra Day O'Connor for the Supreme Court (Kelley, 1991).

In the past, the Christian right in the Republican Party was sometimes viewed as uncompromising and amateurish, but it has also been very good at grassroots efforts, and it has often demonstrated political skill. In many states, New Christian Right groups have simply taken over the state and local Republican Party organizations. With the passage of time, however, it appears that the NCR has devised ways of decreasing the friction between its supporters and the more traditional Republican activists. For one thing, the NCR gives strong support to the kinds of economic positions that have been at the core of the traditional Republican Party agenda.

On the other hand, New Christian Right groups sometimes use the "threat of exit"—a threat to abandon the Republican Party. A front-page Associated Press story (*Muncie Star,* July 22, 1995) reported that James Dobson, president of Focus on the Family, threatened that conservative Christians would leave the Republican Party if it continued to pursue a "big-tent" strategy that avoids taking a stand on moral issues in the interest of party unity. Dobson warned: "We'll see how much unity there is when they have been thrown out of office." However, it does not seem likely that NCR groups will bolt the Republican Party. They did not even give Pat Robertson their complete support in 1988 when he attempted to win the Republican nomination—nor did they give their complete support to Pat Buchanan (a Catholic who espouses many NCR views) in either his 1992 or 1996 efforts to win the nomination. Rather, the "threat of exit" from the Republican Party is probably most useful to the NCR in order to make sure that their views are taken seriously. In the 1992 Republican convention, a number of NCR leaders gave speeches and many of their concerns were incorporated into the platform. In 1996, after losing a string of primaries, Buchanan remained in the race for the Republican nomination even though he acknowledged that he couldn't win. His new rallying cry became: *We're going to write the platform!* While Buchanan himself did not play a dramatic role at the 1996 Republican convention, the NCR did have an impact on the Republican platform—especially on social issues such as abortion.

Oldfield (1996a: 277) sees a fundamental dilemma in coalition building for the Christian Coalition.

> To reach beyond its religious base, the Christian Right needs to present its arguments in broadly acceptable secular language, tolerate compromise, and move beyond a strict social-issue focus. Yet doing so could well undermine the movement's organizational resources that, from the Robertson campaign to the platform battles of 1992, have been the source of the movement's strength.

Rozell and Wilcox (1995: 259) similarly express doubts that the New Christian Right can "maintain their mobilized base while using moderate rhetoric, emphasizing budgetary issues, and compromising on key issues such as abortion." For example, in order to increase the Republican chances of victory in the 1996 presidential elections, Ralph Reed and the Christian Coalition agreed to a statement in the Republican platform that acknowledged that there were different viewpoints within the Republican Party on the issue of abortion and, in effect, downplayed the abortion issue somewhat—although the anti-abortion plank did remain in the platform.

If the NCR compromises on the core issues of its followers, how can it still mobilize followers for the Republican Party? Rozell and Wilcox (1995: 259) observe that many NCR leaders have adopted a "two-track strategy of moderate rhetoric when dealing with Republican leaders and extremist language when mobilizing the faithful." The latter part of this strategy is suggested by an article in *Christian Century* (May 24–31, 1995: 559) that says that in direct-mail campaigns to Christian Coalition members, Pat Robertson complained that the federal government gives millions of dollars to the "homosexual lobby," that Attorney General Janet Reno believes that we should relax laws against child pornography, and that we still have an administration "that is chock full of 1960s-style far-left radicals who have devoted their entire lives to waging an all-out war against just about every moral and spiritual value you and I cherish."

Moen (1992) has argued that the New Christian Right has learned from its mistakes and become much more politically sophisticated. The NCR, at least at the elite level, is no longer amateurish in its strategies and tactics. At the same time, Moen argues that the NCR has become more secular in character. By saying this, Moen does not mean that the people in the NCR have personally become more secularized. Rather he means two things. First, "Christian-Right leaders began incorporating the *trappings* of secularism, dropping religious references from their organizational titles and promotional literature, and soliciting the support of secular organizations sharing their political agenda (Moen, 1992: 4)." Second, from time to time, the NCR leaders sometimes sacrificed their religious principles in order to pursue secular political objectives. More recently, Moen (1994 345) has argued that the NCR has "gradually reconciled and adjusted itself to the secular norms and practices of American politics"—it has forsaken revolution for evolution, as Moen puts it. Further, Wilcox et al. (1996) emphasize that the Christian right is now essentially a political movement rather than a religious movement.

Similarly, Rozell and Wilcox (1995) describe the new pragmatism of the NCR in terms of moderate rhetoric, broader issue concerns, more inclusive coalitions, and compromise on key issues. In contrast with the NCR of the early 1980s, the present NCR has moved its primary efforts from national politics to the state and local level, has focused more on grassroots efforts to win elections and form coalitions, has incorporated training sessions to teach its activists how to be effective in politics, has broadened its agenda to attract others to its coalition, and has learned to use language that will help it attract support. On the latter matter, for example, several scholars (e.g., Hertzke, 1988; Moen, 1994) have noted that the NCR has begun to use "rights" language instead of speaking in terms of moralistic language in dealing with such issues as school prayer (e.g., the NCR supports the *right* of students to pray in school). In a similar vein, Hertzke (1988) noted that one of his most dramatic findings concerning religiously conservative lobbyists was the extent to which they have adopted pragmatic strategies aimed at lobbying success.

Some scholars (e.g., Fowler, 1993; Bruce, 1994) have assessed the New Christian Right as a failure up to this point. The NCR has not gained its major policy goals (prayer in public schools, a ban on abortions, etc.). However, as Kivisto (1994) demonstrates, there is substantial disagreement among scholars as to the future of the New Christian Right. In the 1994 congressional elections, the Republican Party, with the help of New Christian Right groups, gained control of both houses of Congress. While this indicates some degree of success on the part of the NCR, note also that there has not been much in the way of tangible legislative rewards for the NCR. On the other hand, it is apparent that the New Christian Right is now engaged in long-term efforts to achieve its goals and will not give up easily.

Summary and Conclusions

Religious interest groups, like all interest groups, share a particular interest or set of interests and pursue these interests by working within the political system in a variety of ways. The number of such groups has increased steadily since the 1950s and continues to do so. Religious interest groups are currently involved in a wide range of issues that they perceive as having moral or religious dimensions. Although there is a wide variety of such groups, they can be thought of as a continuum ranging from the "peace and justice" cluster on the liberal side to the "traditional values" advocates on the more conservative side.

Religious interest groups are like other interest groups in the techniques they use. They might try to influence how people vote in elections, they might try to shape public opinion, they engage in grassroots efforts to generate communications to public officials, they use the media to present their views, they sometimes seek public office for some of their members, they might lobby public officials, they might use the courts to pursue their goals, and they might engage in protest activities. However, they are different in what they represent: religious interest groups typically represent single religious institutions (such as the Catholic Church), theological traditions and values (for example, pacifism), and/or international religious organizations.

Some religious interest groups are church-based (e.g., those associated with the Methodist Church or the Presbyterian Church) and some, such as the Christian Coalition, are individual membership groups that draw members from a variety of communities of faith. Each types has its relative strengths and limitations.

Religious interest groups lobby public officials through home district pressures and through insider strategies. It has become more important for a religious interest group to be competent in both types of strategies. Religious interest groups must often form coalitions with other interest groups in order to achieve their goals. In order to succeed, it is very important for religious interest groups to achieve access to public officials and use the access aggressively to put forth their agenda. There are rules that are important in order for lobbyists to be effective (e.g., they must be credible, they must have a great deal of knowledge in the issue area, and they must be able to compromise). Additionally, it is important that the skills of the lobbyist are backed up by constituency support and that there is cohesiveness within the religious interest group.

Mainline liberal Protestant religious interest groups have had a problem with regard to cohesiveness because the leaders are more liberal than their members. However, it appears that this gap has decreased over time. Church-based religious interest groups have greater difficulty in achieving cohesiveness than individual membership religious interest groups.

We have examined goals and strategies of Jewish interest groups, mainline Protestant groups, Catholic groups, and conservative Protestant groups. Jewish interest groups have generally supported liberal causes and security for Israel, and they have excelled at the insider strategy. Mainline liberal Protestant groups have generally supported a variety of different liberal causes, but they have not been greatly successful in some of these pursuits because they have often not had great support from their members. Catholic groups have supported liberal causes in terms of some economic matters such as helping the poor, but they have supported the conservative position on social issues such as abortion. Conservative Protestants usually take conservative political positions on the social issues. There are differences, however, among the conservative Protestants. Because of its dramatic growth, we have given particular attention to the Christian Coalition as a representative of the New Christian Right. The history of the Christian Coalition so far suggests that it employs a more conventional interest group strategy than earlier groups such as the Moral Majority did; the Christian Coalition has cast a wider net, attempted to appeal to a wider constituency, and has demonstrated a willingness to compromise in at least certain situations.

This examination of religious interest groups has demonstrated a great deal of diversity among such groups in terms of goals and methods. Some religious groups support liberal views and some support conservative views—and some support liberal views on some issues and conservative views on other issues. And some views are not either liberal or conservative. Although there are times when this diversity turns into unity (e.g., the wide support among many different religious groups for the Religious Freedom Restoration Act), the range of political positions espoused by religious interest groups certainly seems to match the diversity of political views found in the general public. Thus, while some people are concerned about possible problems that might result from the participation of religious groups in politics, it does not seem that religious interest groups pose any problem for maintaining either political or religious pluralism. We now turn to a fuller discussion of views concerning the proper role of religion in public life in the United States.

Important Terms

Interest group	Elite mobilization
Church-based interest group	Direct electoral mobilization
Individual membership interest group	Delegate role of church leaders
Mass constituency mobilization	Trustee role of church leaders
Detail work of lobbying	Christian Coalition

Review Questions

1. Describe each of the strategies used by religious interest groups.
2. What are the strengths and limitations of church-based interest groups? Of individual membership groups?
3. Describe home district pressure lobbying and classic insider lobbying.
4. Why do religious interest groups often form coalitions?
5. How are religious interest groups similar to other interest groups? Different from them?
6. How effective is lobbying by religious interest groups?
7. Why do Jews have influence and access to policymakers far beyond their percentage in the population? For what causes and concerns have they lobbied?
8. Describe the black Americans' lobby in Washington.
9. Describe three important characteristics of mainline Protestant political involvement.
10. Describe the views of Catholic lobbying groups.
11. What causes have evangelicals characteristically championed?
12. What has been the focus of New Christian Right lobbies?
13. How has the New Christian Right become more politically sophisticated over the years?

Discussion Questions

1. Should religious interest groups lobby Washington lawmakers? Why or why not?
2. For each of the strategies described in Review Question 1 above,

discuss whether or not you believe it is an appropriate method for religious groups to use.

3. What might be the advantages and the disadvantages for religious interest groups in forming coalitions with other groups?

4. Do you agree or disagree with the goals of the New Christian Right? Why?

For Further Reading

Hertzke, Allen D. 1988. *Representing God in Washington: The Role of Religious Lobbies in the American Polity.* Knoxville: University of Tennessee Press.

This excellent book is the most comprehensive work on religious lobbying in the United States.

Hofrenning, Daniel J. 1995. *In Washington But Not of It: The Prophetic Politics of Religious Lobbyists.* Philadelphia: Temple University Press.

Basing his study on interviews with religious lobbyists, Hofrenning views such lobbyists as prophets and discusses the implications of this prophetic role for the strategies, goals, and effectiveness of the religious lobbyist.

Moen, Matthew C. 1992. *The Transformation of the Christian Right.* Tuscaloosa: University of Alabama Press.

This work traces the development of the Christian right in politics, focusing on the 1979–1989 time period.

Segers, Mary C. (Ed.). 1990. *Church Polity and American Politics: Issues in Contemporary Catholicism.* New York: Garland.

This edited book contains an excellent selection of articles relevant to Catholic organizations as interest groups.

Stevenson, William R., Jr. (Ed.). 1994. *Christian Political Activism at the Crossroads.* Lanham, Maryland: University Press of America.

This collection of articles by scholars (e.g., Robert Zwier and Allen Hertzke) and religious activists (e.g., Ralph Reed) contains both descriptions of religiously-based political activism and opinions about the proper role of religious activism in the political process.

Wood, James E., Jr., and Derek Davis (Eds.). 1991. *The Role of Religion in the Making of Public Policy.* Waco, Texas: J.M. Dawson Institute of Church-State Studies.

This edited book is very useful in understanding the role of religious groups in the political process.

Relevant World Wide Websites

Remember to visit our website for updates and additional links at:
http://bsuvc.bsu.edu/~00amcorbett/relpol.htm

Here are the webpages for the principal organizations mentioned in this chapter:

http://www.aclu.org/ American Civil Liberties Union
http://www.pfaw.org/ People for the American Way
http://www.cc.org/ Christian Coalition
http://www.cbn.org/ Christian Broadcasting Network
http://www.frc.org/ Family Research Council
http://www.nrlc.org/ National Right to Life Committee
http://www.nvi.net/ncaap_washington_bureau/ Washington Bureau of the NAACP
http://www.nul.org/ The National Urban League
http://www.bread.org/ Bread for the World
http://www.aclj.org/ American Center for Law and Justice
http://nae.goshen.net/ National Association of Evangelicals
http://www.libertynet.org/~esa/ Evangelicals for Social Action
http://www.clsnet.com/ Christian Legal Society
http://www.erols.com/bjcpa/ Baptist Joint Committee for Public Affairs
http://ajc.org/ American Jewish Committee
http://shamash.org/reform/uahc/ Union of American Hebrew Congregations
http://www.aipac.org/ American Israel Public Affairs Committee
http://www.adl.org/ B'nai B'rith Anti-Defamation League

References

Adams, James L. 1970. *The Growing Church Lobby in Washington*. Grand Rapids, Michigan: William B. Eerdmans.

Benson, Peter L., and Dorothy L. Williams. 1986. *Religion on Capitol Hill*. New York: Oxford University Press.

Berry, Jeffrey M. 1977. *Lobbying for the People: The Political Behavior of Public Interest Groups*. Princeton: Princeton University Press.

Bruce, Steve. 1994. "The Inevitable Failure of the New Christian Right." *Sociology of Religion* 55: 229–242.

Corbett, Michael. 1991. *American Public Opinion: Trends, Processes, and Patterns*. New York: Longman.

Davis, Derek. 1991. "The Supreme Court, Public Policy, and the Advocacy Rights of Churches." Pp. 101–125 in James E. Wood, Jr., and Derek Davis (Eds.), *The Role of Religion in the Making of Public Policy*. Waco, Texas: J.M. Dawson Institute of Church-State Studies.

Ebersole, Luke Eugene. 1951. *Church Lobbying in the Nation's Capital.* New York: MacMillan.

Fairbanks, David. 1977. "Religious Forces and 'Morality' Policies in the American States." *Western Political Quarterly* 30: 411–417.

Fairbanks, James D. 1989. "Politics and the Evangelical Press." Pp. 243–258 in Ted G. Jelen (Ed.), *Religion and Political Behavior in the United States.* New York: Praeger.

Fowler, Robert Booth. 1993. "The Failure of the Religious Right." Pp. 57–74 in Michael Cromartie (Ed.), *No Longer Exiles: The Religious New Right in American Politics.* Washington, D.C.: Ethics and Public Policy Center.

Gaffney, Edward M., Jr. 1991. "The Abortion Rights Mobilization Case: Political Advocacy and Tax Exemption of Churches." Pp. 127–158 in James E. Wood, Jr., and Derek Davis (Eds.), *The Role of Religion in the Making of Public Policy.* Waco, Texas: J.M. Dawson Institute of Church-State Studies.

Gelm, Richard J. 1994. *Politics and Religious Authority: American Catholics since the Second Vatican Council.* Westport, Connecticut: Greenwood Press.

Ginsberg, Benjamin. 1982. *The Consequences of Consent: Elections, Citizen Control and Popular Acquiescence.* Reading, Massachusetts: Addison-Wesley.

Glock, Charles Y., and Rodney Stark. 1965. *Religion and Society in Tension.* Chicago: Rand McNally.

Green, John C. 1995. "The Christian Right and the 1994 Elections: An Overview." Pp. 1–18 in Mark J. Rozell and Clyde Wilcox (Eds.), *God at the Grass Roots: The Christian Right in the 1994 Elections.* Lanham, Maryland: Rowman and Littlefield.

Guth, James L., and John C. Green. 1989. "God and the GOP: Religion among Republican Activists." Pp. 223–242 in Ted G. Jelen (Ed.), *Religion and Political Behavior in the United States.* New York: Praeger.

Hadden, Jeffrey K. 1969. *The Gathering Storm in the Churches.* Garden City, New York: Doubleday.

Hanna, Mary T. 1979. *Catholics and American Politics.* Cambridge, Massachusetts: Harvard University Press.

Hanna, Mary. 1989. "Bishops as Political Leaders." Pp. 75–86 in Charles W. Dunn (Ed.), *Religion in American Politics.* Washington, D.C.: CQ Press.

Hertzke, Allen D. 1988. *Representing God in Washington: The Role of Religious Lobbies in the American Polity.* Knoxville: University of Tennessee Press.

Hertzke, Allen D. 1989a. "Faith and Access: Religious Constituencies and the Washington Elites." Pp. 259–274 in Ted G. Jelen (Ed.), *Religion and Political Behavior in the United States.* New York: Praeger.

Hertzke, Allen D. 1989b. "The Role of Religious Lobbyists." Pp. 123–136 in Charles W. Dunn (Ed.), *Religion in American Politics.* Washington, D.C.: CQ Press.

Hertzke, Allen D. 1991. "An Assessment of the Mainline Churches Since 1945." Pp. 43–80 in James E. Wood, Jr., and Derek Davis (Eds.), *The Role of Religion in the Making of Public Policy.* Waco, Texas: J.M. Dawson Institute of Church-State Studies.

Hertzke, Allan D. 1993. *Echoes of Discontent: Jesse Jackson, Pat Robertson, and the Resurgence of Populism.* Washington, D.C.: CQ Press.

Hirschman, Albert. 1970. *Exit, Voice, and Loyalty.* Cambridge, Massachusetts: Harvard University Press.

Hofrenning, Daniel J. 1995. *In Washington But Not of It: The Prophetic Politics of*

Religious Lobbyists. Philadelphia: Temple University Press.

Hutcheson, John D., and George A. Taylor. 1973. "Religious Variables, Political System Characteristics, and Policy Outputs in the American States." *American Journal of Political Science* 17: 414–421.

Jacobson, Gary C. 1985. "Parties and PACs in Congressional Elections." Pp. 131–158 in Lawrence C. Dodd and Bruce I. Oppenheimer (Eds.), *Congress Reconsidered, Third Edition.* Washington, D.C.: CQ Press.

Jelen, Ted G. 1993. *The Political World of the Clergy.* Westport, Connecticut: Praeger.

Johnston, Michael. 1989. "The Christian Right and the Powers of Television." Pp. 203–221 in Michael Margolis and Gary A. Mauser (Eds.), *Manipulating Public Opinion.* Pacific Grove, California: Brooks/Cole.

Jones, Woodrow, Jr., and K. Robert Keiser. 1987. "Issue Visibility and the Effects of PAC Money." *Social Science Quarterly,* 68: 170–176.

Kearns, Laurel. 1996. "Saving the Creation: Christian Environmentalism in the United States." *Sociology of Religion* 57: 55–70.

Kelley, Dean M. 1991. "The Rationale for the Involvement of Religion in the Body Politic." Pp. 159–190 in James E. Wood, Jr., and Derek Davis (Eds.), *The Role of Religion in the Making of Public Policy.* Waco, Texas: J.M. Dawson Institute of Church-State Studies.

Key, V.O., Jr. 1961. *Public Opinion and American Democracy.* New York: Alfred A. Knopf.

Kivisto, Peter. 1994. "The Rise or Fall of the Christian Right? Conflicting Reports from the Frontline." *Sociology of Religion* 55: 223–228.

Langbein, Laura I. 1986. "Money and Access: Some Empirical Evidence." *Journal of Politics* 48: 1052–1064.

Lerner, Robert, Althea K. Nagai, and Stanley Rothman. 1989. "Marginality and Liberalism Among Jewish Elites." *Public Opinion Quarterly* 53: 330–352.

Libby, Ronald T. 1986. "Listen to the Bishops." Pp. 263–278 in Stephen D. Johnson and Joseph B. Tamney (Eds.), *The Political Role of Religion in the United States.* Boulder, Colorado: Westview Press.

Magleby, David B. 1989. "Opinion Formation and Opinion Change in Ballot Proposition Campaigns." Pp. 95–115 in Michael Margolis and Gary A. Mauser (Eds.), *Manipulating Public Opinion.* Pacific Grove, California: Brooks/Cole.

Michels, Robert. 1962. *Political Parties.* Trans. Eden and Cedar Paul. New York: Free Press.

Moen, Matthew C. 1992. *The Transformation of the Christian Right.* Tuscaloosa: University of Alabama Press.

Moen, Matthew C. 1994. "From Revolution to Evolution: The Changing Nature of the Christian Right." *Sociology of Religion* 55: 345–357.

O'Hara, Thomas J. 1990. "The Catholic Lobby in Washington: Pluralism and Diversity among U.S. Catholics." Pp. 143–156 in Mary Segers (Ed.), *Church Polity and American Politics: Issues in Contemporary Catholicism.* New York: Garland.

Oldfield, Duane M. 1996a. "The Christian Right in the Presidential Nominating Process." Pp. 254–282 in William G. Mayer (Ed.), *In Pursuit of the White House: How We Choose Our Presidential Nominees.* Chatham, New Jersey: Chatham House.

Oldfield, Duane M. 1996b. *The Right and the Righteous: The Christian Right Confronts the Republican Party.* Lanham, Maryland: Rowman and Littlefield.

Page, Benjamin I., Robert Y. Shapiro, Paul W. Gronke, and Robert M. Rosenberg. 1984. "Constituency, Party, and Representation in Congress." *Public Opinion Quarterly* 48: 741–756.

Page, Benjamin I., Robert Y. Shapiro, and Glenn R. Dempsey. 1987. "What Moves Public Opinion?" *American Political Science Review* 81: 23–43.

Penning, James M. 1994. "Pat Robertson and the GOP: 1988 and Beyond." *Sociology of Religion* 55: 327–344.

Pierard, Richard V. 1983. "Religion and the New Right in Contemporary American Politics." Pp. 57–75 in James E. Wood, Jr. (Ed.), *Religion and Politics*. Waco, Texas: J.M. Dawson Institute of Church-State Studies.

Pitkin, Hanna Fenichel. 1967. *The Concept of Representation*. Berkeley: University of California Press.

Reed, Ralph. 1994. *Politically Incorrect: The Emerging Faith Factor in American Politics*. Dallas: Word Publishing.

Reichley, A. James. 1985. *Religion in American Public Life*. Washington, D.C.: Brookings Institution.

Rosenthal, Alan. 1993. *The Third House: Lobbyists and Lobbying in the States*. Washington, D.C.: CQ Press.

Rozell, Mark J., and Clyde Wilcox. 1995. "The Past as Prologue: The Christian Right in the 1996 Elections." Pp. 253–263 in Mark J. Rozell and Clyde Wilcox (Eds.), *God at the Grass Roots: The Christian Right in the 1994 Elections*. Lanham, Maryland: Rowman and Littlefield.

Rozell, Mark J., and Clyde Wilcox (Eds.). 1997. *God at the Grass Roots, 1996: The Christian Right in the American Elections*. Lanham, Maryland: Rowman and Littlefield.

Sabato, Larry J. 1984. *PAC Power: Inside the World of Political Action Committees*. New York: W.W. Norton.

Schlozman, Kay Lehman, and John T. Tierney. 1986. *Organized Interests and American Democracy*. New York: Harper and Row.

Segers, Mary C. (Ed.). 1990. *Church Polity and American Politics: Issues in Contemporary Catholicism*. New York: Garland.

Segers, Mary C., and Timothy A. Byrnes (Eds.). 1995. *Abortion Politics in the American States*. Armonk, New York: M.E. Sharpe.

Smidt, Corwin, Lyman Kellstedt, John Green, and James Guth. 1994. "The Characteristics of Christian Political Activists: An Interest Group Analysis." Pp. 133–171 in William R. Stevenson, Jr. (Ed.), *Christian Political Activism at the Crossroads*. Lanham, Maryland: University Press of America.

The Washington Lobby, Fifth Edition. 1987. Washington, D.C.: CQ Press.

Weber, Paul J. 1982. "The Power and Performance of Religious Interest Groups." Paper presented to the Society for the Scientific Study of Religion, Providence, Rhode Island.

Weber, Paul J. 1986. "Religious Interest Groups: An Update." Paper presented to the Society for the Scientific Study of Religion, Providence, Rhode Island.

Wilcox, Clyde, Mark J. Rozell, and Roland Gunn. 1996. "Religious Coalitions in the New Christian Right." *Social Science Quarterly* 77: 543–558.

Zwier, Robert. 1984. "The New Christian Right and the 1980 Elections." Pp. 173–194 in David G. Bromley and Anson Shupe (Eds.), *New Christian Politics*. Macon, Georgia: Mercer University Press.

Zwier, Robert. 1989. "Coalition Strategies of Religious Interest Groups." Pp. 171–186 in Ted G. Jelen (Ed.), *Religion and Political Behavior in the United States.* New York: Praeger.

Zwier, Robert. 1994. "An Organizational Perspective on Religious Interest Groups." Pp. 95–119 in William R. Stevenson, Jr. (Ed.), *Christian Political Activism at the Crossroads.* Lanham, Maryland: University Press of America.

CHAPTER 11

The Debate on the Role of Religion in Public Life

[There] has been no correlation in our own century between Christian belief and liberal democracy. . . . Wherever liberal democracy has taken root and flourished, it has done so owing to the ideas and legacy of the Enlightenment—not to those of any particular faith.
—Aram Vartanian, "Democracy, Religion, and the Enlightenment"

[The] fundamental notions of democracy—of the dignity of the human person, therefore of the necessary limits of the state, of the discrete spheres of influence of economic, political, and cultural life—are rooted in Christianity.
—Richard John Neuhaus, "A Crisis of Faith"

Overview

What should be the role of religion, if any, in the public life of the United States? In Chapter 1 we saw how religion and politics were intertwined in the colonial beginnings of this country. In Chapter 2 we saw that the Founders held differing views on exactly what this role should be. In Chapters 3 and 4 we saw that religion has played a highly visible role in many significant public issues, both past and present. Chapters 5 and 6 examined significant Supreme Court cases, as well as legislation, that have helped to define the role that religion can play in public life. Chapter 7 surveyed the attitudes of the public and of elites regarding this issue. Chapters 8 and 9 examined the ways in which religious and political attitudes are intertwined among white and black Americans. Chapter 10 described the role that religious interest groups play in the American political system.

In this chapter, we will discuss the contemporary debate concerning religious influence in politics. Should the United States become a more secular society? Should it become a more religious society? We will present the different sides of this issue and demonstrate the complexities involved in this question. Individuals and organizations in the United States hold points of view that cover a very wide range. On one end of the continuum are those who assert that religion and politics should remain completely separate, believing that this arrangement is best for both religion and the government. On the opposite end are those who see the ideal situation as one in which religion and politics work closely together in support of common ends. We will survey a number of positions along this continuum.

It should be noted that most discussions of the issue by scholars and most popular debates on the subject assume that the discussion concerns how *Christianity* should or should not participate in public life. Some of the discussion is specific to that religion; for the most part, however, the basic points can be generalized to the discussion of more general *religious* roles and influences in public life. The major questions to guide this chapter are:

- Based on the two religious clauses of the First Amendment to the U.S. Constitution, what four basic types of positions are there on the proper role of religion in public life?
- What arguments have been made for the idea that the participation of organized religion in politics is bad for the political system? Conversely, what arguments have been made for the idea that mixing religion and politics is bad for religion?
- What arguments have been made for the proposition that religion is a necessary support for democracy? And what arguments have been made for the idea that religion is a necessary mediating structure between the individual and the government?
- What arguments have been made for the proposition that the government should serve the purposes of religion?
- What proposals have been made to involve religion in politics without causing church-state problems?
- What is the "culture war" and how does it concern religion and politics?

The Role of Religion in Public Life: Four Theoretical Views

In Chapter 7 you were introduced to a typology of four views held by the public on the proper role of religion in public life: Christian preferentialism, religious nonpreferentialism, religious minimalism, and the religious free-marketeer view (Jelen and Wilcox, 1995). These four types are the result of combining viewpoints on both religion clauses of the First Amendment. Here we want to go back to those viewpoints themselves without combining the two clauses.

We can think about the role of religion in the public life of the nation along two vectors: (1) government support for religion, or the establishment vector, and (2) government noninterference with religious practice, including religious practice in public locales, the free exercise vector.

The two points of view about the establishment clause both have implications for the role of religion in public life. The *accommodationist* position holds that the government should enact policies that favor organized religion. This is, in other words, support for religion over and against secularity. It is based on two assumptions: (1) Religion has beneficial consequences for human behavior, and may even be a necessary undergirding for democracy. (2) Most religions in the Judeo-Christian tradition affirm essentially the same moral values and have similar political effects, providing a "sacred canopy" that is the ethical basis for public life (Burger, 1967).

The *separationist* position believes that religion should be kept in the private realm. It tends to emphasize the problems involved in the absolute nature of religion's claims over and against the compromises required for democratic life. Religious claims thus tend to divide the culture, rather than to unite it. This makes religion a potentially dangerous element in public life, and it should be kept in the private realm.

Let's also review the two approaches to the proper meaning of the free exercise clause. Those who favor a *communitarian* view believe that the scope of religious free exercise should be limited by the actions of state and local legislatures. Because they reflect the consensus of the majority of the citizens of an area, they may impose limits on religious free exercise that violates that consensus. The view that commonly held standards of proper behavior and decency should limit the free exercise of religion is reflected, for example, in the *Reynolds* (polygamy) case discussed in Chapter 6.

On the other hand, a *libertarian* interpretation of free exercise supports the greatest range of free exercise for all, as long as it does not clash with the fundamental rights of other people or bring serious harm to others.

As Jelen and Wilcox point out, there is no necessary connection between the view that someone holds about one clause and the view that person holds on the other. They can be combined in various ways, as we will see.

The High Wall of Separation

The majority of Americans do want religion to have a place in public life. However, there are substantial arguments in favor of keeping public life wholly secular, and we will look at these arguments first. Arguments for keeping religion out of public life—at least in any organized fashion—come from two starting points. (1) The presence of religion in public life, because of its absolute claims, often undercuts the rationality and civility of public discourse. (2) Religion and democracy are based on different and fundamentally incommensurable premises.

The Absoluteness of Religion and the Civility of Public Discourse

First, it may be argued that religion's presence in the political arena adversely affects the style of political discourse. Religion contributes to extremism, intolerance, fanaticism, unwillingness to compromise, and in general undermines the calm and rational way in which political debate needs to be carried out and in which political decisions need to be made. When religion enters the political arena, it may become "too sure it is right" (Frankel, 1994: 108, quoting Judge Learned Hand). One analyst of church-state relations in the United States writes, "No matter how deep your faith, the quality of being 'too sure' resides in the disposition to impose it on others" (Frankel, 1994: 108).

When religious activists plunge into the give-and-take of politics, they may fail to exhibit the capacity for compromise and for treating political opponents with respect, which is deemed crucial for the democratic process. They may find themselves unable to resist translating their heartfelt belief that they know eternal truth into demagoguery (Wogaman, 1988: 171). Religion in the political realm may lead to a tendency for each side to demonize its opponents, as the rhetoric in the current conflicts over abortion and civil rights for gays and lesbians illustrates.

Writing about fundamentalist Christian political involvement, James E. Wood, Jr., editor of the *Journal of Church and State*, observes that when moral absolutes are confused with public policy, anyone who disagrees with the policy is often seen as immoral and ungodly. Such religious grounding of public policy ignores the diversity of American religion and the safeguards essential in a democratic society (Wood, 1987: 250).

Church-state analyst Ronald B. Flowers voices strong appreciation for the Christian Right's role in keeping moral issues before the public and in stimulating national discussion. However, he also notes that advocates on the side of the Christian Right "have often taken intractable positions that have tended to polarize society." He also notes as "more problematic" the movement's tendency to engage in "political efforts to remake the country in its own image" (Flowers, 1994: 127). We note here that taking intractable positions and tending to "demonize" one's political opponents may be engaged in by representatives of other religious perspectives and by secular groups, too.

When religion becomes political, it may well end up acting contrary to its own best insights. As the Williamsburg Charter states,

> Too often, for example, religious believers have been uncharitable, liberals have been illiberal, conservatives have been insensitive to tradition, champions of tolerance have been intolerant, defenders of free speech have been censorious, and citizens of a republic based on democratic accommodation have succumbed to a habit of relentless confrontation ("The Williamsburg Charter," 1988: 15).

Not Just Different, but Incompatible Premises

Another argument for the exclusion of organized religion from participation in organized politics is made on the basis that their underlying values and premises are not merely different, but incompatible (Vartanian, 1991). Vartanian restricts his discussion of religion in politics to *conventional* Christianity.

Conventional Christianity operates in the realm of dogmas that are "nondiscussable and nonnegotiable" (Vartanian, 1991: 12). Democracy, by contrast, requires the readiness for give and take, and willingness to compromise. Democracy requires "rational discourse and the rules of evidence," whereas conventional religion is likely to replace those principles with "obscurantism and willfulness" (Vartanian, 1991: 12), a reflection of the earlier point pertaining to the style of discourse. Religion expects its adherents to surrender to an absolute power that is held to be antithetical to the democratic "faith in freedom, rights and self-rule" (Vartanian, 1991: 14). Thus, "democracy and conventional religiosity . . . have been not merely different but *incompatible* systems of thought and behavior" (Vartanian, 1991: 9).

At the end of his discussion, Professor Vartanian expands his point beyond the incompatibility of conventional Christianity with democracy to include the incompatibility of religion in general with democracy. He also affirms secular humanism or secularism as the only appropriate basis for a political system that affirms individual liberties. He concludes that religion must remain outside public life and church and state must remain altogether separate, "not simply because the Bill of Rights so prescribes but because they do not in fact mix (Vartanian, 1991: 45).

Humanist Manifesto II and *A Secular Humanist Declaration*

Professor Vartanian echoes opinions stated before him in the foundational documents of humanism in the United States. The American Humanist Association has held a consistently separationist viewpoint throughout its history. *Humanist Manifesto II* describes the "separation of church and state and the separation of ideology and state" (Kurtz, 1973: 19) as imperatives. *A Secular Humanist Declaration* makes the point more sharply. It opposes "all varieties of belief that seek supernatural sanction for their values" (Kurtz, 1980: 7). Its authors further hold that any imposition of an exclusive view of what constitutes "truth, piety, virtue, or justice" for a whole society violates liberty. No group should be permitted to make its own views, "whether moral, philosophic, political, educational, or social, the standard for all people" (*A Secular Humanist Declaration*, pages 7 and 12).

The *Declaration* goes on to make several concrete recommendations: tax monies should not be used to benefit or support religious institutions. Properties owned by religious organizations should be taxed, as are other properties. No organized prayers and religious oaths should be permitted in public institutions.

American Atheists and the Freedom from Religion Foundation

Two organizations that have worked intensively for the maintenance of a complete wall of separation between church and state and the complete secularity of public life are American Atheists and the Freedom from Religion Foundation.

American Atheists was founded in 1963 by Dr. Madalyn Murray O'Hare for the purpose of the advancement of atheism and the "total, absolute separation of government and religion." The organization grew out of the Murray family's 1951 challenge to organized prayer and Bible reading in the public schools attended by their children *(Murray* v. *Curlett)*. Dr. O'Hare is perhaps best known for her opposition to the motto "In God We Trust" on coins. She holds that the presence of a religious motto on the official "legal tender" of the nation violates the establishment clause (because it means that the government has selected belief in God as an official stance), the free exercise and free speech clauses (since nonbelievers have to use money), and the equal protection clause of the Fourteenth Amendment.

The Freedom from Religion Foundation (founded in 1978) is an umbrella organization for freethinkers of whatever persuasion. It was formed to "establish an ongoing and authoritative voice for separation of church and state." They believe that organized religion has no place in government and that the Constitution was purposefully written to be a godless document since the only references to religion in it are exclusionary.

Normative or Inevitable?

Secular humanism offers as a normative judgment—what the relationship of religion to politics *should* be—what some theorists see simply as an inevitable state of affairs. The *secularization thesis* when applied to our topic says that as modernization advances, religion's role inescapably declines. Modernization here includes the scientific way of thinking, modern technological advances and complex economic life, mass communication and entertainment, and the growth of government bureaucracies and public education. The secularization theory has two variants. The first says that although religion continues to be a strong force in the general public, cultural elites and the institutions associated with them have become highly secularized. The second variant says that religion does not actually decline in response to modernity; it may even grow stronger. It is, however, relegated to the private sphere of life, increasingly retreating from formal, institutional involvement in political life (Fowler and Hertzke, 1995: 240–243).

Mixing Religion and Politics Is Bad for Religion

The viewpoints described above focus on why it is bad for politics when religion gets too involved. It has also been argued that such involvement is bad for religion. It can lead to idolatry and to attempts to join things that are simply incommensurable.

A Baptist Voice

You learned in Chapters 1 and 2 that Baptists have been strong supporters of religious liberty from colonial times. A recent essay by J. Brent Walker (1997: 3), general counsel for the Baptist Joint Committee, lists four reasons why government support of religion is bad for religion:

- Even though such support may appear to aid religion, it always raises the possibility of government regulation of religion.
- It limits religion's willingness and ability to call government to account in a prophetic way.
- Government financial support encourages people of faith to shirk their own responsibility to support their community of faith financially.
- Government funding can lead to denominational conflict because it raises the specter of favoritism.

The Success of a Free Market

Having religion functioning on its own, without government support or interference, means that all religious groups compete for followers on an equal footing, just as businesses do in a free market economy. It has often been noted that religion flourishes better in the United States than it does in many of the countries in which religion has government support. One explanation given for this is that the free market economy of religion in the United States naturally encourages the development of a large and diverse number of religious groups and styles of religion. This means that religion can appeal to a wide variety of people. It also means that less effective religious groups, those that do not meet people's perceived needs, will fail, just as commercial ventures that do not meet the needs of a constituency fail (Finke and Stark, 1992).

We described the communitarian view above. Communitarians generally believe that a unified "sacred canopy" (Peter Berger) of faith is necessary for a flourishing society and that rampant religious pluralism weakens rather than strengthens religion. The type of economic analysis carried out by Finke and Stark suggests that, far from weakening religion, intense and "market-driven" competition can strengthen its impact on the life of the nation.

The Danger of Idolatry

Religion moves and motivates people. Thus, politicians and political interest groups can be tempted to use its power in people's lives to help them achieve what they might not be able to otherwise. By identifying the limited goals and perspectives of a nation or a political movement with God, the nation or movement becomes an idol. As retiring senator Mark Hatfield said in a recent interview, "I am basically suspicious of anyone who claims to speak for everyone within the Christian faith. And I get so uptight about those who purport to speak for the Lord for political reasons. That to me is saying, Here is the political agenda that is, in effect, a substitute for the biblical gospel" (*Sojourners*, September–October, 1996, page 29).

Even as passionate an advocate of the political involvement of Christians as Philip Wogaman recognizes the danger. While lobbying is a legitimate activity for church groups, it brings with it danger because of the power it can have, power that can extend beyond the immediate issue involved. It also always involves compromise. For this reason, only those who are "thoroughly grounded in the faith and of unimpeachable integrity should . . . be entrusted by the church with that responsibility" (Wogaman, 1988: 203).

That Which God Hath *Not* Joined . . .

It is difficult to summarize the view that politics and true Christian life are simply incommensurable. To mix them is like trying to mix the proverbial oil and water. French sociologist and lay (not ordained) theologian Jacques Ellul provides one approach to this perspective; American Christian theologian John Howard Yoder provides another approach. Both men's views have in common that they see the primary role of the Christian in politics as one of simply "being" rather than "doing." Neither advocates *nonparticipation* in the political world; the Christian *style* of participation should be different. Both take the view that they do on the grounds that Christian faith and politics are two vastly different orders of being and do not properly mix. Individuals motivated by their Christian faith have a definite role within the public realm; organized religion does not, and, if it is true to itself, cannot.

Jacques Ellul: Of Human Bondage and Radical Freedom

Ellul's starting point is that the gift that God makes freely available in Jesus is the gift of radical freedom. That gift delivers human beings from entrapment in the "order of necessity," the state of bondage. However, all human institutions, especially politics, belong to that order of bondage and necessity. Thus, political activity can provide no ultimate solutions, nor can it solve ultimate problems. When people make the mistake of thinking that it can, they mire themselves more deeply in their slavery to necessity. Therefore, trying to use the political order to infuse society with Christian values—or to limit non-Christian ones—is doomed to failure (Ellul, 1967; 1972a; 1972b).

However, Ellul maintains that there is a crucial role for the Christian in politics, that of the *witness*. The state is necessary to see to it that relative freedoms are embodied and evil restrained, but beyond that, it has no use. Its impotence is seen clearly, for example, in the fact that all societies rely on violence to achieve and secure their ends. But violence clearly is one of the defining marks of the "order of necessity" and "unfreedom," a singular element of all that from which Christians have been freed by Christ. By definition, participation in violence cannot be a characteristic of Christian freedom (Ellul, 1972b).

Because it deals in the realm of the relative, the best approach that one living under ultimate freedom can take is simply being there, a constant challenge to political "business as usual." Ellul writes:

> [If] Christians are to be in political life to bear witness, if this is in truth their only motive . . . [others] will then look with astonishment at these odd people who instead of doing like others, i.e., hating one another for political reasons, are full of love for one another beyond these secondary barriers (Ellul, 1976: 396).

From his angle of vision, when Christians plunge into the rough-and-tumble of political compromise and powermongering, they lose their vital capacity to bear witness to the one thing that politics most needs.

John Howard Yoder: The Politics of Inevitable Violence

Mennonite theologian John Howard Yoder provides a different interpretation of this perspective on Christian participation in politics. Like Ellul, Yoder is deeply disturbed by the incompatibility of the use of violence with the Christian vision. (Mennonites have been among the most consistent Christian witnesses for peacemaking and nonviolence.) With Ellul also, he is inclined to see the existence of the state as necessary only to control evil. Even its positive functions—the provision of education and welfare, for example—rely heavily on the use of compulsion to get people to pay the necessary taxes. Relying on compulsion, they rely implicitly on violence (nonpayment can and probably will result in incarceration). From his perspective, the state is something entirely alien to Christianity, to the Kingdom of God, which is founded on peace. He does not advocate disobedience to requirements like paying taxes. Insofar as they can in good conscience, Christians are to be subject to the state and its regulations. But, with Ellul, the unique Christian way of participation in the processes of the state is by witnessing with one's life to a very different reality from the state.

According to Yoder's interpretation, Christians are not called to "manage the world." That is God's business. Given the witness of Christians, God will in time transform the world in accordance with the Kingdom (Yoder, 1972: 236 and elsewhere).

We have seen that belief in the necessity of a "high wall of separation" between church and state can come from the conviction that anything less is a threat to liberty and the civil conduct of public business. We have also examined views that take a strict separationist position because the commingling of religion and government is bad for religion. Others think that the two orders simply do not mix, and in principle cannot. The assertion that religion and politics need to work together, or that religion is necessary for democratic politics, can also be made from either side. It is to these views that we now turn.

A Working Partnership I: Religion as a Necessary Support for Democracy

This point of view holds that democratic values are rooted in Judeo-Christian religious values, and that the values of democracy require this religious grounding to uphold them. In terms of the fourfold distinction with which we began, this is another example of an accommodationist view. Christian neoconservative Richard John Neuhaus (1984: 62) has stated the point succinctly: "[The] fundamental notions of democracy— of the dignity of the human person, therefore of the necessary limits of the state, of the discrete spheres of influence of economics, political, and cultural life—are rooted in Christianity."

Neuhaus also writes that the political realm derives its direction from shared cultural sensibilities. In the United States, moral judgments are usually linked with religious belief for most people. The Judeo-Christian ethic provides the binding thread that brings the nation closer to civility (Neuhaus, 1984).

The Inadequacy of Secular Value Systems

Another proponent of this viewpoint is A. James Reichley. Reichley understands the underlying issue in the discussion of religion in American public life to be that of whether or not "a free society depends ultimately on religious values for cohesion and vindication of human rights" (Reichley, 1985: 8). He distinguishes among three kinds of secular (nonreligious) value systems, and finds each one inadequate to fully support democratic values and practices.

The first of these is *egoism*. Some persons who hold that egoism is a sufficient undergirding for democracy believe that human nature is such that, when freed from oppression and repression, people naturally act in ways that support democracy. Others, the "tougher-minded" egoists, hold that even though human nature cannot be counted on to cause people to behave democratically, the free competition between them will ensure maximum benefits to all. Reichley, on the other hand, says that history will support neither viewpoint. Neither human nature nor the results of free competition can be counted on, and unfettered "egoism is practically guaranteed to cause social disaster" (Reichley, 1985: 341–343).

The second secular system that Reichley reviews is *authoritarianism*, which he sees as "almost by definition hostile to democracy." Even the most benign authoritarian government cannot possibly uphold anything approaching democratic standards of personal liberty (Reichley, 1985: 343–344).

Civil humanism is the third secular value system. It claims that it "legitimizes both individual rights and social authority and establishes a balance between them." Reichley distinguishes two types. *Libertarian* humanism holds that individuals voluntarily give up some of their freedom and civil liberties in order to enjoy the benefits of a civil society. The more *communitarian* version of civil humanism holds that civil liberties are products of the evolution of the social group and hence dependent on it. Reichley thinks that both are unworkable from the outset. The libertarian version falls prey to "atomistic selfishness, obsessive materialism, and personal alienation." The communitarian version tends "toward social indoctrination, state control, and group aggression" (Reichley, 1985: 344–345).

Reichley also identifies a third type of humanism, which he labels "classical civil humanism." Human nature, in this version, "depends for fulfillment on order, justice, and freedom." Since human nature naturally aspires to these goals, they provide adequate moral grounding for a "free and humane society." Reichley sees this approach as inadequate, as well, and not supported by historical evidence (Reichley, 1985: 346–347).

The core of Reichley's critique of all the secular civil humanisms is that a balancing of self and society as dual ultimate sources of value simply cannot be held together without there being a third value source upon which they both rely. Otherwise, one will always overrun the other, because the "essential moral support" for democracy is lacking (Reichley, 1985: 348). Religion provides this third, independent value source, and therefore, "the health of republican government depends on moral values derived from religion" (Reichley, 1985: 340).

Christian Faith and Democratic Values

One listing of specific democratic values that are held to derive from the Judeo-Christian tradition and, ultimately, to depend on it, is provided by Ernest Griffith. Griffith and his co-authors (1956) are interested in the "cultural attitudes or *mores* which will sustain democracy." What sorts of attitudes will provide the necessary psychological undergirding for democracy, and further, will give democracy the "emotional content" that will make its adherents willing to fight for it (Griffith et al., 1956: 101)?

They hypothesize that the Judeo-Christian tradition, and especially Christian faith, is the matrix which best grounds the values necessary for a functioning democracy. Only religious faith can give such attitudes the character of absolutes, a feature that they see as necessary for the survival of democracy (Griffith et al., 1956: 103). They then list seven specific attitudes that they believe are best grounded in Christian faith:

- "Love for and belief in freedom" is supported by the Judeo-Christian belief in the sacredness of each person as a child of God.

- Commitment to active participation in the life of the community is based on a belief in obligation to accept one's responsibility to work cooperatively with all humankind.
- Truthfulness in discussion can be based on belief in truth as the inner light of God's righteousness.
- The obligation of economic groups to serve society is an out-growth of Christian view of society as whole, in which each person has a responsibility for all the rest.
- Leadership and holding office seen as public trusts reflect the biblical examples of prophetic service.
- Religious faiths lead to attitudes that promote a union of individualism and responsibility.
- Cooperation and goodwill among nations grows out of a vision of the world that says we are all children of one Father, God (Griffith et al., 1956: 113).

Reichley's civil humanist might well want to argue that civil humanism is at least as capable of supporting the traits that Griffith et al. deem necessary for democracy, and without the risks posed by grounding such critical features of our common life in the tenets of limited religious thought. From the perspective of the scope of humankind's religions throughout the world, it can also be said that there is nothing in this list that would not be affirmed by the central tradition of them all.

A Broad Consensus of Essential Values

Another variation on the theme of why politics and religion go hand in hand is the view which holds that the United States operates on the basis of a broad consensus on essential values and that religion is an integral part of that consensus. "In this view," says one recent analyst, "we as a people not only agree on a set of rules, but on a substantive set of moral and metaphysical principles with a transcendent basis." Such an arrangement, if one can be shown to exist, clearly does not support unlimited tolerance for differing opinions. Jelen explains that such a consensus would mean that "tolerance for diversity cannot and should not be unlimited." Although the boundaries may be both broad and somewhat vague, violators must not be tolerated. Tolerance should, however, be extended to all those who are within the boundaries (Jelen, 1995: 272–273).

This is a clear statement of an *accommodationist* interpretation of the establishment clause coupled with a *communitarian* view regarding religious free exercise. Organized religion has a definite role in public life, and there are definite cultural norms by which free exercise has to be constrained.

This view has definite implications for public policy issues and for the sorts of questions that we have discussed in Chapters 5 and 6 on the First Amendment. "Religious symbols and imagery" certainly have an important place in those institutions that affirm and inculcate the common culture, such as "schools, public buildings, [and] national holidays." Prayer in the public schools and the public celebration of religious holidays are important for maintaining the consensus. While the government would not be permitted to assist particular religious denominations, aid to religion in general would be encouraged. The religious preferences of the majority could well receive government support (Jelen, 1995: 274–275).

Religion as a Necessary Mediating Structure

A recent group of Christian thinkers takes issue with the privatization of religion that has come about in the wake of modernization and the secularization of American life. Religion and the churches, they argue, are absolutely necessary for the health of a democracy, and the privatization of religion poses a substantial threat to democracy. We will look at the work of Robert Booth Fowler, Richard John Neuhaus, and Stephen L. Carter as representative of this group of thinkers.

The idea that religion and the liberal democratic order are "unconventional partners" goes back at least to Alexis de Tocqueville. On this analysis, religion and culture greatly assist each other. Religion does not engage actively in politics, but is a source for meaning, moral values, and community that the government cannot provide. The relationship, however, remains at a pre-reflective level. The contemporary theorists who think in this vein articulate a vision in which that relationship moves from being unintentional to consciously intentional, and in which religion's role in politics becomes more active.

Religion as an Alternative to the Liberal Democratic Order

According to Robert Booth Fowler, there are two prevailing types of views about the relationship of religion and culture. "Integrationist" views emphasize the ways in which religion reinforces liberal culture, while "challenge" views emphasize the ways in which religion opposes culture. Against both these views, Fowler proposes that religion presents an *alternative* to the liberal order. The liberal order is inherently very individualistic, and thus lacks the dimension of community that human beings must have. By being that community, religion sustains the liberal order by making it possible for people to live with the inevitable inadequacy of liberalism's individualism. By offering believers a sharply alternative reality, religion provides a counterweight to the liberal order that allows believers to sustain and participate in that order as the best way of organizing temporal affairs (Fowler, 1988).

The Naked Public Square

Richard John Neuhaus describes the current situation metaphorically in the title of his book, *The Naked Public Square* (1984). He believes that political practice and doctrine have been operating in such a way that religion and religious values are systematically excluded from the public arena, thus leaving the public square "naked." Such nakedness is both temporary and very threatening to the survival of democracy, because it is a "vacuum begging to be filled," a vacuum that *will* be filled. The only question is, "filled with *what?*"

Neuhaus' concern is that if religious values are excluded from the public square, public morality will be decided by cultural elites whose views do not coincide with those of the majority. We saw evidence of this in our survey of the differences between the views of the mass culture and the elites in Chapter 7. If religion is excluded from a position of influence in the public square, then the realm of public life will be controlled by the government (Neuhaus, 1984).

Part of what Neuhaus contends here is that the moral authority of the democratic state is rooted not so much in individual rights or a concept of "the people," but in those communities which comprise the society and through which "the people" interact with the state. The effective "banning" of religion from the arena of public discourse has left the United States without "an effective and believable linkage between the vast institutions (megastructures) of the public sphere and the values by which people live day-by-day." Thus, despite demanding increasing government services from the growing welfare state, people do not have confidence in the policies of that government, creating problems with both legitimacy and alienation (Kerrine and Neuhaus, 1979: 10–11). Neuhaus writes with a sense of urgency born out of his belief that we face a real crisis of legitimacy that can only get worse unless a "transcendent moral purpose" can focus its judgment on the state and make it clear that the state is simply the servant of the law, not its source (Neuhaus, 1984: 259).

He has a very specific prescription for fixing what he understands is wrong with America: The values that we associate with democracy must not only be sustained, but revitalized. This can only be done by grounding them in biblical faith. He believes that the basic concepts of democracy have their foundation in Christianity, and only by acknowledging this foundation can democracy as we know it survive, since the actual religion of the American people is "overwhelmingly and explicitly Judeo-Christian" (Neuhaus, 1985: 62–65).

Unlike some members of the religious right, Neuhaus does not base his claim of the necessity of the Judeo-Christian tradition for democracy on divine revelation or the words of the Bible. Rather, he argues from the standpoint that Judeo-Christianity provides a necessary grounding for democratic values.

A Culture of Disbelief?

Stephen L. Carter, author of the popular book *The Culture of Disbelief: How American Law and Politics Trivialize Religious Devotion*, also sees an important role for religions as a bulwark against unfettered state power. By being an independent moral voice, religions make claims on their adherents that can be a balance to the competing claims of the government, thus limiting the loyalty of religious persons to the state and providing a point from which the state can be judged (Carter, 1993b: 136).

This makes it possible for religions to be "intermediary institutions" active in the space between the individual and the government, a space that the state might otherwise take over. Strong religious bodies that retain their independence are also able to fulfill their historic function as the transmitters of values and meaning from generation to generation. Religion is uniquely able to meet these needs, since it engages the faithful in thinking about ultimate questions and searching for ultimate answers (Carter, 1993b: 136–137).

According to Carter's thesis, we live in a "culture of disbelief," in which law and politics have joined forces to trivialize religion and relegate it to the private sphere, effectively silencing its public voice. Religious people are expected "to act publicly, and sometimes privately as well, as though their faith does not matter to them." He continues: "Aside from the ritual appeals to God that are expected of our politicians, for Americans to take their religions seriously, to treat them as ordained rather than chosen, is to risk assignment to the lunatic fringe" (Carter, 1993a: 3–4).

Religions are "autonomous communities of resistance and . . . independent centers of meaning" (Carter, 1993a: 40). This makes them "radically destabilizing." It is also what makes them able to stand over against the state. We see this destabilization and moral independence, says Carter, in the civil disobedience of Dr. Martin Luther King, Jr., Gandhi, and the anti-abortion group Operation Rescue (Carter, 1993a: 41).

For persons for whom their religion seems to be ordained—not freely chosen by them, but something given to or laid upon them by an outside agency—religion makes "claims that exist alongside, are not identical to, and will sometimes trump the claims to obedience that the state makes" (Carter, 1993a: 35). It is this possibility of refusal to accept the will of the state and what the majority considers right or reasonable that "leads to America's suspicion toward religious belief" (Carter, 1993a: 41).

Carter also addresses the issue of the separation of church and state. He understands the religion clauses of the First Amendment to have been intended to protect religion from governmental interference, not to insulate government from religious influences (Carter, 1993a: 107). To misinterpret it in the second manner will "carry us down the road to a new establishment, the establishment of religion as a hobby, trivial and unimportant for serious people, not to be mentioned in serious discourse" (Carter, 1993a: 115).

This leads him to very definite views on the proper application of the two clauses. Regarding the establishment clause, he is an accommodationist. He believes that churches and programs run by religious organizations should be "able to compete on the same grounds as other groups for the largess of the welfare state—they should not, on establishment clause grounds, be relegated to a second-class status" (Carter, 1993a: 119). If, for example, a wholly secular drug-treatment program is fundable, so should a religiously-based program that relies heavily on prayer and Bible study. Both should be subject to the same criteria of effectiveness.

A libertarian regarding the free exercise clause, he also argues for a very broad set of exemptions from otherwise applicable laws for religious groups and individuals. This evolves directly out of his conviction that one of the crucial roles that religions play is that of an autonomous source of authority and value that, on occasion, may require that their adherents act otherwise than the law prescribes, or act as it proscribes (Carter, 1993a: 126). The rationale for the accommodation of religion, rather than simply government neutrality, is not primarily to protect the individual conscience, although it also does that. The primary purpose that accommodation serves is the "preservation of the religions as independent power bases that exist in large part to resist the state" (Carter, 1993a: 134).

Carter and Neuhaus have in common a view of religion that sees religion as an absolutely necessary counterweight to the tendency of a secular democratic state to ever enlarge itself at the expense of its own best principles. There are also important differences between them. Neuhaus emphasizes the importance of the Judeo-Christian religious tradition for the *content* of democracy. Carter, by contrast, focuses on the importance of religion and religious groups more generally for the democratic *process*. He frequently uses nonconventional religions as positive examples of religious resistance and is often critical of how the courts have dealt with this opposition.

A Working Partnership II:
The Church and the Maintenance of Civil Order

Protestant reformer John Calvin believed that the best arrangement was one in which civil government supported the worship of the God of Judaism and Christianity, defended correct religious teaching, and protected the church. He also charged the civil government with the responsibility for preventing offenses such as idolatry, blasphemy, sacrilege and other "public offenses against religion." Civil officials were to be responsible for enforcing the Ten Commandments of the Judeo-Christian scriptures. Calvin's city, Geneva, embodied his approach to the role of the Christian church in public life.

One contemporary approach to the necessity of a union between church and state is an outgrowth of Calvin's thought. Rather than asserting that democratic government requires religion as a necessary condition, it begins with the premise that religion requires government's support. It has been given its most consistent formulation in a recent movement referred to as Christian Reconstructionism. There are variations within this movement, but there are certain principles on which nearly all its leaders agree, and we will focus on these.

One of the main institutional centers of Reconstructionist thought is the Chalcedon Foundation think tank, founded by Rousas John Rushdoony. Founded in 1964, the foundation states that its goal is "to educate people in the Biblical standards for life, both individual and social." Its members "believe that there can be no solution to personal or societal problems other than those the Bible offers."

Reconstructionists strive for a total transformation of the United States, and then the world, so that everything and everyone will be brought under the dominion of God as they understand God. Civil magistrates are under a moral and religious obligation to uphold and enforce the law of God as it is recorded in both testaments of the Christian Bible.

Christian Reconstructionism in Outline

A convenient outline of Reconstructionist approach to religion's role in public life can be found in a statement by the Chalcedon Foundation. The full text of the statement is available on Chalcedon's website (http://www.chalcedon.edu). We summarize its main points here.

- Christian Reconstructionism is Calvinistic, understanding itself to be the modern inheritor of the Reformed faith. Christianity must apply to all of life, "to . . . politics no less than to church."
- The law of God has a number of purposes, one of which is to maintain the order of civil society, "restraining and arresting civil evil."
- Reconstructionists believe that Christ will return to the earth only after the church has brought the entire world into submission to Christ.
- Reconstructionists are "dominionists." They believe that everything must be "reconstructed in terms of the Bible." Four things especially are included: the individual, the family, the church, and "the wider society, including the state." They advocate a thoroughly "Christian civilization."

So How *Is* the Church to Be Involved? A Composite Proposal

Thus far we have reviewed a number of *theories* about the proper role of religion in politics. The majority of religious leaders and religious people in the United States believe that religion does have a role to play in the public arena and in the political life of the nation. Their views lie somewhere between those of the ardent secularists and those of the Christian Reconstructionists.

Three relatively recent proposals from Christian writers provide reflections about what the role of the churches in American public life
should be. As we stated before, most of the discussion in the United States
revolves around the role of *Christian* churches, since that is by far the predominant religion. However, we broaden the discussion below to include
organized communities of faith generally. Taking the three authors together gives us a composite list of what such a role might look like
(Reichley, 1985; Wogaman, 1988; Castelli, 1988). We note that not all
people of faith will agree with this composite picture; we have already
seen in this chapter that theologians John Howard Yoder and Jacques
Ellul offer very different proposals.

- Communities of faith are responsible for educating their own
  members, so that they in turn will act individually within the political process in ways that are coherent with their faith commitments. Beyond this, however, communities of faith are called to
  more direct involvement in public life. Being a part of civil society
  entails an obligation to participate in its processes. Faith communities are called upon to oppose moral and social evil and to nurture positive moral values, both among their own members and
  in the society at large. Religious groups in the United States understand the claim of God (or the holy more broadly conceived)
  to be a claim that reaches every area of human life, public and
  private.
- When organized religion chooses to involve itself in this way, it
  "must play by the same rules" (Castelli, 1988: 21) as everyone else.
  This means not relying on appeals to divine revelation or to religious
  authority to bolster their case, and not claiming to speak for God.
- Communities of faith must also realize that the moral relevance
  of government decisions and social issues varies widely. Thus,
  they must choose their issues with care. Faith communities
  should, in other words, take stands on matters in which the outcomes do truly matter in moral terms and on which they are
  most competent to speak.
- Some types of direct political involvement are acceptable. Testimony before legislative committees, friend-of-the-court briefs,
  lobbying, and mail campaigns are examples. Tax laws prohibit
  nonprofit organizations from direct campaigning on behalf of
  candidates, however.

- Civil disobedience is an option that should not be undertaken lightly, but one that may at times be necessary. If so, it must be done with willingness to accept the penalties for illegal actions (as with the civil rights movement, described in Chapter 4).
- Partisan or issue advocacy, "taking sides," is not the only option. Working for reconciliation is also important (see our discussion of common ground politics below).
- Although organized religion must be involved in public life, it must do so with keen awareness of the dangers involved. Becoming too heavily involved in the compromises of politics can impair the ability to maintain an objective moral stance. The greater the involvement, the greater is the danger of tendencies toward the kind of absolutism already discussed as detrimental to public discourse. The danger of idolatry, of equating specific political or social views with the will of God, must be avoided.
- Churches and other faith communities must practice a style of involvement that always reflects respect for both their political opponents and other faith groups.
- On the other hand, a demand that candidates for public office be "godly" or "born-again" violates the constitutional prohibition of religious qualifications for public office. Any stand or action that sends a message of acceptance to adherents of a particular faith, or to religion generally, or that sends messages of "outsider" status to nonadherents is outside the boundaries of what is permissible (Castelli, 1988: 23).

The three ethicists from whom this composite portrait is drawn are moderate in their approach. We have already noted the disagreement of people like Yoder and Ellul on one side. We have described the views of the Christian Reconstructionists, as well. Many in the "religious right" would also take exception to what has been described above and instead press for a style of involvement that would more closely align the nation with their particular view of what makes a society morally good.

"Culture War": Two Religious Cultures at Odds

We discussed the growing difference between liberal and conservative religion in Chapter 4. We now turn to this "culture war" thesis directly. The thesis is not a normative statement about the proper role of religion in public life. It is rather a statement of a conflict that is perhaps inevitable in this particular culture. We will examine the conflict and then look at one proposed solution to it.

The basic thesis is fairly simple. James Davison Hunter (whose book title brought the term "culture wars" into public discourse) uses the terms "orthodox" and "progressive" to define the two poles. The defining feature of *orthodoxy* is its reliance on and commitment to a transcendent authority that is unchanging, consistent, and stands outside both the individual and the culture. *Progressivism,* on the other hand, understands moral authority as more subjective, guided by rationality rather than authority. Truth is more a process than a clearly defined content. Whereas the orthodox base their thinking on the assumptions of the past that are enshrined in tradition, progressives focus more on the "prevailing assumptions of contemporary life" (Hunter, 1991: 44–45).

The division that Hunter observes is rooted in differing moral understandings, each of which desires to dominate all others. It touches the most basic assumptions about how American society should be ordered, and how American individuals should order their lives, as well (Hunter, 1991: 42–43). It is thus at the heart of the discussion of the proper role of religion in American public life.

The Two Opposing Camps

The two opposing camps in the culture war have been identified and labeled differently by different scholars, but usually include at least many of the following: (1) Arrayed on one side are liberals, leftists, modernists, secularists, secular humanists, feminists, gays and lesbians along with their sympathizers, those in favor of the welfare state, big-government advocates, nuclear freeze enthusiasts, religious liberals, ecumenically minded Christians and others (religious people who advocate ecumenism and a broadly pluralistic approach to religion, usually reaching beyond cooperation among Christian churches to include those of other faiths, as well), academics, and the media. They are accused of bulldozing a secular humanist agenda into place against the wishes of the majority of citizens who have not had the political power to prevent it. Organizations that are often named in this category include the American Civil Liberties Union, National Organization for Women, National Abortion Rights Action League, and People for the American Way.

(2) On the other side are those who favor traditional values, who believe in discipline, public decency and order, amendments to protect the American flag from desecration, partisans of United States military superiority, supporters of the traditional two-parent monogamous heterosexual family as the sole locus of sexual expression, traditional gender roles for men and women, the attitude of respect from children to their elders, and public reinforcement of traditional religious beliefs and moral values. The best-known organizational name in this category was the Moral Majority, dissolved in the late 1980s. The current flagship organization is Pat Robertson's Christian Coalition. Many of the issues find a home in Concerned Women for America. There is also a variety of single-purpose organizations dedicated to goals such as limitations on abortion, cleaning up television, reintroducing organized prayer into public school classrooms, and the passage of other legislation designed to enact traditional values into law. Having had only limited success on the national levels, these groups have turned their attention to local school boards, and have been very successful in some instances at getting a majority of their supporters on county boards of education.

There is stereotyping and hostility on both sides of the "theological fence" that separates the two parties to the debate. But how much of it is just rhetoric?

> [Liberals] look across the theological fence at their conservative cousins and see rigid, narrow-minded, moralistic fanatics; conservatives holler back with taunts that liberals are immoral, loose, biblically illiterate, and unsaved. . . . Do tensions between religious liberals and conservatives actually run deep? Or are they merely the work of a few highly articulate pressure groups such as Moral Majority and People for the American Way? (Wuthnow, 1988: 215)

As Wuthnow notes, stereotyping and hostility have often lessened as opposing groups interact with each other; this has been the case, for example, with Jewish-Christian tensions and often with racial tensions as well. In the case of the parties to the current culture war, this has not proven to be the case. Those tensions seem to be "rooted more in the presence of contact than in its absence." Education, traditionally another major factor in lessening prejudice, does not seem to alter liberal-conservative tensions, either. Like contact, it may in fact exacerbate them. The *belief* that such tensions exist seems to have become something of a self-fulfilling prophecy. The tensions do indeed "run deep," creating a "chasm" in American cultural life (Wuthnow, 1988: 217–223).

Not many people identify completely with either side of this conflict; there is, in fact, a continuum that stretches between the two poles. Particularly in the general public, people's views do not fall consistently in one camp or the other. There is greater consistency at the more reflective elite level. However, as Hunter points out, despite the rhetoric, the argument over American culture and who will define "America's soul" (Wuthnow, 1989) has ramifications that will touch everyone. They reflect honest, deeply felt concerns about issues that are central to determining the direction that "American public culture" will take (Hunter, 1991: 33).

The Culture War and the Civil Religion

In Chapter 1, we described civil religion as a religious underpinning that, at least to some extent, unifies the nation. Wuthnow (1988a, 1988b) argues that the noise of the culture war battle reaches the civil religion as well as the churches. Rather than uniting people around a common set of values, it echoes the deep differences reflected by the culture wars thesis.

The conservative version maintains that America stands in a unique relationship to God, with its form of government and economy divinely legitimated. America is responsible for bringing the whole world to Christ, and has been given extraordinary resources and divine favor for that purpose. The liberal version rejects the "one nation under God" concept as an affront to pluralism. America as God's greatest tool for evangelizing the world is not mentioned, and the United States is just as likely to be named as a cause of the problems facing the world as their solution. Basic human rights are cited as the grounds of this civil religion more often than Judeo-Christian particularity (Wuthnow, 1988a).

The two civil religions differ in their presuppositions, their methods, and their end goals. The conservative vision resembles what Max Weber called the *priestly function* of religion, supportive of privilege and the status quo. The liberal vision is more like Weber's *prophetic function* of religion, raising questions and challenging the status quo in light of larger concerns (Wuthnow, 1988a: 398).

As with the ecclesiastical version of the war between the cultures in the United States, there is rhetorical venom on both sides. A letter from the liberal Clergy and Laity Concerned, for example, contrasts the two views of America: "One based on arrogance and a false sense of superiority. The other based on ethical, biblical principles" (cited in Wuthnow 1988a: 397).

Proponents of civil religion in the United States think of it as a unifying religious ethos that underlies and unites the various denominational religions that flourish in such great plurality here. Clearly, a civil religion fragmented along the same lines that ecclesiastical religion is fragmented cannot perform this unifying function. It will, if anything, widen the chasm.

Common Ground Politics: A New Politics Beyond Left *and* Right?

> The old solutions of the Left and the Right and the bitter conflict between liberals and conservatives seem increasingly irrelevant and distasteful to people in their own communities. Many people care both about the moral values that have concerned the conservatives *and* the issues of justice and equity that have preoccupied the liberal agenda. (Wallis, 1996:20)

This statement from Jim Wallis, of the Sojourners organization, provides a summary of the major thrust of a movement that seeks to move beyond the politics of Left versus Right. Sojourners is one of the organizations seeking to bring about an end to the "culture war." The constituency of this movement is diverse, and includes both conservative and more liberal Protestants as well as Catholics and non-Christians. Wallis refers to this as a movement for "common ground politics" (Wallis, 1997).

Three Premises

Advocates of this approach base their thinking on three premises: (1) Both liberals and conservatives have something important to offer, something which the majority of Americans support. (2) Equally, however, both have serious flaws. (3) Although the federal government does have a responsibility for the building of a good society and the moral nurture of its people, especially its youngsters, much more needs to be done at the local level, closer to where people live and work.

What is it that liberals and conservatives offer that is helpful? Liberals have worked hard for "racial, economic, and gender justice." They have stood for peace and against undue corporate power. Liberalism has consistently advocated government provision of a "social safety net" and upheld the importance of individual rights (Gelsey, 1997). Conservatives have demanded a "values-based politics." They have emphasized the need for strong families and for personal responsibility more than reliance on government (Wallis, 1997).

On the other hand, both have serious flaws and have made serious mistakes. Liberal interests have not upheld crucial social and personal moral values, and have not offered adequate support for the "fraying fabric of family life." Too often, their message has been one of moral relativism in the name of individual liberty. They have relied too heavily on government solutions. The conservatives have been in error on important matters, as well. They have not always favored racial justice, nor have they defended the poor and the vulnerable. Although they attack big government, they favor big business and military growth (Wallis, 1997). They have verbally promoted family values and worked to enact policies that undercut families. As a recent Web document on the topic states it, "It is hard to see how resistance to a living wage and a humane workplace, opposition to environmental protection and the Endangered Species Act, support for Uzis and the defunding of National Public Radio will contribute to higher moral values" (Gelsey, 1997).

Finally, people do not believe that the government can solve all the country's problems, especially not without imposing even more burdensome regulations. This approach sees government at all levels—federal, state, and local—and the private sector working together to bring about solutions that transcend the politics of right and left.

Practical Implications

There appear to be at least two practical ramifications of common ground politics. President Clinton, in his 1997 State of the Union address, challenged the churches, as well as other nonprofits and businesses, to "hire someone off welfare." He emphasized that revisions in the law permit the use of welfare money by private employers, including faith groups, to employ and train former welfare recipients.

The other practical ramification is apparent in the American Community Renewal legislation introduced earlier in Congress. This, too, provides for the government helping to fund, through vouchers, religiously-sponsored drug programs as well as religiously-sponsored schools. At least a part of the intention behind the Republican House and Senate "Renewal Alliance" is to advocate proposals that empower groups and governments at the local level to work alongside the federal government in solving problems.

It is not the prospect of more local problem-solving that makes critics of these sorts of programs uneasy. In their practical application, many of the proposals seem to call for a new era of cooperation between government and religion. It is this cooperation that makes opponents of these sorts of programs uneasy, fearing too much entanglement and too much regulation.

Summary and Conclusions

The question of how religion should be involved in politics is, as we have demonstrated, a complex one. In this chapter, we have reviewed the following range of viewpoints:

- Organized religion does not belong in public life. Mixing the two is bad for government, for religion, or for both.
- Government and organized religion both benefit from a working partnership between them. Some theorists hold that religion provides necessary support for democracy. Others believe that religion has within itself the call for cooperation.
- Having reviewed a number of theories about how organized religion might be involved in public life, we looked at a composite proposal that outlined the details of that involvement. In general, we found that, although political involvement is likely to be problematic for religious institutions, there are ways that churches can be involved without compromising either their own beliefs and practices or the constitutionally mandated separation of church and state.
- What appears to many people to be the actual situation is a "culture war" between liberal and conservative interests.
- This situation has led to a call by some for a new politics that transcends both left and right. The practical proposals that arise from this perspective, however, raise difficult questions about the extent of government entanglement with organized religion.

What conclusions can we draw from these reflections? It seems fairly apparent that many theorists want neither an absolute "high wall of separation" between church and state, nor do they want to see the wall torn down completely. This is similar to the situation in the general public which we described in Chapter 7. The most concern comes at the point of the practical application of ideas that would require fairly extensive cooperation between government and organized religion. It seems certain that questions and litigation about the proper role of religion in public life will continue for the foreseeable future, perhaps intensifying.

We began by noting that attitudes toward the role of religion in public life can be described as running along two vectors, one for each of the two religion clauses. It appears to us—although speculation is always risky—that the establishment clause vector will probably take a more accommodationist direction in the near future, encouraging and allowing for the sorts of cooperation between government and religion that have been discussed above.

It is somewhat more difficult to sort out the fate of the free exercise clause vector, because there seem to be forces pulling in both directions. On the one hand, the prevalence of social movements in which previously marginalized groups are demanding full inclusion may lead in the direction of a continued libertarian movement. We see this, for example, in the demands of homosexual couples for marriage ceremonies and for the religious and legal recognition of their partnership. On the other hand, there seems to be an increasing call for community standards that would lead in a communitarian direction (seen, for example, in the resistance to granting these rights). On balance, at least in the near future, a communitarian stance may prevail.

The combination of the religion clauses in the First Amendment with the often noted religiosity of the American people virtually guarantees that the role of religion in public life will be continually renegotiated. It will never be a fixed entity.

Important Terms

Libertarian humanism

Communitarian civil humanism

Classical civil humanism

Culture wars

Christian Reconstruction

Review Questions

1. What are the arguments that people make to support the idea that organized religion does not belong in public life? Remember that there are two types of arguments here.

2. Why do some people claim that religion is a necessary support for democracy?

3. On what basis do some people believe that religion itself requires cooperation between religion and government?

4. What principles should guide churches if they choose to become involved in politics?

5. State the culture war thesis in your own words. Describe its two opposing poles.

6. How does the approach taken by those who advocate common ground politics seek to end the culture war?

Discussion Questions

1. Which of the two quotations given at the beginning of this chapter do you find the most convincing? Why?

2. Should religion stay out of politics or be involved in politics? Why?

3. Do you agree with Neuhaus and Carter that religion is a necessary support for the democratic process? Why or why not?

4. Do you agree or disagree with the views of the Christian Reconstruction movement? Why or why not? What advantages and disadvantages might there be in basing a national morality on the moral principles of Calvinist Christianity?

5. Is there a "culture war" in the United States? With what evidence do you support your answer?

6. Do you think that the views presented by those who advocate a common ground politics that moves beyond both left and right are a good idea, or a bad idea? Why?

7. Go through each of the "rules" for mixing religion and politics discussed in this chapter. Do you agree or disagree with each? Why? Are there any that you would add? Why?

For Further Reading

Baron, Bruce. 1992. *Heaven on Earth? The Social and Political Agendas of Dominion Theology.* Grand Rapids, Michigan: Zondervan.

A thorough review of dominionist and related theologies, including discussion of Regent University. A very balanced treatment of a controversial topic.

Blake, Jack. 1996 *Comes the Millennium.* New York: St. Martin's.

A spirited defense of rationalism as the country approaches the end of the century.

Bork, Robert H. 1996. *Slouching Toward Gomorrah: Modern Liberalism and American Decline.* New York: HarperCollins.

A thorough analysis of what Bork believes is wrong with the country, why we are "slouching toward Gomorrah," and what's needed to fix it.

Carter, Stephen L. 1993. *The Culture of Disbelief: How American Law and Politics Trivialize Religious Devotion.* New York: Basic Books.

A plea for the acceptance of religion in the "public square," both carefully reasoned and impassioned.

Castelli, Jim. 1988. *A Plea for Common Sense: Resolving the Clash between Religion and Politics.* San Francisco: Harper and Row.

A thoughtful discussion of most of the core issues, and a series of proposals for how religion and politics might work together while avoiding the pitfalls that such cooperation may present.

Hunter, James Davison. 1991. *Culture Wars: The Struggle to Define America.* New York: Basic Books.

An account of the history and present contours of the liberal/secular versus conservative/fundamentalist division in American culture.

Neuhaus, Richard John. 1984. *The Naked Public Square: Religion and Democracy in America.* Grand Rapids, Michigan: William B. Eerdmans.

Defense of religion's place in the "public square."

Skillen, James W. 1990. *The Scattered Voice: Christians at Odds in the Public Square.* Grand Rapids, Michigan: Zondervan.

Skillen reviews seven political perspectives held by Christians and then offers his own constructive proposal.

Wogaman, J. Philip. 1988. *Christian Perspectives on Politics.* Philadelphia: Fortress Press.

Thoughtful reflections and proposals on the subject by a well-known United Methodist ethicist. Before presenting his own views, he does an excellent review of several important perspectives.

Relevant World Wide Websites

Remember to visit our website for updates and additional links at:

http://bsuvc.bsu.edu/~00amcorbett/relpol.htm
http://www.infidels.org/org/aha/ American Humanist Association

http://www.atheists.org/ American Atheists
http://www.infidels.org/org/ffrf/ Freedom from Religion Foundation
http://www.chalcedon.edu/ Chalcedon Foundation
http://www.aclj.org/ American Center for Law and Justice
http://www.Sojourners.com/sojourners/home.html Sojourners
http://www.ari.net/calltorenewal Call for Renewal

References

Carter, Stephen L. 1993a. *The Culture of Disbelief: How American Law and Politics Trivialize Religious Devotion.* New York: Basic Books.

Carter, Stephen L. 1993b. "The Resurrection of Religious Freedom?" *Harvard Law Review* 107: 118–142.

Castelli, Jim. 1988. *A Plea for Common Sense: Resolving the Clash between Religion and Politics.* San Francisco: Harper and Row.

"The Courage of Conviction: An Interview with Sen. Mark Hatfield." *Sojourners,* September-October, 1996, pp. 26–29.

Ellul, Jacques. 1967. *The Political Illusion.* New York: Alfred A. Knopf.

Ellul, Jacques. 1972a. *The Politics of God and the Politics of Man.* Grand Rapids, Michigan: William B. Eerdmans.

Ellul, Jacques. 1972b. *Violence: Reflections from a Christian Perspective.* New York: Seabury Press.

Ellul, Jacques. 1976. *The Ethics of Freedom.* Grand Rapids, Michigan: William B. Eerdmans.

Finke, Roger, and Rodney Stark. 1992. *The Churching of America, 1776–1990: Winners and Losers in Our Religious Economy.* New Brunswick, New Jersey: Rutgers University Press.

Flowers, Ronald B. 1994. *That Godless Court? Supreme Court Decisions on Church-State Relationships.* Louisville, Kentucky: Westminster John Knox Press.

Fowler, Robert Booth. 1988. *Unconventional Partners: Religion and Liberal Culture in the United States.* Grand Rapids, Michigan: William B. Eerdmans.

Fowler, Robert Booth, and Allen D. Hertzke. 1995. *Religion and Politics in America: Faith, Culture, and Strategic Choices.* Boulder, Colorado: Westview Press.

Frankel, Marvin E. 1994. *Faith and Freedom: Religious Liberty in America.* New York: Hill and Wang.

Gelsey, Rudi. "Church and State: Give Up Labels and Demand the Politics of Meaning" (http://www.geol.vt.edu/uu/rudi-politics.html).

Griffith, Ernest S., John Plamenatz, and J. Roland Pennock. 1956. "Cultural Prerequisites to a Successfully Functioning Democracy." *American Political Science Review* 50: 107–137.

Hunter, James Davison. 1991. *Culture Wars: The Struggle to Define America.* New York: Basic Books.

Jelen, Ted G. 1995. "Religion and the American Political Culture: Alternative Models of Citizenship and Discipleship." *Sociology of Religion* 56: 271–284.

Jelen, Ted G., and Clyde Wilcox. 1995. *Public Attitudes Toward Church and State.* Armonk, New York: M.E. Sharpe.

Kerrine, Theodore M., and Richard John Neuhaus. 1979. "Mediating Structures: A Paradigm for Democratic Pluralism." Pp. 10–18 in Dean M. Kelley (Ed.), *The Uneasy Boundary: Church and State. The Annals of the American Academy of Political and Social Science,* 446. Philadelphia: The American Academy of Political and Social Science.

Kurtz, Paul (Ed.). 1973. *Humanist Manifestos I and II.* Buffalo: Prometheus Books.

Kurtz, Paul, et al. 1980. *A Secular Humanist Declaration.* Reprinted from *Free Inquiry Magazine,* 1 (No. 1): Winter, 1980.

Neuhaus, Richard John. 1984. *The Naked Public Square: Religion and Democracy in America.* Grand Rapids, Michigan: William B. Eerdmans.

Neuhaus, Richard John. 1985. "A Crisis of Faith." Pp. 61–67 in Raymond English (Ed.), *Ethics and Nuclear Arms: European and American Perspectives.* Washington, D.C.: Ethics and Public Policy Center.

Reichley, A. James. 1985. *Religion in American Public Life.* Washington, D.C.: Brookings Institution.

Vartanian, Aram. 1991. "Democracy, Religion, and the Enlightenment." *The Humanist* 51 (No. 6): 9–14, 45.

Walker, J. Brent. "Church-State Intersection." *The Report from the Capital,* February 1, 1997: 3.

Wallis, Jim. 1996. "A Crisis of Civility." *Sojourners,* September–October, 1996: 16–20. "The Williamsburg Charter: A National Celebration and Reaffirmation of the First Amendment Religious Liberty Clauses." 1988. Washington, D.C.: Williamsburg Charter Foundation.

Wallis, Jim. 1997. "Common Ground Politics." *Sojourners,* January–February, 1997: 7–8.

Wogaman, J. Philip. 1988. *Christian Perspectives on Politics.* Philadelphia: Fortress Press.

Wood, James E., Jr. 1987. "Religious Fundamentalism and the New Right." Pp. 246–250 in John F. Wilson and Donald L. Drakeman (Eds.), *Church and State in American History, Second Edition, Expanded and Updated.* Boston: Beacon Press.

Wuthnow, Robert. 1988a. "Divided We Fall: America's Two Civil Religions." *Christian Century,* April 20, 1988: 395–399.

Wuthnow, Robert. 1988b. *The Restructuring of America Religion: Society and Faith Since World War II.* Princeton: Princeton University Press.

Wuthnow, Robert. 1989. *The Struggle for America's Soul: Evangelicals, Liberals, and Secularism.* Grand Rapids, Michigan: William B. Eerdmans.

Yoder, John H. 1964. *The Christian Witness to the State.* Newton, Kansas: Faith and Life Press.

Yoder, John H. 1972. *The Politics of Jesus.* Grand Rapids, Michigan: William B. Eerdmans.

CONCLUSION

Before you begin reading *our* conclusion to this book, stop and think about how *you* would answer the following question:

Is the United States a secular or a religious nation?

Why did you answer as you did? What evidence have you read in this book that would support each position?

We have covered a lot of ground in this book, and it is now time to summarize and draw some conclusions from what we have done. We have found that the religious and political realms have been thoroughly intermingled throughout the history of the United States. Even before that history began, religion and politics were woven together in the colonies. And before that, they were inextricably united in those countries from which settlers came to what would become the United States.

Politics and Religion: A Common Concern with Values

A significant reason for the close relationship of religion and politics is that they deal with overlapping human concerns. Religion, for example, strongly influences what people take to be good or bad, right or wrong, moral or immoral. Politics exists because people have conflicts concerning these values. Not everyone agrees; hence, values must be authoritatively allocated in the society. This is the reason that politics exists. Its most important role is that of conflict resolution. An issue arises, there is conflict concerning the issue, and at some point a binding decision is reached on the issue (which, however, might not be permanent). An example is the conflict over women's right to legal abortions, an issue on which religious groups and individuals have had a great deal to say. Although "resolved" in the Supreme Court's decision at *Roe* v. *Wade,* the conflict continues today.

The point at which politics and religion often overlap concerns that upon which people place the greatest value; religion provides ways that people can live their lives in conscious relationship with what to them is the highest value. For many people, it seems only natural, right, and reasonable that *their* highest values should be the ones chosen for the culture in which they live, and that is where politics comes in. As we noted in Chapter 1, politics provides one way in which people can work to have their values become the values of the public arena. We have traced this enduring concern with values throughout the book. For example:

- In Chapter 1, we saw that some people came to this country because of their values, and in some cases they attempted to impose their values on others.

- In Chapter 2, we saw that the founders had different values about what the new nation should be. Further, contemporary scholars do not agree on just what those values were.

- Throughout history, reviewed in Chapters 3 and 4, religious values were interwoven in the issues of the day, many times being used to support opposing viewpoints and strategies. For example, some people supported the war in Southeast Asia as a battle against "godless communism," while others demonstrated for peace based on their religious convictions.

- In examining the ways in which the Supreme Court has interpreted the two religion clauses of the First Amendment (Chapters 5 and 6), we saw that the justices have been guided by diverse values, resulting in distinctive interpretations at different times in the history of religious liberty litigation.

- In Chapter 7, we saw that public opinion about the proper relationship between religion and politics reflects a wide range of values on the part of the American public. We saw in Chapters 8 and 9 that religious commitments sometimes lead to differing political values among black and white Americans.

- Chapter 10 dealt with how religious groups function as political interest groups, attempting to translate their particular values into public policy.

Culture Wars . . . And Beyond?

In the last half century, there has often been polarization between the values upheld by the "conservative right" and those of the "liberal left." Some authors have even described this as a "culture war," as we saw in Chapter 11. The debate concerns both the core values of the two sides and their views about how those values should affect the public realm. There are, in other words, both content and process differences between them.

One of the ways that religion and politics have been intertwined throughout much of the history of the United States is expressed by the concept of "civil religion," a public religiousness that combines religious and patriotic values. Civil religion was originally thought of as an underlying commonly accepted fund of religious and patriotic sentiment that unified the nation despite its many religious and political outlooks. Recent investigators have highlighted the extent to which the civil religion—or, in this case, religions—have themselves become involved in the fragmentation that has characterized values in the United States since the 1960s. There are now at least two civil religions, a conservative and a liberal version, with quite different views of the nation and where it should be heading.

As we saw in Chapter 11, common ground politics is one attempt to resolve this conflict and bring about a new politics beyond the divisions of left and right. To us, it seems reasonable to suggest that *both* dimensions of political and religious discourse in the United States will continue. The dialectic between the two poles has been a feature of our national life for some time, and cannot easily be resolved. At the same time, there does seem to be genuine interest in resolving it, and we can expect efforts to continue in that direction.

The Proper Role of Religion:
Private, Public, or Both?

Another ongoing issue will be where religion belongs. Is its only proper location the private sphere of life—family and home and community of faith—or does it have a place in the "public square" as well? For those who hold, as most people currently do, that religion does indeed belong in the public square, what is its presence there to be? How is it to relate to the other actors who occupy that space? This discussion will surely continue, and shows signs of intensifying, it seems to us.

Again we can cite a successful book by way of illustration. Stephen L. Carter's *The Culture of Disbelief,* discussed in the previous chapter, is a thoughtful, scholarly work that demands its readers' attention and concentration. It is not a "popular" book as that word is often used. Nevertheless, it has had great success in the market, helped by a virtual endorsement from President Bill Clinton. Carter's major concern is the extent to which the secularity of the United States crowds religion out of the public square, or at least trivializes it and reduces it to the level of a private hobby.

The majority of citizens believe that religion does have a role to play in the public realm. Although some people maintain that religion and politics simply cannot or should not mix, most people do not take this position. The question for the majority then becomes just what that influence should be and how it will be exercised. A second question concerns how to give politics the benefits that religion can have for it, while recognizing as well that religion can have a negative impact on politics. From the side of religion, there is concern over how to have religion participate in the secular politics of the nation without compromising religion itself.

Interpreting the Religion Clauses

Another perennial concern in the United States is how the two religion clauses of the First Amendment are to be interpreted and related to each other. In the final analysis, do they work together, or do they come into inevitable conflict with each other? What kinds of interpretations are best for politics? For religion? Again, these questions will continue to be raised as the Supreme Court struggles to define the boundaries of the relationship between religion and politics, and the role of religion in the life of the nation. Given the tendency to turn increasingly to legal solutions through the courts, First Amendment cases can reasonably be predicted to increase.

The question of the standard by which the meaning of the free exercise clause is to be interpreted and applied was thrown open again when the Religious Freedom Restoration Act was declared unconstitutional in 1997. Its supporters have indicated they will mount a new effort to restore religious freedom to its pre-*Smith* level. As you recall, prior to the *Smith* decision, the government had to show a compelling interest if it interfered with religious practice. After *Smith*, it had only to demonstrate a rational basis for doing so. Since the Supreme Court struck down the act, the rational basis standard currently applies. This issue continues to be debated among both lawmakers and religious leaders.

In terms of public opinion about church-state relations, the public shows very mixed attitudes. People favor the separation of church and state more in the abstract, while being more likely to favor accommodation in concrete instances such as support for school prayer. Public support for free exercise depends largely on the perception of the group involved; people are more likely to support free exercise for groups with which they are relatively comfortable, and to favor restrictions on groups about which they have concerns. Cultural elites—both religious and secular—are more likely to favor separation and to support free exercise. All three of these patterns—the mixed attitudes of the general public and the stronger support for both separationism and free exercise among the elites, and hence the discrepancy between the two groups—can be expected to be a permanent feature of the discussion.

Religion Variables as Predictors of Political Attitudes and Identifications

We found that three religious variables—religious identification, biblical literalism, and religious commitment—are important predictors of political attitudes and identification. The religious variables are certainly not the only predictors, and sometimes they are not even the strongest ones. However, to varying degrees, religious factors will continue to influence what people think and how they act politically. Numerous factors influence exactly what that relationship will be; two of the most important are race and the political or social issue itself. The values that women and men hold will continue to be shaped in part by their religious attitudes and participation, and these values in turn will help to motivate their political decisions and actions. Religion is among the most intensely personal of all human characteristics; it can also become intensely political, a dynamic that has been demonstrated repeatedly throughout American history and will be in the foreseeable future.

Religious Groups as Political Interest Groups

One of the major ways that religion has been and continues to be involved in politics is that religious groups function as interest groups and attempt to influence the political process in a variety of ways. For example, in relatively recent history, religious groups have functioned as interest groups in trying to affect public policy concerning abortion rights, the civil rights movement, prayer in public schools, apartheid in South Africa and aid to Israel, to name but a few.

The Millennium

The new calendric millennium in the year 2000 appears to have activated people's interest in a *religious* millennium, a sense that something important, perhaps cataclysmic, is going to happen. That speculation has been encouraged by dramatic changes and events around the world—famine in Africa, nuclear disaster at Chernobyl, the disintegration of the former Soviet Union and the conflicts that have followed in its wake, and earthquakes and hurricanes of climactic magnitude. Some people, at least, see more than natural events here, interpreting them as evidence of significant *super*natural happenings. For those who think along these lines, the new millennium imparts a special urgency to questions about values, and thus to questions about politics and religion.

A Secular or Religious Nation?

We turn finally to the question of whether the United States is a religious nation, a secular one, or somehow, both. Although the latter answer is by far the most complex, it is the only one that accurately describes the United States in the 1900s as well as throughout most of its history.

The United States is a secular nation. There is clearly no established church. Tax monies do not go to support religious organizations, and people of any religious persuasion or of none can hold public office. The founding documents of the nation were conceived and written by people who held many different religious views, including free thought and deism, as well as agnosticism. Religion may be taught about, but not preached, in the public schools, which are barred from advocating for or against any religion. Public education—arguably the greatest means a culture has for inculcating its values—is notably secular. The elites and gatekeepers of culture—the media, academics, and business elites—are consistently more secular or liberal than the mass public. Survey research indicates that a substantial segment of the population has low religious commitment, and those with low commitment are very much like their secular counterparts. Thus, the social and political views of even "religious" people may be effectively secular. Adherents of all of humankind's religions live in this country on an equal legal footing with each other, and with those of no religion. By and large, people support civil liberties such as free speech for those who are against churches and religion, and some, although a minority, report that they would be willing to vote for an atheist for president.

The United States is a religious nation. Churches, temples, and synagogues thrive. Adherents of all the world's religions live here, and many attract American converts. Books on religious topics appear on the bestseller list. People continue to turn to their communities of faith for support, especially in times of crisis and important life passages such as birth, marriage, and death. College students are interested in religion, and parachurch organizations flourish on campuses around the country. At our own university, student religious fellowships sponsor daily prayer meetings at an hour of the day when most students are still asleep—and some students attend. As we write this concluding chapter—Holy Week for Western Christians—three major weekly newsmagazines featured cover stories dealing with the Christian belief in Jesus' resurrection and contemporary scholarly work on the biblical accounts of it. Television programs dealing with religion draw large audiences. Even a hasty tour of the World Wide Web reveals a tremendous collection of sites pertaining to religion. Conservative and fundamentalist religious organizations, especially, have become much more active in politics in the past several decades. Religion motivates individuals to work and to protest for causes that concern the religious values that are important to them. Theologians and ethicists discuss the "how to" of religion's involvement in the public

life of the nation. Promise Keepers, an evangelical Christian men's organization, has grown rapidly and continues to do so. A parallel organization for women is in the planning stage. Many people think of this as "one
nation under God," and our coins proclaim trust in a divine being. Presidents routinely include religious themes in their remarks, and the last
several presidents have spoken quite openly about their Christian faith.

What are we to make of all of this? Are we living in a religious or a
secular country? In sum, it seems to us, the United States is a secular nation populated mostly by religious people. Some are profoundly religious,
more may be nominally so. But most *are* religious, and have found a
home in this secular nation.

APPENDICES

APPENDIX A Profiles of Religious Groups in the United States

Overview

This Appendix presents basic information about the major religious groups in the United States. We do not attempt to cover all religions or groups—an impossible task. Instead, we concentrate on the major groups that are heavily invested in the relationship between politics and religion. These major groups include approximately 90 percent of the population. The remaining 10 percent is distributed among a nearly countless variety of alternatives to the religious affiliations of the majority. Their relative numbers are so small that except in isolated instances they do not have a significant impact on the relationship of politics and religion.

Religious Identification

There are a number of ways to differentiate religious groups in a nation as religiously diverse as the United States. One way is in terms of major religious traditions such as Protestantism, Catholicism, and Judaism. We will begin with this type of division.

Surveys of the public often ask people to select from a number of possible religious preferences. These survey results are not completely accurate. Each survey has a *margin of error,* the amount by which any figure given for the sample may vary from the comparable figure for the entire population. Beyond the statistical margin of error, self-identification with a religious group can mean different things. Some respondents who say that they are Protestant, for example, will be very active in the programs of their church and support its goals financially. Other respondents may mean nothing more than that they were raised as Protestants.

In spite of this, the information we gain from these surveys helps to provide a meaningful picture of religion in the United States. Protestants make up about 65 percent of the population of the United States. About 25 percent are Catholic and about 2 percent are Jewish. Religious "nones" account for about 10 percent.

The Judeo-Christian Tradition

Jews and Christians have several significant beliefs in common. Most of these beliefs have as their starting point shared scripture. The Hebrew Bible or Tanakh is found in Christian Bibles as the Old Testament, with almost no change of content. The primary difference is in the order of the books.

According to both, the one personal God is the Creator of the world and all that is in it. Some Christians and a small percentage of Jews take the biblical account of creation literally, while others take it as a narrative embodying important religious truths without understanding it literally. Either way, the belief that the world is created and sustained by God colors how Jews and Christians see and live in the world. Jews and most Christians believe that the world, as a part of God's creation, is essentially good, although certainly not without problems. Although for some Christians, it is necessary to avoid "worldliness" in order to live an upright life, this is not the view of most Christians in the United States.

Human beings are believed to have been created with intelligence, free will, and other attributes that make people different from the rest of the created order and give them special responsibility. Christians and Jews believe that people are created in God's image, although exactly what is meant by this varies.

Jews and Christians think of time as beginning when God created the world and running forward until some point in the future when God will intervene in the affairs of the world in a decisive way to bring to fruition what was begun with creation. In this "linear" view of time, progress is possible and the imperative to work for progress becomes natural. This view of creation and of time also makes history very important, because it is the stage on which God's purposes for the world are played out. As

with the creation narratives, not all believers in either tradition understand these things literally, although some do. The meaningfulness of history, however, transcends differences in interpretation.

Morality and ethics are what they are for Jews and Christians because
God is a holy and righteous God who has high expectations for people.
People can know the will of God because God has chosen to reveal it.
Moral acts are those that conform with God's will, while immorality violates God's will. An important feature of both is their belief that God requires of people that they help to care for those who cannot care for
themselves; a strong sense of social morality is deeply ingrained in both,
beginning with the writings of the Hebrew prophets.

The Ten Commandments, or Decalogue, found in the book of Exodus are the foundation for morality for both Jews and Christians. Some
commandments have to do primarily with people's relationship with
God: avoiding idolatry and using God's name as a curse, or observing the
Sabbath. Others focus on interpersonal relationships: honoring parents,
not murdering, not committing adultery, not stealing, not bearing false
witness, and not coveting what one does not have.

Most of what has been said in this section applies to Muslims—
members of the Islamic faith—as well as to Jews and Christians. Like
their Jewish and Christian counterparts, Muslims emphasize the importance of obedience to the one God in morality and proper worship. Although there is no Decalogue as such in the *Quran* (the Muslim scripture), the moral content is very similar.

The Predominant Majority: Christianity

Christianity includes four subcategories: Protestantism, Catholicism,
Eastern Orthodoxy (primarily Greek Orthodox and Russian Orthodox
churches), and a variety of other Christian communities of faith that are
not part of any of these three larger groupings. The best-known of this
last group of churches is the Mormons (Latter-day Saints and Reorganized Latter Day Saints). The last group also includes Seventh-day
Adventists and Christian Scientists, as well as Jehovah's Witnesses. Eastern Orthodox Christians account for about 1 percent of the population,
and Mormons, 2 percent.

There is, of course, considerable variation in the beliefs and practices
of Christians. However, the "religious life of Christians . . . centers on the
person, life, death, and resurrection of Jesus. Christians are those people

who are defined by their faith in Jesus as their Lord and Savior" (Corbett, 1997: 34). However, especially in the United States, the commonalities among Christian denominations far exceed their differences. One summary of Christian belief and practice is the Nicene Creed, one of the earliest creeds that the Christian Church formulated (Figure A–1). It is a product of the Council of Nicaea in 325 C.E.

Protestant Christians

Protestants are largest group of Christians in the United States. While there is a tremendously wide range of Protestant beliefs, styles of worship, and church organization, there are significant similarities, as well. Protestants usually focus on a direct, personal relationship with God through

---

FIGURE A–1

The Nicene Creed

We believe in one God, the Father, the Almighty, maker of heaven and earth, of all that is, seen and unseen.

We believe in one Lord, Jesus Christ, the only Son of God, eternally begotten of the Father, God from God, Light from Light, true God from true God, begotten, not made, of one Being with the Father. Through him alll things were made. For us and for our salvation he came down from heaven: by the power of the Holy Spirit he became incarnate from the Virgin Mary, and was made man. For our sake he was crucified under Ponitus Pilate; he suffered death and was buried. On the third day he rose again according to the Scriptures; he ascended into heaven and is seated at the right hand of the Father. He will come again in glory to judge the living and the dead, and his kingdom will have no end.

We believe in the Holy Spirit, the Lord, the giver of life, who proceeds from the Father [some add, "and the Son"]. With the Father and the Son he is worshiped and glorified. He has spoken through the prophets.

We believe in one holy and apostolic Church. We acknowledge one baptism for the forgiveness of sins. We look for the resurrection of the dead, and the life of the world to come.

Jesus the Christ, unmediated by the church. The church remains important as the fellowship of believers, the coming-together of those who have placed their faith and trust in Jesus. But the church and its leadership are not responsible for officially interceding between God and people.

This view of the church is a corollary of two other distinctive Protestant beliefs. Most Protestants emphasize that salvation from sin and its effects comes to people by God's grace alone. In other words, there is nothing that human beings can do to "earn" salvation and redemption. God through Jesus, the Christ, has overcome the separation in an act of grace which people can only accept in faith.

Because the church does not mediate the relationship between God and people, the church does not have final authority over the lives of the faithful in matters of religious truth. For Protestants, the Bible is the sole source of religious truth. The church's interpretation and explanation may well be helpful and insightful, but the final authority is the believer's own interpretation of what he or she reads. Protestants believe that their understanding is guided by the Holy Spirit and informed by the teaching of their church, but the church in the final analysis is not authoritative.

Protestant worship emphasizes God's word as read from the Bible, read responsively by the worship leader and congregation, sung in hymns, and explained and applied in the sermon. The sermon is usually the most prominent feature of Protestant worship. This emphasis on God's word links Protestants' worship with their belief in the authority of the Bible.

It is not possible to go into detail about the multitude of separate Protestant denominations found in the United States; that would be a book in itself. In varying degrees and with varying nuances, the information given about Protestantism applies to them all. A few notes are in order, however.

The largest group of Protestants in the nation is the Baptists, with about 20 percent of the entire population and about 33 percent of the Protestant population. There are a large number of groups that make up this diverse Protestant family. Many of them are very conservative in their religious outlook, although not all are. Several of the historic black churches are part of the Baptist tradition. While we find Baptists everywhere in the United States, they are strongly concentrated in the Southeast.

Other major Protestant groups include the Methodists, Lutherans, Presbyterians, Christian Church/Disciples of Christ, United Church of Christ, and Episcopalians. Each of these groups includes 10 percent of the population or less. All of these churches are home to a wide range of styles of belief and worship, and draw their members from almost every social class and area of the country. Like the Baptists, the Methodist family of churches includes some of the historic black churches. All but the Disciples of Christ trace their roots back to European churches during the Protestant Reformation period in the 1300s through the 1500s. The Disciples' history began in the pre–Civil War United States.

There are also "nondenominational Protestant" churches that have no ties with a larger denomination. They tend to favor a very traditional approach to Christian belief and morality, although not all do.

Catholic Christians

About 25 percent of the population of the United States claims Catholicism as their religious preference. Over half live in the Northeast and the Midwest. Over one third reside in four states: New York, California, Pennsylvania, and Texas (Kosmin and Lachman, 1993: 55–56). Long identified with blue-collar jobs and lower than average socioeconomic status and education, Catholics now equal or surpass non-Catholics in the United States in these demographic dimensions. Although Catholic family size exceeded that of non-Catholics for many decades, this difference has equalized, as well.

Although the Second Vatican Council brought about extensive changes in the Catholic Church, there are things that remain distinctive about Catholicism. Several of these have to do with the Catholic view of the church and the role of its leadership. The Catholic Church regards itself as one worldwide church with a single leader, the pope, whose headquarters are in the Vatican City. According to church teaching, the authority of the pope goes back to Jesus himself. In the Gospel recorded by Matthew (16:18–19), Jesus is reported to have said to Peter, "You are Peter, and upon this rock I will build my church, and the gates of hell will not overcome it. I give you the keys of the kingdom of Heaven. Whatever you bind on earth will be bound in heaven, and whatever you loose on earth will be loosed in heaven." The office of the papacy (which is distinguished from particular popes) exists in an unbroken line that goes back to Jesus himself. This is the doctrine (official belief) of apostolic succession.

The affirmation of the "teaching authority of the church" goes along with apostolic succession. Unlike Protestantism, which emphasizes the importance of individual interpretation of the Bible, Catholic teaching understands the church as the official interpreter of the Bible. The official teachings of the church, along with the Bible itself, make up a unified body of authoritative tradition in which both elements are equal. On a very few matters that are believed to be crucial for Catholic faith, the pope is said to speak *ex cathedra*. When he does so, the church teaches that the Holy Spirit protects him from error, in order that he not lead the entire church astray.

Survey data indicate that, even though many Catholics in the United States have serious reservations about some of the official policies of their church, and many do not follow its teachings closely, they remain loyal to the pope and are basically satisfied with their church's ability to meet their spiritual needs.

The Catholic Church differs from most Protestant churches in that the Catholic Church has official teachings about many issues of personal lifestyle that its members are supposed to follow. It is about these issues that Catholics in the United States disagree with their church the most. Over 75 percent feel that divorced Catholics should be permitted to remarry in the church. Over 80 percent believe that Catholics should be permitted to use artificial means of conception control, and over half believe that the church's stance on abortion should be relaxed. All of these things are against church teaching. Only half agree with their church that extramarital sex and homosexual sex are always wrong. Nearly two thirds think that women should be able to be ordained as priests, and three fourths favor allowing priests to marry, both of which are forbidden by the church (Moore, 1993).

Catholic worship is much more focused on the sacraments than is Protestant worship. Baptism and Holy Communion (Eucharist) are the primary sacraments for Catholics. In addition, they observe as sacraments five rites of the church that, for most Protestants, do not have sacramental significance. These are confirmation, marriage, reconciliation, ordination to the priesthood, and anointing of the sick and dying.

Jews in the United States

Jews are the next-largest single religious group in the United States (after Christians). Nationally, persons of Jewish faith account for about 2 percent of the population. There is, however, a problem encountered in evaluating the Jewish response to the religious self-identification question on surveys. As a recent major study of religious identification in the United States emphasizes, Jews tend not to separate Judaism as a religious faith from Jewishness as an ethnic and cultural identification (Kosmin and Lachman, 1993: 299). Sometimes, people may use "Jewish" to indicate identification with the State of Israel. Therefore, people who are ethnic and cultural Jews may or may not self-identify as "Jewish."

Probably the most obvious difference between Jews and Christians, and the one that creates the greatest misunderstanding, is that Jews do not accept Jesus as the savior of humankind. Most Jews, like most non-Christians generally, do not doubt the existence of Jesus as a historical person, which is corroborated by historical sources outside the bibles of either group. Where Jews differ is that, for them, Jesus is not the Christ (Messiah). There are several reasons for this.

The first has to do with the Jewish understanding of the nature of God. According to Jewish thought, God is pure spirit, without form and without body. In terms of how Jews think about God, there cannot be an incarnation of God—God becoming fully human as Christians believe happened in Jesus. God could not become human without simultaneously ceasing to be God.

The prophecies of a coming messiah that are found in the biblical book of Isaiah are part of the Hebrew scriptures as well as of the Christian Old Testament. The links between the messiah foretold by Isaiah and the person Jesus of Nazareth are made in the Christian New Testament only; they do not exist in the Tanakh. Thus, they are not relevant to the Jewish viewpoint.

Jesus was not the kind of messiah that most of the Hebrew people anticipated. According to Hebraic thought on the topic, the messiah would be a political deliverer who would lead the entire House of Israel out of oppression, and bring about an age of peace and plenty. They did not expect a divine figure whose life and death would save individual people from sin and its effects, the work Christians attribute to Jesus.

Sin, for most Christians, is a state of being that precedes and leads to specific sinful acts. The Jewish understanding of sin is different in that it begins with the acts themselves. People are sinners because they sin, rather than sinning because they are sinners. There is no fundamental alienation from God that must be overcome. Thus, in the Jewish religious framework, there is no need for a savior to do for people what people cannot do for themselves.

There are a number of subdivisions within Judaism in the United States. We discuss the three major ones here. *Orthodox* Jews follow all of the moral and the ceremonial law strictly, and believe that the entire Tanakh is God's literal word and has absolute authority. Orthodox Jews believe that their way of being Jewish best embodies historical Jewish be-lief and practice.

At the other end of the spectrum are *Reform* Jews, who represent the most modernized and liberal major sector of American Judaism. Reform Jews make a clear distinction between the moral law and the ceremonial or ritual law (such as Sabbath observance and the kosher dietary rules), and believe that only the moral law is binding. The observance of ritual and ceremony is a matter of personal choice.

Conservative Jews take a middle position between Orthodoxy and Re-form. Conservative Jews seek to preserve their tradition and remain in continuity with the past, but allowing for some adaptation and change. There are more Conservative and Reform Jews in the United States than there are Orthodox.

Secular and Nominally Religious Persons

A minority of persons in the United States, around 10 percent or less, claim to have no religious preference. They may be atheists, agnostics, freethinkers, humanists, or simply not be involved in religion. Recent re-search also indicates that those whose religious commitments are very nominal function more as secular than as religious persons. When these nominally religious persons are added to the professed seculars, the pro-portion of people in the United States who are essentially irreligious is nearly one third, at 30 percent (Kellstedt et al., 1993). Thus, the irreligious are in themselves an important "religious group." In the main, these people are not actively hostile to religion; they are not *anti*religious, merely *non*religious (Davenport, 1991).

One recent study operationalizes irreligiousness in terms of five vari-ables: (1) ritual practice, measured by attendance at public worship, (2) private devotion, measured by the frequency of private prayer, (3) the im-portance of religion in the respondent's daily life measured by a direct question, (4) religious belief, measured by belief in life after death, and (5) religious affiliation, measured by membership in a community of faith. They develop an index of religious commitment that ranges from 1 to 7. Analysis demonstrates that people with commitment scores of 3 and below are effectively secular (Kellstedt et al., 1993: 8–10).

Who, then, are the unreligious in the United States? In most ways, they are not as different from their more religious counterparts as popu-lar wisdom often assumes. They have about the same educational level.

The one difference is that more of the nonreligious have at least some graduate or professional school; 5 percent of the religious and 9 percent of the nonreligious have more than sixteen years of education. They are found in all occupational categories, as well as in all income categories. They are slightly less likely to be married, and, if married, they have slightly fewer children, on the average. The differences are slight, but statistically significant. They are more urban than rural and small-town in where they live (Davenport, 1991).

Usually, people are not nonreligious from birth, but become nonreligious, whether by a simple drift away from religion or a sort of "reverse conversion" experience, in which they make a conscious turn away from religion. Socialization may be the key factor. In this case, the attitude is acquired from people in one's social environment. Spouses are particularly important in this regard, as are other "significant others" (Davenport, 1991).

The Changing Shape of Religion in the United States: Liberals and Conservatives

The last several decades have seen a restructuring of religion in the United States in ways that are very important for the interaction of religion and politics. In the period following World War II in 1945, there were three major ways in which people interpreted religious difference: the difference between Catholics and Protestants, between Christians and Jews, and among the various Protestant denominations.

Changes in the attitudes of the religious groups themselves, as well as changes in the larger culture, brought about a shift. No longer are these major divisions drawn between communities of faith in the traditional sense, although remnants of them still remain. Rather, the division is between secularists and religious liberals on one side, and religious conservatives and fundamentalists on the other (Wuthnow, 1988 and 1989).

We will discuss this division in terms of three categories: liberalism, conservatism, and fundamentalism. About half the people in the United States are religious conservatives. About one third are fundamentalists, and the remainder are liberals (Corbett, 1997: 19). It is important to understand, however, that these are what sociologists call "ideal types," constructs that are usually not found in pure form in the world of lived experience. The religious picture in the United States is also one of a continuum with these three points as markers along it. Individuals and groups, however, are distributed all along the continuum without interruption. If these two qualifications are kept in mind, however, looking at these three positions helps us to understand religion in the United States.

Social scientists do not agree on the definition of any of these three terms. One way of distinguishing among these three religious attitudes is to examine what people think about the Bible. One question in the National Opinion Research Center's General Social Survey asks respondents to indicate which of the following three views comes closest to their own:

1. The Bible is the actual Word of God and is to be taken literally, word for word.
2. The Bible is the inspired Word of God, but not everything in it is to be taken literally.
3. The Bible is an ancient book of stories, legends, and precepts written by men.

We take this distinction among views of the Christian Bible as our starting point and further define the terms in the discussion below.

Fundamentalist Christians

Fundamentalist Christians take the Bible literally and believe that it means what it says and says what it means. There is little room for human interpretation. Except for obvious instances in which Jesus taught in stories or parables, its language is not to be taken figuratively. It is important from a fundamentalist's standpoint that the Bible not contain any possibility of error, and the way to ensure this is through complete verbal inspiration. The fundamentalist view of human nature emphasizes human sinfulness. If human influence were allowed to affect the words of the Bible, then there would be no possible way of guaranteeing that its core message about God, Jesus, and human sin and salvation would not be compromised. Although this literal view of the Bible is often noted as the core tenet of fundamentalism, it is a means to an end, that end being the assurance that the message that God seeks to convey to the world will get through correctly.

Fundamentalists stress the importance of certain basic beliefs that must be held by those who consider themselves Christians. There are a number of lists of these fundamentals of belief, but one common list includes the following:

- The verbal inspiration and inerrancy of the Bible.
- The literal virgin birth of Jesus
- The visible, physical, bodily raising of Jesus from the grave after the crucifixion
- The visible, physical, bodily, return of Christ to the earth at what is called the Second Coming
- An interpretation of the work of Jesus Christ that holds that his death was a substitute for the death due to all of humankind for sin (the "penal substitutionary" view).

For fundamentalists, only the traditional views are correct, and there can be no alteration. Personal faith in Jesus as one's lord and savior is held to be the only way to salvation. Because these views are so important to fundamentalists, they are reluctant to work cooperatively with others who do not share them.

Fundamentalist morality emphasizes that there are absolute standards of right and wrong, equally applicable in all situations. Moral decisions are not "good," "better," or "best," but only "right" or "wrong." They believe that issues of personal morality are the most crucial.

Christian Liberals

Christian liberals are at the other end of the spectrum, and their views merge seamlessly into those of their secular counterparts. They emphasize the human influences at work in the writing of the Bible, and are more likely to understand it as the record of humanity's search for God than as God's divinely guaranteed revelation to humankind. Because it is a product of people who lived in a particular time and culture, it, too, is historically and culturally relative. To interpret it, people have the responsibility to use the best human knowledge available through science and reasoning.

Liberals are not as concerned as the fundamentalists that the human role in the production of the Bible will imperil its essential message. They also do not think that it is necessary to spell out specific beliefs that one must hold. While specific beliefs are important, their chief importance lies in their influence on how people choose to live their lives. Behaving is more central than believing.

The liberal approach to morality outlines broad moral and ethical guidelines, but these guidelines must be applied in each situation. Depending on the situation, the application may differ. There are decisions that are good, those that are better, and those that are best under a given set of circumstances. In their approach to morality, most liberals believe that personal moral issues are best left up to the individual's conscience, rather than being legislated by either church or civil law. They focus more on the large issues of social morality and justice. The goal of individual salvation is less important than building a better society.

Life in this world is important in and of itself. Heaven and hell, although understood in various ways, are often taken by liberals as metaphors for states of mind that people create by how they live in this life. Some liberals take them as figurative expressions for life with and without God after death, as well.

Liberals are usually quite open-minded and tolerant of other religions and points of view. They understand Christianity to be one religion among many, and do not believe that it has an exclusive claim on either religious truth or salvation.

Christian Conservatives or Moderates

As you might expect, Christian conservatives or moderates take positions that are in between the other two. For that reason, this position is not as clear-cut. Conservatives usually hold that the Bible is inspired by God and emphasize its role as the revelation of God to humankind, but believe that some interpretation is necessary. While the crucial message about human sin and salvation is held to be without error, historical and cultural relativity is believed to have brought about errors in things that are not essential. Thus, revelation and human reason are both important.

While conservatives are cautious in their estimate of human nature, they are more optimistic than their fundamentalist counterparts. This translates to a similar attitude toward secular values, as well. Most conservatives believe that people do better with traditional standards of personal morality, but there can be some flexibility in their application. For example, while most fundamentalists say that abortion is always wrong, and liberals usually say that it should be up to the woman herself, moderates may hold that abortion is wrong except when the pregnancy is the result of rape or incest, or when there is solid medical evidence that the unborn child has a serious defect. Building a better society, one as much in line with God's wishes for the world as possible, is held to be as important as personal morality. From this standpoint, faith in Jesus offers the fullness of salvation and religious truth, but Christianity is not believed to be the only religious truth.

Other Religions in the United States
Latter-day Saints (Mormons)

Although more traditional Christians sometimes are unwilling to include the Mormons among the varieties of Christianity, two things require that they be understood as an alternative interpretation of Christianity: In the first place, Mormons identify themselves as Christians. Second, they affirm the basic Christian belief in the saving grace of God through the life, death, and resurrection of Jesus Christ.

Latter-day Saints believe that God's self-revelation to people did not stop with the books of the Bible. Alongside the Christian Old and New Testaments, they believe that other books contain the record of God's ongoing revelation to their founder, Joseph Smith, and those who came after him. The main record of this revelation is the Book of Mormon. This revelation continues into the present, since the First Presidency of the church is believed to receive revelation in the same way that Smith did.

In other ways as well, Mormons are very similar to their non-Mormon neighbors. They share with other people in the United States a strong belief in the work ethic and in the importance of economic success. They have an extensive system for providing for the needs of members and others who have fallen on financial hard times. Those who receive such help are expected to respond in kind when they are able. Self-sufficiency is highly valued. Mormons are active in relief efforts for nonmembers, as well, particularly in the face of natural disasters such as floods and earthquakes.

They support education for all people through both public education and their own colleges and universities, the best-known of which is Brigham Young University. Mormons emphasize the importance of strong families, and most families set Monday evenings aside for Family Home Evening, a program supported by their church. The church provides materials and suggestions for activities in which the entire family can participate, some of which are religious in nature and some not. The focus is on the family spending time together, talking, and enjoying one another's company. Most Mormon churches provide many social, educational, religious, and recreational activities for their members throughout the week.

The Mormon Church encourages its members to live by a health code known as the Word of Wisdom, a part of the revelation to Joseph Smith. This code forbids the use of tobacco in any form, illegal drugs, alcohol, and drinks containing caffeine (such as coffee, tea, and many soft drinks). It encourages a balanced life of study, work, worship, and attention to physical health through recreation and exercise

Mormons distinguish between local churches and their temples, special buildings set apart for the most sacred rites of the church. Once a temple is consecrated (set apart), non-Mormons may not enter it, and even Mormons must have an interview with their bishop and other church officers to assess their worthiness to enter. The rites carried out in the temples are sacred, and those who participate in them do not divulge details to others. There are endowment rituals that must be completed before other rituals may be undertaken. A series of very important rituals joins husbands and wives together, and their children as well, for eternity. In contrast to the more common belief that marriage is until "death do us part," Mormons believe that families can remain together throughout eternity.

Other World Religions in the United States

All the major world religions are represented in the United States. Many of them include less than 2 percent of the population. According to a recent survey, two tenths of 1 percent of the population is Hindu; four tenths of 1 percent is Buddhist, and one half of 1 percent is Muslim. Many people may tend to associate these religions with specific ethnic groups. For instance, many people assume that the majority of the Muslim (Islamic) population in the United States is Arab-American. This is not the case. Most Americans of Arab ethnic background are Christians rather than Muslims, and most Muslims in the United States are not of Arab descent. Similarly, most Asian-Americans are neither Hindu nor Buddhist. Two thirds of Asian-Americans are Christians (Kosmin and Lachman, 1993). In all of these cases, there are at least two factors at work. The people most likely to immigrate to the United States in the first place are those who are already Christians in their native countries. And, for those for whom this is not the case, there is a tendency to assimilate once they arrive here.

There is also a tendency for these very small groups to accommodate and take on the characteristics of American religiousness, even when these are remarkably foreign to their own ways of doing things. Hindu and Buddhist religious life has taken on a "congregational" style in the United States, in part because that is the way religion here tends to be organized. Congregational worship is often held on Sunday, the day of worship for the Christian majority. The people that gather are more of a congregation, a group of people united in a collective act of worship, than would be common in Asian countries, in which people worshiping in a temple are usually offering their own individual worship. Muslims, on the other hand, have maintained their communal Friday noon Jummah prayer service as their congregational worship.

Small and relatively newer communities of faith in the United States, such as Muslims, Hindus and Buddhists, are today faced with many of the same issues that faced Catholicism, and later Judaism, in an earlier period of United States history. To what extent will they modify their traditional rituals and lifestyles in order to assimilate more easily into the larger culture of the United States? To what extent will they uphold their unique identity? All three of the groups we have discussed are highly educated and disproportionately represented in professional and upper managerial occupations, both of which encourage assimilation. Intermarriage does, as well. Conversely, for all three, religion is a central element of personal identity, and this leads toward efforts to maintain the tradition. How these two polar forces balance out remains to be seen.

Owing in large part to their small size, these groups usually do not attempt to influence public policy in an organized way. There is no Hindu or Buddhist lobby in Washington, for example. Although Muslims have traditionally remained apart from the political process in the United States, there are some Muslims now who advocate increasing involvement. A recent article in *Islamic Horizons* urged Muslims to stop making excuses for avoiding participation in leadership and start bringing an Islamic perspective to bear on public policy issues alongside other viewpoints (*Islamic Horizons*, Summer, 1992, pages 22–39).

For Further Reading

Corbett, Julia Mitchell. 1997. *Religion in America, Third Edition.* Upper Saddle River, New Jersey: Prentice Hall.

A thorough yet accessible survey of major and minor religious groups and movements in the United States, written for college undergraduates.

Melton, J. Gordon. 1997. *The Encyclopedia of American Religions, Sixth Edition.* Detroit, Michigan: Gale Research.
Descriptions of over two thousand groups, plus essays on religion in the United States. An excellent resource that your college library probably has.

Relevant World Wide Websites

http://www.abc-usa.org/ American Baptist Churches
http://www.cs.cmu.edu/People/spok/catholic.html Catholic Resources on the Net
http://www.tricycle.com Buddhism
http://www.ecusa.anglican.org/ Episcopal Church
http://www.elca.org/ Evangelical Lutheran Church in America
http://www.HinduismToday.kauai.hi.us/ashram Hinduism
http://www.optisol.com/imenu.htm Islam
http://www.jcn18.com/ Judaism
http://www.lds.org/ Latter-day Saints
http://www.pcusa.org/ Presbyterian Church (USA)
http://www.rlds.org/ Reorganized Latter Day Saints
http://www.sbcnet.org Southern Baptist Convention
http://www.ucc.org/ United Church of Christ
http://www.umc.org/ United Methodist Church

References

Corbett, Julia Mitchell. 1997. *Religion in America, Third Edition.* Upper Saddle River, New Jersey: Prentice Hall.

Davenport, Thomas A. 1991. *Virtuous Pagans: Unreligious People in America.* New York: Garland.

Kellstedt, Lyman A., John C. Green, James L. Guth, and Corwin E. Smidt. 1993. "Religious Traditions and Religious Commitments in the USA." Paper presented to the XXIIth International Conference of the International Society for the Sociology of Religion, Budapest, Hungary, July.

Kosmin, Barry A., and Seymour P. Lachman. 1990. *One Nation Under God: Religion in Contemporary American Society.* New York: Harmony Books.

Moore, David W. 1993. "Catholics At Odds With Church Teachings." *Gallup Poll Monthly,* August, pages 21–31.

Wuthnow, Robert. 1988. *The Restructuring of American Religion: Society and Faith Since WW II*. Princeton: Princeton University Press.

Wuthnow, Robert. 1989. *The Struggle for America's Soul: Evangelicals, Liberals, and Secularism*. Grand Rapids, Michigan: William B. Eerdmans.

APPENDIX B Further Information About NORC GSS Question Wording

In several chapters we used questions from National Opinion Research Center General Social Surveys (NORC GSS). For some questions, we provided the exact wording in the text, but for others, we simply provided the general nature of the question. Here we will give further information on those questions not fully reproduced in the text.

Political Tolerance Questions
During the 1950s, Samuel Stouffer (1955) asked three questions about each of three hypothetical persons: "somebody who is against all churches and religion;" "somebody who favors government ownership of all the railroads and big industries;" and "a man who admits he is a Communist." Later NORC GSS surveys added three other hypothetical persons (but dropped the socialist questions): "a person who believes that blacks are genetically inferior;" "a person who advocates doing away with elections and letting the military run the country;" and "a man who admits that he is a homosexual." Thus, these questions basically concern an atheist, a Communist, a racist, a militarist, and a homosexual.

For each hypothetical person, three questions were asked that concerned allowing a speech, teaching in college, and removing a book from the library. We will demonstrate these questions below with the series concerning the atheist; the questions about the other persons followed the same format with small variations.

There are always some people whose ideas are considered bad or dangerous by other people. For instance, somebody who is against all churches and religion.

If such a person wanted to make a speech in your community against churches and religion, should he be allowed to speak, or not?

Should such a person be allowed to teach in a college or university, or not?

If some people in your community suggested a book he wrote against churches and religion should be taken out of your public library, would you favor removing this book, or not?

Social Issues

Would you favor or oppose the death penalty for persons convicted of murder?

Do you think the use of marijuana should be made legal or not?

Would you favor or oppose a law which would require a person to obtain a police permit before he or she could buy a gun?

Which of these statements comes closest to your feelings about pornography laws?

(1) There should be laws against the distribution of pornography whatever the age.

(2) There should be laws against the distribution of pornography to persons under eighteen.

(3) There should be no laws forbidding the distribution of pornography.

The United States Supreme Court has ruled that no state or local government may *require* the reading of the Lord's Prayer or Bible verses in public schools.

What are your views on this—do you approve or disapprove of the court ruling?

Should divorce in this country be easier to obtain, more difficult to obtain, or stay as it is now?

Do you strongly agree, agree, disagree, or strongly disagree that methods of birth control should be available to teenagers between the ages of fourteen and sixteen if their parents do not approve?

Do you think a person has a right to end his or her own life if this person has an incurable disease?

Abortion

Please tell me whether or not you think it should be possible for a pregnant women to obtain a legal abortion (*Yes* or *No* for each of the following situations):

If there is a strong chance of serious defect in the baby?

If she is married and does not want any more children?

If the woman's own health is seriously endangered by the pregnancy?

If the family has a very low income and cannot afford any more children?

If she became pregnant as a result of rape?

If she is not married and does not want to marry the man?

If the woman wants it for any reason?

Racial Equality

Do you think there should be laws against marriages between blacks and whites?

White people have a right to keep blacks out of their neighborhoods if they want to and blacks should respect that right.

Suppose there is a community-wide vote on the general housing issue. There are two possible laws to vote on. Which law would you vote for?

A. One law says that a homeowner can decide for himself whom to sell his house to, even if he prefers not to sell it.

B. The second law says that a homeowner cannot refuse to sell to someone because of their race or color.

Sexual Equality

Please tell me whether you agree or disagree with the following statement: Most men are better suited emotionally for politics than are most women.

If your party nominated a woman for president, would you vote for her if she were qualified for the job?

Do you approve or disapprove of a married woman earning money in business or industry if she has a husband capable of supporting her?

Do you agree or disagree with this statement: Women should take care of running their homes and leave running the country up to men.

Support for Social Welfare

Some people think that the government in Washington ought to reduce the income differences between the rich and the poor, perhaps by raising the taxes of wealthy families or by giving income assistance to the poor. Others think that the government should not concern itself with reducing this income difference between the rich and the poor. Here is a card with a scale from 1 to 7. Think of a score of 1 as meaning that the government ought to reduce the income differences between the rich and the poor, and a score of 7 meaning that the government should not concern itself with reducing income differences.

    What score between 1 and 7 comes closest to the way you feel?

Some people think that the government in Washington should do everything possible to improve the standard of living of all poor Americans; they are at Point 1 on this card. Other people think it is not the government's responsibility, and that each person should take care of himself; they are at Point 5.

    Where would you place yourself on this scale, or haven't you made up your mind on this?

Some people think that the government in Washington is trying to do too many things that should be left to individuals and private businesses. Others disagree and think that the government should do even more to solve our country's problems. Still others have opinions somewhere in between.

    Where would you place yourself on this scale, or haven't you made up your mind on this? (Respondents were given a 1–5 scale on a card, similar to the situation in the previous question.)

In general, some people think that it is the responsibility of the government in Washington to see to it that people have help in paying for doctors and hospital bills. Others think that these matters are not the responsibility of the federal government and that people should take care of these things themselves.

    Where would you place yourself on this scale, or haven't you made up your mind on this?

Religious Commitment

How often do you attend religious services?

Never	Less than once a year	About once or twice a year
Several times a year	About once a month	2–3 times a month
Nearly every week	Every week	Several times a week

Would you call yourself a strong (*religious preference selected in a previous question*), or a not very strong (*religious preference*)?

About how often do you pray?

| Several times a day | Once a day | Several times a week |
| Once a week | Less than once a week | Never |

INDEX

('i' indicates an illustration; 't' indicates a table)